Critical Discourse Analysis

Critical Discourse Analysis

Theory and Interdisciplinarity

Edited by

Gilbert Weiss
University of Salzburg, Switzerland

and

Ruth Wodak
University of Lancaster, UK

palgrave
macmillan

First published in hardback in 2003
This paperback edition first published 2007 by
PALGRAVE MACMILLAN
Houndmills, Basignstoke, Hampshire RG21 6XS and
175 Fifth Avenue, New York, N.Y. 10010
Companies and representatives throughout the world

PALGRAVE MACMILLAN is the global academic imprint of the Palgrave
Macmillan division of St. Martin's Press, LLC and of Palgrave Macmillan Ltd.
Macmillan® is a registered trademark in the United States, United Kingdom
and other countries. Palgrave is a registered trademark in the European
Union and other countries.

ISBN-13: 978–0–333–97023–2 hardback
ISBN-10: 0–333–97023–3 hardback
ISBN-13: 978–0–230–55514–3 paperback
ISBN-10: 0–230–55514–4 paperback

This book is printed on paper suitable for recycling and made from fully
managed and sustained forest sources. Logging, pulping and manufacturing
processes are expected to conform to the environmental regulations of
the country of origin.

A catalogue record for this book is available from the British Library.

Library of Congress Cataloging-in-Publication Data
    Critical discourse analysis: theory and interdisciplinarity/edited by Gilbert
Weiss and Ruth Wodak.
        p. cm.
    Includes bibliographical references and index.
        ISBN 0–333–97023–3 (cloth)   0–230–55514–4 (pbk)
    1. Discourse analysis. 2. Interdisciplinary approach to knowledge. I. Weiss, Gilbert.
II. Wodak, Ruth, 1950–

P302.C6858 2002
401'.41—dc21   2002030260

10   9   8   7   6   5   4   3   2   1
16   15   14   13   12   11   10   09   08   07

Printed and bound in Great Britain by
CPI Antony Rowe, Chippenham and Eastbourne

Contents

Preface

Gilbert Weiss and Ruth Wodak

This volume was inspired by a stimulating conference in Vienna in July 2000. Most of the contributors to this volume and some other colleagues discussed intensively problems and issues of Critical Discourse Analysis and Interdisciplinarity for three days. However, many issues remained unresolved. This fact triggered the idea to request the contributors to revise their papers and to reflect their positions. Moreover, we invited several other colleagues in the field to discuss the central notions of 'inter/trans/multidisciplinarity' in the Social Sciences with us as well.

The possibility of publishing this volume gave us a chance to frame this discussion more broadly, to set it into a long development of theory and empirical work in the Social Sciences. The questions which arise lead us from abstract reflections on theory building to aspects of application of empirical results and to political practice.

We would like to thank all the contributors to this volume for their contributions. We would also like to thank the publishers for their support and patience. We are very grateful to Lieselotte Martin for her help in organizing the conference in July 2000. Heidemarie Markhardt checked the non-native English papers and translated some of our work in a most efficient and remarkable way. Lastly, we would like to thank the Austrian Science Foundation (FWF) for awarding the Wittgenstein Prize to Ruth Wodak which made the work on this book, the conference and our teamwork possible.

Vienna, March 2002

Acknowledgements

We are grateful to the following copyright holders for permission to reproduce material.

In Chapter 13, Abril Editoras, Sao Paulo, Brazil for the use of illustrations and page layouts from issues of the magazine *Veja* and to the *Daily Mail*, London, for permission to reproduce the text of the article on José. In Chapter 14, *Cape Argus*, South Africa, for permission to reproduce the list of detainees and a cartoon, and the *Mail and Guardian*, South Africa, for permission to reproduce page layouts and a letter from the *Weekly Mail*.

The authors have attempted to clear use of all copyright material reproduced in the volume. In the event that any copyright holder has inadvertently been overlooked, the publisher will make amends at the earliest opportunity.

Notes on Contributors

Christine Anthonissen is an Associate Professor and Chairperson of the Department of General Linguistics at Stellenbosch University, South Africa. Her research interests include critical discourse analysis, media discourses, discourses in primary health care, as well as multilingualism and intercultural communication, most recently focussing on HIV/AIDS clinics in South Africa.

Michael Billig is Professor of Social Sciences at Loughborough University. He is the author of numerous books and articles, which reflect his parallel concerns with theory and with studying ways of thinking, especially ideological thought. Among his recent book publications are *Freudian Repression: Conversation Creating the Unconscious* (Cambridge, 1999) and *Rock'n'Roll Jews* (Nottingham, 2000).

Carmen Rosa Caldas-Coulthard, formerly Professor of English Language and Applied Linguistics at the Federal University of Santa Catarina, Brazil, is now Senior Lecturer in the Centre for English Language Studies, Department of English, at the University of Birmingham. She has published widely in the areas of Critical Discourse, Media and Gender Studies. She is the author of *News as Social Practice* (UFSC, 1997) and editor of *Texts and Practices: Reading in Critical Discourse Analysis* (London, 1996).

Marcelo Dascal is a Professor of Philosophy at Tel Aviv University. His research interests include the philosophy of language, pragmatics, the history of modern philosophy (especially Leibniz), and the role of controversies in the evolution of knowledge, as well as in sociopolitical conflicts. He is the editor of *Pragmatics & Cognition*, published twice a year in Amsterdam. He has authored and edited about 25 books.

Concepción Gómez Esteban is Associate Professor in Sociology, Faculty of Political Science and Sociology, Universidad Complutense de Madrid. She has carried out research in the fields of Sociology of Knowledge, Sociology of Death and, since 1993, she has dedicated most of her research work to fields related with women and their labour situation, especially when holding positions of management and leadership.

Carlos A.M. Gouveia is an Assistant Professor at the Department of English, Faculty of Letters, University of Lisbon, and a researcher at the Centre for English Studies of the same University. His research areas are Discourse

Analysis, Critical Discourse Analysis and Systemic Functional Grammar. His published work includes, among several articles in these areas, both in Portuguese and in English, a co-edited book on current issues in General and Portuguese Linguistics and a co-authored one on Language and Linguistics.

Phil Graham is Professor of Communication and Culture in the Creative Industries Faculty of Queensland University of Technology. He has written numerous articles and several books. He is on the international advisory board of *New Media & Society*, and is interested in critical social theory, new media research, economic history of communications, and discourse analysis methods. His most recent book publications are *The Digital Dark Ages* and *Hypercapitalism*.

Marianne W. Jørgensen is an Assistant Professor in the Department for Studies of Social Change and Culture at Linköping University, Sweden. She analyses social research as discursive practice, focussing on the democratizing and critical potentials of new interactive research strategies. She is co-author (with Louise Phillips) of *Discourse Analysis as Theory and Method*.

Jay L. Lemke is Professor of Educational Studies at the University of Michigan, USA. His research interests include discourse linguistics, social semiotics, language in education and science education. He has published numerous books and articles in these fields, including *Textual Politics: Discourse and Social Dynamics* (London, 1995).

J. R. Martin is Professor of Linguistics (Personal Chair) at the University of Sydney, Australia. His research interests include systemic theory, functional grammar, discourse semantics, register, genre, multimodality and critical discourse analysis, focussing on English and Tagalog. Recent publications include *The Language of Evaluation* (with P. R. R. White, 2005), *Genre Relations* (with David Rose, 2006) and *Knowledge Structure* (edited with Fran Christie, 2007).

Luisa Martín Rojo is Associate Professor in Linguistics, Faculty of Philosophy, Universidad Autónoma de Madrid. She is also senior researcher in various research projects in gender studies and in multilingual and multicultural education. She is a member of the editorial boards of *Discourse & Society* and *Language and Politics*.

Patricia O'Connor is Associate Professor in the Department of English at Georgetown University. Her major research interests include theory and practice of learning and teaching, especially in regards to new technologies, as well as prison research. Most recently she published the book *Speaking of Crime: Narratives of Prisoners* (Lincoln, 2000).

Suzanne Scollon is an independent scholar based in Haines, Alaska, who consults and Lectures on geosemiotics and nexus analysis, the subjects of two recent books co-authored with Ron Scollon: *Discourses in Place: Language in the Material World* (2003) and *Nexus Analysis: Discourse and the Emerging Internet* (2004).

Teun A. van Dijk is Professor Emeritus at the University of Amsterdam and since 1999, Visiting Professor at the Universitat Pompeu Fabra, Barcelona, Spain, where he also lives. He has published some 30 monographs and edited books and more than 150 scholarly articles. He has founded several international journals: *POETICS, TEXT, Discourse & Society, Discourse Studies* and most recently, *Discourse & Communication* and *Discurso & Sociedad*.

Gilbert Weiss is Assistant Professor of Political Science at the University of Salzburg, Austria. He is the author or editor of several books, including *Theorie, Relevanz und Warheit, Eine Rekonstruktion des Briefwechsels zwischen Eric Voegelin und Alfred Schütz (1938–1959), European Union Discourses on Un/employment* (with Peter Muntigl and Ruth Wodak, 2000). He has also edited (with William Petropulos) Volume 4 (*The Authoritarian State*), and Volumes 32 and 33 (*Miscellaneous Papers 1921–1938, 1939–1985*) of *The Collected Works of Eric Voegelin*.

Ruth Wodak is Professor of Discourse Studies at Lancaster University, UK and head of the Wittgenstein Research Centre "Discourse-Politics-Identity" at the University of Vienna. Among other honours, she was awarded the Wittgenstein Prize for Elite Researchers in 1996. She has published many books; among the most recent are: *The Discursive Construction and Representation of Politics in Action, The Discursive Construction of History: Remembering the Wehrmacht's War of Annihilation* (with H. Heer, W. Manoschek, A. Pollak, translated from the German) and *Voices of Migrants* (with G. Delanty, P. Jones).

1
Introduction: Theory, Interdisciplinarity and Critical Discourse Analysis

Gilbert Weiss and Ruth Wodak

The aim of this volume is to critically examine the foundation and basic elements of discourse-analytical research as it has been developing for roughly two decades. The focus is therefore on the elementary and paradigmatic. This is both an opportunity and a danger. There is the danger of virtually losing contact with the ground, that is, the concrete reality of research, in the Olympian spheres of the fundamental. At the same time this offers an opportunity to go beyond one's own research practice, to reflect for a moment on the basis of this very research practice and, by doing so, ultimately reap a benefit for this practice. The range of contributions included in this volume and the quality of the authors will hopefully guarantee that the opportunity will prevail against the danger.

The concepts 'theory' and 'interdisciplinarity' refer to the conceptual and disciplinary framework conditions of discourse-analytical research. Discourse analysis has concentrated on the process of theory formation and has stressed the interdisciplinary nature of its research since its beginning (Fairclough and Wodak, 1997; van Dijk, 1997; Wodak, 2001b). It seems therefore appropriate to focus on these two aspects when examining fundamental principles and analysing the status quo. This is of particular importance as these are the very points for which discourse analysis is often criticized (see van Dijk, 1995). In the following we elaborate on the problem horizons associated with the two concepts.

Theory

Theory and practice, theory and methodology, theory and empirical research, theory and myth, theory and *Weltanschauung*, theory and research goals, theory and construction – the concept of 'theory' seems to provoke dualistic comparisons. On a very general level 'theory' could be defined as a coherent series of individual and universal statements, going beyond a mere description and making it possible to substantiate, explain or understand, or even (re-)construct the object of theory as well as to establish causal relations between specific phenomena. What exactly this means is, however, hotly disputed. The two concepts of 'explaining' and 'understanding', for instance, imply two completely different approaches to the constitution of theory. These different approaches – a hermeneutic-reconstructive one on the one hand (understanding) and a nomothetic-deductive one on the other hand (explaining) – have practically drawn a dividing line through the modern social sciences. The differentiation between explaining and understanding was introduced by Wilhelm Dilthey (Rodi and Lessing, 1984), whose primary objective had been to make a distinction between the natural sciences and the humanities. Based on this approach, the natural sciences use explanation by formulating a theory of an all-embracing, causal natural relation against the background of a number of individual observations. The humanities and social sciences do not have to take this bypass but have direct access to the nexus of conscious life and culture because we are supposed to understand our own conscious life and our own cultural products 'from within'. The differentiation between explaining and understanding was however reproduced in the social sciences, above all under the title 'objectivism versus subjectivism' (Giddens, 1979).

From antiquity (Plato, Aristotle) to the twentieth century, the theoretical, contemplative attitude was distinguished from a practical, action-oriented position. Even the most influential Continental philosophical approach of the last century, that is, Edmund Husserl's phenomenology, centres on a differentiation between a theoretical attitude and a 'relative-natural *Weltanschauung*' (Janssen, 1976). According to Husserl, this natural attitude, which makes us accept the existence of the world without questioning it, has to be put in the parentheses of a 'phenomenological reduction' so as to radicalize the Cartesian doubt and to gain theoretical knowledge in the strict sense (Husserl, 1993). However, since the nineteenth century an increasing number of approaches have been developed (by, inter alia, Marx, Nietzsche, Heidegger, Horkheimer, Adorno, Habermas) which claim that every theory is determined by practical research goals. The main representatives of present-day Critical Discourse Analysis (CDA) (see Van Dijk, 1984; Fairclough, 1989; Wodak, 1989) adhere to this school of thought as well. This approach is essentially based on a critical-dialectical concept of theory that is not limited to formulating and examining general statements about the laws of social reality. Moreover, the focus is on a criticism of scientific-theoretical results. They are challenged with other options, examined for contradictions and considered in an overall context. The aim of theoretical work in this sense is true and instructional enlightenment about the historical and social situation. This approach emphasizes the fact that the scientific work process instituted by the human has always formed part of the historical-social context it strives to identify by acts of cognition. Therefore theory in the social sciences must always be an object-adequate form of knowledge subject to reflection and prescribed by the 'thing' itself. Theory should not be considered an *instrument* of knowledge but rather a social reality that has taken on a different shape (Berger and Luckmann, 1966). Academic interests and thus the selection and objectives of theories are deemed closely connected with the relations and contradictions between varying social interests. In the recent past this interrelation between theory and practice has been explored against the above background mainly by the sociologist Pierre Bourdieu (Bourdieu, 1977; Chouliaraki and Fairclough, 1999, p. 99).

Plato, Aristotle and – as one of the last – Schelling considered intuition or the intellectual penetration of a complex unity the supreme form of theoretical knowledge. However, since the beginning of modern times and due to the triumph of the natural sciences theory has come to be understood as a deductive system consisting of definitions, principles (axioms), final propositions and inferential statements (theorems). Hence, it must be possible to verify a theory either empirically or logically. Traditionally, a theory is required to be substantiated. Therefore a terminological distinction is made between theory and hypothesis. Unlike a hypothesis, a theory was verified and is therefore an expression of knowledge (Hügli and Lübcke, 1991, p. 569).

Due to this deductive-axiomatic model of theory, with which the natural sciences were operating highly successfully, the humanities and social sciences came under severe pressure. This was even increased by schools of scientism such as logical positivism (Carnap, 1928). As is generally known, this philosophy did not accept any theory unless it was verifiable. An opposite point of view was, for example, taken by Karl Popper, who stipulated that a theory had to meet the following requirements: (a) it need not be verifiable but it must be possible to establish its falsity; (b) it must solve more problems than any alternative theory; (c) it must have been subject to tests, and (d) must have passed them successfully (Popper, 1935). Popper's hypothetical-deductive methodology shows optimum results if the following procedure is adopted: formulation of a problem (that is, 'new', surprising observations regarding recognized theories), formulation of a hypothesis (that is, proposals for a possible explanation of the problem), logical deduction of assumptions based on the hypothesis, and verification (test) of the hypothesis by observation and/or experiment.

In many respects Popper's model is still deeply rooted in a natural-scientific model of theory. The fact that the process of establishing the truth or falsity is basically one determined by society is underrated. The intersubjectivity of theoretical positions is a problem hardly considered. Moreover, the pre-theoretical world of experience, in which every theory needs to be substantiated, is uncoupled from questions of theory as if free from problems.

It is particularly an achievement of the phenomenological-hermeneutic approach of Alfred Schutz (Schutz, 1932, 1962; Schutz and Luckmann, 1973) that intersubjectivity and the pre-theoretical world of experience were recognized and formulated as basic questions of the constitution of theory. Based on Max Weber's concept of a *Verstehende Sozialwissenschaft* and Edmund Husserl's idea of the *Lebenswelt*, Schutz made one of the earliest and most significant attempts to free theory formation in the social sciences from the constraints of naturalistic and positivistic assumptions. In his essay 'Concept and theory formation in the social sciences' (1954) Schutz made it clear that *Verstehen* (understanding) in the social sciences has to be founded primarily on everyday understanding, for '*Verstehen* is ... primarily not a method used by the social scientist, but the particular experiential form in which common-sense thinking takes cognizance of the social cultural world' (Schutz, 1962, p. 56). Schutz expounded:

> the common-sense knowledge of everyday life is the unquestioned but always questionable background within which inquiry starts and within which alone it can be carried out. It is this *Lebenswelt*, as Husserl calls it, within which, according to him, all scientific and even logical concepts originate; it is the social matrix within which, according to Dewey, unclarified situations emerge, which have to be transformed by the process of inquiry into warranted assertability; and Whitehead has pointed out that it is the aim of science to produce a theory which agrees with experience by explaining the thought-objects constructed by common sense through the mental constructs or thought objects of science. For all these thinkers agree that any knowledge of the world, in common-sense thinking as well as in science, involves mental constructs, syntheses, generalizations, formalizations, idealizations specific to the respective level of thought organization. The concept of Nature, with which the natural sciences have to deal is, as Husserl has shown, an idealizing abstraction from the Lebenswelt, an abstraction which, on principle and of course legitimately, excludes persons with their personal life and all objects of culture which originate as such in practical human activity. Exactly this layer of the Lebenswelt, however, from which the natural sciences have to abstract, is the social reality which the social sciences have to investigate. (Schutz, 1962, p. 57ff.)

This statement stresses the *Lebenswelt* foundation of theory formation in the social sciences. To make a scientific understanding of social actions possible, an 'understanding' sociology as formulated by Schutz has to explicate how understanding works in everyday life, prior to any science. There is a direct interrelation between the objective understanding focusing on the 'external horizons' of action and the subjective understanding of 'everyday activities'. The approach developed by Schutz determined the theoretical understanding of qualitative trends in the social sciences, for example, ethnomethodology, grounded theory, conversational analysis and discourse analysis (Cicourel, 1973; Strauss, 1978; Garfinkel, 1984; Heritage, 1984; Wodak, 1996; Titscher et al., 2000).

Alfred Schutz also reformulated the interrelations of problem, theory and relevance. He distinguished three forms of 'relevance': (1) thematic relevance, (2) interpretational relevance and (3) motivational relevance (Schutz and Luckmann, 1973, p. 186ff.). Thematic relevance refers to the basic question, 'What is the problem to be studied?' According to Schutz, this level of relevance is basically characterized by the fact that the study topic, the 'problem-object', the 'question-able' must always be considered against the background of an 'order established naturally and without questioning' (Voegelin et al., 1993, p. 56). In this respect the relevance of a theoretical problem does not differ from the 'practical relevance' of an everyday problem. The differentiation between the question-able and the order established without questioning is indispensable to provide the sociology of knowledge with a tool of formally dealing with questions of problem selection. According to Schutz, the next level is interpretational relevance that deals with the question, 'Which elements of our knowledge are relevant for the interpretation of the problem subject to study?' The relevance of a specific method is decided on this level. This is also considered the point where 'an ideal (that is, never fully developed) method can provide guidance on the interpretative steps to be taken and the material to be used for interpretation' (ibid., p. 57). However, the third concept of relevance, that is, motivational relevance, focuses on the question, 'To what extent should the problem be investigated?' In other words, 'at what point should I content myself with the findings of the study; when do I have to stop and declare everything beyond a specific scope as "irrelevant" or at least not relevant for the problem studied?' In the same way as he had done with regard to 'thematic relevance', Schutz also pointed out explicitly in respect of the other two concepts of relevance that they should be applied not only to scientific thinking but also to 'everyday life'. The different relevance levels are not at all independent from one another but directly interrelated. This interrelation determines every theoretical study. For a problem-oriented and reflexive approach such as discourse analysis this differentiation of relevance levels is therefore imperative (Cicourel, 1964; Grathoff, 1995).

So far we have addressed the questions of theory formation only on a very general level. On this general level different types/concepts of theory can be distinguished. To summarize them once more: (1) ontological-normative, (2) deductive-axiomatic, (3) critical-dialectical, (4) phenomenological-hermeneutic. Other types or subtypes of theories could certainly be listed and, of course, the four types mentioned could be named differently (for example, empirical-nomological instead of deductive-axiomatic, and so on). Nevertheless, theory formation of the last two centuries is basically covered by listing these four types.

Let us now turn to specific theory formation in CDA. First of all, one can state that CDA has its roots in the latter two (critical-dialectical and phenomenological-hermeneutic) of the four theory types mentioned, but apart from this it is quite difficult to make consistent statements about the theoretical foundation of CDA. There is no such thing as a uniform, common theory formation determining CDA; in fact, there are several approaches. Michael Meyer came to the conclusion that 'there is no guiding theoretical viewpoint that is used consistently within CDA, nor do the CDA protagonists proceed consistently from the area of theory to the field of discourse and then back to theory' (2001, p. 18; see also Wodak and Ludwig, 1999, p. 11). Meyer also points out that not only epistemological theories but also general social theories, middle-range theories, microsociological theories, sociopsychological theories, discourse theories and linguistic theories can be found in CDA. It would be outside the scope of these introductory remarks to present the different aspects stressed by the different CDA representatives in their respective approaches (although an overview will be given in this volume) or to reconstruct the individual theoretical bases (see Lemke, 1995; Chouliaraki and Fairclough, 1999; Wodak, 2000a; Wodak and Meyer, 2001). Attention should however be drawn to the fact that it is essential to be aware of the different levels of theory types proposed by Meyer. This is of particular importance since in the discourse of applied sciences the concept 'theory' refers to all levels without any further qualification. Let us take two philosophers as an example who undoubtedly had a strong influence on the development of CDA: Michel Foucault and Jürgen Habermas (see Foucault, 1972; Habermas, 1981; Wodak, 1996, p. 24ff.). The different levels of theory are often mixed up in the CDA reception of both Foucault and Habermas. For example, Foucault's tools are used on both the epistemological level and the level of discourse theory (Fairclough, 1992; Lemke, 1995, p. 29; Wodak, 1996, p. 26). The approach developed by Habermas is applied as a general social theory, a microsociological interaction theory and a discourse theory (Chouliaraki and Fairclough, 1999, p. 88ff.). Of course, this indiscriminate mixing leads to inconsistencies in terms of concept and category which in turn have an adverse effect on systematics. Under the influence of other so-called 'grand theories' (for example, those developed by Bourdieu (1980), Giddens (1984), and Luhmann (1997)), this problem has become even more acute. On the whole, the theoretical framework of CDA seems eclectic and unsystematic. However, this can also be viewed as a positive phenomenon. The plurality of theory and methodology can be highlighted as a specific strength of CDA, to which this research discipline ultimately owes its dynamics (Wodak, 2002). Chouliaraki and Fairclough (1999, p. 16ff.) described this as follows:

> We see CDA as bringing a variety of theories into dialogue, especially social theories on the one hand and linguistic theories on the other, so that its theory is a shifting synthesis of other theories, though what it itself theorises in particular is the mediation between the social and the linguistic – the 'order of discourse', the social structuring of semiotic hybridity (interdiscursivity). The theoretical constructions of discourse

which CDA tries to operationalise can come from various disciplines, and the concept of 'operationalisation' entails working in a transdisciplinary way where the logic of one discipline (for example, sociology) can be 'put to work' in the development of another (for example, linguistics).

This statement underlines the direct connection between theory and inter-disciplinarity/transdisciplinarity that is typical of discourse analysis and explicitly addressed in this volume. We will look at transdisciplinarity in more detail below. Even if plurality of theory is undoubtedly a strength, attention has to be drawn to the fact that it is crucial to be aware of the different levels and types of theories – as, for example, listed by Meyer – and the respective operational levels.

The 'mediation between the social and the linguistic', referred to by Chouliaraki and Fairclough in the above quotation, is highly relevant for the theory formation process in CDA. Major difficulties of operationalization in the research process are usually related to this mediation problem (Fairclough and Wodak, 1997; Wodak, 2001b, p. 12). The CDA representatives agree to a large extent that the complex interrelations between discourse and society cannot be analysed adequately unless linguistic and sociological approaches are combined. The problem is however that sociological and linguistic categories are basically not compatible as they tend to have diverging *Horizontgebundenheit* – the term Husserl used to describe the fact that they were dependent on different horizons. In sociological contexts the term 'representation' usually denotes something different (or has a wider meaning) than in specific linguistic analyses. The term 'institution' is used in discourse-analytical concepts and sociological theories with a completely different meaning. A theoretical basic structure capable of reconciling sociological and linguistic categories (mediation) is therefore required. No such uniform theoretical framework of mediation has been created in CDA to date. However one can speak of a theoretical synthesis of conceptual tools developed in different theoretical schools, as practised to a certain extent by Chouliaraki and Fairclough. Tools of this kind are, for example, Foucault's discursive formations, Bourdieu's habitus, or register and code as defined by Halliday and Bernstein (Lemke, 1995, p. 19ff.). This synthesis of theories is by no means a monistic theory model and it does not claim to be 'more true' than the individual theories from which conceptual ideas are drawn. It is primarily committed to a 'conceptual pragmatism' (Mouzelis) focusing on 'criteria of utility rather than truth' (Mouzelis, 1995, p. 9). Such a pragmatic approach would not seek to provide a catalogue of context-less propositions and generalizations, but rather to relate questions of theory formation and conceptualization closely to the specific problems that are to be investigated. In this sense, the first question we have to address as researchers is not, 'Do we need a grand theory?', but rather, 'What conceptual tools are relevant for this or that problem and for this and that context?' With this question, due regard is given to the fact that the context of discursive practices needs to be addressed adequately. Hence, some CDA representatives have concentrated on the issue of the context and the development of a context model in recent years (Wodak, 2000a; van Dijk, 2001).

The above statement by no means renders the question as to the truth of knowledge futile. However, it should not be asked on the level of the 'conceptual tools' if a constructive connection is to be successfully established between different theoretical approaches on the one hand and theory and empirical research on the other hand. The question of the truth or, in more general terms, the possibility of knowledge in the social sciences basically has to be dealt with on a metaconceptual level. There the focus will be on the ontological character of the social, the constitution of the subject, and so on. On the conceptual level a decision has to be made on the plausibility, that is, the usefulness of specific 'tools' for a specific question or specific object of research. An object of research can be characterized by different dimensions requiring conceptual tools of different theoretical contexts. Basically, the use of heterogeneous tools of different theories should not be rejected provided they may be integrated on the conceptual level.

To sum up, one could say that in order to develop an integrated theoretical framework capable of reconciling different (sociological and linguistic) perspectives without reducing them to one another (and this is where we get to the heart of the problem of interdisciplinarity) the following steps are necessary:

1. Clarification of the basic theoretical assumptions regarding *text, discourse, language, action, social structure, institution and society*. This is done on a level preceding the actual analysis. It constitutes the framework for developing conceptual tools, for establishing categories and for analytical operationalization. This step is vital for sociology and linguistics to arrive at a 'mutual understanding'.
2. The development of conceptual tools capable of connecting the level of text or discourse analysis with sociological positions on institutions, actions and social structures. Conceptual tools are elements of theory allowing a connection in both directions (linguistics and sociology). As analytical interfaces (for example, the concepts of discursive formation, order of discourse, habitus, register and code) they guarantee a sociolinguistically integrated model in the strict sense. Their plausibility determines whether further categorization will be successful. In other words, if these tools do not work, it will not be possible to reconcile the respective positions in the research strategy at a later date.

   Conceptual tools do not represent a self-contained edifice of theories. They are elements that may be adopted from different theoretical approaches, schools and traditions. The principle of 'conceptual pragmatism' applies also here: theory formation is not a process leading up to a final product valid for all times representing in itself the total truth of the world, but rather a continued development of tools and resources designed to help us understand the world. In this context, Pierre Bourdieu uses the phrase 'cumulative conceptualization work':

> The striving for originality at all costs, sometimes favored by ignorance, and the religious devotion to this or that canonical author, which often ends up in ritual recitation, have in common that they often prevent an appropriate attitude vis-à-vis a theoretical tradition that consists in affirming continuity and rupture, conservation and innovation at the same time, that relies on the entirety of the available thinking – without fear of being accused of mere imitation or eclecticism – in order to go beyond the predecessors by using the tools to whose production they contributed in a new way. The ability to actively reproduce the best products of the thinkers of the past by applying the production instruments they left behind is the access requirement of really productive thinking. (Bourdieu, 1997, pp. 64–5)

This statement by Bourdieu can be considered the programmatic basis for all efforts to develop an integrated theoretical framework. If we adopt instruments or tools from different theories, among them also those of Bourdieu, and integrate them into the research process, this does not necessarily have to lead to eclecticism in a negative sense. On the contrary, it could be the very characteristic of an innovative and productive theory formation, albeit a characteristic that has to prove its productivity in empirical applicability. One should however add that an eclecticism marked by incoherent and unrelated concepts and categories can in fact be found in the research practice.

As we pointed out before, the most important task of conceptual tools is to integrate sociological and linguistic positions, that is, to mediate between text and institution, between communication and structure, and between discourse and society. This problem of mediation not only refers to the hyphen in socio-linguistics but also pinpoints the central problem of modern social science, the 'wound' of sociological thinking in the twentieth century, so to speak (Weiss, 1996, p. 90ff.). This 'wound' has been given many names: subjectivism versus objectivism, individualism versus collectivism, voluntarism versus determinism, and so on. In essence, all these dualities deal with the micro/macroproblem of the reference context of player and structure: is it actions, practices, strategies, intentions of players that explain social phenomena or is it structural characteristics of a specific social formation (class structures, social and cultural codes, normative systems)? This fundamental question divided the social sciences into two camps. On the one hand, there are approaches focusing on the understanding of actions taken by the individual; on the other, there are structural-functionalist approaches concentrating on the determining structures overpowering the players and leaving them little room to manoeuvre. State-of-the-art approaches of social theory do however try to conceptualize the context of reference of action and structure as being mutually determined/recursive and, consequently, try to treat both levels as having equal status in analysis. In the following we would like to provide some hopefully useful details.

Communicative actions, social and symbolic *practices* are things that happen *within* wider frames of reference and contexts, such as *in* social *systems*, in a way that microcontexts would take place within macrocontexts or be embedded *in* them; hence it is not a box system in which one box contains another. Therefore it is misleading to state that players engage in their actions within structures and systems and it is equally inappropriate to claim that the individual is a part of society. These phrases convey the substantialist conception that social systems or societies are self-contained entities containing other self-contained entities, such as players or individuals, that is, the box system (Luhmann, 1984, 1997). This has to be rejected flatly: symbolic practices do not take place within social systems. Instead, they reproduce the latter simply by taking place; the systems reproduced in this way then retroact on the conditions of action. This means that *engaging in an action equals system reproduction, or in our concrete case, text production equals system reproduction.* In this sense microcontexts cannot be placed within macrocontexts – from an ontological perspective microcontext *equals* macrocontext. For analytical purposes it is however useful to distinguish between microlevel and macrolevel.

This reasoning is only comprehensible if a 'duality of structure' (Giddens, 1984) is assumed: structure as the *medium* and *result* of behaviour which it organizes in a recurrent process. The structural factors of social systems do not exist outside action but are continuously engaged in the production and reproduction of action, or, in the more drastic wording of Mouzelis (1995, p. 139): 'rules (or structures, in Giddens' terminology) are 100 per cent the medium and outcome of action'. Discursive practices should always be regarded as both structuring and structured actions. In text production the players reproduce the conditions that make text possible. Hence, also Pierre Bourdieu (1990) refers to 'structured and structuring structures'.

3. After clarifying the theoretical assumptions and identifying the conceptual tools, the third basic step is the *defining of categories, that is, of analytical concepts, to denote the content of specific phenomena.* Categories are based on disciplinary or methodological borders only to a minor extent; they depend primarily on the object of research, that is, questions and content to be subject to study. Categories of this kind include, for example, public space, identity, legitimacy, prejudice, discrimination, power, racism, and so on. It is important to identify both parallels in and differences between the

process of analytical category formation on the one hand and categorization in everyday discourses on the other. Category formation is not the exclusive privilege of scientific theorists, it is also an important and pervasive part of people's discourse. As Eric Voegelin (1987, p. 27) has said, 'man does not wait for science to have his life explained to him, and when the theorist approaches social reality he finds the field pre-empted by what may be called the self-interpretation of society'.

The question of how categories are constituted in everyday discourse and what functions they satisfy is therefore – in the strictest sense of the word – a fundamental question regarding the categorization of theories. However, even though analytical categories are very closely linked to categories constructed by players in conversations, for example, to include or exclude specific social groups, they differ in one important aspect: they are instruments of an observer 'relieved of action'. In this respect they are, to put it in the words of Alfred Schutz, *second-grade constructions*, as opposed to the *first-grade constructions*, that is, the categories of 'everyday discourse' (see Schutz, 1962, p. 3ff.).

This background information has been provided to present the key aspects of the complex of problems 'theory' in CDA at least in broad outline. Before addressing the questions of interdisciplinarity directly related to it, we would like to make a last general remark on the basic theoretical task in the social sciences. By referring to Schutz and Ricoeur, the English sociologist David Levy (1981, p. 14) established a standard which is still valid:

> An objective science of social reality has a task of interpretation which encompasses several levels. It must give a true account of the systems of meanings by which men in society make sense of their lives. Then it must seek to understand the variations between such systems by reference to to the particular historical circumstances of the societies in which they arise. It must relate these different systems to universal symbolic patterns of the type suggested by Schutz, And, finally, it must refer these universal symbolisms to the character of the human condition as rooted in reality that can neither be dreamed nor defined away. It must move through intersubjectivity to the objective world of which we are conscious and on which the work of consciousness builds. To use Paul Ricoeur's terms, an interpretation of social reality cannot rest before it has shown the way in which 'my world', or 'our world', is always an aspect of 'the world'.

Cornerstones of CDA: discourse, ideology, power

The roots of CDA lie in classical Rhetoric, Textlinguistics and Socio-linguistics, as well as in Applied Linguistics and Pragmatics. The notions of ideology, power, hierarchy, gender and sociological variables were all seen as relevant for an interpretation or explanation of text. The subjects under investigation differ for the various departments and scholars who apply CDA (see Wodak 2002 for an extensive discussion of the development and characteristics of CDA). Gender issues, issues of racism, media discourses, political discourses, organizational discourses or dimensions of identity research have become very prominent. The methodologies differ greatly in all these studies on account of the aims of the research and also the methodologies applied: small qualitative case studies can be found as well as large data corpora, drawn from fieldwork and ethnographic research (see the chapters by Caldas-Coulthard, Martín Rojo and Anthonissen in this volume).

CDA takes a particular interest in the relationship between language and power. The term 'CDA' is used nowadays to refer more specifically to the critical linguistic approach of scholars who find the larger discursive unit of text to be the basic unit of communication (see Anthonissen, 2001). This research specifically considers more or less overt relations of struggle and conflict in all the domains mentioned above.

Deconstructing the label of this research programme means that we have to define what CDA means when employing the terms 'critical' and 'discourse'. Michael Billig in this volume clearly points to the fact that CDA has become an established academic discipline with the same rituals and institutional practices as all other academic disciplines. Ironically, he asks whether this might mean that CDA has become 'uncritical' – or if the use of abbreviations such as CDA might serve the same purpose as in other traditional, non-critical disciplines – to exclude outsiders and to mystify the functions and intentions of the research. We cannot answer Billig's questions extensively here, but we do believe that he points to some interesting and potentially very fruitful and necessary debates for CDA, which will hopefully arise as a result of this volume.

At this point, we would like to stress that CDA has never been and has never attempted to be or to provide one single or specific theory, and one specific methodology is not characteristic of research in CDA. On the contrary, studies in CDA are multifarious, derived from quite different theoretical backgrounds and oriented towards very different data and methodologies. Researchers in CDA also rely on a variety of grammatical approaches (see the contrast between the approaches of Jim Martin, Teun van Dijk and Jay Lemke in this volume). The definitions of the terms 'discourse', 'critical', 'ideology', 'power', and so on, are also manifold (see Wodak, 1996). Thus, any criticism of CDA should always specify which research or researcher they relate to because CDA as such cannot be viewed as a holistic or closed paradigm. We suggest using the notion of a 'school' for CDA, or of a programme which many researchers find useful and to which they can relate. This programme or set of principles has changed over the years (see Fairclough and Wodak, 1997).

Such a heterogeneous school might be confusing for some, but on the other hand it allows for open discussion and debate, for changes in the aims and goals, and for innovation. In contrast to 'total and closed' theories (such as Chomsky's Generative Transformational Grammar or Michael Halliday's Systemic Functional Linguistics), CDA has never had the image of a 'sect' and does not want to have such an image.

This heterogeneity of methodological and theoretical approaches that can be found in this field of linguistics would tend to confirm van Dijk's point that CDA and Critical Linguistics, (CL) 'are at most a shared perspective on doing linguistic, semiotic or discourse analysis' (van Dijk, 1993, p. 131). CDA sees 'language as social practice' (Fairclough and Wodak, 1997), and considers the context of language use to be crucial:

> CDA sees discourse – language use in speech and writing – as a form of 'social practice'. Describing discourse as social practice implies a dialectical relationship between a particular discursive event and the situation(s), institution(s) and social structure(s) which frame it: the discursive event is shaped by them, but it also shapes them. That is, discourse is socially constitutive as well as socially conditioned – it constitutes situations, objects of knowledge, and the social identities of and relationships between people and groups of people. It is constitutive both in the sense that it helps to sustain and reproduce the social status quo, and in the sense that it contributes to transforming it. Since discourse is so socially consequential, it gives rise to important issues of power. Discursive practices may have major ideological effects – that is, they can help produce and reproduce unequal power relations between (for instance) social classes, women and men, and ethnic/cultural majorities and minorities through the ways in which they represent things and position people. (Fairclough and Wodak, 1997, p. 258)

The term 'discourse' is, of course, used very differently by different researchers and also in different academic cultures. In the German and Central European context, a distinction is made between 'text' and 'discourse', relating to the tradition in text linguistics as well as to rhetoric (see Vass, 1994; Brünner and Gräfen, 1995; Wodak, 1996 for summaries). In the English-speaking world, 'discourse' is often used for both written and oral texts (see Schiffrin, 1992). Other researchers distinguish between different levels of abstractness: Lemke (1995) defines 'text' as the concrete realization of abstract forms of knowledge ('discourse'), thus adhering to a more Foucauldian approach (see also Jäger et al., 2001). The discourse-historical approach elaborates and links to the sociocognitive theory of Teun van Dijk (1984, 1993, 1998) and views 'discourse' as a form of knowledge and memory, whereas text illustrates concrete oral utterances or written documents (Reisigl and Wodak, 2001).

The shared perspective and programme of CDA relate to the term 'critical', which in the work of some 'critical linguists' could be traced to the influence of the Frankfurt School or Jürgen Habermas (see above). Nowadays this concept is conventionally used in a broader sense, recognizing, in Fairclough's words, 'that, in human matters, interconnections and chains of cause-and-effect may be distorted out of vision. Hence "critique" is essentially making visible the interconnectedness of things' (Fairclough, 1995, p. 747; see also Connerton, 1976, pp. 11–39).

References to the contribution of Critical Theory to the understanding of CDA and the notions of 'critical' and 'ideology' are of particular importance (see Anthonissen, 2001, for an extensive discussion of this issue). Thompson (1990) discusses the concepts of ideology and culture and the relations between these concepts and certain aspects of mass communication. He points out that the concept of ideology first appeared in late eighteenth-century France and has thus been in use for about two centuries. The term has been given a range of different functions and meanings at different times. For Thompson, ideology refers to social forms and processes within which, and by means of which, symbolic forms circulate in the social world. Ideology, for CDA, is seen as an important means of establishing and maintaining unequal power relations. CDA takes a particular interest in the ways in which language mediates ideology in a variety of social institutions. For Eagleton, moreover, the study of ideology has to bear in mind the variety of theories and theorists that have examined the relation between thought and social reality. All the theories assume 'that there are specific historical reasons why people come to feel, reason, desire and imagine as they do' (1994, p. 15).

Critical theories, and thus also CDA, are afforded special standing as guides for human action. Such theories seek not only to describe and explain, but also to root out a particular kind of delusion. Even with differing concepts of ideology, Critical Theory seeks to create awareness in agents of their own needs and interests. This was, of course, also taken up by Pierre Bourdieu (1989) in his concepts of '*violence symbolique*' and '*méconnaissance*'. One of the aims of CDA is to 'demystify' discourses by deciphering ideologies.

For CDA, language is not powerful on its own – it gains power by the use powerful people make of it. This explains why CDA often chooses the perspective of those who suffer and critically analyses the language use of those in power; those who are responsible for the existence of inequalities and who also have the means and the opportunity to improve conditions. In agreement with its Critical Theory predecessors, CDA emphasizes the need for interdisciplinary work in order to gain a proper understanding of how language functions in constituting and transmitting knowledge, in organizing social institutions or in exercising power.

An important perspective in CDA related to the notion of 'power' is that it is very rare that a text is the work of any one person. In texts discursive differences are negotiated; they are governed by differences in power which is in part encoded in and determined by discourse and by genre. Therefore texts are often sites of struggle in that they show traces of differing discourses and ideologies contending and struggling for dominance.

Thus, defining features of CDA are a concern with power as a central condition in social life and efforts to develop a theory of language which incorporates this as a major premise. Close attention is paid not only to the notion of struggles for power and control, but also to the intertextuality and recontextualization of competing discourses in various public spaces and genres. Power is about relations of difference, and particularly about the effects of differences in social structures. The constant unity of language and other social matters ensures that language is entwined in social power in a number of ways: language indexes power, expresses power, is involved where there is contention over and a challenge to power. Power does not derive from language, but language can be used to challenge power, to subvert it, to alter distributions of power in the short and the long term. Language provides a finely articulated vehicle for differences in power in hierarchical social structures. Very few linguistic forms have not at some stage been pressed into the service of the expression of power by a process of syntactic or textual metaphor. CDA takes an interest in the ways in which linguistic forms are used in various expressions and manipulations of power.

Power is signalled not only by grammatical forms within a text, but also by a person's control of a social occasion by means of the genre of a text. It is often exactly within the genres associated with given social occasions that power is exercised or challenged.

Thus, CDA might be defined as fundamentally interested in analysing opaque as well as transparent structural relationships of dominance, discrimination, power and control as manifested in language. In other words, CDA aims to investigate critically social inequality as it is expressed, constituted, legitimized, and so on, by language use (or in discourse). Most critical discourse analysts would thus endorse Habermas' claim that 'language is also a medium of domination and social force. It serves to legitimize relations of organized power. Insofar as the legitimizations of power relations ... are not articulated ... language is also ideological' (1967, p. 259).

Interdisciplinarity

'Interdisciplinarity', 'transdisciplinarity' and 'multidisciplinarity' have become catchwords of academic discourse, just like the 'theory concepts' cited above. (A website of a students' competition in Calgary (www.ucalgary.ca/evds/intervention/1996ss/interdisciplinarity.html) presents ironical rhymes, drawings and prints alluding to the fact that in job applications one is expected to give account of one's experience with interdisciplinarity, or at least show some interest in it: 'If we want jobs so we don't look like slobs – They tell us we're going to need Interdisciplinarity.')

In an important work by Peter Weingart and Nico Stehr (2000) the authors point out that scientific jargon has changed in the last few years. According to them, the above catchwords have to be used to 'belong to' the *academic community*. A new 'jargon of authentic being' (Adorno) seems to be evolving. In his contribution Weingart outlines the concepts of a traditional discipline and of interdisciplinary research. 'Fields' of specialization are defended by resorting to territorial metaphors, while interdisciplinary research uses images associated with innovation, progress and flexibility. He concludes that 'in fact, it reveals the seemingly paradoxical mechanism that the more differentiation of knowledge production the more intense will be the call for interdisciplinarity' (Weingart, 2000, p. 30). Finally Weingart states that interdisciplinarity can be seen as the result of opportunism in the production of knowledge: researchers seize interdisciplinary opportunities to produce new knowledge; practitioners grab these opportunities as well and provide the necessary resources. From this perspective, specialization and interdisciplinarity complement each other; they are not opposites or new dichotomies, but rather they coexist. Weingart and Stehr free the concept of 'interdisciplinarity' from jargon-like vagueness. They also stress that the existing matrix of traditional academic disciplines is dissolving and that significant changes in the traditional canon of knowledge are imminent.

What does this mean for CDA? How can demands for interdisciplinarity or transdisciplinarity be put into practice? What are the preconditions? And what are the consequences for the theory and practice of CDA and discourse analysis in general?

Of course these questions are not new. In feminist theory and cultural studies these questions and demands have existed for some years (see, for example, *L'Homme*, 1995). Since its inception in the early 1990s, CDA has waved the flag of interdisciplinarity (see Wodak, 1996; Chouliariki and Fairclough, 1999). The new anthology published by Helmut Gruber and Florian Menz (2001) with the promising title *Interdisziplinarität in der Angewandten Sprachwissenschaft. Methodenmenü oder Methodensalat?* (Interdisciplinarity in Applied Linguistics. Methodological Menu or Hotchpotch?) addresses not only methodological questions. In the Preface the two editors outline the most important debates within discourse analysis, which all require interdisciplinary responses: questions concerning the interpretation of discourses, questions concerning the definition of 'context' and questions as to an 'exhaustive description' versus 'abstinence from theory'. It is especially Martin Reisigl's (2001) contribution to this volume based on a study of secondary interjections that exemplifies how much extradisciplinary knowledge is necessary to interpret individual interjections and their use.

Here we will list some reasons why interdisciplinary research may be fertile and useful.

Innovation and creative environment

Roger and Ellen Hollingsworth, renowned American sociologists and historians, have been examining the questions of where creativity is thriving and how research should be conducted for many years. In 'Major discoveries and biomedical organizations: perspectives on interdisciplinarity, nurturing leadership, and integrated structure and cultures' (2000) they arrived at the conclusion that interdisciplinary teamwork at a very intensive level, that is, teams working together at the same place, is an important prerequisite for creativity. In addition they stated that these teams should include scientists of different disciplines and traditions. The Hollingsworths also emphasized that traditional hierarchical structures have an adverse effect on innovative research. 'Nurturing leadership' is required, a concept that stands for a very respectful, cooperative but at the same time firm stance of the project management: 'organizations require distinctive structural and cultural characteristics if scientists are to make major discoveries repeatedly'. The Hollingsworths investigated mainly institutions and teams in the field of natural sciences; nevertheless, we can ask ourselves to what extent their findings and proposals may also be applied to research and university institutions in the area of the social sciences and the humanities.

In this context it is also important to clarify what creativity and innovation could mean in the social sciences, for in the social sciences it will never be possible to make a 'new discovery' comparable to the relativity theory. According to the epistemological literature (see Kuhn, 1976), changes of paradigms are observable and possible also in social sciences although their quality differs from that of the natural sciences. Paradigms may coexist, different attempts at explanation may compete, and contexts may be interpreted and explained differently. In linguistics we find Noam Chomsky's pioneering approaches paralleled by structural and also descriptive, systemic theories. One theory does not replace another. Undoubtedly it can be considered an innovation to identify new causal relations, to weigh known causal relations differently or to highlight new dimensions of a study object. For example, women could be taken into account in historical, sociological, philosophical and linguistic research so as to end the attributing of universal validity to findings based on studies of white middle-class men. The step from the sentence to the text could also be interpreted as an innovation; and there are many other examples.

Why interdisciplinarity?

As can be seen from the above, there is a wealth of literature both for and against interdisciplinarity. Our brief remarks on this subject are based on, inter alia, Axeli Knapp and Hilge Landweer (1995), Roger and Ellen Hollingsworth (2000), Peter Weingart and Nico Stehr (2000), on some lectures at the conference 'Interdisciplinarity and the Organization of Knowledge in Europe' (Cambridge, 2000), on the debate between multidisciplinarity and interdisciplinarity in the cognition sciences (Yvonne Rogers, Mike Scaife and Antonio Rizzo), on Chouliaraki and Fairclough (1999), who present an extensive programme for CDA, on Gruber and Menz (2001), as well as on Moti Nissani

(1997) of the Interdisciplinary Studies Program at Wayne State University, who vehemently advocates interdisciplinary research in the social sciences and who drew up a ten-item programme. The science sociologist Helga Nowotny outlines the concepts up for discussion briefly and very accurately:

> Pluri(multi-)disciplinarity shows in the fact that the manifold disciplines remain independent. No changes are brought about in the existing structures of disciplines and theories. This form of academic cooperation consists in treating a subject from differing disciplinary perspectives.
>
> Interdisciplinarity may be recognized in the explicit formulation of a standardized transdisciplinary terminology. This form of cooperation is used to treat different subjects within a framework of an interdisciplinary or transdisciplinary design.
>
> Transdisciplinarity manifests itself when research across the disciplinary landscape is based on a common axiomatic theory and the interpenetration of disciplinary research methods. Cooperation leads to a bundling or clustering of problem-solving approaches rooted in different disciplines and drawing on a pool of theories. (Nowotny, 1997, p. 188ff.)

All authors agree in one respect: the difference between multi(trans)disciplinarity and interdisciplinarity is that interdisciplinary research ideally integrates theoretical approaches and thereby creates new holistic approaches, while multidisciplinary research does not modify the approaches of individual academic branches and applies them separately. Integration may however reach several levels both in the theory and the practice of research, which we describe in more detail below.

Axeli Knapp (Knapp and Landweer, 1995) presents five arguments in favour of interdisciplinary research within feminist theory. Slightly modified, they also fit applied theoretical and practice-oriented linguistics as well as CDA:

- A historical argument: the clear differentiation and specialization of individual disciplines is suited to solve individual problems very accurately and comprehensively within a specific debate in 'normal science', but complex new problems, such as identity research, racism research, and so on, require more than the expertise of an individual discipline. To address a current conflict without hesitation we have to point out that this triggers territorial fears and results in new borders.
- An argument related to the sociology of science: competition and careers often determine the progress in individual sectors of the traditional canon of disciplines. This progress no longer meets the requirements of the problem areas identified. Another consequence is that university training and the institutionalization of disciplines has to be re-examined and adjusted. This implies that new occupational profiles and models have to be developed and accepted.

- An epistemological argument: longstanding conventions of data gathering, theory formation and validation increasingly prove an obstacle in constructing new knowledge. It becomes necessary to transcend old-established modes of thinking. These steps often break taboos and are therefore perceived as threats. Moreover, in an attempt to arrive at a holistic innovation many specialized details have to be ignored, which provokes the valid criticism of the individual disciplines. Today another Leonardo da Vinci has become impossible: the classical model of the humanist scholar and the example of academia has become obsolete due to rapid technological and social developments. In fact there is a real danger of 'doing an amateur job', that is, of superficially dipping into other disciplines. This is another argument in favour of teaming up specialists from different disciplines.
- An argument relating to the content: cooperative and interdisciplinary research projects become the more important, the more complex social relations are. New problems are considered to be of relevance. In many cases this demand is met by resorting to eclecticism and the indiscriminate copying of approaches of individual disciplines.
- Finally, a political argument: critical thinking and critical practice point to new forms and organizations as well as applications of knowledge. For example, feminists or CDA researchers are of the opinion that traditional organizational structures cannot be respected in this process. It is an open question as to whether this applies also to other disciplines.

'Hyphen linguists'

Within applied linguistics, such as socio-linguistics or psycho-linguistics, interdisciplinary research per se was necessary and implied in the names of these research branches. William Labov and Basil Bernstein had already drawn on sociological layer models, linguistic theories (Labov, 1966; Bernstein, 1990) and psycho-linguistics, for example, in studying therapeutic communication, psycho- and social-psychological theories (Wodak, 1981, 1986). Therefore in these fields of study the fundamental question regarding interdisciplinarity no longer arises. In these branches of linguistics interdisciplinarity has to be taken into account at all levels, from theory through to methodology.

Which models are we faced with in 'hyphen linguistics'?

1. Additive models: approaches from various disciplines and areas are added up. Here the two traditional socio-linguistic approaches mentioned above may be given as an example. In the case of Labov, sophisticated linguistics were combined with static long-established sociological variables. In the case of Bernstein, elaborate structural sociological approaches were associated with some – simple – linguistic variables. In both cases, the specialized disciplines responded with immediate criticism, and the creative potential of the two approaches was therefore often overlooked or swept aside.

2. Eclectic ad hoc models: in exaggerated terms, one could say that every-thing is accumulated that 'comes in handy', without questioning its epis-temological origin and compatibility. For example, the 'grand theories' of Giddens, Habermas, Bourdieu, Foucault and Laclau are combined with systemic linguistics, a fact many specialized scholars view with scepti-cism, and rightly so. In most cases – and now we refer to our own expe-rience of the routine practice of team research – this works as follows: somebody reads an interesting book, or hears about it; this book then develops a dynamics of its own, and – purely by accident – will soon appear in mainstream research. The more this work is quoted, the more everybody will be convinced that this book or this study is in fact a clas-sic. Admittedly, we cannot be expected to know or to be able to assess the state of art of all disciplines involved. This is how fashions and trends develop that blur our vision of many other important works or prevent us from perceiving them.

3. Integrative (problem-oriented) models: based on research questions and problems, approaches are applied that provide meaningful, adequate and transparent interpretations and explanations. And with this we come to speak of our own work within the Research Centre for Discourse, Politics and Identity based on many individual projects conducted at the Department of Linguistics, where we jointly developed the so-called 'dis-course historical approach' (see Reisigl and Wodak, 2001; www.oeaw.ac.at/ wittgenstein). This approach is based on a pragmatic strategy similar to the one developed by Mouzelis (1995).

Interdisciplinary approach in this case is not limited to theory formation but extends to the practice of research and application. The team itself is recruited on an interdisciplinary basis. The dynamics within the team reflects all aspects and problems in microcosm that would otherwise come into play in the individual research disciplines. To give a more detailed account would go beyond the scope of this Introduction; but the degree of complexity is considerably higher than in monodisciplinary research pro-jects. The mere fact of having to agree on a common terminology poses problems (see above): it is not merely an act of definition but implies that specific subjects, theories and perspectives have to be agreed on. And this requires time: time to read, to learn, to discuss and to analyse.

In our study on unemployment and employment policies (Muntigl et al., 2000) political scientists, sociologists and linguists teamed up. However, these were not just plain linguists but socio-linguists, conversational analysts and critical discourse analysts. The linguists' team itself was there-fore required to learn intercultural communication. We held team meet-ings on a regular basis to present concepts relevant to us all and to agree on a basic stock of common literature. With that, a general consensus and a canon of common knowledge was established. In long sessions we jointly analysed and interpreted text sequences; the sociologists and political scientists were familiarized with grammar theory and discourse analysis, while we acquired basic knowledge of sociological theories. Economic consultants were called in to present theories in workshops and to support us in analysing texts. In order to acquire international know-how, we invited other experts to hold guest lectures and seminars. Supervision at regular intervals helped us to reflect on conflicts arising and to address them. Hence, the participants' willingness to learn, their ability to deal with criticism, openness and curiosity, as well as their willingness to treat other team members as equal partners, are the indispensable requirements of the interdisciplinary research practice which make 'innovation' (as defined in the social sciences) possible. Other key factors are a 'creative environment', office space, resources, money and time.

However, in many cases we do not have that time. And this takes us to a difficult aspect, the institutional setting. If the project findings need to be available within a short period of time it will not be possible to use this approach. The institutions responsible for commissioning research projects should therefore take into account the conditions of knowledge construction and creative research. Teamwork has to be taught and learned. The model of 'nurturing leadership', as formulated by Hollingsworth, requires many social competencies we do not acquire systematically in traditional studies and professional careers.

Perspectives: theory, interdisciplinarity, context

A 'symptomatology' is associated with the aforementioned pragmatic approach by Mouzelis (1995). Problems manifest themselves in 'symptoms'. Attempts are made to show systematic relations between manifestations, which do not necessarily have to be causal: social phenomena are too complex to be thought of as chains of causes and effects. The question of *context* is of particular relevance. If 'context' is understood not as a mere 'setting' in space/time or 'situational framework' but rather as something that requires a more comprehensive theoretical explanation to allow an analysis of texts and discourses, an interdisciplinary approach is almost a logical consequence (Wodak, 2000a). (Here we allude to the recent debate engaged in by Emanuel Schegloff, Michael Billig and Margaret Wetherell in *Discourse & Society* (1997–99), but without presenting it here in more detail.)

In the following we present a brief outline of our own approach to 'mediation' between discourse and society. For this purpose differentiation of the context concept within the discourse-historical approach is indispensable (Wodak, 2001c, 2002). One methodical way for critical discourse analysts to minimize the risk of critical baseness and to avoid simply politicizing, instead of accurately analysing, is to follow the principle of 'triangulation'. One of the most salient features of the discourse-historical approach is its endeavour to work interdisciplinarily, multimethodically and on the basis of a variety of different empirical data as well as background information (see Wodak and Meyer, 2001). Depending on the respective object of investigation, it attempts to transcend the pure linguistic dimension and to include more or less systematically the historical, political, sociological and/or psychological dimension in the analysis and interpretation of a specific discursive occasion.

In investigating historical and political topics and texts, the discourse-historical approach attempts to integrate much available knowledge about the historical sources and the background of the social and political fields in which discursive 'events' are embedded. Further, it analyses the historical dimension of discursive actions by exploring the ways in which particular genres of discourse are subject to diachronic change, that is, the intertextuality and interdiscursivity.

In accordance with other approaches devoted to CDA the discourse-historical approach perceives both written and spoken language as a form of social practice (Fairclough and Wodak, 1997). A *discourse* is a way of signifying a particular domain of social practice from a particular perspective (Fairclough, 1995, p. 14). As critical discourse analysts we assume a dialectical relationship between particular discursive practices and the specific fields of action (including situations, institutional frames and social structures) in which they are embedded. On the one hand, the situational, institutional and social settings shape and affect discourses, and, on the other, discourses influence discursive as well as non-discursive social and political processes and actions. In other words, discourses as linguistic social practices can be seen both as constituting non-discursive and discursive social practices and, at the same time, as being constituted by them.

Our triangulatory approach is based on a concept of 'context' which takes into account four levels. The first level is descriptive, while the other three levels constitute part of our theories on context:

1. the immediate, language or text internal co-text
2. the intertextual and interdiscursive relationship between utterances, texts, genres and discourses
3. the extralinguistic social/sociological variables and institutional frames of a specific 'context of situation' (middle-range theories)
4. the broader sociopolitical and historical contexts, which the discursive practices are embedded in and related to (see Figure 1.1).

The main challenge facing CDA representatives is to highlight gaps between theory and empirical research, between discourse and context – gaps which will in any case be unbridgeable. Theory formation has to manifest itself in an explanation of the structural and linguistic facts; discourse analysis is not practicable without integrating the theoretical approaches (see above, regarding mediation and macro/microproblems; important steps). Thus the

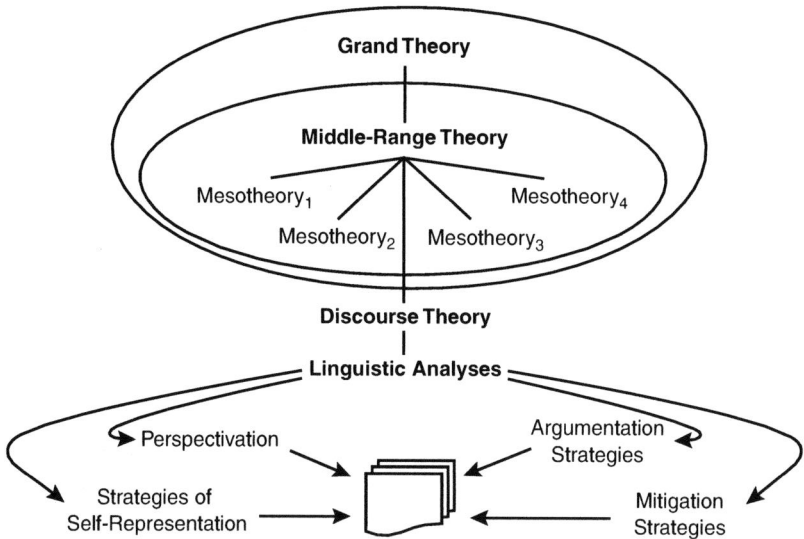

Figure 1.1 Levels of context

analysis of relevance presents a new problem: innovation by interdisciplinarity becomes possible if new relevance levels are defined by mixing new perspectives of theoretical context and discourse analyses. Ideally, this approach should be implemented consistently from the structural context analysis to the analysis of discursive practices, as demonstrated in some studies (see Muntigl et al., 2000; Wodak and Meyer, 2001). In Wodak and Meyer (2001) some CDA representatives present their respective theoretical and methodological steps by focusing on different aspects (see Fairclough, 2001; Jäger, 2001; Scollon, 2001; van Dijk, 2001; Wodak, 2001b, 2001c). We continue this debate in this volume.

The structure of the volume

Chapter 2, by Michael Billig, is a critical reading of the story of Critical Discourse Analysis. Billig recapitulates the basic claims of CDA and particularly calls for reflexivity and self-criticism in CDA vis-à-vis its own development. It is emphasized that 'CDA itself must be subjected to critique, and this includes the very symbol "CDA". In particular, one might ask whether the general processes of marketization are reflected in Critical Discourse Analysis' own passage from being a "critical approach" to the capitalised entity of "CDA".'

After a *tour d'horizon* through 'critical' approaches in the history of philosophy, Billig identifies crucial features giving particular meaning to the current use of 'critical'. He then focuses on 'dilemmas of success' in the academic world as well as the social context of academic work. Finally, a certain tension between interdisciplinary or even anti-disciplinary positions (as represented by CDA approaches) on the one hand and the establishment of an academic discipline (represented by the three capitals 'CDA') on the other is revealed. For the author, this tension shows that 'academic disciplines are social and institutional practices rather than inherent qualities of academic texts'.

In Chapter 3 Carlos Gouveia also asks for the specific quality of criticism in CDA. For him, the relevance and success of the latter depends on how scientific knowledge and common sense are brought together. Gouveia reflects on the emergence of CDA embedded in a broader history of epistemological breaks, starting with a first break constituting the very beginning of modern sciences, namely the Cartesian *divisio mundi*. The reductionism of modern science in approaching human realities is rooted in this break, which, according to Gouveia, represents also the break between scientific knowledge and common sense. However, the author identitifies another epistemological break at the end of the twentieth century which itself breaks with the first epistemological break, so to speak. The emerging 'new science', for him, is represented by theorists like Prigogine, Capra, Maturana and Varela – and not least also by the formation of CDA. In this context, theory and methodology of CDA are 'examples of tentative responses (not all of them entirely successful, though) to key factors in the general crisis that has been affecting the paradigm of modern science in the last decades of the twentieth century'. Finally, Gouveia claims that, in linking scientific knowledge to common sense again, interdisciplinarity is an important task – although not so much an advocated concept as the actual deconstruction of 'taken-for-granted, naturalised, discourses of the disciplines'.

In Chapter 4 Marianne W. Jørgensen applies discourse analysis to epistemological problems. In particular, the author is interested in the creation of scientific subject positions in the field of anthropology. Building on Foucault's diagnosis of 'modern man' and using tools from CDA, Jørgensen, although acknowledging the achievements of constructivist epistemology and 'reflexive' knowledge research, develops also a systematic criticism of the latter. She asks questions such as, 'What makes the debate on reflexivity make sense?', 'What are its conditions of possibility?', 'Which view of the world is constructed?', 'How are the relations between knowledge, the object of knowledge and the knowledge producer constituted in reflexive texts?', and 'Which subject positions are thus created; from which discursively constituted positions do knowledge producers claim validity and legitimacy for their knowledge?'

Finally, Jørgensen argues that an interdisciplinary approach to the question of reflexivity provides us with a common denominator for the discussions of scientific knowledge in a number of disciplines, enabling us to analyse a range of contributions as different solutions to the same problem concerning the status of knowledge. Jørgensen then focuses on the discipline of anthropology, first sketching different anthropological negotiations of the problem, and then putting the developed tools at work in a closer analysis of one example, Talal Asad's article 'The concept of cultural translation in British social anthropology'.

Teun van Dijk, in Chapter 5, approaches one fundamental problem in CDA, namely the relation or interface between discourse and knowledge. Van Dijk demonstrates the relevance of multidisciplinary perspectives and theoretical substance par excellence. In order to grasp the complexity of the problem of knowledge, a variety of disciplines and perspectives must be included: epistemology, psychology, cultural anthropology, cognitive anthropology, sociology and linguistics. What is true for knowledge is also true for the notion of discourse. So, for van Dijk, it is evident that the interface between discourse and knowledge also needs to be multidisciplinary. This is not surprising when we realize that they need and presuppose each other mutually: Discourse production and understanding is impossible without knowledge, and knowledge acquisition and change usually presupposes discourse. Van Dijk follows aspects of knowledge and social cognition, knowledge and representation, comprehension and discourse processing. Finally, a typology of knowledge is developed which, together with an explicit theory of context, serves as a critical model of knowledge-discourse processing. What all this means for concrete texts and contexts is illustrated by a systematic analysis of an editorial in the *New York Times*.

In Chapter 6 Phil Graham approaches the problem of interdisciplinarity in the most direct manner. He argues that the trend towards academic specialization in social science is most usefully viewed from the perspective of evaluative meaning, and that each new discipline, in emphasizing its aspect of a broken conception of humanity, emphasizes one aspect of an already broken conception of value. Graham analyses the development of disciplines in the social sciences as the result of 'historically constituted practices of evaluating the social world in different ways'. For him, it is precisely these different ways of evaluating the world that constitute the disciplinary boundaries. This is then the point where, for Graham, CDA comes in, because it has the analytical potential to make these evaluations transparent. CDA, qua critical social science, may therefore benefit firstly by proceeding from the perspective of evaluative meaning to understand the dynamics of social change and overcome the damage to understanding entailed by intensive specialization across the sciences. Graham then applies his critical instruments by closely following the genre-specific values and the formation of sciences. In particular, he provides examples from the disciplines of economics, political science, psychology and ethics by analysing first-issue journals of the respective disciplines.

Jay Lemke, in Chapter 7, is interested in questions of social change. According to him, texts play a crucial role in processes of social change 'because they are the link across time and space that binds a social system together; they are both material and semiotic objects, they have physical properties which enable their semantic content to span time and space'. Accordingly, texts can be seen as indices of changing modes of social organization and control. Lemke shows the necessity of an interdisciplinary approach to these questions. He provides a theoretical perspective integrating advanced social theory and semiotics, especially social systems theory and models of social change and linguistic analyses of texts. Within this frame he is able to identify recent developments in textuality and the respective changing modes of social organization. In particular, he investigates the development from standardized discourses to what he calls 'hypertextual traversals' (for example, hypertexts, web surfing, mall cruising, career surfing, and – last but not least – academic transdisciplinarity itself). He follows different forms of textscales and timescales at different levels of social organization, such as television series and film sequels. Finally, crucial aspects of textual mediation of social control in today's globalized telecratic regimes become transparent.

In Chapter 8 Marcelo Dascal places CDA tools in the wider frame of philosophy as an 'essentially critical endeavour'. In his eyes, the major purpose of such a critical endeavour is 'to detect and clear up conceptual difficulties that are often responsible for what seem to be insurmountable obstacles for the solution of practical conflicts'. The conflict approached by Dascal here is one that is observed with increasing helplessness and despair today, namely the conflict between Arabs and Jews and the respective identities in the Near East. The author makes it quite plain that interdisciplinarity is unavoidable in approaching this case. After showing the difficulties accompanying the claim for interdisciplinarity, he performs a critical analysis of the concept of 'identity'. Out of this conceptual clarification, Dascal proposes eight points affording new horizons for the relations between Arabs and Jews in Israel. Finally, a number of obstacles making the implementation of conceptual 'solutions' so difficult in the case of this conflict are detailed.

Suzanne Scollon, in Chapter 9, discusses interdisciplinary practice in research extensively, using her own studies on the notion of 'social practice' in Tai Chi groups in Hong Kong and China as point of departure. She describes in detail how her own position and approach slowly developed, while applying eclectically important and relevant theories and parts of these theories when starting to describe and investigate Athabaskan speech communities and intercultural communication. Her approach finally ends, together with Ron Scollon, in a school of Critical Discourse Analysis – Mediated Discourse Analysis. In contrast to other CDA methodologies, Suzanne Scollon emphasizes the role of ethnography and also of semiotics. She discusses the notions of 'habitus' and 'practice', integrating important concepts of Pierre Bourdieu and Norbert Elias. Her elaborate investigation of even the smallest actions (for instance hanging your gym bag on a tree or putting it on a blanket on the ground) make it very clear how embedded such seemingly trivial actions are in cultural and ideological traditions. They have meaning and signify certain stances. Such research is a perfect example for the necessity of an interdisciplinary approach, both in theory and in methodology.

In Chapter 10 Jim Martin takes a completely different point of departure: he compares modernist and postmodernist approaches to intercultural interaction in Australia between the white population and the Aborigines. He endorses the voicing of the powerless, and how minorities gain access to the media and to the perspective of the majority. The approach is interdisciplinary in that he has to take account on the one hand of the writings and histories of the minorities, and, on the other, of the power play between social groups. He emphasizes different modes of depicting minorities and the impact of multimodal meanings. Martin is critical of CDA pointing mostly to the powerless and de-masking the powerful. His approach is to be seen as a 'positive' approach: he wants to give voice to the powerless.

In Chapter 11 Patricia O'Connor suggests that an 'activist socio-linguistics' can emerge from certain empirical work of linguists. She has been concerned with discourses of violence and abuse for many years while investigating narratives of prisoners. O'Connor explicitly endorses a position where Critical Discourse Analysis should apply its results and actively participate in social processes. In her research on maximum-security prisoners and addicts she examines the ways in which people agentively present themselves in autobiographical discourse, not only positioning themselves in their criminal or errant pasts but also narratively constructing past selves and potential new selves in society. She claims that elements of agentive discourse are clustered in sites of reflexive language, particularly in frame breaks and in meta-talk or evaluative references to one's knowledge state. Such breaks interpenetrate the narratives and complicate the determination of personal, moral agency because they reveal an epistemic grappling with the action taken (in the past) while showing agentive manipulation of the story (in the present). Such constructivist work places the speaker and the linguist in an interesting nexus of practice that could effect change. The reconstruction of life stories is thus seen as a possibility for changing motivations and identities, after having reflected on past actions. This, of course, reminds us in some ways of a kind of therapeutic methodology, but without the characteristic setting of psychotherapeutic discourses. Discourse serves, in these cases, not only as transmitter of information, but also as a vehicle for change.

After a presentation of examples from institutional data, O'Connor considers the issue of subjectivity when the researcher herself is part of that reflexivity in a community of uptake. She discusses her methods for beginning new research projects into narratives from those in substance-abuse treatment. People in prison have often entered such places because of drug use, addiction or illicit drug sales. This research suggests that long-term involvement in such a setting leads to a thicker and richer interpretation of data that can contribute to social change.

Interdisciplinarity is hence emphasized on at least two levels: on the level of discourse analysis and participation research, drawing multiple methodologies together; and on the level of research and political practice. Questions to be pursued in such an approach include, 'How do attachments to (or detachment from) speakers affect data?', 'How can informants become co-researchers?', 'How do researchers form partnerships with communities?', and 'Does participatory action research allow for continuing relationships of inquiry?'

Luisa Martín Rojo and Concepción Gómez Esteban illustrate in Chapter 12 very precisely what it means to integrate different theoretical and methodological approaches from linguistics, gender studies, organisation studies and sociology while investigating women in management positions.

The chapter is part of an interdisciplinary research project into management models and gender. The main aim of the study is to explore whether and to what extent new theoretical models of management were encouraging the promotion of women to positions of responsibility in companies, and also leading to a correlative improvement of the image of women managers. New studies emphasize that 'female' models defend a more democratic view of management, and communicative and relational skills (showing empathy and requesting compliance) versus an assertive style. Specifically, as the data stem from Spanish firms, the impact of Spanish culture has to be observed as well. The analysis focuses on the way people adapt these new 'soft' models to traditional management situations – showing differences depending on whether the managers are men or women – and on the effects of this adaptation on the image of women managers.

The theoretical framework focuses, inter alia, on power relations in organizations. This is in fact an essential object of interest in sociological studies, which cannot be ignored when analysing the role of gender in social life. At the same time, the approach focuses on discursive practices and the ideological production, reproduction and justification of the gender relations of domination. Following this sociodiscursive approach, discursive practices are viewed as an expression of organizational structure as well as the means by which organization members create this structure and give coherence to everyday practices. Organizations are understood here not only as a social collective where shared meanings and practices are produced, but also as a 'battlefield' where different groups compete to try to shape the organization in ways that serve their own interests. Gender is clearly involved in this competition, and organizations thus appear as fundamentally gendered structures.

Moreover, a very practice-oriented aspect is also endorsed. The authors study this topic to be able to support models which could introduce positive action to end the discrimination experienced by female managers and indeed the entire female workforce.

Thus, interdisciplinarity is not considered – in this chapter – as the mere superposition of analyses, by different disciplines, of the same object of study, but rather as the attempt to integrate them. What underlies this sociodiscursive approach is the shared assumption that to reduce the complexity of phenomena to a single disciplinary approach, or level of analysis, would mean reducing the comprehension and interpretation of social life. At the same time, the construction of the object of study and the analysis itself are based more than ever now on an ongoing discussion of the basic concepts and principles used.

In Chapter 13 Carmen Caldas-Coulthard examines news in the UK about Brazil and other postcolonial countries. Her approach is interdisciplinary in many respects: she employs and integrates theories from media studies, postcolonial studies, multimodality and discourse analysis. Her methodology stems by and large from functional systemic linguistics. Specifically, she focuses on processes of recontextualization and legitimation.

In all cases she investigates, the representations in the news are never neutral, without a point of view. In the age of globalization, the international distribution of power tends to make the First World a powerful transmitter of cultural ideas and ideologies. The Third World, however, appropriates these ideas and reverses them in terms of self-referentiality. She illustrates how media discourses construe states of affairs that can be harmful to many people. The awareness of their processes, strategies and points of view is of utmost importance. The discursive-analytical view taken in this chapter, together with key notions of intertextuality, recontextualization and multimodality, allow the deconstruction of discrimination through language and image. By examining textual and visual evidence, nationalistic, racist and gender-biased discourses could be unravelled. Thus, the analysis tries to demonstrate that one should be aware of the power of representation and of the goals and evaluations of any given recontextualization.

In Chapter 14 Christine Anthonissen investigates the role of censorship in South African print media before the transition to democracy. In investigating media, she applies multiple approaches: discourse analysis, the multimodal analysis of Gunther Kress and Theo van Leeuwen, and a sociopolitical interpretation of the social developments in South Africa. She labels her approach as Critical Discourse Analysis, which – she claims – must be interdisciplinary when taking on such complex objects of investigation. Her analysis uncovers several important strategies aimed at circumpassing censorship, using diverse linguistic realizations as well as semiotic modes. This case study illustrates the application of CDA while analysing a very complex political setting such as the South African media. On the other hand the study lends itself to generalization, because such strategies and modes of dealing with suppression and censorship are common in other authoritarian regimes.

References

Anthonissen, C. (2001) 'On the Effectivity of Media Censorship: An Analysis of Linguistic, Paralinguistic and Other Communicative Devices Used to Defy Media Restrictions'. Unpublished PhD thesis, University of Vienna.

Berger, P.L. and Luckmann, T. (1966) *The Social Construction of Reality*. New York: Doubleday.
Bernstein, B. (1990) *The Structure of Pedagogic Discourse: Class, Codes and Control*, Vol. VI. London: Routledge.
Bourdieu, P. (1977) *Outline of a Theory of Practice*. Cambridge: Cambridge University Press.
Bourdieu, P. (1980) *Le sens pratique*. Paris: Les Éditions de Minuit.
Bourdieu, P. (1989) *Symbolische Formen*. Frankfurt am Main: Suhrkamp.
Bourdieu, P. (1990) *Was heißt Sprechen? Die Ökonomie des sprachlichen Tausches*. Vienna: Braumüller.
Bourdieu, P. (1997) *Der Tote packt den Lebenden. Schriften zu Politik und Kultur 2*. Hamburg: VSA.
Brünner, G. and Gräfen, G. (eds) (1995) *Texte und Diskurse*. Tübingen: Niemeyer.
Carnap, R. (1928) *Scheinprobleme in der Philosophie*. Wien: Springer.
Chouliaraki, L. and Fairclough, N. (1999) *Discourse in Late Modernity: Rethinking Critical Discourse Analysis*. Edinburgh: Edinburgh University Press.
Cicourel, A. (1964) *Method and Measurement in Sociology*. New York: Free Press.
Cicourel, A. (1973) *Cognitive Sociology: Language and Meaning in Social Interaction*. London: Penguin Books.
Connerton, P. (1976) *How Societies Remember*. Cambridge: Cambridge University Press. (1996 reprint).
Eagleton, T. (1994) (ed.) *Ideology*. London: Longman.
Fairclough, N. (1989) *Language and Power*. London: Longman.
Fairclough, N. (1992) *Discourse and Social Change*. Oxford, UK, and Cambridge, MA: Polity Press and Blackwell.
Fairclough, N. (1995) *Critical Discourse Analysis: The Critical Study of Language*. London: Longman.
Fairclough, N. (2001) 'Critical discourse analysis as a method in social scientific research', in R. Wodak and M. Meyer (eds), *Methods of Critical Discourse Analysis*. London: Sage, pp. 121–38.
Fairclough, N. and Wodak, R. (1997) 'Critical discourse analysis', in T. van Dijk (ed.), *Discourse Studies: A Multidisciplinary Introduction*. Vol. 2. London: Sage, pp. 258–84.
Foucault, M. (1972) *L'ordre du discours*. Paris: Gallimard.
Garfinkel, H. (1984) *Studies in Ethnomethodology*. Cambridge: Polity Press.
Giddens, A. (1979) *Central Problems in Social Theory*. London: Macmillan.
Giddens, A. (1984) *The Constitution of Society. Outline of the Theory of Structuration*. Cambridge: Polity Press.
Grathoff, R. (1995) *Milieu und Lebenswelt. Einführung in die phänomenologische Soziologie und die sozialphänomenologische Forschung*. Frankfurt am Main: Suhrkamp.
Gruber, H. and Menz, F. (eds) (2001) *Interdisziplinarität in der Angewandten Sprachwissenschaft. Methodenmenü oder Methodensalat?* Bern: Lang Verlag.
Habermas, J. (1967) *Erkenntnis und Interesse*. Frankfurt am Main: Suhrkamp.
Habermas, J. (1981) *Theorie des kommunikativen Handelns*. 2 Vols. Frankfurt am Main: Suhrkamp.
Heritage, J. (1984) *Garfinkel and Ethnomethodology*. Cambridge: Polity Press.
Hollingsworth, R. and Hollingsworth, E. (2000) 'Major discoveries and biomedical organizations: perspectives on interdisciplinarity, nurturing leadership, and integrated structure and cultures', in P. Weingart and N. Stehr (eds), *Practising Interdisciplinarity*. Toronto: University of Toronto Press.
Hügli, A. and Lübcke, P. (1991) *Philosophielexikon. Personen und Begriffe der abendländischen Philosophie von der Antike bis zur Gegenwart*. Reinbeck: Rowohlt.

Husserl, E. (1993) *Arbeit an den Phänomenen.* Ausgewählte Schriften. Frankfurt am Main: Fischer.

Jäger, S. (2001) 'Discourse and knowledge: theoretical and methodological aspects of a critical discourse and dispositive analysis', in R. Wodak and M. Meyer (eds), *Methods of Critical Discourse Analysis.* London: Sage, pp. 32–62.

Jäger, S. et al. (2001) *Kritische Diskursanalyse.* Duisburg: DISS Verlag.

Janssen, P. (1976) *Edmund Husserl. Einführung in seine Philosophie.* Munich: Alber.

Knapp, G.A. and Landweer, H. (1995) 'Interdisziplinarität in der Frauenforschung: Ein Dialog', *L'Homme,* 6(2), pp. 6–38.

Kuhn, T. (1976) *Die Struktur wissenschaftlicher Revolutionen.* Frankfurt am Main: Suhrkamp.

L'Homme. Zeitschrift für Feministische Geschichtswissenschaft (1995), Special Issue, Vol. 6(2), Interdisziplinarität (eds G. Axeli-Knapp and E. Saurer).

Labov, W. (1966) *The Social Stratification of English in New York City.* New York: Center for Applied Linguistics.

Lemke, J. (1995) *Textual Politics. Discourse and Social Dynamics.* London: Taylor and Francis.

Levy, D.A. (1981) *Realism. An Essay in Interpretation and Social Reality.* Manchester: Carcanet Press.

Luhmann, N. (1984) *Soziale Systeme.* Frankfurt am Main: Suhrkamp.

Luhmann, N. (1997) *Die Gesellschaft der Gesellschaft.* 2 Vols. Frankfurt am Main: Suhrkamp.

Meyer, M. (2001) 'Between theory, method, and politics: positioning of the approaches to CDA', in R. Wodak and M. Meyer (eds), *Methods of Critical Discourse Analysis.* London: Sage, pp. 14–31.

Mouzelis, N. (1995) *Sociological Theory: What Went Wrong? Diagnoses and Remedies.* London: Routledge.

Muntigl, P., Weiss, G. and Wodak, R. (2000) *European Union Discourses on Un/Employment. An Interdisciplinary Approach on Employment Policy-Making and Organizational change.* Amsterdam: Benjamins.

Nissani, M. (1997) 'Ten cheers for interdisciplinarity', *Social Science Journal,* 34, pp. 201–16.

Nowotny, H. (1997) 'Transdisziplinäre Wissensproduktion – eine Antwort auf die Wissensexplosion?', in Friedrich Stadler (ed.), *Wissenschaft als Kultur. Österreichs Beitrag zur Moderne.* Vienna and New York: Springer, pp. 188–204.

Popper, K. (1935) *Logik der Forschung.* Wien: Springer.

Reisigl, M. (2001) 'Intradisziplinarität, Transdisziplinarität und Interdisziplinarität – Einige Überlegungen am Beispiel der sekundären Interjektionen', in H. Gruber and F. Menz (eds), *Interdisziplinarität in der Angewandten Sprachwissenschaft. Methodenmenü oder Methodensalat?* Bern: Lang Verlag, pp. 79–106.

Reisigl, M. and Wodak, R. (2001) *Discourse and Discrimination.* London: Routledge.

Rodi, F. and Lessing, H.-U. (1984) *Materialien zur Philosophie Wilhelm Diltheys.* Frankfurt am Main: Suhrkamp.

Schiffrin, D. (1992) *Approaches to Discourse Analysis.* Oxford: Blackwell.

Schutz, A. (1932) *Der sinnhafte Aufbau der Sozialen Welt.* Vienna: Springer.

Schutz, A. (1962) *The Problem of Social Reality.* Collected Papers. Vol. 1. The Hague: Martinus Nijhoff.

Schutz, A. and Luckmann, T. (1973) *The Structures of the Life-World.* Vol. 1. Evanston, IL: Northwestern University Press.

Scollon, R. (2001) 'Action and text: towards an integrated understanding of the place of text in social (inter)action, mediated discourse analysis and the problem of social action', in R. Wodak and M. Meyer (eds), *Methods of Critical Discourse Analysis.* London: Sage, pp. 139–83.

Strauss, A.L. (1978) *Negotiations: Varieties, Contexts, Processes and Social Order.* San Francisco: Jossey-Bass.

Thompson, J.B. (1990) *Ideology and Modern Culture.* Cambridge: Polity Press.

Titscher, S, Meyer, M., Wodak, R. and Vetter, E. (2000) *Methods of Text and Discourse Analysis.* London: Sage.

van Dijk, T.A. (1984) *Prejudice in Discourse: An Analysis of Ethnic Prejudice in Cognition and Conversation.* Amsterdam: Benjamins.

van Dijk, T.A. (1993) 'Principles of critical discourse analysis', *Discourse & Society,* 4(2), pp. 249–83.

van Dijk, T.A. (1995) 'Discourse semantics and ideology', *Discourse & Society,* 6(2), pp. 243–89.

van Dijk, T.A. (ed.) (1997) *Discourse Studies: A Multidisciplinary Introduction.* 2 Vols. London: Sage.

van Dijk, T.A. (1998) *Ideology. A Multidisciplinary Study.* London: Sage.

van Dijk, T.A. (2001) 'Multidisciplinary CDA: a plea for diversity', in R. Wodak and M. Meyer (eds), *Methods of Critical Discourse Analysis.* London: Sage, pp. 95–120.

Vass, E. (1994) 'Probleme des diskurskonzeptes'. MA thesis, University of Vienna.

Voegelin, E. (1987) *The New Science of Politics. An Introduction.* Chicago: University of Chicago Press.

Voegelin, E., Schutz, A., Strauss, L. and Gurwitsch, A. (1993) *Briefwechsel über 'Die Neue Wissenschaft der Politik'.* Munich: Alber.

Weingart, P. (2000) Foreword, in P. Weingart and N. Stehr (eds), *Practicising Interdisciplinarity.* Toronto: University of Toronto Press.

Weingart, P. and Stehr, N. (eds) (2000) *Practicising Interdisciplinarity.* Toronto: University of Toronto Press.

Weiss, G. (1996) 'Die Atemnot der Wissenschaft', *Tumult,* 20, pp. 90–102.

Wodak, R. (1981) *Das Wort in der Gruppe. Linguistische Studien zur therapeutischen Kommunikation.* Vienna: Akademie der Wissenschaften.

Wodak, R. (1986) *Language Behavior in Therapy Groups.* Los Angeles: University of California Press.

Wodak, R. (ed.) (1989) *Language, Power and Ideology.* Amsterdam: Benjamins.

Wodak, R. (1996) *Disorders of Discourse.* London: Longman.

Wodak, R. (2000a) 'Does sociolinguistics need social theory? New perspectives on critical discourse analysis', *Discourse & Society,* 2(3), pp. 123–47.

Wodak, R. (2001b) 'What CDA is about – a summary of its history, important concepts and its developments', in R. Wodak and M. Meyer (eds), *Methods of Critical Discourse Analysis.* London: Sage, pp. 1–13.

Wodak, R. (2001c) 'The discourse-historical approach', in R. Wodak and M. Meyer (eds), *Methods of Critical Discourse Analysis.* London: Sage, pp. 63–94.

Wodak, R. (2002) 'Aspects of Critical Discourse Analysis', *Zeitschrift für Angewandte Linguistik.*

Wodak, R. and Ludwig, C. (1999) Introduction, in R. Wodak and M. Meyer (eds), *Challenges in a Changing World. Issues in Critical Discourse Analysis.* Vienna: Passagen, pp. 11–20.

Wodak, R. and Meyer, M. (eds) (2001) *Methods of Critical Discourse Analysis.* London: Sage.

Part I
Critical ≠ Critical ≠ Critical

2
Critical Discourse Analysis and the Rhetoric of Critique

Michael Billig

It is not difficult to make claims for the academic success of Critical Discourse Analysis. Chouliaraki and Fairclough begin their new book *Discourse in Late Modernity* with the statement: 'Critical discourse analysis ... has established itself internationally over the past twenty years or so as a field of cross-disciplinary teaching and research which has been widely drawn upon in the social sciences and the humanities (for example, in sociology, geography, history and media studies), and has inspired critical language teaching at various levels and in various domains' (1999, p. 1). One sign of this success has seen the establishment of the term 'Critical Discourse Analysis', together with its abbreviation CDA, to denote a distinct and substantial body of work.

Much of the success of Critical Discourse Analysis can be traced to the pioneering works of analysts such as Norman Fairclough, Teun van Dijk and Ruth Wodak. If one wished to chart the emergence of the term 'Critical Discourse Analysis', one could point to the work of Norman Fairclough. In his 1992 book, *Discourse and Social Change*, Fairclough did not use the term as such. In this book, Fairclough outlined 'critical approaches' to discourse analysis. These critical approaches included 'critical linguistics' (Fowler et al., 1979) and Althusserian approaches to the study of ideology. Fairclough was also using other terms such as Critical Language Awareness, which was abbreviated to CLA, and Critical Language Studies or CLS. However, Fairclough (1992b), in his edited book *Critical Language Awareness*, was using the term 'critical discourse analysis' without specially abbreviating it to 'CDA'. In that work, he positioned 'critical discourse analysis' as a form of CLS. Three years later, a decisive terminological shift was made when Fairclough published his book *Critical Discourse Analysis* (Fairclough, 1995). The book bore the subtitle *The critical study of language*. The use of the definite article in the subtitle was emblematic: it was as if the multiplicity of 'critical approaches', which were outlined in Fairclough (1992a), had coalesced into a uniformity which could be identified as *the* critical study.

This change in nomenclature is not mentioned merely for historical purposes, but in order to raise questions about the success of Critical Discourse

Analysis in becoming a recognized field within the current academic context. The questions are not whether success has been achieved: that will be taken for granted, both in terms of genuine intellectual advances as well as achieving international visibility within the academic world. The questions concern the consequences of academic success for a critical endeavour, for it will be suggested that in the present climate success is double-edged.

These considerations are related to two basic concerns that are posed by critical discourse analysts. First, as Fairclough has stressed, contemporary capitalist society is characterized by deep-seated processes of marketization, which are leading to the emergence of new patterns of discourse (Fairclough, 1995; Chouliaraki and Fairclough, 1999). Fairclough has been particularly concerned with the effects of marketization within university contexts, for, as Chouliaraki and Fairclough write, 'universities these days are under increasing pressure to operate as a market that is shaped by its service relation to other markets' (1999, p. 8). In this regard, Fairclough has noted the need for critical discourse analysts to be critical of the marketing discourse that is produced by the institutions in which they operate.

This leads to a second concern: the need to be reflexively self-critical. As Chouliaraki and Fairclough note, 'CDA, like other critical social sciences... needs to be reflexive and self-critical about its own institutional position and all that goes with it' (ibid., p. 9). This involves critically examining its own discourse. As Gunther Kress wrote, 'all signs are...equally subject to critical reading' for 'no sign is innocent' (1993, p. 174). Therefore the signs of CDA itself must be subjected to critique, and this includes the very symbol 'CDA'. In particular, one might ask whether the general processes of marketization are reflected in Critical Discourse Analysis' own passage from being a 'critical approach' to the capitalized entity of 'CDA'.

One preliminary point should be stressed. The raising of such questions and the turning of the critical approach upon critical analysis itself do not indicate a stance that is opposed to critical discourse analysis. Certainly, there have been approaches to the study of talk and texts that have explicitly criticized the critical approach for containing a political stance (for example, Widdowson, 1995; Schegloff, 1997). I have been concerned with counteracting some of the claims made by opponents of the critical study of discourse (for example, Billig, 1999) and, more generally, with supporting the notion that the analysis of ideology must, and should, be based upon ideological presuppositions itself (Billig, 1991). Thus, my stance here is not a hostile attack from outside, but one that follows the demand that critical analysts be self-critical. This means that we cannot use critical terminology unreflexively, as if our own words are somehow magically innocent. If we do, then we run the risk of ignoring the political economy in which we operate. As Fairclough has written, ' "critical" implies showing connections and causes that are hidden' (1992a, p. 9). This means decoding the operations of ideology, for the discursive patterns of ideology can conceal features of the social world (Billig, 1996; van Dijk, 1996a, 1998). As will be suggested, if critical analysts fail to be self-reflexive then the critical enterprise can be compromised, to the extent that the critical limits of critique become ignored and thereby hidden.

Critical studies

The emergence of Critical Discourse Analysis has occurred at a time that co-incides with the growth of other critical paradigms/theories/disciplines in the social sciences, such as 'critical psychology', 'critical social policy' and 'critical anthropology'. As has been mentioned, Critical Discourse Analysis initially had alternative labels such as 'critical language awareness' or 'critical language studies'. Fairclough (1992a) also used the label 'critical linguistics'. In this context, the term 'critical' can be seen to mark out a specific genre of academic studies and one can ask what implications are carried by this label.

There is a long history of academics describing their approach as 'critical'. Most notably, Kant, in the Preface of his great *Critique of Pure Reason*, described his work as constituting 'a Critical Investigation of Pure Reason' (Kant, 1781 [1964], p. 3). He explained his use of 'critical' by stressing that he was not referring to 'a criticism of books and systems', but to the analysis of reason which would be conducted by rational a priori principles '*without the aid of experience*' (ibid., emphasis in the original). Despite Kant's disclaimer, the term 'critical' inevitably bears a rhetoric of criticism. This is because the formulation of an academic theory inevitably occurs in the context of argumentation, so that the propounding of a theory involves the explicit, and sometimes implicit, criticism of alternative theories (Billig, 1987). Thus, Kant, who did not specifically argue with his philosophical opponents, nevertheless could not forbear in his Preface from casting aspersions on the 'dogmatists', who promise 'to extend knowledge beyond the limits of possible experience' (1781 [1964], p. 4). In this way, Kant was employing a rhetorical antithesis, contrasting his own critical philosophy with the uncritical dogmatism of others.

In this sort of context, the label 'critical' bears a rhetoric of self-praise, for it is invariably a term that is applied to the self. 'Uncritical' or 'non-critical' are reserved for others. No doubt the theorists who were judged to be 'uncritical' by Kant would not have happily accepted such a label. Nor would they have accepted the criterion that Kant proposed for distinguishing between the critical and the uncritical. Years after Kant, Karl Popper was to describe his own work as 'critical rationalism', claiming that metaphysicians, Marxists and those who believed in the principle of induction were all, in some way, uncritical dogmatists (Popper, 1976; see also Notturno, 1999). Historically, the claim to be 'critical' has not been confined to philosophers. As Erica Burman (1996) points out, the developmental psychologist,

Jean Piaget, called his approach 'critical'. By this he meant that his psychology contained its own standards of validation and that rival approaches to which he was contrasting his own approach lacked such standards.

The critical approaches that emerged in the 1990s do not claim to be the inheritors of all previously self-labelled critical approaches. Critical discourse analysts do not tend to position themselves as Kantians or Popperians. As Burman (1996) makes plain, her own critical developmental psychology is very different from Piaget's. If the various recent critical paradigms/theories/disciplines do claim a common critical inheritance, then it tends to be from the 'critical theory' of the Frankfurt School. Kenneth Gergen, one of the most influential figures in the movement of critical psychology, sees his work and that of other critical psychologists as following the example of the Frankfurt School, despite advocating a very different sort of psychology than that used by Frankfurt School theorists. According to Gergen, today's critical psychologists share with the Frankfurt School a sense that academic work should aim to criticize existing conditions of social life in the hope of transcending those conditions (Gergen, 1994, p. 197ff.).

More specifically, it is possible to identify several crucial features which the recent critical paradigms/theories/disciplines claim to possess and which gives particular meaning to the current use of 'critical'.

The first and most important factor is that critical approaches claim to be critical of the present social order. Van Dijk (1993) writes that the targets of Critical Discourse Analysis are power elites that sustain social inequality and injustice. Critical discourse analysts do not see themselves as conventional discourse analysts who happen to have radical or progressive views, as if social or political criticism were something additional to their academic work. Instead, Critical Discourse Analysis is seen to be a means of criticising the social order. This delineates today's critical studies from Kantian, Popperian or Piagetian critical study. Critical Discourse Analysis does not claim to be 'critical' because of a technical or methodological difference from other approaches to the study of language. It is claimed that Critical Discourse Analysis, like critical psychology or critical social policy, is critical because it is rooted in a radical critique of social relations.

Second, following from the commitment to radical critique, critical approaches position themselves as being critical of other academic approaches that are not primarily addressed to the critique of existing patterns of dominance and inequality. In particular, critical approaches contrast themselves with disciplines/paradigms/theories whose theoretical and methodological assumptions seem to exclude direct political or radical analyses. Fairclough writes that 'critical approaches differ from non-critical approaches in not just describing discursive practices, but also showing how discourse is shaped by relations of power and ideologies' (1992a, p. 12). Critical discourse analysts are likely to view the approaches of both traditional linguistics and conversation analysis as being 'non-critical', because their perspectives seem to ignore the connections between language and power. Both such approaches focus on technical aspects of language so that the analytic tools are devoted to examining discrete pieces of language rather than placing these pieces in a wider political and social context (Wetherell, 1998). For example, the conventional linguist might focus on details of grammar without seeking to link the occurrence of particular grammatical constructions within ideological practices and the maintenance of power relations (see, for instance, Widdowson's 1995 critique of critical approaches). Schegloff (1997) argues that the strength of conversation analysis lies in its refusal to impose political or other categories on the data of conversational interaction. The imposition of such categories, according to Schegloff, would obstruct the task of analysing the details of talk as they appear to participants. For critical analysts, the resulting focus is too narrow, for the wider political issues give way to detailed, technical analyses of interpersonal communication (Wetherell, 1998; Billig, 1999).

In such debates, the term 'critical' can become an object of contestation, for the supposedly 'non-critical' or 'uncritical' cannot be expected to accept the ascribed label without protest. Jonathan Potter, in a discussion of Critical Discourse Analysis, points out that CDA treats 'criticism as if it were intrinsic to the enterprise (and, implicitly, absent from other forms of discourse analysis)' (1996, p. 227). Potter recommends types of discursive analysis which might or might not produce social criticism, depending on what emerges from the particular examination of particular pieces of discourse. The avowedly critical approaches take a different stance. For them, social critique is not something that may or may not result from analysis: it is the *raison d'être* for analysis. As such, the critical approach claims to have the aim of political critique inbuilt into its theoretical and methodological tools of analysis.

Third, critical approaches assert that academic work is related to the social conditions of domination. This assumption leads to a specific sort of critique that is directed against supposedly non-critical approaches. It is argued that non-critical approaches tend to constitute the dominant position within particular academic disciplines. Certainly, at present non-critical linguistics is much more widely practised and firmly established than Critical Discourse Analysis, and so is mainstream experimental psychology, as compared with critical psychology. Given that critical theorists see a link between academic work and social relations of domination, then the critique of mainstream, non-critical approaches takes on an extra edge. It is not merely argued that mainstream approaches fail to place their particular findings in a wider social context, but this gap is seen to be highly ideological. The mainstream approach, often by attacking the critical endeavour as 'politically biased' or 'non-rigorous', is said to preclude systematic social critique. This omission, according to critical theorists, is not innocent but has the function of maintaining existing power relations. Thus, the critical approach's critique of mainstream approaches cannot be confined to discussing technical questions of theory and methodology. Critical approaches not only seek to expose gaps in the supposedly non-critical orthodoxy but then seek to show how these gaps are neither neutral nor haphazard. According to critical discourse analysts, mainstream non-critical approaches to the study of language are themselves discourses whose ideological nature needs to be studied.

What this means is that the critical approach will view the existing discipline, which it is criticising, as being too narrow. Other forms of analysis, perhaps from other disciplines, need to be incorporated into the traditional disciplinary basis. Thus, critical discourse analysis implies that it is insufficient merely to study discourse as linguists have traditionally done. Linguistic analysis needs to be augmented by critical social analysis. Moreover, the tools of social analysis should be directed to studying conventional linguistics as a discipline. In this sense, the critical endeavours must go beyond the boundaries of the academic disciplines from which they emerge. Teachers of Critical Discourse Analysis or critical psychology will direct their students to read texts that seem to belong to other academic disciplines – to sociology, to social theory, to the history of ideas, and so on. The result is that the critical approach will appear to be interdisciplinary, since it cannot accept the disciplinary structure of the approach that it is criticizing.

Social context of academic work

The analysis of power relations, which is central for a critical approach, starts close to home. The critique of the non-critical paradigms is also typically an analysis of the power relations within the academic context, for the non-critical Other is assumed to constitute the mainstream dominant way of doing the discipline. In the case of critical psychology, the power relations are clear. In today's academic context, psychology has a complex, well-developed economy in Europe and North America. Large numbers of fee-paying students are to be trained each year; expensively funded research is booming; the discipline is part of a major publishing industry, as thousands upon thousands of textbooks, journals and academic books are issued each year. The vast bulk of this economy is devoted to mainstream, experimental-based psychology. By comparison, critical psychology – in terms of the personnel involved in production, the potential customers and economic turnover of the product – is a mere cottage industry.

It is at this point that claims about the success of a critical approach should start to raise problems. What does it mean to say that a critical discipline is establishing itself successfully? The opening statement by Chouliaraki and Fairclough (1999) hints at the meaning of such success. They suggest that CDA is now being drawn upon by teachers and researchers across the social sciences and humanities. One might say, then, that CDA is entering the political economy of contemporary academic teaching and research. CDA specialists are being hired by universities. Fee-paying undergraduate students are enrolling in their courses. Postgraduates are being trained in CDA studies and seeking posts in universities. Publishers are issuing CDA books and journals, presumably doing so because of satisfactory profit margins. CDA researchers are attracting research grants, obtaining sponsorship for setting up specialist conferences, and so on. In short, the success of a critical subdiscipline such as CDA involves capturing some of the resources and markets occupied by the main discipline that is being criticized. The more successful the critical discipline, the more people will be professionally involved in its maintenance and the greater will be its economy.

Critical theorists seldom discuss these matters. It is easier and more comfortable to discuss critically the position of the mainstream – to point to its economy and its unbalanced relations of power. However, critical academics, by and large, operate in the same economic context as their supposedly noncritical colleagues. Fairclough (1995) has shown how the language of marketization is affecting documents such as prospectuses of job advertisements. It is possible to take the analysis two uncomfortable stages further. In the first step, one might wish to examine the rhetoric of product promotion within academic texts. This would involve examining how academics promote their own research wares, seeking to attract customers for their academic products. One might note the use of brand names. A conventional rhetoric encourages academics to package their products as part of a range issued by a theoretical perspective. The branding of the theory can be accomplished by the use of abbreviations. Rival theories are to be downgraded, as the academic seeks to attract customers (whether graduate students, research sponsors, potential collaborators or admiring readers) to their product. Thus, the unique selling point of the theory will be proclaimed.

Of course, the promotion of one's own academic product and the claiming of its academic advantages has always occurred. However, in the last 20 years the process seems to have become particularly marked, especially in relation to 'academic branding'. An example of this branding process can be given briefly. In social psychology, one of the major approaches to the study of intergroup relations goes under the heading of 'Social Identity Theory' and is conventionally abbreviated to 'SIT'. Social Identity Theory is explicitly derived from the work of Henri Tajfel, whose major book *Human Groups and Social Categories* was published in 1981. In that book Tajfel did not explicitly label his ideas as 'Social Identity Theory', let alone 'SIT'. Re-reading that work, and especially noting its title, one can see how little concerned Tajfel was with the branding of his ideas. A recent book introducing research in this area starts with the statement 'it is now 21 years since the first published statement of social identity theory (Tajfel, 1978)' (Brown and Capozza, 2000, p. vii). Yet the early statements by Tajfel did not present his ideas as 'social identity theory'. Even the introductory chapter of his edited book *Social Identity and Intergroup Relations* did not use the term, although some of the younger contributors were beginning to use it (Tajfel, 1982). Today the label is easily available, as researchers today can identify their own particular investigations as belonging (or not belonging) to the established and well-tested brand of Social Identity Theory or its relaunched offshoot 'Self-Categorization Theory' (SCT).[1] In such ways, ideas are not themselves sufficient but become successfully marketed as branded and identifiable intellectual products in today's academic world.

The emergence of Critical Discourse Analysis needs to be placed in these growing trends towards academic marketization. In one sense Critical Discourse Analysis has been a response to such trends, as Norman Fairclough and others have turned their critical focus upon the language of academia. Yet, in a literal sense the emergence of 'CDA' has itself been a product of the spread of marketing discourse within academic institutions. To be sure, there have previously been radicals who have sought to analyse the linguistic details of dominant and dominating language. However, these ideas are now presented as coalescing into a distinct project that can be labelled 'Critical Discourse Analysis' or 'CDA'. As such, the critical ideas about language appear a product, a 'thing'. This has occurred at a precise time, when this type of rhetorical labelling is becoming common in academic work.

This is not mentioned in order to downgrade the importance of critical approaches to the study of contemporary discourse. Quite the reverse, it follows from the assumption that a critical approach must seek to place the analysis of particular discursive formations in a wider social context, particularly an economic context. In this regard, it must be acknowledged that critical academic endeavours operate in the same broad economic context as uncritical approaches. If the context affects the nature of discourse, then one must expect critical and non-critical approaches to share common rhetorics. Certainly, critical texts tend to bear the hallmarks of conventional contemporary academic writing. A journal such as *Discourse & Society*, which specializes in critical studies of discourse, has similar publishing, refereeing and referencing styles to non-critical journals. Its format and style contains few, if any, overtly distinguishing features. It would be naive to think that the rhetorical processes of marketization, that might affect other aspects of the contemporary academic world, would somehow leave critical approaches untouched. However, the implications of the context, in which critical approaches operate, need to be assessed clearly. And this is one reason why, as Fairclough and others have stressed, critical approaches should be self-reflexive. If they are not, the limits of critique may be ignored.

Dilemmas of success

If the success of an endeavour such as Critical Discourse Analysis must occur within an academic context of power and economic relations, then this is not a matter of good or bad intentions by the critical analysts. However, it is all too easy for critical analysts, in their critiques of the mainstream Other, to ignore, or indeed wish away, this aspect of their endeavours. For example, there have been a number of discussions by critical social scientists about teaching critical approaches. Sometimes such writers talk about the necessity for creating the type of classroom discussions that enable students to enter discussions on terms of equality (see, for instance, McGuire's 2001 discussion of critical classroom practice, or Nightingale and Neiland's 1999 thoughtful account of the way that critical students and teachers can introduce the themes of critical psychology into their curricula). Typically such accounts contain a crucial omission. While they discuss how previously silenced voices might be empowered in the teaching of university courses, they do not address a central dilemma in the position of the critical university teacher.

The scope for egalitarianism is crucially limited and does not hinge upon the conduct of tutorial discussions.[2] University teachers not only operate within a system of inequality, but they also have key responsibilities for administering and thereby reproducing inequalities. Critical and non-critical teachers share in these responsibilities. Typically, university teachers are required to examine and grade the performance of students on their courses. This is expected by university employers, students and prospective employers of the students. Grading and examining involves both the operation of power and the necessity of discriminating between students in order to accomplish a record of inequality of performance. The accounts of critical pedagogy are typically silent about the exercise of power through grading students taking critical courses: it is as if social analysis gives way to the critical academic's protestations of good intentions.

Teachers of university courses in 'Critical Discourse Analysis' will have to engage in the practice of power that results in the grading of students. The more successful CDA is in establishing itself within the university curriculum, the more students will take CDA courses and the more critical analysts will be hired to teach and to grade these students. Success will bring more records of the unequal achievements in CDA. These records will be of use to prospective employers within and without the university sector. Thus, CDA teachers, who may be committed to egalitarianism, will find themselves professionally reproducing inequalities as a consequence of their professional commitments. Such is the dilemma of the professional critical analyst.

Dilemmas affect not only the teaching of a critical perspective, but also the establishment of the perspective as a research activity. As a critical paradigm establishes itself so it takes on many of the characteristics of an established discipline. It has its graded courses, textbooks and doctoral programmes. These courses, books and programmes will cite the texts of established critical writers in ways that promote some academics as 'leading figures', whose work is to respected and followed by the juniors. The discipline will also have its established journals, in which the young trained critical academics will compete to have their papers published. The result is that many young critical discourse analysts, and critical academics working in other subdisciplines, will be working in different circumstances from their teachers. Unlike those teachers they will not be struggling to break free of the disciplinary assumptions that they were taught. The young critical academics, by contrast, will find themselves working within a paradigm and its career structures. In short, success will bring a 'critical orthodoxy', which will have its own institutional and economic bases.

The question is whether this matters. Perhaps, it is inevitable that a sense of intellectual excitement must diminish as, to paraphrase Kuhn, revolutionary 'critical science' becomes normal 'critical science'. So one might envisage the pages of a critical journal such as *Discourse & Society* becoming filled with worthy pieces that make up for a missing creative excitement with technical proficiency as an already created paradigm is applied to an expanding range of problems.[3] Perhaps this is not something to worry about. One might justifiably talk of progress: the establishment of a critical paradigm, even as an intellectual orthodoxy, can be seen as an improvement of what came before and what goes on elsewhere. The critical academic may even point to a greater proportion of minority figures in established positions in the critical endeavours. The critical hierarchies, it might be suggested, are more permeable, although they still are hierarchies in a wider class system.

Or, by contrast, one might worry that the growth of respectability entails the loss of critique as an intellectual creativity, especially if there is a lack of self-reflexive analysis or, worse still, if self-reflexive analyses systematically omit uncomfortable, but key, factors. In structural terms, the critical endeavour by its own success runs the risk of becoming a discipline with all that entails. It may have been liberating for early critical linguists to read outside their own disciplinary base and to turn this reading against the presuppositions of that base. However, what was once external is incorporated into critical courses of instruction. As courses in Critical Discourse Analysis are established, so radical works of social analysis that never were considered by conventional linguists to be part of linguistics become transformed into set texts for the next generation of students. Thus, the movement of success may be from a position that was interdisciplinary, even radically anti-disciplinary, to one that is itself disciplinary. This occurs because academic disciplines are social and institutional practices rather than inherent qualities of academic texts.

Maybe there is a need for continual intellectual revolution. If that is the case, then, perhaps critical discursive studies must be open to new forms of writing and to beware of its own linguistic orthodoxies. There may be a need to draw back from treating 'Critical Discourse Analysis' as if it were a recognizable product and to unpick the rhetoric that has lead from 'critical approaches' to the abbreviated and capitalized 'CDA'. Young academics should not seek to identify themselves with a defined way of doing academic research, but should see themselves as engaged in the critical analysis of discourse. The return of pronouns and the lower case to the description of that activity would itself carry a rhetorical message. Above all, there is a need to encourage young academics, especially those without established positions, to criticize the language and rhetoric of the established critical writers – even to expose the self-interest and political economy of the sign 'critical'. The results would not be comfortable for the critical experts; nor should they be if the activity of social critique is to continue into the future.

Notes

1. Condor (1996) acutely points out that Tajfel's ideas on social identity and inter-group relations do not actually have the formal properties of a theory.
2. In fact, the detailed discursive evidence of Edwards and Mercer (1987) suggests limitations to the equality and empowering that critical teachers might claim for their pedagogic methods. Analysing liberal teachers in junior schools, Edwards and Mercer showed how teachers subtly retain control over the classroom agenda, even when ostensibly seeking to impose knowledge on the pupils (see Billig et al., 1988, for a discussion of the dilemmas facing teachers who claim not to be imposing discipline). There is little reason to suppose that detailed study of interaction in university settings would not provide analogous findings.
3. This is a problem about which the editor of *Discourse & Society* has repeatedly expressed concern. In a series of editorials he has warned against the journal becoming tied to a single established paradigm, which becomes established as a fixed way of doing critical analysis with a detrimental effect on succeeding generations of scholars (see, for instance, van Dijk, 1995 and 1996b). The present chapter, in fact, began as a brief invited editorial for *Discourse & Society* (Billig, 2000).

References

Billig, M. (1987) *Arguing and Thinking*. Cambridge: Cambridge University Press.
Billig, M. (1991) *Ideology and Opinions*. London: Sage Publications.
Billig, M. (1996) 'Discourse, opinions and ideologies: a comment', in C. Schäffner and H. Kelly-Holms (eds), *Discourse and Ideologies*. Clevedon: Multilingual Matters.
Billig, M. (1999) 'Whose terms? Whose ordinariness? Rhetoric and ideology in conversation analysis', *Discourse & Society*, 10, pp. 543–58.
Billig, M. (2000) 'Editorial: towards a critique of the critical', *Discourse & Society*, 11, pp. 291–2.
Billig, M., Condor, S., Edwards, D., Gane, M., Middleton, D. and Radley, A.R. (1988) *Ideological Dilemmas: A Social Psychology of Everyday Thinking*. London: Sage.
Brown, R. and Capozza, D. (2000) 'Social identity theory in retrospect and prospect', in D. Capozza and R. Brown (eds), *Social Identity Processes*. London: Sage.
Burman, E. (1996) 'Continuities and discontinuities in interpretive and textual approaches to developmental psychology', *Human Development*, 39(6), pp. 330–45.
Chouliaraki, L. and Fairclough, N. (1999) *Discourse in Late Modernity*. Edinburgh: Edinburgh University Press.
Condor, S. (1996) 'Social identity and time', in W.P. Robinson (ed.), *Social Groups and Identities*. London: Butterworth/Heinemann.
Edwards, D. and Mercer, N.M. (1987) *Common Knowledge*. London: Methuen.

Fairclough, N. (1992a) *Discourse and Social Change.* Cambridge: Polity.
Fairclough, N. (ed.) (1992b) *Critical Language Awareness.* London: Longman.
Fairclough, N. (1995) *Critical Discourse Analysis.* London: Longman.
Fowler, R., Hodge, B., Kress, G. and Trew, T. (1979) *Language and Control.* London: Routledge.
Gergen, K.J. (1994) *Toward Transformation in Social Knowledge* (2nd edition). London: Sage.
Kant, I. (1781 [1964]) *Critique of Pure Reason.* London: Dent.
Kress, G. (1993) 'Against arbitrariness: the social production of the sign', *Discourse & Society,* 4, pp. 169–91.
McGuire, P. (2001) 'The congruency thing: transforming psychological research and pedagogy', in D.L. Tolman and M. Brydon-Miller (eds), *From Subjects to Subjectivities.* New York: New York University Press.
Nightingale, D. and Neiland, T. (1999) 'Understanding and practising critical psychology', in D. Fox and I. Prilleltensky (eds), *Critical Psychology.* London: Sage.
Notturno, M.A. (1999) 'Popper's critique of scientific socialism, or Carnap and his co-workers', *Philosophy of Social Sciences,* 29, pp. 32–61.
Popper, K. (1976) *Unended Quest.* London: Fontana.
Potter, J. (1996) *Representing Reality.* London: Sage.
Schegloff, E.A. (1997) 'Whose text? Whose context?', *Discourse & Society,* 8, pp. 165–87.
Tajfel, H. (ed.) (1978) *Differentiation between Social Groups.* London: Academic Press.
Tajfel, H. (1981) *Human Groups and Social Categories.* Cambridge: Cambridge University Press.
Tajfel, H. (ed.) (1982) *Social Identity and Intergroup Relations.* Cambridge: Cambridge University Press.
van Dijk, T.A. (1993) 'Principles of critical discourse analysis', *Discourse & Society,* 4, pp. 249–83.
van Dijk, T.A. (1995) Editorial: 'Interdisciplinarity'. *Discourse & Society,* 6, pp. 459–60.
van Dijk, T.A. (1996a) 'Discourse, opinions and ideology', in C. Schäffner and H. Kelly-Holms (eds), *Discourse and Ideologies.* Clevedon: Multilingual Matters.
van Dijk, T.A. (1996b) Editorial: 'On schools', *Discourse & Society,* 7, pp. 451–2.
van Dijk, T.A. (1998) *Ideology.* London: Sage.
Wetherell, M. (1998) 'Positioning and interpretative repertoires: conversation analysis and post-structuralism in dialogue', *Discourse & Society,* 9, pp. 387–412.
Widdowson, H. (1995) 'Discourse analysis: a critical view', *Language and Literature,* 4, pp. 157–72.

3
Critical Discourse Analysis and the Development of the New Science[1]

Carlos A.M. Gouveia

When looking back over the last three or four decades of the twentieth century, one cannot avoid noticing some widespread signals of a deep crisis that is affecting the model of scientific rationality that governs us. Revealing itself more and more at the core of the configurative lines of that model of rationality, this crisis has been identified (Santos, 1987, 1989, 2000, for instance) as the result of both societal and theoretical conditions that have developed interactively. In the light of this reading, and following the work of authors who have addressed the subject from different perspectives (Capra, 1982, 1996; Santos, 1987, 1989, 2000; Lemke 1995; Horgan 1996), my purpose in this chapter is threefold. First, I will propose a reading of the development of linguistics as reflecting attitudes and ways of looking at the experience of language that, if not ahead of, have been homologous with the new conditions undermining the paradigm of modern science. I will argue that the discursive turn in (social) science(s), being the result of the crisis of the paradigm of modern science, is itself a condition for that crisis. Second, I will try to show that some issues in linguistics, particularly the ones brought about by the theory and methodology of Critical Discourse Analysis (CDA), are examples of tentative responses (not all of them entirely successful, though) to key factors in the general crisis that has been affecting the paradigm of modern science in the last decades of the twentieth century. Third, I will defend the view that in the new paradigm of science some pairs of concepts and oppositions need to be redefined in view of their integration and synonymy. For instance, I will claim that, in the context of the present crisis, one of the most important epistemological acts to be registered is the break with the first epistemological break of modern science, which separated scientific knowledge from common sense (see Santos, 1987, 1989, 2000). In the emerging new science being developed on the fringes of modern science, scientific knowledge aims at being common sense itself. It will be a new common sense with more sense, though less common, where one uncovers and accepts more disagreement and conflict concerning the nature of scientific knowledge and where one recognizes only relative autonomy with regard to the scientific community. Also, as a characteristic of the new paradigm, the validity of science must not be separated from its usefulness and utility which will help to define its internal consistency and cogency.

I will start by defining the main characteristics of the paradigm of modern science, then moving on to the characterization of the emerging new science, in the light of the symptoms of crisis and definitions of the present paradigm. I will then try to establish some relations between CDA as the most comprehensive theory reflecting the discursive turn in linguistics, and the emerging new science, looking at CDA as a contradictory example of a crisis creating theory and methodology in the beliefs of the present scientific paradigm. Finally, some tentative conclusions will be drawn.

The paradigm of modern science

As is well known, the rationale underlying the paradigm of modern science was constructed in opposition to common sense; but apart from causing this separation, the rationale of modern science was also highly reductive in its understanding of reality, favouring theories in which causality is the dominant explanatory principle. Furthermore, basing itself on the principle of power over life, of man over nature, it originated a progressive disconnection between human beings and the natural world, aiming at giving the former the means to control the latter. Even though it was formulated in its essential outlines in the sixteenth and seventeenth centuries, this rationale still informs the worldview and value system that lies at the basis of our culture. In fact, as Fritjof Capra (1982, p. 37) has put it:

> Between 1500 and 1700 there was a dramatic shift in the way people pictured the world and in their whole way of thinking. The new mentality and the new perception of the cosmos gave our Western civilisation the features that are characteristic of the modern era. They became the basis of the paradigm that has dominated our culture for the past three hundred years...

Incorporating the social sciences in the nineteenth century, this model of rationality definitely split knowledge into three different types. First, there was scientific knowledge – as rational, objective and devoted to quantification and to the reduction of complexity. Second, there was common sense. And, third, there was the knowledge of the humanities – including historical, philological, juridical, literary, philosophical and theological studies (Santos, 1987, p. 10). The particularity of this separation is the fact that both common sense and the humanities were looked at as non-scientific, non-objective, which were the fundamental characteristics of scientific knowledge. With this splitting in the value of knowledge, scientific knowledge became the only true form of knowledge. In other words, this epistemological turn in the rationale underlying modern science made scientific knowledge a totalitarian model for apprehending reality, the only free and unbiased form of knowledge for the so-called systematic and rigorous observation of reality, the ultimate goal of science.

Referred to by Santos (1987, 1989, 2000) as the first epistemological break in modern science, the separation from common sense of scientific knowledge, as the only valid form of knowledge, opened up the way to several developments and consequences identified as intrinsic to modern scientific reasoning. For instance, it was this separation that led to both a specialization and a professionalization of knowledge as one of the main characteristics of the paradigm. As a consequence, a new symbiosis between power and knowledge was established and the producers of common sense knowledge, the ordinary individuals, were constructed as expropriated of the cognitive and scientific competences necessary for a correct evaluation of reality and all the power related to them. The fact that, for instance, there is an increasingly widespread consensus among social scientists that contemporary Western societies are ruled by knowledge and expertise confirms that this model still dominates our cultural system. As has been pointed out (Cetina, 1999, p. 5), 'the power of the nation-state is undermined not only by multinational corporations and a capitalist economy, but also by transnational social units whose ties are based upon technologically usable knowledge'. In fact, knowledge governs modern societies in the form of expert systems, expert processes, scientific-technical elites or scientific beliefs. Epitomized by science, they continuously give rise to new forms of exclusion, such as info-exclusion, for instance, in its interpretation, appropriation and action on (Giddens, 1990), by individuals in everyday life.

The way reality was understood by the model of rationality underlying the dominant paradigm of modern science constitutes another fundamental aspect for its characterization. Science became Cartesian, mechanistic in its understanding of reality. The world was seen as too complex for the understanding of the human mind, and the only way of learning about it was to become aware of its mechanical clockwork complexity and proceed accordingly. Only by acquiring a part of it, reducing it to a number of small, simple pieces that are easy to understand, and then analysing them and putting them all back together again, could one understand the whole. In other words, reality was scientifically looked at in terms of its structural constituency, and it was made known first by operations of analytical decomposition and then by synthetic and generalized recompositions (Reis, forthcoming). In this knowledge/understanding of the object, scientific rigour equated the rigour of measurements, where the qualities of the object were only considered if translated into quantity: what was not quantifiable was non-relevant scientifically (Santos, 1987, p. 15). In this model of science, mathematics naturally came to be a multileveled tool that offered scientific knowledge not only a perfect instrument of analysis, but also the coherence to back up the research and the model for representing the structure of matter.

The development and transformations undergone by this model during the twentieth century, initially due to Einstein's theory of relativity and later to the developments of quantum and subatomic physics, have left mechanistic thinking behind but not its consequences in scientific knowledge. In fact, the pendulum has been replaced by a tiny quartz crystal; mechanical pieces have almost turned into microscopic chips whose potentialities are increased year after year; the world has become a global village; the end of ideology has been proclaimed; but the way reality is perceived has not suffered any substantial changes. In other words, along the path of modern science we find several symptoms of a crisis that are mirror reflections of a single crisis: a crisis of perception, a crisis in our understanding of reality, from which we have been radically separated by modern science.

The emerging new science

As pointed out by Santos (1987, 2000), the first obvious symptom of the general crisis affecting modern science was introduced by Einstein and by his demonstration that the simultaneous nature of far-away events cannot be verified, only defined. As Einstein himself has described (1920 [1954], pp. 26–7):

> Every reference-body (co-ordinate system) has its own particular time; unless we are told the reference-body to which the statement of time refers, there is no meaning in a statement of the time of an event. Now before the advent of the theory of relativity it had always tacitly been assumed in physics that the statement of time had an absolute significance, *i.e.*, that it is independent of the state of the motion of the body of reference.

Einstein's theory came to revolutionize our conceptions of time and space, in the sense that Newton's absolute time and space ceased to exist. It thus introduced the necessity of local measurements, as two simultaneous events in a reference system are not simultaneous in another reference system (Santos, 1987, p. 25). Opening the way to quantum physics, the necessity of local measurements informed the way microphysics has been established and developed. The exploration of the atomic and subatomic world forced scientists to think about completely new ways, because 'Every time they asked nature a question in an atomic experiment, nature answered with a paradox, and the more they tried to clarify the situation, the sharper the paradoxes became' (Capra, 1982, p. 64). Werner Heisenberg and Niels Bohr – the former with his uncertainty principle; the latter with his notion of complementarity – showed that at the atomic level there are aspects, or pairs of concepts that cannot be defined separately in a precise way. They are interrelated, and the properties they show are dependent on their environment, which 'will depend on the experimental situation, that is, on the apparatus it is forced to interact with' (ibid.). In other words, there is a structural interference of the subject in the object under observation, which leads to the ultimate fact that we can only learn from reality whatever we bring into it (Santos, 2000, p. 66; my translation hereafter):

> The idea that we do not know from reality except whatever we introduce in it ... is well expressed in Heisenberg's principle of uncertainty: the errors of measurement of speed and the position of particles cannot be reduced simultaneously; whatever is done to reduce the error of one of the measurements increases the error of the other ... This principle, and thus the demonstration of the structural interference of the subject with the object under observation, has important implications. On the one hand, as the rigour of our knowledge is structurally limited, we can only aspire to approximate results and thus the laws of physics are only probabilistic. On the other hand, the hypothesis of mechanistic determinism is ruled out as the totality of reality is not reduced to the sum of the parts we divide it into in order to observe and measure it. Lastly, the distinction subject/object is much more complex than it may seen at a first glance. The distinction loses its dichotomist contours and takes on the shape of a *continuum*.
>
> Correspondingly, modern physics stopped asserting final principles, since events do not occur according to deterministic laws that govern changes in time, but according to a set of probabilities at different dimensions.

Another definite warning about the flaws of modern science was introduced by Gödel's Undecidability and Incompleteness Theorems. These proved respectively that within a formal system, questions exist that are neither provable nor disprovable on the basis of the axioms that define the system, and that in a sufficiently rich formal system in which decidability of all questions is required, there will be contradictory statements. As Santos (2000, p. 67) stresses, Gödel's investigations made it possible to dispute the preciseness of mathematics, which has come to be questioned creatively. Today, it is recognized that mathematics lies on a selectivity principle and, as such, it has both a constructive and a destructive side.

All these results have only come to be appreciated during the last decades of the twentieth century, along with others from several new theories, disciplines and postulates. For instance, Maturana and Varela's theory of autopoiesis (1980, 1987), the investigations of Ilya Prigogine (1980), the investigations of António and Hanna Damásio in neuropsychology (Damásio, 1994), the theory of complex self-organizing systems (Prigogine, 1996 [1997]) or, for that matter, the problems raised by genetics, with its implications in bio-ethics, form a core of conditions that show the limitations of scientific knowledge in the dominant paradigm. (For an appreciation of these investigations and, in some cases, an application of their postulates in other areas of investigation, see, for instance, Kenny, 1989; Santos, 1987, 2000; Lemke, 1995; Graham and McKenna, 2000.)

What this revolution has shown us is that when an object, a system, is dissected either physically or theoretically into isolated elements, its systemic properties are destroyed. We can in fact discern individual parts in any system or object, but the nature of that system or object is always different from the mere sum of those individual parts. In fact, the behaviour of the system as a whole is a complex aggregation of the interactions of all its compositional interacting parts.

Therefore, in the new science that is emerging, one never ends up with things, one always deals with interconnections because there are no things in reality but interconnections between things, which in their turn are interconnections between other things (Capra, 1982, pp. 69–70). With consequences on the way scientific knowledge is conceived, this notion of interconnection, together with the notion of probability, has far-reaching implications in physics. It has also implications in the general way reality is perceived.

In this new paradigm, reality is looked at in terms of relationships and integration. Every system is an integrated whole whose properties cannot be reduced to ones of smaller parts, because these smaller parts only exist in interconnection. A system does not exist independently of its principles of organization and of its basic building blocks, of its smaller parts. However, as a complex whole, it cannot be reduced to its principles of organization or to the properties of its constitutive parts. As Capra (1982, p. 83) has put it:

> In modern physics, the image of the universe as a machine has been transcended by a view of it as one indivisible, dynamic whole whose parts are essentially interrelated and can be understood only as patterns of a cosmic process. At the subatomic level the interrelations and interactions between the parts of the whole are more fundamental than the parts themselves. There is motion but there are, ultimately, no moving objects; there is activity but there are no actors; there are no dancers, there is only the dance.

CDA and the emerging new science

According to Fritjof Capra, there is no well-established framework to accommodate the formulation of the new paradigm that has been developed on the fringes of the dominant paradigm. What one can see is that 'the outlines of such a framework are already being shaped by many individuals, communities, and networks that are developing new ways of thinking and organizing themselves according to new principles' (1982, p. 285). This framework, informed by a principle of transdisciplinarity, refuses the simplicity of laws that reduce reality to an arbitrary simplification beyond which other aspects of reality are dismissed, thus remaining unknown in their interconnection to what we came to know.

Such has been the case with CDA since it appeared around twenty years or so ago (cf. Gouveia, 1997b, p. 156; Chouliaraki and Fairclough, 1999, p. 1). The development of CDA into multiple trends that interact with each other has shown a tendency which will predictably be characteristic of the new scientific paradigm. In fact, within CDA 'several schools are integrated with very different methodologies and very different theoretical claims' (Wodak, 1996, p. 33, n. 10; cf. also Wodak, 2001). Whereas within one discipline or across disciplines, the multiple trends that are characteristic not only of CDA but mainly of the new science progressively aim at putting together a network of interconnected concepts, theories, models and methodologies. As Capra (1982, p. 285) has stressed, this characteristic of new science goes beyond the conventional disciplinary distinctions:

> None of the theories and models will be any more fundamental than the others, and all of them will have to be mutually consistent. They will go beyond the conventional disciplinary distinctions, using whatever language becomes appropriate to describe different aspects of the multi-leveled, interrelated fabric of reality.

Therefore, far from being negative, the presence of 'competing and uncontrolled' methodologies within CDA (see Fowler, 1996), may be seen as an important condition for increasing communication. It also may be a necessary condition for 'bringing to bear shifting sets of theoretical resources and shifting operationalisations of them', to use Chouliaraki and Fairclough's words (1999, p. 17). This dialogic nature of CDA seems to have worked only one way, though. Not only has CDA been confined to its own limits in terms of influence on other disciplines and theories, but, as has been pointed out (Widdowson, 1995, 2000; Fowler, 1996; Stubbs, 1997), it is also closely reminiscent of work from other areas of research which has not always been acknowledged as such. And although one can see it as an example of the interconnectedness of subatomic particles when applied to disciplines, that is, as the continuum of an essential disciplinary trend of a discursive nature, CDA is still far from being totally understood as the result of a new move in the way scientific knowledge is conceived. It is exactly because of this that Chouliaraki and Fairclough's concept of operationalization (1999, p. 16) as entailing work 'in a transdisciplinary way where the logic of one discipline (for example, sociology) can be "put to work" in the development of another (for example, linguistics)', must not only be taken into account, but also grasped (even if by redefinition).

In fact, the fragmentation one may see in CDA, and in fact not totally advocated by everybody working in the area (see Fowler, 1996, and my comments in reaction in Gouveia, 1997b), is nothing but the consequences of a new scientific perception. Besides revealing a considerable diversity of positions regarding approaches that are labelled 'Critical Discourse Analysis' (Chouliaraki and Fairclough, 1999, p. 7; Wodak and Meyer, 2001), this fragmentation is the outcome of a valuable heterogeneity in terms of roots, theories and aims within CDA. Rather than being the result of personal histories of research interests and motivations on the part of CDA researchers, the varying approaches are the outcome of different configurations and patterns of interdisciplinary action. According to Wodak (2001, p. 11) 'CDA emphasises the need for interdisciplinary work in order to gain a proper understanding of how language functions in, for example, constituting and transmitting knowledge, in organising institutions or in exercising power.' It is worth mentioning, though, that the way interdisciplinarity is activated depends on the aims of the research, which are not ultimately discipline-dependent but thematically motivated.

The fragmentation of CDA, or rather its heterogeneity, is then not disciplinary (and thus not motivated by interdisciplinarity), but thematic, in exactly the sense in which Santos (1987, 2000) refers to the notion. In Santos' reading (1987, p. 47), in the new science, themes are galleries where different systems of knowledge develop in interconnection. In contrast to what is stressed by beliefs in the present paradigm, Santos asserts that in the new paradigm knowledge develops as the object is amplified; similar to that of a tree, this amplification proceeds by differentiation and by spreading its roots in search of new, different interfaces. What better metaphor is there to describe what has happened in linguistics in the past 40 years?

In truth, among other synergies, the discursive turn one may discern in the social sciences, linguistics included, is itself the result of the amplification referred to above. The central role that discourse plays in our lives has been recognized by different researchers working in diverse fields, areas or disciplines (see Sarangi and Coulthard, 2000). Nevertheless, one tends to look at this as the result of interdisciplinarity, sometimes failing to see that the whole matter transcends disciplines and reflects a new and more dynamic way of perceiving reality that refuses the de-unifying character of science and the disciplines and advocates thematic fragmentation. We do need to move forward, as stressed by different researchers, such as, for instance, Cetina (1999, pp. 2–3):

> The differentiating terms [disciplines and scientific specialty] we have used in the past were not designated to make visible the complex texture of knowledge as practiced in the deep social spaces of modern institutions. To bring out this texture, one needs to magnify the space of knowledge-in-action, rather than simply observe disciplines or specialties as organizing structures.

It is rather awkward that nowadays interdisciplinarity has given way to transdisciplinarity. The whole thing is constructed as if in that move one can actually make a difference in terms of understanding the specificity of the new kind of knowledge and methodology one is advocating. If one accepts that the fragmentation is not disciplinary but thematic, one can only talk of interconnectedness between theories and methodologies when these are looked at from the point of view of themes. In fact, one should bear in mind, as Santos does (1987, p. 46), that the fragmentation and specialization of disciplines has turned the scientist into a specialized ignoramus. Ultimately this has brought with it a de-responsibility in failing to see the forest, seeing only the trees, and the destructive impact that specialization has introduced in the ecosystem. As opposed to discipline fragmentation, thematic fragmentation involves the migration of local concepts and ways of reading to other contexts in a localized but total and interconnected description. In other words, thematic fragmentation involves *operationalization*.

In representing of a different attitude in perceiving language from that of the dominant formal paradigm in linguistics, CDA may well prove to be the catalyser of a new model of understanding what happens when one uses language. In order to understand this, language has to be seen as a set of multilevelled layers of meaning in interconnection, which may only be defined by the interconnections they establish with yet other interconnections. As in physics, linguistic events do not occur according to deterministic laws but according to a set of probabilities in different dimensions. This understanding may dictate the end of formal linguistics as it is, but it does not necessarily dictate the end of CDA. In view of this, the notion of discourse should be understood in CDA as a probability pattern of a continual exchange of meaning in an inseparable web of relationships that include language, people, events, situations, institutions, social structures, and so on. Each of these relationships should be understood, in turn, as constituting another set of relationships or interconnections with yet other interconnections. In short, discourse manifests its existence in probability patterns just as any physical particle or system of particles.

As a probability pattern of interconnections, discourse opens itself not only to analysis but also to interpretation. I mean, of course, interpretation-2, as defined by Fairclough (1996) in his reply to Henry Widdowson (1995), since interpretation-1, as also defined by Fairclough (1996, pp. 49–50), is itself another interconnection in the probability pattern of interconnections of discourse:

> Interpretation-1 is an inherent part of ordinary language use, which analysts, like anyone else, necessarily do: make meaning from/with spoken and written texts. People make meanings through an interplay between features of a text and the varying resources which they bring to the process of interpretation-1. Interpretation-2 is a matter of analysts seeking to show connections between both properties of texts and practices of interpretation-1 in a particular social space, and wider social and cultural properties

of that particular social space. Notice that interpretation-1 is part of the domain of interpretation-2; one concern of interpretation-2 is to investigate how different practices of interpretation-1 are socially, culturally and ideologically shaped.

Like electrons, protons and neutrons, language manifests its existence between potentiality and reality, or one might say, following Halliday (1994), between a meaning potential and its realization in discourse. But this realization in discourse has to be analysed in relation to its potential, through the consciousness of the one who analyses it. That is to say that nothing in discourse has meaning as an isolated entity but can only be understood as interconnections between various processes of observation and measurement. Again, as in physics, 'the observed phenomena can be understood only as correlations between various processes of observation and measurement, and the end of this chain of processes lies always in the consciousness of the human observer' (Capra, 1982, pp. 76–7).

Paraphrasing Capra, one could then say that the crucial feature in CDA is that the analyst is not only necessary to observe the properties of a discursive phenomenon, but is necessary even to bring about these properties, since discursive phenomena do not have objective properties independent of the analyst's mind. In his critique of the critical approaches in linguistics, in a seldom quoted book, Thompson provides a touchstone for a correct appraisal of this issue, by means of what he calls a methodology of interpretation. Claiming that critical discourse analysts should take this methodology of interpretation into account, Thompson (1984, p. 133) characterizes it by highlighting two fundamental considerations:

> The first consideration has to do with the inescapable situation of that which forms the object of interpretation: *discourse* – that is, language realized in speech and writing – *is already an interpretation*. Events, actions and expressions are constantly interpreted and understood by lay actors in everyday life, who routinely employ interpretative procedures in making sense of themselves and others. To undertake an analysis of discourse is to produce an interpretation, to re-interpret a pre-interpreted domain ... The second consideration to which I want to call attention concerns *the creative character of the interpretative process*. The analysis of discourse can never be merely an analysis: it must also be a synthetic construction, a creative projection, of a possible meaning.

In other words, everything is interpretation, which does not exactly mean that in CDA, as Widdowson (1995, p. 169) has mistakenly put it, what 'is actually revealed is the particular discourse perspective of the interpreter' and that CDA 'cannot provide analysis but only partial interpretation'. Widdowson's critique is, in fact, missing the point, as probably is Fairclough's reply to Widdowson. There is nothing wrong in providing only a partial interpretation, if one considers that there are no static structures in discourse and that one cannot ascribe it a definite reading because its potentiality is what lies in between readings, or observations and measurements, to use *more scientific* words.

Widdowson is, strangely enough, missing the fact there is no value-free CDA, that, ultimately, there is no value-free science. And even if one does not want to claim the postulates of the whole tradition of critical theory, in the sense of work done by the Frankfurt School, regarding the impossibility of objectivity in science (see, for instance, Wodak, 1989), one cannot avoid noting, however, the findings of modern physics. Once again as Capra has put it (1982, p. 77):

> In transcending the Cartesian division, modern physics has not only invalidated the classical ideal of an objective description of nature but has also challenged the myth of a value-free science. The patterns scientists observe in nature are intimately connected with the patterns of their minds; with their concepts, thoughts, and values. Thus the scientific results they obtain and the technological applications they investigate will be conditioned by their frame of mind. Although much of their detailed research will not depend explicitly on their value system, the larger paradigm within which this research is pursued will never be value-free.

But again, for CDA, the fact that the research is not value-free does not mean that one should impose readings on discourse or that no alternative readings are possible. That is, in fact, the danger of activist linguistics or, in this particular case, of activist CDA, particularly when, aiming at being critical, it does not provide a critique of critical knowledge (see Gouveia, 1996, 1997a, pp. 27–31).

As stressed before, modern science has been highly reductive in its understanding of reality which was kept apart and separate from any explanation one might scientifically provide about it. The new science aims at inverting this radical separation. In fact, the idea that science, and for that matter, of theoretical linguistics, to quote Widdowson (1997, p. 146), 'cannot do otherwise than idealise reality and produce abstract models which bear no direct resemblance to the actual experience of language' is a dogmatic principle that has been questioned, not only in linguistics but also in other sciences for a long time now. Along with Prigogine (1996 [1997], p. 7), one can in fact say that we are and have been 'observing the birth of a science that is no longer limited to idealized and simplified situations but reflects the complexity of the real world, a science that views us and our creativity as part of a fundamental trend present at all levels of nature'.

Thinking about CDA, one can say that although it corresponds to a novel way of looking at language, CDA risks not totally understanding its role in the new science project. In fact, there has not been enough epistemological enquiry into the role of CDA at the core of this new way of understanding scientific knowledge. Following the lines of thinking of Hyland (2000, p. 167), if one considers that 'The social interactions in the writings of academics not only negotiate community knowledge and credibility, but help produce and sustain status relationships, exercise exclusivity and reproduce interests which lead to an unequal distribution of influence and resources', then there is something for CDA to work on in CDA. In fact, one should bear in mind that, through its research and discourse practices, the academy – and CDA with it – help reproduce and transform the identities and boundaries of disciplines and the relationships between them. Instead of advocating inter-disciplinarity (itself a disciplinary concept and practice), an important task for CDA, along the lines of development of the new science, would be to try to deconstruct the taken-for-granted, naturalized, discourses of the disciplines. New ways of thinking about CDA in relation to itself and in relation to other 'disciplines' are thus needed. By this, I mean not only thinking about CDA in terms of what it can take from and give to other 'disciplines', theories and methodologies, but also in terms of how it relates to them when it comes to the value of the knowledge it aspires to.

As with the case of disciplines, the discoursal resources of CDA are not ordinarily available to outsiders (Hyland, 2000). The social and cultural distance between members and non-members of a discipline, on the one hand, and between members of a discipline and the larger community, on the other, is a reality that opposes integration and favours expertise and discrimination. Particularly because of its motivations and aims, CDA needs to be fully aware of how, inadvertently, it may be contributing to certain negative and compromising practices.

Although he is not writing from the point of view of CDA, Santos (2000, p. 29) raises the issue in a very accurate way that may also be useful for CDA:

> Every act of knowledge is a trajectory from a point A, which we call ignorance, to a point B, which we call knowledge. In the modernity project one can distinguish between two forms of knowledge: regulative-knowledge, whose point of ignorance is called chaos and whose point of knowledge is called order; and emancipatory-knowledge, whose point of ignorance is called colonialism and whose point of knowledge is called solidarity... By not looking at the epistemological critique of modern science, critical theory, though it aspired to be a form of emancipatory-knowledge, ended up as regulative-knowledge.

It seems fair to recognize that this is a critique one can make not only as regards critical theory but also of CDA, in the sense that CDA seems to have failed to promote emancipatory-knowledge. The knowledge it achieves, though aspiring to become emancipatory, has transformed itself in regulative-knowledge, like scientific knowledge in the modern science paradigm. In fact, like the model of scientific rationality that has governed us, CDA has stressed its separation from common sense. By calling attention to the latter's mystified and mystifying nature, to its conservative and prejudiced characteristics, and devaluating its positive aspects, CDA has failed to go beyond the dualisms that constrain modern reasoning.

Activist CDA, if one chooses to use such a label, must aim at transforming its emancipatory-knowledge into common sense: a new common sense, as I stressed in the introduction, with more sense, though less common, that is, a prudent knowledge for a decent life. In other words, a prudent knowledge that does not objectify things, thus refusing to accept the destructive impact that objectification has on reality; and a decent life based in principles of solidarity and the end of monopolies of interpretation, and in non-discriminatory practices that favour integration. That can only happen through a valuation of common sense in dialogue with emancipatory-knowledge. The old common sense was constructed as a determination of cause and effect in the dense world of separate events. In the new common sense, 'science is no longer identified with certitude and probability with ignorance' (Prigogine, 1996 [1997], p. 7). Thus, the new common sense is the result of the resolution of both the dilemma of determinism and of the dualism that considers ourselves as distinct from the natural world. The outcomes are: (1) a wisdom of life that is dialogically motivated by sustained technological development in a world of interconnections; and (2) a scientific knowledge that will be an applied, shared, efficient, democratic (and thus non-professional) knowledge, that, ultimately, will be common sense. And so I reach my conclusions.

Conclusions

If, by following Santos (2000, p. 101), we look at the distinction between science and common sense not from the perspective of the former, a negative perspective, but from the perspective of the latter, a positive perspective, we may end up with a set of characteristics that help us to configure emancipatory-knowledge.

First, common sense brings together cause and intention, manifesting a worldview that stresses creativity and individual responsibility. Second, common sense is practical and pragmatic, reproducing itself in connection with the life experiences of a group and thus inspiring trust and security. Third, common sense is transparent and evident, refusing to consider the opacity and the esotericism of technological objectives and of knowledge, thereby manifesting a principle of equality in leading to discursive, cognitive and linguistic competences. Fourth, common sense is undisciplined and non-methodical and it is not the result of a practice specifically oriented to reproduce it, it is reproduced spontaneously in the flow of our daily lives. Fifth, common sense prefers actions that do not produce ruptures in reality.

As Santos stresses (2000, p. 102), when left on its own, common sense is conservative; but if transformed by emancipatory-knowledge, common sense is fundamental to intensifying the trajectory from the moment of colonialism – the moment of ignorance, to the moment of solidarity – the moment of knowledge.

All these aspects should guide the new science, including CDA, in the development of a new kind of knowledge. But in order to obtain this, one has to break definitely with the first epistemological break of modern science, and bring together scientific knowledge and common sense. This will constitute the second epistemological break in modern science, and it is a necessary condition for the development of the new science. CDA, which has come a long way, has all the reasons and motivations to help produce such a break. As Fairclough stated (1995, p. 20), CDA has 'passed the first flush of youth and is embarked upon the maturation process'. This maturation process, though, should go on free of constraints from postulates that do not serve its configuration as a possible representative of a new way of making science, a new way of apprehending reality, a new way of bringing interconnections in its mode of looking at a world that is made of interconnections.

CDA has not been and is not exempt from criticism. In fact, over the years several central questions have emerged requiring attention and denoting a need for discussion (see, for instance, Schegloff, 1997). The maturation process CDA is undergoing must take these questions into account, addressing them not as critiques that are to be dismissed as irrelevant and *indefensible* (cf., for instance, Beaugrande, 1998, 2001; Chouliaraki and Fairclough, 1999) but as issues demanding an adequate discussion of the frameworks that motivated them, regarding CDA's theoretical constructions and in relation to critical claims of a more epistemological nature concerning research and institutional practices. If necessary, CDA must be able to incorporate critiques into theory as open questions and perspectives while welcoming the search for a better understanding (cf. Wodak, 2001). With the benefit of hindsight, it seems clear that a fully epistemological critique of the way knowledge has been and is accomplished, produced and transmitted is central to the understanding of the conditions of possibility which bring about the development of science in our late modernity.

Confronting the transformations the world has undergone, both at a societal level and at an epistemological level, CDA will help to produce what Santos (1987, 1989, 2000) calls 'prudent knowledge for a decent life'. And contrary to what Widdowson (1997, p. 166) has argued, *it is* for the linguist to decide whether a linguistic theory is useful or not. This will not be a matter of designing a theory 'expediently to suit a particular purpose', as Widdowson deceitfully writes of Critical Discourse Analysis and of Systemic Functional Linguistics, but a matter of conceiving scientific research and scientific knowledge as emancipatory, and thus prudent, that will produce models for understanding reality – models that will guide us in the decent and real-life experience not only of language but also of all social and natural phenomena.

Note

1. I would like to express my deepest thanks to Luísa Azuaga and Vicky Hartnack for their constructive reactions to an earlier version of this chapter. None of them should be blamed for any inadequacy of this final version, only given credit for whatever adequacy it may have.

References

Beaugrande, R. (1998) 'On "usefulness" and "validity" in the theory and practice of linguistics: a riposte to H.G. Widdowson', *Functions of Language*, 5(1), pp. 85–96.

Beaugrande, R. (2001) 'Interpreting the discourse of H.G. Widdowson: a corpus-based critical discourse analysis', *Applied Linguistics*, 22(1), pp. 104–21.

Capra, F. (1982) *The Turning Point: Science, Society, and the Rising Culture.* London: Flamingo.

Capra, F. (1996) *The Web of Life: A New Synthesis of Mind and Matter.* London: Flamingo.

Cetina, K.K. (1999) *Epistemic Cultures: How the Sciences Make Knowledge.* Cambridge, MA: Harvard University Press.

Chouliaraki, L. and Fairclough, N. (1999) *Discourse in Late Modernity: Rethinking Critical Discourse Analysis.* Edinburgh: Edinburgh University Press.

Damásio, A.R. (1994) *Descartes' Error: Emotion, Reason, and the Human Brain.* New York: G.P. Putnam's Sons.

Einstein, A. (1920 [1954]) *Relativity: The Special and the General Theory* (15th edition, revised and enlarged). London: Methuen & Co.

Fairclough, N. (1995) *Critical Discourse Analysis: The Critical Study of Language.* London: Longman.

Fairclough, N. (1996) 'A reply to Henry Widdowson's "Discourse Analysis: A Critical View"', *Language and Literature*, 5(1), pp. 49–56.

Fowler, R. (1996) 'On Critical Linguistics', in C.R. Caldas-Coulthard and M. Coulthard (eds), *Texts and Practices: Readings in Critical Discourse Analysis.* London: Routledge, pp. 3–14.

Giddens, A. (1990) *The Consequences of Modernity.* Cambridge: Polity Press.

Gouveia, C.A.M. (1996) 'How critical can we be? Some notes on Marian Meyers's "Defining Homosexuality"', *Discourse & Society*, 7(1), pp. 155–9.

Gouveia, C.A.M. (1997a) 'O Amansar das Tropas: Linguagem, Ideologia e Mudança Social na Instituição Militar'. Unpublished PhD thesis, University of Lisbon.

Gouveia, C.A.M. (1997b) 'Review of: C.R. Caldas-Couthard and M. Coulthard (eds) (1996), *Texts and Practices: Readings in Critical Discourse Analysis.* London: Routledge', *Discourse & Society*, 8(1), pp. 156–8.

Graham, P. and McKenna, B. (2000) 'A Theoretical and Analytical Synthesis of Autopoiesis and Sociolinguistics for the Study of Organisational Communication', *Social Semiotics*, 10(1), pp. 41–59.

Halliday, M.A.K. (1994) *An Introduction to Functional Grammar.* London: Edward Arnold.

Horgan, J. (1996) *The End of Science: Facing the Limits of Knowledge in the Twilight of the New Scientific Age* (British Edition). London: Little, Brown & Co.

Hyland, K. (2000) *Disciplinary Discourses: Social Interactions in Academic Writing*. London: Longman.

Kenny, V. (1989) 'Life, the multiverse and everything: an introduction to the ideas of Humberto Maturana', in A.L. Goudsmit (ed.), *Self-Organisation in Psychotherapy*. Heidelberg: Springer-Verlag.

Lemke, J.L. (1995) *Textual Politics: Discourse and Social Dynamics*. London: Taylor & Francis.

Maturana, H. and Varela, F. (1980) *Autopoiesis and Cognition: The Realisation of the Living*. Dordrecht: Reidel.

Maturana, H. and Varela, F. (1987) *The Tree of Knowledge*. Boston: Shambhala.

Prigogine, I. (1980) *From Being to Becoming*. San Francisco: W.H. Freeman.

Prigogine, I. (1996 [1997]) *La Fin des Certitudes*. English translation: *The End of Certainty: Time, Chaos, and the New Laws of Nature*, 1997. New York: The Free Press.

Reis, J.E. (forthcoming) 'Mindwalk no Castelo do Barba Azul – Notas para uma redefinição da cidadania'. Paper presented at *XXI Encontro da APEAA, Viseu, 6–8 April, 2000*.

Santos, B. de S. (1987) *Um Discurso sobre as Ciências*. Porto: Edições Afrontamento.

Santos, B. de S. (1989) *Introdução a uma Ciência Pós-Moderna*. Porto: Edições Afrontamento.

Santos, B. de S. (2000) *Para um Novo Senso Comum: A Ciência, o Direito e a Política na Transição Paradigmática*. Volume 1: *A Crítica da Razão Indolente: Contra o Desperdício da Experiência*. Porto: Edições Afrontamento.

Sarangi, S. and Coulthard, M. (2000) 'Discourse as Topic, Resource and Social Practice: An Introduction', in S. Sarangi and M. Coulthard (eds), *Discourse and Social Life*. London: Longman, pp. xv–xli.

Schegloff, E. (1997) 'Whose text? Whose context?', *Discourse & Society*, 8(2), pp. 165–87.

Stubbs, M. (1997) 'Whorf's children: critical comments on Critical Discourse Analysis (CDA)', in *Evolving Models of Language*. Clevedon: BAAL/Multilingual Matters, Ltd, pp. 100–16.

Thompson, J.B. (1984) *Studies in the Theory of Ideology*. Cambridge: Polity Press.

Widdowson, H.G. (1995) 'Discourse Analysis: a critical view', *Language and Literature*, 4(3), pp. 157–72.

Widdowson, H.G. (1997) 'The use of grammar, the grammar of use', *Functions of Language*, 4(2), pp. 145–68.

Widdowson, H.G. (2000) 'Critical practices: on representation and the interpretation of text', in S. Sarangi and M. Coulthard (eds), *Discourse and Social Life*. London: Longman, pp. 155–69.

Wodak, R. (1989) Introduction, in R. Wodak (ed.), *Language, Power and Ideology*. Amsterdam: John Benjamins, pp. i–ix.

Wodak, R. (1996) *Disorders of Discourse*. London: Longman.

Wodak, R. (2001) 'What CDA is about – a summary of its history, important concepts and its development', in R. Wodak and M. Meyer (eds), *Methods of Critical Discourse Analysis*. London: Sage, pp. 1–13.

Wodak, R. and Meyer, M. (eds) (2001) *Methods of Critical Discourse Analysis*. London: Sage.

4
Reflexivity and the Doubles of Modern Man: The Discursive Construction of Anthropological Subject Positions

Marianne W. Jørgensen

Scientific knowledge is situated, it has been argued in recent decades, and in debates on scientific knowledge, whether natural, social or human scientific, reflexive writers[1] have focused their attention on the social and cultural context of knowledge production. The common argument is that knowledge is not just a passive reflection of an object 'out there' but also a projection of forces working from 'within' the author, the academy or Western culture at large. Knowledge is seen as shaped, or even as exclusively determined, by shared conventions for knowledge production, and 'truth' is understood to be more a matter of providing a culturally recognizable representation of reality than a direct correspondence with reality. This constructivist epistemology has prompted a large amount of reflexive research into the conditions of possibility of traditional scientific knowledge and extensive discussions of what scientific knowledge is and should be.

The debate on reflexivity has revolved around the core question of how to understand and evaluate our own knowledge. If all knowledge is socially situated, what claims can we then make for the knowledge we produce ourselves as scientific knowledge producers? I share this concern as well as the constructivist epistemology of reflexive research, and I suggest that a discourse analytical approach can give new input to the discussion – though not so much by providing an answer as by reformulating the question.

Discourse analysis is characterized by an interdisciplinary integration of perspectives from the human and the social sciences, whereby representations of the world are seen as related to a social context (for example, Fairclough, 1992). Thus, knowledge is understood as knowledge production, that is, as a socially situated discursive practice with its own regulative mechanisms and with social consequences. Similar understandings of knowledge are also forwarded in the debate on reflexivity, but, as I shall later demonstrate, they often seem to be forgotten when it comes to the understanding of the knowledge presented in the reflexive texts themselves. Thus, discourse analysis does not provide an 'outside' view of reflexivity. Rather it offers a perspective and a vocabulary with which to map out the discursive processes within reflexive research whereby the debate on reflexivity is 'turned back on itself'. A discourse analytical investigation of reflexivity involves questions such as, 'What makes the debate on reflexivity make sense?', 'What are its conditions of possibility?', 'Which view of the world is constructed?', 'How are the relations between knowledge, the object of knowledge and the knowledge producer constituted in reflexive texts?', and 'Which subject positions are thus created: from which discursively constituted positions do knowledge producers claim validity and legitimacy for their knowledge?' Such investigations into the reflexivity debate itself, I believe, will renew the discussion of what claims we (can) make for our own knowledge within a constructivist epistemology.

This chapter proposes a discourse analytical framework for the investigation of scientific subject positions. With a starting point in Michel Foucault's diagnosis of 'modern man' I argue that an interdisciplinary approach to the question of reflexivity provides us with a common denominator for the discussions of scientific knowledge in a number of disciplines, enabling us to analyse a range of contributions as different solutions to the same problem concerning the status of knowledge. I then turn to the discipline of anthropology, first sketching different anthropological negotiations of the problem, and, finally, putting the developed tools at work in a closer analysis of one example, namely Talal Asad's article 'The concept of cultural translation in British social anthropology' (Asad, 1986).

Modern man

Michel Foucault's book *The Order of Things* is probably best known for its prophecy that *man*, as we know him, is perhaps about to disappear, 'erased, like a face drawn in sand at the edge of the sea' (1966 [1974], p. 387). Here, I shall not be concerned with the possible disappearance of man and the question of what might follow as it seems to me that the man Foucault detected in the modern era still lives on as our predominant matrix for understanding human beings and their knowledge.[2] Instead, I want to suggest that Foucault's conceptualization of this modern man can, first, illuminate one set of conditions of possibility for the debates on reflexivity, and, second, when operationalized, provide discourse analytical tools with which to investigate the various subject positions assigned to human beings as knowledge producers.

The Order of Things is, as the subtitle states, 'an archaeology of the human sciences'. Among the human sciences Foucault includes, for instance, sociology, ethnology, history and psychology. These sciences emerged in their modern form during the nineteenth century simultaneously with their object of knowledge, man. According to Foucault, it would be a mistake to think that, first, man existed, and then gradually developed the human sciences that could make him understandable to himself. Rather, the modern episteme[3] gave rise to both a specific constitution of the human being, man, *and* to the human sciences that through their knowledge production canvassed this new creature.

Before proceeding with the description of man in Foucault's rather convoluted terminology, a more impressionistic rendering might be helpful. In the modern age, man emerged as a mystery to himself. On the one hand, man sees himself as producing knowledge about the world and about himself, and as such he is the master of the world: able to see it, to describe it, to understand it and explain it. On the other hand, modern man is always suspicious as to the status of the knowledge he obtains, because he conceives of himself as a historical, cultural and biological being. His thoughts and ideas are governed by laws he is only dimly aware of. This means that a piece of knowledge supposed to grasp a certain object might be distorted by the knowledge producer's particular worldview, and, hence, behind his back yield as much information of himself as a particularly situated subject, as of the object he intended to produce knowledge about. How is he to separate the two, the valid knowledge of the object, and the bias – beyond his reach – that his contingency upon time and space induce? He never fully can; he becomes an epistemological problem to himself, and the question of the conditions of knowledge production becomes a major concomitant to all knowledge production.

Let me now try to outline the contours of modern man in a terminology closer to Foucault's. To get to know himself, modern man needs to make a detour. He understands himself as a living, working and speaking being – and life, work and language are in turn understood as domains governed by their own interior laws that extend themselves into all human beings. Biology is concerned with the laws governing man as a living organism, economics looks for the rules that determine his needs and desires, his production of goods, and his exchange with others, and philology maps the words he speaks onto long histories of languages (Foucault, 1966 [1974], p. 313). These laws are determining man as if from the outside, but at the same time their contents define the inner depth of empirical living men.

In one sense, man is governed by labour, life, and language: his concrete existence finds its determinations in them; it is possible to have access to him only through his words, his organism, the objects he makes – as though it is they who possess the truth in the first place (and they alone perhaps); and he, as soon as he thinks, merely unveils himself to his own eyes in the form of a being who is already, in a necessarily subjacent density, in an irreducible anteriority, a living being, an instrument of production, a vehicle for words which exist before him (ibid.).

This means, first, that man is exterior to himself, governed by laws that exist outside and before him, of which he only holds a vague awareness.

Second, it means that to gain access to these laws he has to turn to his own empirical being as a specific example of the general laws. As an empirical being, man understands himself as *finite*: he is a specific historical particularity, representing a possible instance of the general laws. The finitude is seen as the very condition for gaining knowledge at all: man can only experience things because he has a particular body, he can only bestow things with a value because he has particular desires, and he can only speak of things because he masters a particular language. Thus, man's access to the world, and to knowledge of the world, is dependent upon his particularity, his finitude (ibid., p. 314). At the same time the finitude makes it difficult for modern man to establish the general laws of human existence. The general laws he seeks to reveal are always only available through specific empirical manifestations, and he can never be certain of what, in the specific empirical instance, represents the particularity of just that instance, and what represents the general rule.

According to Foucault, this general matrix of modern man's self-understanding can be specified as three interrelated doubles characterizing and constituting man's knowledge production about himself: man is an empirico-transcendental double, man is a double of the cogito and the unthought, and man is caught between the retreat and return of the origin. In the form of these three doubles man has sought knowledge about his thought, his being and about the meaning of life. But, as Foucault argues, modern man's self-understanding prevents him from ever producing final answers. As such, the three doubles constitute paradoxes that cannot be dissolved within the modern episteme.

In the first double man constitutes himself as a simultaneously empirical and transcendental being (ibid., p. 318ff.). The question modern man asks himself here is, 'What makes knowledge possible at all?' He seeks the transcendental forms of all knowledge production, but, according to Foucault, the knowledge he produces about such forms will remain unstable. Since the transcendental forms only can be extracted through particular empirical contents, and since knowledge about the forms always is produced by particular empirical individuals, modern man can never be certain that a specific account of the transcendental actually is of universal validity, that is, that the account is not itself determined by other transcendental forms. Instead, the final capture of the transcendental forms is continuously displaced in an endless regress.

The second double, of the cogito and the unthought, frames modern man's investigation into his own being and consciousness (ibid., p. 322ff.). Modern man's thought is always haunted by a suspicion of an unthought remainder yet to be discovered – the conditions that render a thought possible and, hence, the criterion on which to evaluate this specific thought escapes him. Thus, 'the whole modern thought is imbued with the necessity of thinking the unthought', Foucault says, 'straining to catch its endless murmur' (ibid., p. 327).

The third double is the retreat and return of the origin (ibid., p. 328ff.). In this double questions are asked about man's history and origin, and, in turn, about the meaning of life and history. Again, modern man cannot establish stable knowledge about these issues, as the origin continuously retreats into a more and more distant past. On the other hand, the origin returns as a promise that some near future investigation will make it possible finally to fathom the mystery of origin. However, the retreat of the origin is twofold; it also 'retreats' into the future as the promise of final knowledge remains unfulfilled.

Reflexivity

With his diagnosis of modern man, Foucault characterizes a certain under-standing of man and his knowledge, common to the constitution of all the modern human sciences. His interdisciplinary discourse analysis, reworking disciplines such as history, philosophy and the history of ideas, allows him to take a step back from the individual human scientific disciplines in order to excavate a common epistemological denominator. As I shall argue below, this denominator is also constitutive of reflexive research. Therefore, with Foucault we might bring together different claims to knowledge often kept apart in reflexive research. Whereas reflexive research often reproduces the disciplinary division of knowledge production, Foucault points to the com-mon conditions of possibility, and whereas reflexive research often repre-sents itself as a radical break with modern epistemology, Foucault allows us to see lines of continuity between now and then.

Reflexive research often establishes the individual scientific discipline as its horizon of investigation. Through reflexivity, researchers explore the context of scientific knowledge production, asking how the context has shaped the scientific representation of the world. In some cases this results in an inves-tigation of the personal context of the individual researcher, in others, Western science or Western culture at large is made the appropriate object of investigation. But a widespread tendency has been to focus on the indi-vidual scientific discipline whereby reflexivity has been carried out as genealogies of specific disciplines in order to expose their worldviews, their taken-for-granted assumptions and their specific procedures for knowledge production. Thus, anthropologists have reflected on anthropology (for exam-ple, Clifford and Marcus, 1986; Weston, 1997), social psychologists on social psychology (for example, Parker, 1989), and science studies researchers have reflected on science studies (for example, Ashmore, 1989). Although illumi-nating, such studies have reproduced the division of scientific knowledge into individual disciplines within reflexive research. Later on, I shall also sin-gle out one such discipline for further investigation, namely anthropology, but I suggest that formulating the problem of reflexivity as a problem common to all of the human sciences enables us to compare and discuss different contributions to the debate – within and across disciplines.

My argument is, thus, that Foucault's diagnosis of the modern human sciences and their constitution of man and knowledge provides a neat framework for recent debates about reflexivity in a range of disciplines. This implies a continuity between modern science and reflexive research that counters a widespread self-representation in reflexive writing. Here, the reflexive concern is often articulated as a better alternative to a previous human scientific practice which supposedly favoured a paradigm of naive representation, and thus achieved the appearance of objectivity by ignoring the epistemological complication of the knowledge producer (for example, Bourdieu and Wacquant, 1996; Denzin, 1997; Haraway, 1996). Reflexive writers have deconstructed previous scholars ad lib in order to expose the discrepancy between their claims to objective knowledge and their situatedness as knowledge producers (for example, White, 1978; Clifford and Marcus, 1986). A few exceptions apart, we are presented with an image of a modernist era, by now antedated, suppressing the bearing on knowledge of the social and cultural context of knowledge production.

If, however, we apply Foucault's conception of modern man, the reflexive turn can itself be understood as a truly modern enterprise. The lesson reflexive research teaches is that to assess knowledge and to qualify what it is knowledge about, we need to learn about its mode of production. In terms of the cogito and the unthought, an unthought situatedness has supposedly dominated knowledge production within the human sciences hitherto, but now it is being excavated in order to bring about either better knowledge, or a more adequate status claim for the knowledge produced. Also, the double of the empirical and the transcendental is being activated insofar as it is argued that all knowledge (a transcendental principle) is situated (is empirically contingent).

My aim here is not so much to enter into the general debate on 'modernity' and 'postmodernity' or to discuss if there has been a dramatic change or not. What I want to establish is merely that Foucault's framework applies to the reflexive turn on important points and that applying this abstract framework can provide us with a common denominator for 'modern' and 'reflexive' work alike across the individual disciplines. Foucault's diagnosis of modern man points to the modern episteme as a common condition of possibility for both the modern human sciences *and* the contemporary discussions of reflexivity. Does this mean, then, that in terms of the conception of knowledge producers and knowledge production reflexivity is old news? That we are still stuck with the same insoluble modern paradoxes? The short answer is yes. But whereas Foucault tends to emphasize the apories of the modern knowledge project, not without discontent, yearning for a different understanding of self and knowledge (for example, Foucault, 1966 [1974], p. 342ff.), I suggest a bit more sympathy with modern man. Foucault demonstrates that modern man's self-understanding provides for three doubles, and that these three doubles are insoluble paradoxes. In itself, this demonstration serves as his critique of the modern episteme. But if modern man is still with us, with no substitute in sight, what is interesting is not so much a repeated demonstration that the paradoxes are in principle insoluble as an inquiry into the ways in which they are nonetheless temporarily settled in human scientific writing.

Although the sharp contrast established between now and then in reflexive writing probably partly serves as boundary work, opening space for a new generation of scholars (cf. Sangren, 1988, p. 414), the ardent deconstruction of canonical texts also suggests that a number of different positions are available within the modern episteme. Foucault's focus is not on such differences, but, as I shall now argue, a reworking of his framework can provide a scaffolding within which to analyse the different positions and their struggles to settle the paradoxes in specific ways.

Dispersion

When assessing Foucault's archaeological work, discourse analysts have often found his concept of practice wanting. His focus on the discursive structures underemphasizes the variation and possibilities for contestation inherent in concrete discursive practice (Fairclough, 1992), and the discourses he points to appear as abstract preformed and coherent entities (Potter, 1996; cf. Wetherell, 1998). This criticism also applies here: in order to turn Foucault's doubles into analytical tools enabling investigations of dispersed discursive practice we need to climb down one step of Foucault's ladder of abstraction.

Foucault's analysis of modern man and the human sciences aims to reveal the modern episteme, that is, the totality regulating the discursive practices and their dispersion at a given time (Foucault, 1997, p. 91). As such, his diagnosis maps out the contradictory field in which specific statements about man and his knowledge make sense at all in modernity. In *The Order of Things* specific discursive practices only interest Foucault insofar as they lead him to the underlying epistemic unity and all specific practices are thus condensed in their common epistemic denominator, where any differences between them tend to disappear. In my view, the effect is that Foucault tends to overemphasize the instability of modern man's understanding of himself and his knowledge.

At the epistemic level I agree that all modern claims to knowledge in principle are unstable, as any claim always might be displaced by claims to an even deeper understanding. But at the level of discursive practice, statements are continuously proposed about man and his knowledge, and some of these become hegemonic for a while or in certain contexts before they perhaps, in turn, are subverted. Foucault's diagnosis outlines a field of possibilities, but in order to investigate how these possibilities are invested, how specific understandings became naturalized, and the consequences of such naturalization, we need to focus on the level of specific discursive practice where claims to knowledge are dispersed in time and space. It is here, in the struggle between specific practices that we can follow how concrete understandings are either subverted immediately or are constituted as relatively stable knowledge.

One aspect of the attempt to 'disperse' Foucault's diagnosis is thus to enable an analysis of temporary closures of the principally undecidable modern paradoxes. Another aspect concerns the distribution of the poles of the paradoxes. Foucault tends to describe modern man as always suspicious about his own knowledge, always both producing knowledge and undermining it. At the contrary, analysis of specific discursive practice demonstrates that the two sides of the doubles often are distributed among groups of people, so that some people are constituted as knowledgeable whereas the knowledge of others is rejected as distorted by underlying mechanisms.

Let me give an example illustrating a temporary fixing of the paradox of the cogito and the unthought. Steven Shapin has analysed the emergence of experimental natural science in seventeenth-century England (Shapin, 1988). The condition for production of legitimate knowledge here was that the experiment should be carried out successfully in the presence of adequate witnesses. While people from a number of different social categories were allowed to attend the experiment, only gentlemen counted as sufficiently credible and objective to be appropriate witnesses. The lower classes, such as merchants, were disqualified as unfree; too entangled in their worldly interests to see reality without prejudice (ibid., p. 396).[4] Shapin's analysis shows that even if the generalized modern man on the epistemic level is caught in an endless oscillation between the cogito and the unthought, specific human beings can still on the level of discursive practice be unambiguously distributed between the two poles of the double: the gentlemen were endowed with the cogito's insight, whereas everyone else was locked in the delusions of the unthought.

Foucault precludes this kind of analysis of the social distribution of the privilege to knowledge in his insistence on the unity of the episteme whereby the cogito and the unthought become two inseparable sides of modern man's self-image. If, as I have suggested, the cogito and the unthought are unfolded as two poles of a paradox or two forms of discursive resources that discourse users can navigate with(in), then an analytical field is opened for the investigation of struggles over who might produce legitimate knowledge of what, and whose accounts might be rejected as distorted. The poles of the paradoxes are inseparable in the epistemic abstraction, but by dispersing the doubles we can analyse how the poles nevertheless might by distributed socially (culturally, historically) on the level of situated discursive practice.

Anthropological negotiations of the doubles

Returning to my empirical area of interest, the reflexivity debate in anthropology, I am now able to pose the question of the different positions as a question of dispersion, rather than as a question of modernity or not. Before proceeding with an analysis of a specific anthropological contribution to the debate, I will first more generally address the question of reflexivity as it has appeared within anthropology.

As I have suggested, in Foucault's framework the debate on reflexivity can be understood as part of the modern episteme. Still, recent anthropology has displayed a widespread agreement that something has recently changed. Before, we are told, the paradigm of representation ruled almost unquestioned, the problem of the knowledge producer was seen as a problem of bias, and thus the conditions of knowledge production were relegated to forewords, diaries and personal letters. Now, it is argued that representation is always shaping and constituting the object of knowledge, the knowledge producer is often made a central object of study, and the conditions of knowledge production are thus thought to have pervasive bearing on the knowledge produced.

Aware of the danger of monumentalizing these two modes of anthropological knowledge production – we might call them 'high modernity' and 'reflexivity', respectively – I suggest that we have here (at least) two different negotiations of the modern episteme. The question still to be answered is that if the reflexivity debate fits so well into the modern episteme, why hasn't anthropology always been reflexive, the way it has been in the last few decades? Michael Herzfeld's deconstruction of high modern anthropology in *Anthropology through the Looking-Glass* (1987) provides some answers that articulate well with my suggestion to re-disperse the Foucaultian episteme.

According to Herzfeld, anthropology has worked as a discourse of identity, constituting hierarchical differences between the societies that created anthropology and the societies anthropology studies (ibid., pp. 3, 18). In the societies studied, anthropologists deemed the local knowledge dependent upon context, while the privilege of producing absolute, context-free knowledge was reserved for the anthropologists themselves (ibid., pp. 13ff., 51ff.). 'The others' were portrayed as passive carriers of culture, obliged to perform its commands, whereas the Westerners were presented as individualistic and original, able to see and actively manipulate the underlying structures (ibid., p. 56ff.). On a time scale, Herzfeld argues, 'the others' were represented as a common past of all humanity. But whereas 'they' have stayed in homogeneous and static cultures, 'we' have developed into differentiated and complex societies. And whereas they have remained ignorant of the structures ruling their life and knowledge, we have liberated ourselves from the structures to such an extent that we can both see them for what they are and manipulate them for our purposes (ibid., p. 61ff.).

Translating Herzfeld's analysis into the vocabulary of the doubles, we can explicate high modern anthropology's specific way of fixing the three paradoxes. Transcendental knowledge was regarded possible, but only through the liberation from cultural and social structures that the Western complex societies facilitate. Thus, legitimate knowledge in high modern anthropology rested on making the unthought structures visible – and the Western cogito was granted the capacity to do so, both in the own society and in the others'. The ensuing 'division of labour', the anthropologists' context-free knowledge production against the indigenous context-bound and passive executions of underlying structures, was in turn founded in a history of origin, where 'they' represented the common origin of passivity and delusion, from where 'we' have developed into knowledgeable agents.

Relying on Herzfeld's analysis, we might then characterize the high modern anthropological negotiation of the paradoxes as a distribution of their poles onto two groups. The anthropologists (and the West in general) occupied the transcendental pole in the transcendental-empirical double and the pole of the cogito in the double of the cogito and the unthought.[5] Belonging to the other group, the others' knowledge claims were represented as empirical instances of underlying, unthought structures. The history of origin, with us in the lead, and the others still in the past, framed these high modern knowledge claims in an evolutionary scheme.

In contrast to this, perhaps somewhat stereotyped, image of high modern anthropology, the reflexive turn can be described as an attempt to keep the opposing poles of the paradoxes together in the same object. The transcendental condition for knowledge production is taken to be that knowledge is always produced by particularly situated knowledge producers – and this applies to both the anthropologists and their informants. And thus, the knowledge produced by the cogito is always embedded in a never fully recoverable unthought. As far as the origin is concerned, it is now widely agreed that different communities produce partly imaginary ancestries and myths of origin to support their claims, anthropologists and informants alike. At least as far as the explicit declarations go, these are the starting points of most reflexive research. But keeping the poles of the paradoxes closer together is not the same as resolving them, and the reflexive turn itself displays a number of different negotiations of the doubles, resulting in a number of different subject positions constructed for the authors.[6] In the following I shall analyse one such negotiation.

Talal Asad: 'The concept of cultural translation in British social anthropology'

James Clifford's and George E. Marcus' edited volume *Writing Culture: The Poetics and Politics of Ethnography* (1986) has become almost metonymic with the reflexivity debate within anthropology. This does not mean, however, that *Writing Culture* has autonomously set the standards for reflexivity in anthropology – often providing the starting point for discussions of reflexivity, it has been praised as well as harshly criticized (see, for example, Sangren, 1988; Watson, 1991); nor is it in itself a unison recipe of how to be reflexive. While all contributions in *Writing Culture* attempt to explore domains so far unthought in anthropological knowledge production, they differ markedly in the conclusions they draw about the possibilities for knowledge and the future task of anthropology. Here, I shall focus on Talal Asad's contribution, 'The concept of cultural translation in British social anthropology'.

Asad's article is an investigation into the constitution of subject positions within anthropological texts, and as such the same kind of analysis as I want to engage in – except that in Asad's paper (as in *Writing Culture* in general), this feature of texts is called authority construction, rather than subject positions. However, the aim is similar: to characterize the position that the anthropologist creates for him/herself as a producer of knowledge, and to examine how that position rhetorically enhances the credibility of the text. First, I follow Asad's analysis of a specific authority construction in British anthropology – we might call it 'authoritative cultural translation' – and then I analyse Asad's alternative in the framework derived from Foucault above.

Authoritative cultural translation

As Asad notes, many British anthropologists have seen the ethnographic task as one of cultural translation, where the ethnographer must translate the foreign culture into his or her home language. While agreeing with this definition of the ethnographic practice, Asad criticizes its traditional execution. Anthropologists have tended to represent themselves as people with privileged access to the meanings of other cultures; only they have been able to tell the truth of the culture – a truth that the participants cannot see themselves. To make this point, Asad criticizes anthropologists like Ernest Gellner and Mary Douglas.

Gellner has done fieldwork among Moroccan Berbers. In the Berber society a privileged minority of people, called *igurramen*, are attributed religious powers and work as arbitrators among people. The Berbers believe that it is God who selects the people who are to become *igurramen*, but Gellner argues that: 'The reality of the situation is, however, that the *igurramen* are in fact selected by the surrounding ordinary tribesmen who use their services.'[7] To Asad, this is a perfect example of the kind of authority construction he wants to expose. Full of irony, he spells out the implications of Gellner's argument:

> [W]hat they [the Berbers] believe is quite wrong: thus, the Berbers believe that God 'selects' *igurramen*; we know God does not exist (or if some of us still 'believe' he does, we 'know' he does not intervene directly in secular history); ergo the 'selector' must be another agent whom the tribesmen do not know as the agent – in fact, the surrounding tribesmen themselves. (1986, p. 154ff.)

Asad concludes that Gellner sees cultural translation as bringing out the *real* meaning of the foreign culture; in the example, the real meaning of what the Berbers say, in spite of what the Berbers think themselves. Thereby Gellner constructs a specific and important position for himself. Not only can he report about foreign cultures, unknown to his home audience, he can do so even better than a native might have done, because he can tell what the culture in question *really* is about. Hereby, the ethnographer accords himself a privileged access to knowledge as it is only he who can produce adequate knowledge.

In terms of Foucault's doubles, we here see the cogito and the unthought at work. Native knowledge is being dismissed as illusions in Gellner's ethnographic practice and replaced with the anthropological uncovering of an unthought, invisible to the natives themselves. Asad's criticism resembles Herzfeld's, and in Foucault's terms his argument may be formulated as a criticism against using the double of the cogito and the unthought as a motor for dismantling native knowledge, because the discursive effect is an asymmetrical relationship between anthropologist and native, both in terms of knowledge and power as the anthropologist retains the privileged access to the unthought.

Translation and power relations

In order to establish an alternative to this authoritative subject positioning, Asad suggests that we begin by reconceptualizing the process of translation into a framework of power (1986, p. 156ff.). A good translator, Asad argues, must 'stretch' or transform his or her own language in order to capture the specificity of the foreign language. Unfortunately, he continues, it is not all languages that lend themselves to this form of transformation, and this has to do with relations of power. Western countries, the traditional audiences of anthropology, dominate Third World countries, the traditional locus of anthropological studies, and the knowledge inherent in the languages of the Third World is not valued in Western countries. This power relationship induces restrictions on the extent to which Western languages will transform themselves in order to understand Third World cultures; for instance, the extent to which publishers and audience will accept alternative ways of representing Third World cultures. The conclusion is that

> the process of 'cultural translation' is inevitably enmeshed in conditions of power – professional, national, international. And among these conditions is the authority of ethnographers to uncover the implicit meanings of subordinate societies. Given that it is so, the interesting question for enquiry is ... how power enters into the process of 'cultural translation,' seen both as a discursive and as a non-discursive practice. (ibid., p. 163)

Hence, Asad argues that anthropologists like Gellner and Douglas in effect reproduce the unequal power relations between the West and the Third

World countries, and he promotes an enquiry into these power relations as an alternative.

Asad here himself draws on the double of the cogito and the unthought in order to disqualify the knowledge produced by Gellner and Douglas. He does this by introducing a social theory of knowledge, namely the theory that people and the knowledge they produce are conditioned by power and sociocultural context. This social theory is commonplace in anthropology, but here it is used to deconstruct Gellner's and Douglas' knowledge as determined by a, for them, unrealized unthought. Asad brings this displacement about by investing in another of the doubles, the empirico-transcendental, in which the conditions of knowledge are investigated. Asad's claim, so far, is that the transcendental condition for knowledge is that it is shaped by the sociocultural context of the knowledge producer. But, as we shall see, this does not apply equally to all knowledge producers involved in the text.

Fieldwork

According to Asad, the practice of cultural translation can be separated into two processes: the fieldwork in the other culture, and the representing of the results for the home audience. Of fieldwork, Asad says:

> In the field … the process of translation takes place at the very moment the ethnographer engages with a specific mode of life – just as a child does in learning to grow up within a specific culture. He learns to find his way in a new environment, and a new language. And like a child he needs to verbalize *explicitly* what the proper way of doing things is, because that is how learning proceeds … When the child/anthropologist becomes adept at adult ways, what he has learnt becomes *implicit* – as assumptions informing a shared mode of life, with all its resonances and areas of unclarity. (1986, p. 159)

The beginning of this passage brings together two metaphors of fieldwork. On the one hand, fieldwork is a process of translation, and translation must be between two registers, presumably between the new culture and the home culture. On the other hand, the ethnographer is compared to a child learning a way of life. Normally, we would conceive of children as empty slates, or at least not from birth possessing a second register into which they translate their experiences. Let us look at the implications of the conception of fieldwork as translation and as the ethnographer-as-child respectively.

Following Asad's above-mentioned social theory of the sociocultural conditioning of people, the implications of seeing fieldwork as translation might be that the anthropologist, brought up in a different culture, would acquire the new culture in a certain way. That is to say that the preconditioning of the anthropologist would somehow effect *how* he or she sees and learns the new culture. If this is the case at all (Asad does not discuss it), the preconditioning does not seem to hinder the full acquisition of the new culture: the end of the quote makes clear that the result of fieldwork is that the anthropologist has learned the new culture as if he or she had been a child in that culture. Hence, in the negotiation of the two metaphors, Asad plays down the translation part of fieldwork in favour of the metaphor of the ethnographer-as-child.

Earlier, we saw how Asad settled the empirico-transcendental double through his theory of knowledge that knowledge is shaped by the sociocultural context. The metaphor of the child-anthropologist makes way for a seemingly unauthoritative conception of fieldwork that coheres with this theory of knowledge – a result that would be difficult to achieve if the anthropologist was seen as an adult. The question is that if knowledge is socioculturally shaped, how and to what extent can the (socioculturally shaped) anthropologist gain adequate knowledge of the foreign culture? With the image of the child this question disappears. The anthropologist-as-child is socioculturally shaped by the foreign culture and there is no sociocultural baggage on his or her part to account for. When fieldwork is conceptualized as learning a culture the way a child does, it implies that the anthropologist (when adept) knows the culture the way natives do. If the anthropologist, by contrast, were seen as an adult from the beginning, already shaped by a sociocultural context, this would complicate the argument in two ways. One thing is the above-mentioned disposition of the anthropologist to learn the new culture in a certain way. Another thing is his or her reception in the new culture. The anthropologist is unlikely to be regarded as a child in the new culture and responded to as a child by the natives. Given the anthropologist's different, typically Western, background, it is much more likely that the natives will form some opinion of him or her in that capacity, and hence 'teach' their culture accordingly (cf. Herzfeld, 1983).

These are questions that Asad avoids by settling for the metaphor of the child, and consequently he is able to deal with the issue of fieldwork in just a few lines. The discursive effect is that the fieldworker is detached from any previous sociocultural conditioning. This allows for a seemingly unauthoritative construction of the knowledge gained through fieldwork: since the anthropologist has temporarily 'gone native', his or her understanding of the foreign culture can hardly be controversial to the members of this culture.

Back home

As the anthropologist returns home, the global power relations are again foregrounded in Asad's text:

> When anthropologists return to their countries, they must write up 'their people', and they must do so in the conventions of representation already circumscribed (already 'written around,' 'bounded') by their discipline, institutional life, and wider society. (1986, p. 159)

The power relations seem to be unidirectional: the West dominates the rest of the world and this asymmetry is reproduced at all levels of society. Hence, they determine ethnographic writing through conventions of representation that hinders the smooth translation of the foreign culture into the home language, conventions that are difficult, perhaps even impossible to overcome (ibid., p. 158). But whereas anthropologists like Gellner and Douglas were incarcerated in these conventions and could only reproduce them, Asad sees another possibility for anthropologists like himself:

> [A]nthropologists need to explore these processes [of power] in order to determine how far they go in defining the possibilities and the limits of effective translation. (ibid., p. 164)

This is Asad's reflexive call for an anthropology that takes the global power relationships seriously. Anthropological representation is conditioned by relationships of power, and thus anthropologists need to explore how far this conditioning goes. But how? Let me try to pull out the implications of the quote. First the anthropologist must know what an effective translation would be, if unequal power relations did not exist, in order to measure the effects of power on actual translations. Moreover, to judge what the effective translation would be, the anthropologist must know both registers: the culture being translated and the language translated into – but not from the viewpoint of either. Since both the culture translated from, and the language translated into are implicated in the global power relations, the anthropologist needs a third position outside the power relations from where he or she can recognize the power relations and their effects on translation.

Distributing the doubles

In Foucault's terms, Asad's suggestion encourages anthropologists to uncover an unthought that has so far ruled anthropological representations of other cultures. But the possibility of doing so is founded in a complex negotiation of the empirical and the transcendental in Asad's text. This becomes clear when we look at Asad's ascription of conditions of possibility for knowledge production to different actors in the text. One such actor is anthropologists like Gellner and Douglas. As we have seen, Asad constructs their knowledge as socioculturally conditioned. This also applies to another actor in the text, the Third World people. Their knowledge is to some extent explained as effects of the global power relations: 'industrial capitalism transforms not only modes of production but also kinds of knowledge and styles of life in the Third World' (1986, p. 158).

A third actor in the text is the fieldworker. Here, the principle of the sociocultural conditioning of knowledge both applies and does not. With the image of the child, Asad cuts the strings to the fieldworker's sociocultural conditioning previous to entering the field. On the other hand, this leaves room for a new sociocultural conditioning of the fieldworker *in the field*, as he or she is 'brought up' to know the new culture as the natives do.

The last actor in the text is the critical anthropologist carrying out Asad's programme of disclosing the power relations. There are no signs in the text indicating any sociocultural conditioning of this actor. Rather, Asad implies a position for himself from where to produce unconditioned knowledge *about* the power relations and sociocultural constraints conditioning everyone else's knowledge.

Thus, the question of the transcendental conditions for knowledge production is answered ambiguously in Asad's text. As far as Third World people and other anthropologists go, the transcendental condition seems to be that all knowledge is produced within sociocultural relationships of power. But when it comes to Asad's own knowledge another possibility is launched. Without specifying the conditions of possibility, Asad constructs for himself a position above power while everyone else is confined to speaking the language of power.

Asad's subject position as knowledge producer is thus established through the distribution of the poles of two of Foucault's doubles on the actors in the text. The empirico-transcendental double is distributed to the effect that everyone else's knowledge is determined by their empirical, situated being, while Asad himself is granted transcendental insight. Thus, he can also represent the cogito and uncover the unthought that conditions his colleagues and informants.

If this subject positioning was consistent right through Asad's text, though, it would produce some asymmetrical differences between the actors of the text, unacceptable to Asad's pursuit of an unauthoritative anthropological subject position. If Asad throughout constructed himself as a cogito vis-à-vis a native unthought he would merely repeat Gellner's and Douglas' authoritative stance. The metaphor of the ethnographer-as-child serves as a detour from the main metaphor governing the text, ethnography-as-translation, and effects a minimization of difference between anthropologist and native when it comes to fieldwork. And at the same time it facilitates Asad's construction of a position from where to acquire knowledge without distorting sociocultural constraints.

The metaphor of the child might also be interpreted as Asad's investment in Foucault's last double, the retreat and return of the origin. Becoming a child, the fieldworker sheds his or her sociocultural conditioning and returns to his or her own original state as the unconditioned child ready to grow up in a new culture and internalize its practice and knowledge uncontaminated.

Compared to 'high modern' anthropological accounts of knowledge, Asad shifts the emphasis of the unthought and the empirical situatedness from the natives to fellow anthropologists. The knowledge of other anthropologists is contextualized and disqualified with reference to the conditions under which it is produced. Native knowledge, on the other hand, is upgraded, as the natives are the teachers (or upbringers) of anthropologists. Where 'high modern anthropologists' reserved the privilege of adequate knowledge for themselves, the knowledge of anthropologists and natives share the same conditions of possibility in Asad's text – but only when it comes to other anthropologists. In his own knowledge claims Asad comes close to the high modern subject position of producing knowledge from nowhere (cf. Haraway, 1996).

Conclusion

The point of this analysis is primarily to show a specific construction of a human scientific subject position, and only secondarily to criticize it. All writers construct subject positions for themselves, and negotiating the doubles and fixing their paradoxes in specific ways is inevitable as long as the modern episteme is our framework for producing knowledge. To use the doubles as discursive resources in knowledge production is not in itself open to criticism (until an alternative to the modern episteme perhaps comes along), since the doubles provide the conditions of possibility for knowledge of human beings and their knowledge at all.

What I find interesting is *how* the doubles are negotiated and how their paradoxes are fixed in specific texts, *which* subject positions are thus constructed, and how they are discursively accomplished. Such analyses might provide the basis from which to continue the discussion of academic subject positions and their consequences. Thus, my analysis of Asad's text is intended to contribute with one shred of an investigation of which subject positions reflexive research makes available.

Foucault's analysis of modern man as well as my derived analytical framework and the application of this on Asad's text might itself be interpreted as a negotiation of the doubles. Concerning the conditions of possibility of knowledge, that is, the empirico-transcendental double, I share with Foucault the assumption that knowledge is produced within historical discursive structures, even if his understanding of the episteme is rather more monumental than the one I have suggested. Moreover, Foucault's diagnosis of modern man can be read as a disclosure of an unthought in modern man's understanding of himself and his knowledge,[8] and this in turn applies to my treatment of Asad. But whereas Foucault impatiently looks into the future for a different understanding of man and knowledge, I have suggested that insofar as we are still modern we might as well use the doubles to analyse and critically discuss academic subject positions as from within the modern episteme.

The critical evaluation of Asad's text therefore does not take its starting point in the fact that he uses the doubles to construct his argument and his own subject position, but rather in his particular negotiation of the doubles that prevents him from convincingly delivering the promised alternative to the authoritative stance he criticizes. Asad's own subject position is authoritative itself, as it provides knowledge from nowhere of what no one else can see.

Whereas everyone else's knowledge is conditioned, the positive conditions for Asad's knowledge production remain unexplicated.

It would be possible, though, to combine Asad's critical project with a less authoritarian subject position. This would include a reference to a sociocultural basis that could provide the context for Asad's knowledge production. And such a reference could only be made, if Asad's theory of power was reformulated. In Asad's text the global power relationships seem hegemonic and without room for 'counter-knowledge'. Hence, a sociocultural basis for Asad's knowledge is wanting. Therefore Asad's subject position becomes one where knowledge from nowhere uncovers the power that is everywhere. Instead, power could be theorized as dispersed, so that the dominating relationships of power were only understood as partially determining. In such a theory the sociocultural reality would be seen to be constructed contradictorily, and it could thus be the basis for different kinds of knowledge production, some reproducing the dominant relations of power, and some trying to subvert them. In that case one could try to single out a sociocultural 'pocket' as a basis for the kind of knowledge production Asad is suggesting.[9]

But social theory and subject positioning often go together, and thus such a reformulation of Asad's theory would also change his subject position. If everyone, including Asad, was equally constrained (though in different ways according to their position in the sociocultural landscape), this would make his position less authoritative. Like anyone else, he would be socioculturally situated, and his knowledge would be produced from a certain sociocultural perspective. But for the same reason, this would also be a weakening of his subject position, since the claim to transcendental knowledge would become impossible: Asad's knowledge of the world would become one of many possible representations.

This thought experiment with Asad's theory and subject position is intended to show that reflexive thinking leaves room for different negotiations of the doubles – 'reflexivity' itself does not settle the doubles once and for all. The reflexive focus on the knowledge producer brings the doubles and their paradoxes to the foreground of knowledge production, but it does not dissolve them. What it does, though, is to keep us alert to the ongoing negotiation of subject positions – in our own texts as well as in the texts of others – and, thus, in a good modern spirit, helps us to uncover the unthought.

Notes

1. In my use of the term, 'reflexive research' covers research that emphasizes and explores the situated production of scientific knowledge as a necessary context for understanding and assessing this knowledge and its consequences.
2. I here follow Foucault's terminology and speak of the modern human being as 'man' and in the masculine.
3. The episteme is Foucault's term for the totality that regulates the discursive practices at a given time (Foucault, 1997, p. 191).

4. It might be noted that Shapin's analysis in this respect problematizes Foucault's epochalization, since it demonstrates that man was already conceived as an epistemological problem in the seventeenth century. According to Foucault the modern episteme first emerged at the end of the eighteenth century, and before this time 'there was no epistemological consciousness of man as such', he claims (Foucault, 1966 [1974], p. 309).
5. This human scientific subject position is similar to the one found by Steve Woolgar (1988) in the natural sciences. Woolgar investigates how scientists construct their accounts to be accounts of an external reality rather than projections of the author.
6. See Jørgensen and Phillips (forthcoming, ch. 6) for a discussion of a range of attempts across the human scientific disciplines to establish more symmetrical theorizations of the relationship between researcher and researched.
7. Ernest Gellner, 'Concepts and Society', in B.R. Wilson (ed.), *Rationality*. Oxford: Blackwell, 1970; quoted in Asad (1986, p. 154).
8. In the preface to *The Order of Things*, Foucault thus formulates his aim as to 'uncover the deepest strata of Western culture' (1966 [1977], p. xxiv), and quite parallel to Asad's argument, he asks rhetorically: 'I should like to know whether the subjects responsible for scientific discourse are not determined in their situation, their function, their perceptive capacity, and their practical possibilities by conditions that dominate and even overwhelm them' (ibid., p. xiv).
9. This suggested strategy for subject positioning parallels the ones adopted by, for example, Abu-Lughod (1991) and Weston (1997).

References

Abu-Lughod, L. (1991) 'Writing against culture', in R.G. Fox (ed.), *Recapturing Anthropology*. Santa Fe/Washington: School of American Research Press.

Asad, T. (1986) 'The concept of cultural translation in British social anthropology', in J. Clifford and G.E. Marcus (eds), *Writing Culture: The Poetics and Politics of Ethnography*. Berkeley/Los Angeles: University of California Press.

Ashmore, M. (1989) *The Reflexive Thesis*. Chicago: University of Chicago Press.

Bourdieu, P. and Wacquant, L. (1996) *An Invitation to Reflexive Sociology*. Cambridge: Polity Press.

Clifford, J. and Marcus, G.E. (eds) (1986) *Writing Culture: The Poetics and Politics of Ethnography*. Berkeley/Los Angeles: University of California Press.

Denzin, N.K. (1997) *Interpretive Ethnography*. Thousand Oaks: Sage Publications.

Fairclough, N. (1992) *Discourse and Social Change*. Cambridge: Polity Press.

Foucault, M. (1966 [1974]) *The Order of Things: An Archaeology of the Human Sciences*. London: Routledge.

Foucault, M. (1997) *The Archaeology of Knowledge*. London: Routledge.

Haraway, D. (1996) 'Situated knowledges', in E. Fox Keller and H.E. Longino (eds), *Feminism and Science*. Oxford: Oxford University Press.

Herzfeld, M. (1983) 'Looking both ways: the ethnographer in the text', *Semiotica*, 46(2/4), pp. 151–66.

Herzfeld, M. (1987) *Anthropology through the Looking-Glass*. Cambridge: Cambridge University Press.

Jørgensen, M.W. and Phillips, L.J. (forthcoming) *Discourse Analysis as Theory and Method*. London: Sage Publications.

Parker, I. (1989) 'Discourse and power', in J. Shotter and K.J. Gergen (eds), *Texts of Identity*. London: Sage Publications.

Potter, J. (1996) *Representing Reality*. London: Sage Publications.

Sangren, P.S. (1988) 'Rhetoric and the authority of ethnography', *Current Anthropology*, 29(3), pp. 405–35.

Shapin, S. (1988) 'The house of experiment in seventeenth-century England', *ISIS*, 79, pp. 373–404.

Watson, G. (1991) 'Rewriting culture', in R.G. Fox (ed.), *Recapturing Anthropology*. Santa Fe/Washington: School of American Research Press.

Weston, K. (1997) 'The virtual anthropologist', in A. Gupta and J. Ferguson (eds), *Anthropological Locations*. Berkeley: University of California Press.

Wetherell, M. (1998) 'Positioning and interpretative repertoires: conversation analysis and post-structuralism in dialogue', *Discourse and Society*, 9(3), pp. 387–412.

White, H. (1978) *Tropics of Discourse*. Baltimore: Johns Hopkins University Press.

Woolgar, S. (1988) *Science: The Very Idea*. London: Tavistock Publications.

Part II

Debating and Practising Interdisciplinarity

5
The Discourse-Knowledge Interface
Teun A. van Dijk

Discourse and knowledge as multidisciplinary phenomena

One of the major challenges of Critical Discourse Analysis (CDA) is to make explicit the relations between discourse and knowledge. Both discourse and knowledge are very complex phenomena studied in virtually all disciplines of the humanities and social sciences. Thus, we may expect that also a theory of their relationships has philosophical, linguistic, psychological, sociological and anthropological dimensions.

The philosophical enquiry, developed in epistemology, focuses on fundamental issues of the nature of knowledge, traditionally defined as 'justified true beliefs' (for a selection of work in epistemology where this concept is discussed and criticized, see, for example, Bernecker and Dretske, 2000). I shall deviate from this orthodoxy as well as from most other approaches by defining knowledge as the consensual beliefs of an epistemic community, and shall reserve truth as a property of assertions. Only situated talk or text may be said to be true or false; for instance, when the beliefs expressed by them are asserted to correspond to the facts. Beliefs themselves may, or may not, correspond to 'reality', but have no truth values unless discursively asserted.

Linguistics has traditionally ignored knowledge, and it is only in cognitive grammar that knowledge has appeared as an important category (see, for example, Langacker, 1983; Fauconnier, 1985). In linguistic discourse analysis, it is especially the late Paul Werth who has made interesting proposals on the role of knowledge in discourse (Werth, 1999). In the theory of generative grammar, knowledge appears especially as implicit knowledge of the (rules) of grammar, shared by the members of a language community. Cognitive approaches explore the relations between meaning and knowledge, thus blurring the classical distinction between language and thought. For instance, in modern metaphor theory, it is assumed that virtually all meanings are organized by underlying metaphorical concepts and processes, whose 'embodied' nature also shape the ways we know the world (Lakoff and Johnson, 1980, 1999).

Psychology and Artificial Intelligence (AI) have undoubtedly contributed most to our contemporary knowledge about knowledge, defined as mental representations in memory (Schank and Abelson, 1977; van Dijk and Kintsch, 1983; Britton and Graesser, 1996; Bechtel and Graham, 1999; Markman, 1999). Although 'representational' formats also have their critics, knowledge representation theories have meant a major advance in our understanding of discourse processing. Producing and comprehending discourse not only involves the processing of meaning, form and action, but presupposes vast amounts of knowledge; for instance, during lexicalization, stylistic variation, and especially for the processing of meaning. Notions such as topics, global and local coherence, implication, presupposition, schematic structures and a host of other properties of discourse, all require a knowledge component. And not only the meaning of discourse requires a knowledge component, but also its forms. However, in order to further limit the size of a potentially vast area, I shall focus in this chapter on only some of the semantic properties of the discourse-knowledge interface.

Knowledge is not only mental, but also social, as many contemporary directions in pragmatics and discourse studies show (Gumperz and Levinson, 1996; Potter, 1996; Wodak, 1996; see also the early work of Kreckel, 1981). Knowledge is acquired, shared and used by people in interaction, as well as by groups, institutions and organizations. Indeed, without such a social basis, knowledge would be no more than personal belief. Consensus, common sense or common ground are among the many notions that define this social dimension of knowledge (Clark, 1996). It is this social nature of shared knowledge that defines presupposition and that allows discourse to be understandable without making all relevant knowledge explicit all the time. Like all other scarce social resources, knowledge may be a power resource, that is, the 'symbolic capital' of specific groups (Bourdieu, 1988). Knowledge may be dominant, and may (have to) be ratified and legitimated, or may be challenged as such by alternative forms of beliefs (Foucault, 1972). Knowledge is expressed, conveyed, accepted and shared in discourse and other forms of social interaction. It may be spread and acquired through talk and text of social institutions such as governments, media, schools, universities and laboratories. In sum, many fundamental properties of knowledge need to be dealt with in a sociological approach.

Finally, knowledge has an important cultural dimension, and hence needs an anthropological or ethnographic account (Holland and Quinn, 1987; D'Andrade, 1995; Shore, 1996). Epistemic communities are not merely social groups or institutions, but also communities of practice, thought and discourse. More than any other property of humans, knowledge has been used to define the very basis of cultures: one belongs to the same culture, and one can only act competently as a member of such a culture when one shares its knowledge and other social cognitions. The epistemic common ground that allows discourse production and understanding needs definition in terms of culture. Even when we speak of the knowledge shared in an organization or by a group, we often do so in terms of 'culture'. Whereas in several other disciplines the cognitive and the social dimensions of knowledge have seldom been fruitfully combined, cognitive anthropology is one of the interdisciplines where such an integration has proved to be very successful.

Similar remarks may be made for the notion of discourse, which also has philosophical, linguistic, cognitive, social and cultural dimensions – and of course historical ones (instead of providing a vast bibliography here, I may refer to the chapters contributed to van Dijk, 1997). That means that also the interface between discourse and knowledge needs to be multidisciplinary. This is not surprising when we realize that they mutually need and presuppose each other: discourse production and understanding is impossible without knowledge, and knowledge acquisition and change usually presupposes discourse. Indeed, it has been claimed that whatever is socially relevant of knowledge is usually also expressed in text or talk.

Given the obvious limitations of a single chapter, we can only examine some of the many properties of this complex interface between discourse and knowledge. Although all dimensions mentioned above are closely interrelated, I shall focus on the cognitive and semantic aspects of the discourse-knowledge interface, also because the social aspects of knowledge are much better known in CDA, as is the case for the work of Foucault, Gumperz and Bourdieu among others. It is in this interface that we are able to bridge the fundamental gap between knowledge (and hence the mind), and discourse meaning (and hence social interaction), and hence between discourse and society and discourse and culture.

Knowledge analysis and CDA

It is not the main task of this chapter to spell out extensively the relationships between what we may call 'epistemic analysis' and CDA. We first have to establish what epistemic analysis is in the first place, since in discourse analysis that is not a very common enterprise.

However, there are some obvious links between CDA and the study of the relations between knowledge and discourse structures. One of the general aims of CDA is to study the discursive reproduction of dominance (power abuse) and its consequences on social inequality (van Dijk, 1993b). Such social power relations are based on the preferential access to or control over scarce social resources by the dominant group. These resources are not only material, but also symbolic (see also Bourdieu's (1988) notion of 'symbolic capital'), and knowledge as well as access to public discourse are among the major symbolic power resources of contemporary society. In order to study power and its abuse, it is therefore crucial to understand how exactly powerful groups and institutions (such as media, universities, and so on) manage and express their knowledge in public discourse. This is what I shall do in the illustrative analysis below.

There are many ways such an epistemic analysis of dominant group discourse can be further focused on in a critical perspective. Power abuse or domination, as we define it, is ultimately based on the breach of human or social rights, that is, of laws, principles or norms regulating the relations between people, or the public actions of groups or institutions. Thus, of a newspaper it may normatively be expected that it does not deliberately lie, that it provides essential information about news events and does not provide irrelevant personal information that might hurt people or groups (such as the ethnic group membership of perpetrators of crimes). This variant of the Gricean principles, duly made more explicit, may be applied to the management of knowledge by all powerful groups and institutions. Thus, of scholars, politicians, journalists and legal specialists we may expect that they do not use their specialized knowledge in order to harm, exclude or marginalize citizens, but on the contrary that they only use such knowledge in order for citizens (clients) to benefit from such knowledge. For each group or institution, we may thus formulate an applied ethics that also regulates the acquisition, uses and application of knowledge in various forms of public discourse (for the media, see, for instance, my own study on racism and what knowledge should and should not be included in news reports: van Dijk, 1991; see also van Dijk, 1993a, for a similar study of other forms of elite racism, also involving breaches of laws, norms and rules for the treatment of minorities by elites).

Similarly, an essential part of a critical approach to knowledge is also a study of the relations between knowledge and social groups and institutions: which groups or institutions have preferential access to various kinds of knowledge, which groups or institutions set the criteria for the very definition or legitimization of knowledge, and which are especially involved in the distribution of knowledge – or precisely in the limitation of knowledge in society. This more general, sociological and philosophical approach to knowledge, often associated with the work of Foucault and Bourdieu, is well-known and need not be discussed further here. Our task as critical discourse analysts is to spell out these general social strategies of dominance and knowledge management at the more detailed level of cognitive knowledge structures and strategies and how these affect discourse structures, and vice versa; how these discourse strategies may in turn affect the cognitive and then the social properties of the audience and society at large.

Knowledge and social cognition

In the same way as it would be wrong to reduce knowledge to individual, mental representations, we should not merely view knowledge as a discursive, social or cultural phenomenon. In my view, knowledge is both cognitive and as such associated with the neurological structures of the brain, as well as social, and thus locally associated with interaction between social actors and globally with societal structures. For social knowledge to have an impact on discourse, however, we necessarily need a sociocognitive interface, according to all we know today in cognitive science.

In this chapter I shall thus explore some of the cognitive properties of the way knowledge and discourse are related. This does *not* mean, however, that cognition here is merely understood as 'individual' cognition. Although it is quite plausible and in line with our firmest intuitions that people also have personal or 'private' knowledge, the kind of 'knowledge of the world' studied most in discourse analysis is clearly social. Therefore, in order to guarantee the possible integration with sociological and anthropological approaches to knowledge I also define such knowledge in terms of *social cognition*.

'Social cognition' I shall define as the system of mental structures and operations that are acquired, used or changed in social contexts by social actors and shared by the members of social groups, organizations and cultures. This system consists of several subsystems, such as knowledge, attitudes, ideologies, norms and values, and the ways these are affected and brought to bear in discourse and other social practices. Although what counts as knowledge for a specific epistemic community may be based on attitudes, ideologies and norms and values, we shall largely ignore these other components of social cognition. Indeed, the overall architecture of the 'social mind' is still on the agenda.

Note that in social psychology, 'social cognition' is usually associated with the (largely experimental) research tradition in the US (see, for example, Fiske and Taylor, 1991). This approach is often accused of having an individualistic slant that ignores the social dimensions of the acquisition, usage, and so on, of knowledge (Augoustinos and Walker, 1995). In Europe, alternatively, much (especially qualitative) work on shared knowledge has been done in terms of 'social representations' (Farr and Moscovici, 1984; Moscovici, 2000).

Fortunately, there have recently been attempts at integration of these two traditions, a development that is in line with my multidisciplinary framework. I shall therefore use the more general term 'social cognition' in a broader sense than has hitherto been the case in social psychology, that is, as a perspective that combines the cognitive and the social aspects of knowledge and other fundamental properties of the 'social mind' or the 'thinking society' (see also Bar-Tal and Kruglanski, 1988; Fraser and Gaskell, 1990; Breakwell and Canter, 1993; Flick, 1998).

Types of knowledge

The explicit formulation of the discourse-knowledge interface first of all requires a typology of knowledge. Instead of reducing knowledge to just one type, and thus having to find other terms for other types of knowledge, I shall maintain the general term for all types and differentiate between them with various adjectives. Since a typology of knowledge is not a main aim of this chapter, I shall be brief about it and merely enumerate and succinctly define various types of knowledge. However, it is strange that, as far as I know, neither epistemology nor psychology has provided such a typology before, apart from mentioning some of the distinctions referred to below.

- *Declarative vs procedural knowledge.* In both philosophy and AI a distinction is often made between 'declarative' and 'procedural' knowledge, that is, between 'knowing that' and 'knowing how to' (Ryle, 1949), sometimes also described as 'explicit' vs 'implicit' knowledge (Wilkes, 1997). In this chapter I shall only be concerned with 'declarative' knowledge, also because 'knowing how' is an ability or capacity, and not knowledge as we define it. Such knowledge may be expressed explicitly in discourse or be presupposed (remain implicit). Hence we do not use the oppositional pair explicit vs implicit knowledge to refer to declarative vs procedural knowledge. Nor do we use the notion of 'declarative' because knowledge need not be 'declared' or expressed in discourse at all: indeed, it may also be presupposed by our actions or social practices.
- *Personal vs social knowledge.* Many properties of discourse and interaction require a distinction between 'private' and 'shared' knowledge. It is only the latter knowledge that can be presupposed in discourse. Personal knowledge is acquired by personal experiences and used only as a condition for personal action, and as a source for personal storytelling.
- *Types of social knowledge.* Social knowledge also comes in different types, depending on who shares such knowledge, that is, depending on its 'scope'. Thus, we may distinguish between interpersonal, group and cultural knowledge, depending on whether such knowledge is shared and discursively presupposed by two or a few people (typically in a conversation), a whole group, such as a profession or institution, or a whole culture. The traditional concept of 'knowledge of the world' is usually a form of cultural knowledge, that is, all knowledge being shared by all competent members of a culture. We might also speak of national knowledge when it is shared by the members of a nation; it is typically acquired through schooling and through the mass media of a country, and presupposed by all competent members of a nation. And finally, there might be a form of 'universal' knowledge if there is knowledge shared and presupposed by all competent members of all cultures. In these brief characterizations we already see that the sociocognitive definitions of these kinds of knowledge are closely related to discourse, namely through their typical acquisition by various discourse genres and contexts, as well as by their discursive uses, as is the case for presuppositions.
- *General vs specific knowledge.* The types of knowledge distinguished above may be specific or general. Personal knowledge about one's own experiences tends to be specific, and so is knowledge about historical events shared by members of a group, nation or culture. Socially shared knowledge, however,

is usually general, and can thus be used or 'applied' in many different contexts. Different, but closely related, is the difference between *abstract* vs *concrete* knowledge, which, however, is not defined in terms of the knowledge itself but in terms of the things we have knowledge *about*. This distinction is relevant, among other things, for the application of 'truth criteria', such as personal observation, for knowledge: 'I know it, because I have seen (heard, and so on) it myself.'

Why this typology?

The point of this knowledge typology is first of all to make us more aware of the fact that knowledge is not just some unitary 'knowledge of the world' but many different things, each with their own typical mental representation, memory storage, usage and expression in discourse. Second, we have already seen some typical correlates of these types with properties of discourse, that is, potential characteristics of the discourse-knowledge interface. It needs little argument that an explicit typology would need to be much more explicit, but for this chapter this first account will do.

Knowledge and representation

I shall also be brief about the representational formats of knowledge in the mind or in memory. It was already suggested that the very concept of 'representation' is controversial. The concept is usually made more explicit as 'X representing Y for Z', where X is the representation (often in some kind of language, code or other representational medium), Y is something represented by X (usually something concrete 'in the world'), and Z is a person or group. This is already pretty vague, but it will have to do here (for details, see Markman, 1999). For our discussion, it only needs to be stressed that knowledge need not 'represent' any 'outside' things, reality or world at all, but may be limited to mere mental 'constructs'; for example, as acquired, used or expressed by discourse or other forms of semiotic communication. Yet, intuitively, members usually define knowledge as something they believe *about* something (in or of the world), and in that sense knowledge is often said to be 'intentional' or indeed 'representational', whereas 'mere beliefs' (fantasies, and so on), are not. Similarly, I shall ignore the neuropsychological aspects of knowledge, for example, in terms of its realization in specific regions or overall properties of the brain and its activities (see, for example, Gazzaniga et al., 1998).

Nor shall I take a position in the debate between 'representationalists' and 'connectionists', except by suggesting that many of the properties of knowledge and the discourse-knowledge interface as yet cannot be (well-) accounted for in terms of a connectionist theory of the mind (see Levy, 1995; Dijkstra and Smedt, 1996). That is, for practical purposes, I shall simply assume that knowledge as mental construct is schematically represented in various forms, for example, as scripts and various other socially shared schemas, such as schemas for things, people, events, phenomena, and so on. Thus, personal experiences (biographical memories, and so on) are usually represented in mental models that have event schema structure (Johnson-Laird, 1983; van Dijk and Kintsch, 1983; van Oostendorp and Goldman, 1999). On the other hand, general and socially shared knowledge may be represented in generalized event/action schemata such as scripts (Schank and Abelson, 1977) or in terms of frames or schemata for objects, people, groups, phenomena and many other types. The same is obviously true for others forms of social cognition, such as attitudes, norms, values and ideologies (van Dijk, 1998). Note finally that depending on the theory or uses of such knowledge, such different 'formats' of knowledge may be more or less *static* or *dynamic*, that is, as a finished construct, shared (and presupposed) by people, or as an ongoing process of construction, as it is typically manifested in concrete conversation and interaction and its processes of knowledge construction or interpretation.

A unified theory of the structures of such different mental constructs, as well as of the strategies of knowledge construction (acquisition, use), is still on the agenda. We have only some general insights in terms of the uses, accessibility, connections, hierarchies, and so on, of such constructs and their components. Such a theory should obviously combine the neurological evidence of brain research with the mental evidence of psychological research. The latter should be connected to a social theory of knowledge, since we have seen that knowledge can only properly be defined in terms of epistemic communities and their criteria.

Discourse processing

One of the important advances of the cognitive theory of discourse processing has been the recognition of the fundamental role of knowledge in production and comprehension. Whether at the level of words or sentences or at the level of whole discourses, language users need vast amounts of knowledge in order to be able to produce or understand meaningful text and talk. Indeed, as we shall see in a moment, discourses are in many respects icebergs of which only the most relevant information is actually expressed as meaning. Thus, language users need social and cultural knowledge in order to establish local coherence, to derive global topics, to know what parts of sentences or propositions are asserted and which ones are presupposed, and so on. They need knowledge about specific events in order to monitor what they already know about the event, what is new information, what is foreground and background, and in general they need knowledge in order to establish whether a discourse is meaningful.

Ignoring for a moment the fundamental problem of the formats of the mental representation of knowledge, I shall merely summarize some of the relevant aspects of this crucial role of knowledge in text processing.

The knowledge typology we have proposed above suggests that there are basically two kinds of knowledge we need to attend to in discourse processing:

- personal or group knowledge about specific events: mental models
- socially or culturally shared, general knowledge: social representations.

Personal knowledge is usually represented in episodic memory, as part of our 'personal history' of experiences. In discourse processing it is the typical source of personal storytelling, and knowledge that is not presupposed but asserted. Once asserted, it may become shared interpersonal knowledge or local 'common ground'; for example, among friends and spouses, and in that case it is presupposed in later interpersonal discourse.

The same is true at the group level for the kind of event knowledge shared by a collectivity or nation, such as prominent political or historical events (the Holocaust or the terrorist attacks of 11 September 2001 on the World Trade Center and the Pentagon, for example), typically asserted and later presupposed in news discourse and other forms of public discourse.

Socially or culturally shared, general knowledge is the result of a process of learning and is presupposed in all public discourse. It is part of the 'public sphere' and typically asserted in all forms of didactic discourse for young or new members of an epistemic community. Such knowledge is usually represented in social memory, and assumed to be used for the understanding of all meanings of discourse and for the construction of mental models, that is, of the personal interpretations of discourse by individual language users.

In other words, discourse comprehension and production at all levels involve the activation, use, change or updating of various kinds of personal and social knowledge. In this process, the understanding of words, clauses, sentences, paragraphs or larger parts of text and talk requires the activation of usually implicit, socially or culturally shared knowledge; for instance, in the construction of the mental models we build of our experiences in everyday life. These mental models may again be generalized and abstracted from when constructed as more general knowledge about the world.

So far, this is standard theory in the psychology of discourse processing, and one of the main controversies is about the amount of knowledge being activated, used and applied in the construction of mental models, that is, in the interpretation of specific events. For instance, in order to understand stories about the terrorist attacks of 11 September 2001, do we need to activate all we know about airplanes, skyscrapers, terrorists, and so on, or just activate relevant parts of such knowledge, just enough to establish local and global coherence or to construct a mental model? And if so, how much is 'relevant' in such a case? (See, for example, Kintsch, 1998; van Oostendorp and Goldman, 1999.)

We have seen, however, that there is not merely one type of 'world' knowledge, but many different types of knowledge and, depending on the structures, strategies and contexts of text and talk, these may differently be addressed, used, asserted, presupposed, implied, and so on. In some situations it is better or even necessary to make one's personal knowledge explicit in discourse (for example, in interrogations, testimonies, and so on); in other situations divulging one's personal knowledge may be irrelevant, taboo or simply uninteresting. And whereas cultural knowledge for competent members may always be presupposed in all public discourse, specialized group knowledge may only be used and presupposed by competent group members, such as professionals or members of an organization, institution or sect. That is, there is a permanent, and dynamic relationship between the cognitive processes of knowledge activation and use in discourse production and comprehension, and the properties of the communicative contexts, such as settings, types and roles of speakers, ongoing actions, intentions, genres, and so on, as we shall see below.

As we have seen for the definition of knowledge above, which also cannot be limited to an abstract epistemological or cognitive dimension but needs a sociocultural dimension in terms of epistemic communities and their criteria and practices, the psychology of text processing thus needs a sociocultural basis in which we can explain how various kinds of knowledge affect processing in different ways. Indeed, such a sociocognitive interface may result in different kinds of mental representations, specialization, modules, forms of activation, and so on. General, cultural knowledge that is usually presupposed in all discourse may not only be socially learned, overlearned, routinely used many times and hence easily accessible, but such processes of specific use may also neurologically and mentally have their consequences for the construction of such knowledge in the brain/mind. Unique personal memories of one's individual life or political events, on the one hand, or specialized general group knowledge, on the other, may have a quite different form of mental representation or brain manifestation, depending on their different use, in discourse processing. Indeed, unlike general cultural knowledge such personal, specific or specialized group knowledge is often more easily forgotten. We need much more theorizing, experiment and discourse analysis in order to find the details of this cognitive-social interface of knowledge on the one hand and discourse structures and their processing on the other.

Knowledge, context and cognition

From a discourse-theoretical point of view, knowledge is a property of participants of communicative events, and hence part of the context. As is the case for all context properties, knowledge thus controls part of the properties of text and talk as part of the process of contextualization. As we have seen above, this theoretical point of view is consistent with a cognitive account of discourse processing.

However, since we still lack an explicit theory of context, this relation between knowledge and context needs further comment. Context is usually defined in terms of the (relevant) properties of the social situation of discursive language use, including such features as Setting (Time, Location), Participants and their various roles or identities, Actions and Goals, among other categories (in this chapter we do not review work on context; for references and further arguments on the nature of contexts as mental models, see van Dijk, 1999).

The problem with this analysis is that properties of a social situation are not directly related to the conditions of discourse processing. That is, psychologically speaking a direct context–text relationship does not make sense. Also, such an account would make contextualization deterministic: all people in the same social situation would then speak, write or understand the discourse the same way.

We need an interface between text and social situation, and again for theoretical reasons such an interface must be cognitive. In line with contemporary views on the psychology of discourse processing, I have therefore proposed to define this interface in terms of a mental model (van Dijk, 1999). That is, a context is *not* a social situation but a subjective mental model that participants construct of the relevant properties of the social situation. Such *context models* explain many aspects of contextualization, such as the personal and hence individually variable interpretation of social constraints, as well as the fundamental notion of *relevance*. Indeed, a mental model theory of context *is* a theory of relevance (see also Sperber and Wilson, 1986). Thus, it is not location, time, gender, age, profession or other social properties of the social situation that influence how we speak, write and understand, but rather our subjective interpretations or *constructions* of such social dimensions. This also allows us to explain that sometimes such social dimensions are (constructed to be) relevant, and sometimes not.

Finally, classical analyses of contexts often had some 'cognitive' properties, such as the goals and beliefs of the participants. In our mental model approach, these cognitive conditions find a natural place – plans, goals, and so on, are also mental models, namely of future actions or states of affairs.

Knowledge, then, is one of the 'cognitive' properties of context, and hence in our approach they are part of context models. What exactly does this mean, and what does it describe or explain? The basic idea is simple: we only know what knowledge to express or to leave implicit or presupposed when we know (or have reason to believe) what our recipients know. That is, we need a representation of the knowledge of our recipients – as we also need to know something about their other characteristics. Of course, since this knowledge is vast, and we can hardly be expected to know all our recipients know, this 'common ground' knowledge must be limited to knowledge that is *relevant* for the understanding of the ongoing discourse. More in general, then, the context model that manages the knowledge side of text processing provides the overall and specific strategies applied by language users during their understanding. How does this device limit a potential infinite set of hearer-knowledge to a manageable amount? How do language users adapt their discourses to the (vast) knowledge of their recipients, usually adequately and sometimes within a fraction of a second?

Fortunately, as we have seen above most knowledge is socially shared with other members of the same group or culture so that the speaker/writer needs no additional knowledge representation of recipients if these are known to be competent members of the same epistemic community. In other words, the contextual strategy for interaction with co-members is to presuppose the same knowledge as the speaker has.

The same is true for memory of past communicative events shared with the recipients, which also allow the speaker to activate previously shared knowledge (though far from completely, and hence possible repetitions of information). That is, the speaker may strategically presuppose that recipients share all socially and much interpersonally shared knowledge, and thus may focus especially on what recipients are most likely *not* to know as yet (news about recent events, situations in which recipients were not present and cannot have read or heard about, and so on).

In other words, as part of the context model we find what we may call a *knowledge model* or K-device which, for each text or talk, and ongoing during discourse, keeps track of what recipients know and do not yet know. This allows speakers/readers to select the relevant information from their mental models of events they want to tell or write about. Such mental models of events may be quite extensive (all people know about an event), and we know that only a tiny fragment of such knowledge is *relevant* for recipients. The knowledge component of context models thus operates as a selection device in the production of semantic meaning of discourse on the basis of mental models of events. It is this device that controls what mental model information remains implicit or presupposed in the discourse. The detailed structure and operation of this device is beyond the scope of this chapter, but the general strategy is that all relevant unknown information may be selected for inclusion in the semantic representation of the discourse.

Of course, mental model information (knowledge, opinions, and so on) about events may also be selected or excluded for other than epistemic reasons; for instance, when it is assumed to be bad for one's self-image, or when it violates politeness constraints. It is also the context model that provides the information about such social constraints on knowledge expression or suppression in discourse.

This account of context–knowledge relationships at the same time provides us with fragments of a more adequate, context-sensitive cognitive theory of discourse processing, and hence with the interface between text and social situation we need. This means that in discourse production and comprehension, it is not the text which is first produced, but rather the model of the social situation which we have called 'context'. This context model is a routine part of our daily experiences – continually represented as our subjective models of all events in which we participate and which define our consciousness. Also, context models are dynamic and continuously updated as a function of the (interpreted) changes in the social situation as well as by the interpretations of the ongoing discourse – and the knowledge conveyed by it. It is in this way that the discourse and its understanding are adapted to the environment of the participants, merging the relevant mental and social aspects of this environment. And perhaps most importantly, context models explain how social aspects of situations are able to condition discourse structures and, conversely, how discourse structures are able to affect properties of social situations. Context models thus act as the fundamental interface between social and cognitive dimensions of discourse; and we have seen that knowledge plays a fundamental role in this context model, controlling many important aspects of discourse meaning and interpretation.

Knowledge and discourse structures

Unfortunately, there is no systematic procedure that allows us to find the structures of discourse that are controlled by the knowledge structures identified above, though given the postulated cognitive unity of meaning and knowledge, we may assume that this relationship will most clearly be exhibited in meaning. However, since meaning in turn may control grammatical or discursive form (such as word order, pronouns, or the headline of news reports or the conclusion of an argument), knowledge might at least also indirectly be related to formal aspects of text and talk that at first sight are less dependent on underlying knowledge structures.

Depending on how we define knowledge, we may also count context models as knowledge, as models of the current situation – just like mental models of events count as specific knowledge of such events. And when we take context models as forms of knowledge, and context models control many other aspects of discourse including its form and variation, then the scope of knowledge control on text is much wider. For instance, when adult speakers modify their intonation when speaking to a child, this means that intonation may vary with our knowledge of whom we are speaking to. Since, however, this would (not quite so trivially) be the case for all aspects of context, all contextualization cues of discourse would be knowledge-based, in a way that needs no further analysis here.

Another obvious and trivial link between knowledge and discourse is of course the relation between *all* discourse structures and our general (linguistic, and so on) knowledge about such structures. Reading a headline not only activates knowledge about some political event such as a civil war, but of course also knowledge about headlines – as we can readily ascertain when the headline has a position or form that is totally deviant from the usual ones. The same is true for all aspects of grammar, but this well-known relationship between discourse processing, structures and our knowledge about discourse is also beyond the scope of this chapter.

A more productive way to examine discursive expressions of knowledge is to study the ways that different types of knowledge are mapped into discourse. Thus, we have seen that we need to distinguish between mental models of specific events on the one hand, and socially shared representations on the other. We have already suggested that the first typically are expressed in stories of various types, and the latter typically in various forms of abstract, generic discourses. This implies that different types of knowledge may be related to different (classes of) discourse genres. But we have also seen that *all* discourse processing needs general, cultural knowledge, even for the interpretation of specific expressions, and that the same genre may mix specific and generic expressions so that a discursive extrapolation of types of knowledge is not as straightforward as one would hope. Thus, instead of starting with properties or types of knowledge and finding evidence for them in discourse structures, let us begin by exploring some discourse structures and examining how these are linked to underlying knowledge structures. We shall start with the more obvious semantic structures and then examine some formal structures. It need not be repeated that such an exploration is tentative, and that in a single chapter only a few aspects of the very complex relations between discourse and knowledge can be investigated.

Example

By way of example, I shall use an editorial that appeared in the *New York Times*, 17 May 2001, 'SETBACK ON MEDICAL MARIJUANA'. The article was about the unanimous Supreme Court decision to ban marijuana as a medical drug, which went against an earlier decision on the part of some US states.

As suggested above, the knowledge activated (by journalist or reader) in the processing of this article is controlled by the knowledge device of the context model of the journal or reader. That is, the journalist writing this editorial activates what he or she thinks the readers know or should know on the issue, and which knowledge thus can be presupposed or left implicit. Note also that the context model activates the knowledge of the journalist about editorials as a genre, about the *New York Times* (henceforth *NYT*), as the purported medium, on the probable other social cognitions of the readers (such as their attitudes and ideologies about drugs and marijuana), as well as the social or political goals of the journalist, such as influencing the opinions of the readers or of the government. All this contextual knowledge will potentially be relevant also in the control of the knowledge device of the context model. For instance, assumptions on the ideology of the readers also affect what we expect them to know (for example about marijuana, or their experiences with marijuana) and what they will probably infer from the editorial.

Headline

One of the most important properties of the semantics of discourse, as well as of its schematic conventional form, is the headline, which literally heads an article, is printed in bigger type and hence calls attention, is generally read first, and expresses the (intended) main topic of the article, that is, the top of its semantic macrostructure, also in strategic cognitive processing. The proposition expressed by the headline is also a strong strategic suggestion to the readers to construct this as the top macro proposition of their mental model of the event to be represented – or to add or modify an opinion already formed in an earlier model when readers heard about this case. That is, this proposition may be interpreted as the summary of the current opinion of the *NYT* on the Supreme Court's decision to ban marijuana as a medical drug, and hence as one of the top macro propositions of the mental model of the current opinion editorial about this event. Note, though, that a headline as part of the text is also a clause, with its own lexical (for example) properties, and is not merely a global proposition. This means that even if the headline *expresses* a major proposition, it is not the same as that proposition. That is, the actual formulation of the headline is also a function of the context model, in particular of the social or political aims of the editorial and the newspaper. Since this editorial is a critique of a Supreme Court decision, and a newspaper of record such as the *NYT* is not expected to attack the Supreme Court head on, let alone with aggressive language, we may expect that contextual constraints will control the expression of its negative opinion about this verdict, which will thus be formulated in mitigated terms – as is indeed the case in the choice of *setback* in the title, instead of, for instance 'disastrous decision'.

We see how the contents of some categories of the context model (such as opinions about the political role of the *NYT* and the relationship between the *NYT* and the Supreme Court – part of the Participant category of the context model) influence the transformation of the (probably) negative opinion of the event model of the journalist into a mitigated formulation in the actual text itself. And since this actual formulation of the headline is the input for the readers, we may expect a persuasive mitigating effect on the top (opinion) proposition of the model of the readers on this decision.

Apart from the complex relationships between headline, context model and event models of journalists and readers, the headline also expresses and activates general social knowledge, in this case on marijuana and in particular its medical uses. The knowledge involved here is not only more general – widespread knowledge about marijuana as a drug, but also more specific – more recent knowledge about proposals to use marijuana for medical purposes in easing the pain of patients suffering from cancer or AIDS. This knowledge is general and abstract, and socially shared at least by 'informed citizens', but is still closely related to actual 'cases' people may also remember, that is, with mental models. We here find an area of knowledge that lies at the borders of episodic (specific) and social (general) memory: years later the cases may have been forgotten (mental models have become inaccessible) but the general knowledge about the medicinal properties of marijuana may have become common knowledge. The headline here addresses, expresses and activates this area of knowledge at the border of mental models of concrete events and the social representation of marijuana. And since most readers will also have ideologically based attitudes about marijuana – attitudes that have probably been activated and updated in relation to the recent cases in the US where the medical use of marijuana was advocated – these evaluative forms of shared social cognitions will also probably be activated by the headline. Conversely, we may assume that the reverse is the case for the journalist: expressing an opinion on the medical use of marijuana in an editorial presupposes that the journalist (and perhaps the collectivity of the *NYT*) has attitudes and ideologies about marijuana and its medical uses, and not just an isolated opinion on this Supreme Court decision.

Although we try to be rather precise in our analysis of the probable cognitive processes involved in the production and comprehension of this headline, and in particular about the role of knowledge in these processes, it needs to be emphasized that if we were required to spell out all the detailed knowledge items and inferential steps involved, we would need to write down many pages of 'code', which I shall refrain from in order not to hamper the readability of this chapter.

Next, consider the first paragraph of this editorial:

> The federal government won a major legal victory Monday in its benighted efforts to prevent the use of marijuana to relieve the symptoms of pain, nausea or loss of appetite in desperately ill patients. But the Supreme Court's unanimous verdict against a California cooperative set up to supply marijuana to qualified patients need not terminate all efforts to help those who have no reasonable alternative treatment. The verdict simply shifts the onus to individual patients or to compassionate state governments to obtain marijuana for medical purposes and test the limits of federal intransigence.

The first clause of the paragraph, and especially the use of the definite article of the (definite) noun phrase *the federal government*, presupposes that the readers know what the federal government is, and that there is only one such government, but also what *a* government, and *a* federal government are. That is, in order to know what specific government the editorial is referring to, the readers obviously need to activate their general political knowledge about governments. This example also nicely shows the omnipresent role of the context model, which needs to supply the presupposed, implicit information 'in the United States of America'. This information may be left implicit for readers of the *NYT*, precisely because it will be contained in their context models as readers of this US newspaper. And since the knowledge model of the author(s) of the editorial also features pointers to the assumed knowledge of the readers (including their knowledge that the *NYT* is a US newspaper, and so on), they can leave this information implicit also in the textual realization of the information in the event model about the federal government. Note how the strategic formulation or understanding of a simple phrase like this involves mental models of events (about what the government did), common ground political knowledge about governments, and about the US having a federal government, as well as context model knowledge about what editorial writers and readers know (also about each other). Again, writing all this knowledge and mental operations down would be a major task of codification.

It needs little further analysis to deduce that the interpretation of the adverbial expression *Monday* presupposes a context model with a Setting category for time, which specifies that 'today' is Wednesday, 17 May. This allows the inference that the decision was two days ago, and hence can be called 'recent', which is consistent with the general knowledge about editorials as a genre, which specifies that editorials are usually about recent events. This general genre knowledge about editorials will itself also be activated and applied in the context model of this particular communicative event, necessary to be able to interpret and categorize this particular text in the newspaper or on the internet. Note finally that the reference to the day of the Supreme Court decision (not yet referred to in the text) which meant a victory for the US government, will occupy the Time category of the event model being formed by the readers. In other words, inferences from context models (for example, about the time of events) may provide information (knowledge) about the time of event models that constitute the readers' interpretation of a text. Again we see how context models are at work in the formation and control of the formation of event models, and hence in understanding.

The interpretation of the next phrase, *won a major legal victory*, similarly combines several kinds of knowledge. First, the past tense of *won* calls the Time categories of both context model and event model, and is thus consistently interpreted as an event that happened (past) Monday. Second, general political and legal knowledge is activated in the interpretation of this phrase, namely in order to be able to construct that the event of a government winning a legal battle can actually be modelled (understood) by the readers. Such a predicate would not be applicable to (say) federal taxes or my cat. This is the well-known and most straightforward relation between discourse and knowledge, namely that such knowledge is necessary for the very interpretation of expressions (like the predicate phrase here) and more specifically for the construction of mental models: are governments the kind of things that can win legal battles?

Note that, although readers may have little problem understanding this phrase, it is not likely that they have a ready-made proposition in their knowledge about the federal government that it may engage in litigation, no more than for most people or institutions. That is, it is likely that some inferences are needed in order to establish the interpretability of this phrase; for instance, that legal battles are usually engaged in by people or collections of people, such as organizations, institutions or states (and not objects or animals), and that the government is an institution and hence belongs to the set of things that can engage in legal battles. Such inferences are instantaneous and can and must be derived in milliseconds in order for this phrase to be understood and construed as part of a 'possible' mental model of the event (for details, see Graesser and Bower, 1990).

Finally, also note that the general and specific knowledge involved is metaphorical: being vindicated by a court decision is 'winning' and hence conceptualized as a 'victory', which presupposes that legal conflicts may be represented as a game or a battle. Indeed, it is rather difficult to describe the positive outcome of a legal decision in terms other than 'winning'. If this metaphorical conceptualization of our knowledge about legal trials in terms of games or battles is part of the very knowledge structure about such trials, it may also affect the further interpretation of the text in the same metaphorical terms, that is, as a battle between the (conservative) Bush government, and (more liberal) state governments or medical organizations, with the (predominantly conservative) Supreme Court as ally of the government. Incidentally, the expression *winning a victory* might normatively be considered to be tautological and a contraction of 'winning a battle' and '(having a) victory'.

The next phrase, *its benighted efforts to prevent the use of marijuana*, the predicate of the US government, first of all continues and confirms the activation of the knowledge about marijuana, which is consistent with the knowledge about 'using (drugs)' and the knowledge about prevention, which in turn is compatible with efforts or policies of a government responsible for upholding the laws that limit the use of drugs. Indeed, part of the knowledge complex activated by marijuana may feature information about prohibition, government policies, and so on, and hence be directly applicable in the mental model construction of the readers understanding this fragment.

The use of the stylistically formal word *benighted* in this case, expressing a negative opinion about the government's intellectual or moral virtues, and attributing to it backwardness in its efforts to prevent the medical use of marijuana, signals the first explicit opinion of this paragraph. That is, it is not only knowledge that is expressed or activated here, but also opinions or attitudes. Part of the knowledge structure of marijuana is that its use in many countries is prohibited or controversial but that as a soft drug it does not do much harm, and that many liberal people advocate freedom of use, especially in medical situations when people need it. That is, the meaning of 'benighted' is consistent with the normative, moral aspect of the knowledge we have about the prohibition of the use of marijuana. As an opinion it is a manifestation of the negative opinion of the (relatively liberal) *NYT* about the current (conservative) US government. However, this calls for knowledge represented in the context model of the journalist and the readers about the political and ideological orientation of the *NYT* and about its likely relations with the current government. All this information provides for the plausibility of the critical opinion expressed by *benighted*. That is, even for the understanding of evaluative meanings in terms of underlying opinions or attitudes, we need to activate and apply general social knowledge in order to be able to judge whether the opinions are relevant. Note finally that the very lexical selection of *benighted* (instead of, say, 'reactionary') also indexes the formality of the communicative event and the written/printed dimension of the genre, and the formality of the relations between a major newspaper and the Supreme Court, as indicated above.

The last phrase of this sentence, *to relieve the symptoms of pain, nausea or loss of appetite in desperately ill patients* briefly describes the nature of the medical uses of marijuana. Its concepts ('symptoms', 'pain', 'ill', 'patients', and so on) are all consistent parts of our knowledge about the 'medical' application of drugs, and would only need a few inferences to be fully interpreted. Of course, this phrase does more than merely describe some medical uses of marijuana. Indeed, the editorial could simply have abstracted from this knowledge and written, 'prevent the medical use of marijuana'. It does not, and gets down to the (painful) details of illness, and in addition adds 'desperate' to 'illness'. In other words, even at the abstract level of a Supreme Court case and government policies, we find a change of *level of description* to a much more detailed, concrete description of the medical uses of marijuana as a drug. Such a stylistic change has rhetorical and persuasive functions. Rhetorically, it calls on the feelings (pity, sympathy) of the readers by confronting them with the details of serious illness in an effort to influence their opinion about the medical use of marijuana. Implied in this case is the opinion that its morally backward stance on the use of marijuana is more important for the government than the plight of terribly ill people – thus legitimating the critical use of *benighted*.

In this last example, we see how concrete, everyday reader knowledge about illness is activated in order to obtain a preferred opinion in a mental model, through the manipulation of the readers, emotions triggered by reading about the misery of very ill people. Just one phrase activates knowledge at various levels, social attitudes and personal opinions about ill people, social and political attitudes and personal opinions about the (conservative) government, as well as emotions that may be used in the construction of the ongoing even model. We have seen that discursively these processes are expressed and signalled by the use of specific (emotion-arousing) words such as 'desperately' by the rhetorical device of an enumeration and by the change from a high/abstract to a lower level of description.

Although the government is explicitly described and judged as being *benighted*, it is not said but *implied* that it is also hard and heartless in preventing the use of a drug in order to relieve suffering. It is also not said but implied that such a policy is typical of a conservative government, and hence ideologically consistent. And finally, it is implied that if the *NYT* thinks that prohibition of the medical use of marijuana is 'benighted', propagating its use is liberal, progressive, modern and especially humane, and since its critical position against the government presupposes such an attitude about marijuana, it is also implied that the *NYT* has these positive properties – which is part of the self-identity category in the context model of the journalists of the newspaper. In the context model of most readers of the *NYT* its attitude would simply be consistent with their own attitude about the newspaper, and hence the editorial would hardly be an ideological surprise.

We see that such a conclusion operates largely in terms of a rather impressive set of inferences and bodies of knowledge. Thus, really understanding the editorial is not limited to understanding its words or sentences, and not even limited to the knowledge needed merely to understand these words, but also involves complex sequences of inferences about social and political presuppositions and the implications of these interpreted meanings as constructed in the mental model of an event. Very much present in these political implications are the contents and inferences drawn from the mental model the journalists and the readers have of the context, that is, of themselves, of the media, of government, of the relations between government and media, about their own attitudes about marijuana, and so on. These implications are controlled by the overall (genre) goal of editorials to give an opinion on recent events and to criticize important organizations, institutions or persons.

Systematic analysis

After this more detailed but still informal and unsystematic description of the relations between discourse and knowledge, we shall be more succinct and more systematic in the analysis and 'epistemic interpretation' of the rest of the paragraph. After the type of knowledge indicated, we only mention one or two general knowledge propositions needed to establish coherence or to derive a meaningful interpretation. The list of actual knowledge activated could run into many dozens, and sometimes hundreds, of relevant propositions. Below, bold italics indicate the word or phrase that is being analysed in each line. Where a whole phrase is analysed, the quote is just in italics.

1. ***But** the Supreme Court's*   Semantic contrast. General political knowledge: Legal victory of government. Makes use of marijuana difficult.

2. *the Supreme Court's **verdict***   Definite description. Presupposition. General/National political knowledge about legal affairs: Legal victory. Verdict. Specific knowledge (mental model): Readers know about the verdict.

3. *Supreme Court*	Name of institution. General/National political knowledge; scriptal knowledge: Legal victory of government because of Supreme Court decision.
4. *unanimous verdict*	Topic. Nominalization. Legal knowledge about Supreme Court: Unanimous decisions presuppose consensus.
5. *against a California cooperative set up*	Participant. Legal knowledge: The losing party of the trial. Social-political knowledge: California is (more) liberal in drug matters. Specific knowledge (public mental model): Readers know about the California plans.
6. *to supply marijuana to qualified patients*	New social knowledge: Marijuana is a useful medicine for seriously ill people. Specific knowledge: People know about these actions of the California cooperative. Medical knowledge: Patients are beneficiaries of treatment. Implication: 'qualified'. Legitimization of drug use.
7. *need not terminate all efforts*	Predicate. Causal relation. Legal-Political knowledge: Supreme Court prohibition implies problems for a social programme.
8. *to help those who have no reasonable alternative treatment*	Social knowledge: Goal of actions of participant. General-Medical knowledge: Patients' Treatment. Causality: *No reasonable alternative*: Implication: Marijuana is morally/medically necessary.
9. *the verdict*	Definite expression. Topic. Specific knowledge: Verdict known while mentioned before.
10. *simply shifts the onus to individual patients*	Predicate. Legal knowledge: Official prohibition does not end 'illegal' practices. Implication: Individual patients are victims of verdict. Opinion implication: Government and Supreme Court are immoral.
11. *or to compassionate state governments*	Participant. Legal-Political knowledge: States have some freedom to act independently of Supreme Court decision. General knowledge: To help very ill patients is compassionate. Implication: Government/Supreme Court not passionate.

12. *to obtain marijuana*   Predicate. Goal.
    for medical purposes   Global coherence: to get marijuana for
                            terminally ill patients.
13. *and test the limits of*   Predicate. Goal.
    federal intransigence   Presupposition: Federal government is
                            intransigent.
                            Social-Political knowledge: Conflict States:
                            Government.
                            General knowledge: Intransigence is
                            immoral.
                            Social knowledge: Not helping patients
                            is immoral.

This brief analysis shows the following about the relations between discourse and knowledge:

(a) Comprehension of this passage first of all requires a huge amount of general knowledge; in this case, especially political, legal and medical knowledge
  - about the role of the (federal) government, the possible conflicts with the states, and so on
  - the implications of (unanimous) Supreme Court decisions
  - how to treat seriously ill patients
  - the role of marijuana in such treatment.

(b) Local and global coherence requires specific (mental model) knowledge about a specific event (this particular case). For instance, this allows the editorial to mention the Supreme Court only in the second sentence, although already presupposed in the expression 'legal victory' in the first sentence. 'The verdict' similarly presupposes that the reader already knows the case. In sum, reading an editorial usually means that readers already have a mental model about an event, and the editorial may presuppose this knowledge to be known to many readers.

(c) Knowledge is being presupposed and asserted also as part of expressing and constructing opinions, as is the case for the use of expressions such as 'benighted efforts', 'desperately ill patients', 'qualified patients', 'no reasonable alternative treatment', 'compassionate' and 'intransigence'. These expressions (in context) all imply that the government (and even the Supreme Court) is immoral.

(d) Context model knowledge is being presupposed in the use of explicit opinion expressions (in principle excluded in news reports) and hence the critique of the government by the newspaper, the presupposed knowledge of the readers (about the California marijuana experiments, about the decision of the Supreme Court, and so on), general-political knowledge (about government, and so on) that resolves referential expressions (*the government*); and the social implications of the editorial – support for patients in an important social issue (the medical use of marijuana).

These, and many more types of relationships that need to be researched further, are not merely semantic-cognitive but also show up in formal structures; for instance, in definite expressions (*the federal government*), definite articles (*the verdict*), nominalizations (*effort*), connectives (*but*), embedded clauses vs main clauses (*in its benighted efforts to prevent*), adjectives that express opinions (*desperately ill; qualified patients*). In addition, for these many properties of discourse we need to examine in more detail how they show the ways that language users express, signal, emphasize or hide knowledge and other social cognitions.

Conclusion

In this chapter it has been argued that CDA and discourse studies in general need a detailed theory of the role of knowledge in discourse production and comprehension. Current work on knowledge in several disciplines often ignores the results of research in other disciplines. Against this background, this chapter has pleaded for a broad, multidisciplinary theory of knowledge in order to be able to describe in detail the interface between discourse and knowledge. Even a simple typology of discourse, as presented here, shows how complex a theory of discourse processing becomes when we take into account different types of knowledge and how they influence discourse production and comprehension. And since knowledge must (also) be defined in the social terms of beliefs shared and ratified by an epistemic community, this means that a cognitive theory of text processing needs an important social and cultural dimension: what is being expressed and presupposed in discourse depends on the social nature of the (members of) groups so that a true, integrated sociocognitive theory of knowledge-discourse processing can be developed. It has also been shown that a context model, that is, the mental representation (stored in episodic memory) of the communicative context, is an indispensable theoretical device for such a development. Knowledge is an important category of context models, the device that regulates pragmatic (deictic) interpretation, the adequate use of many pronouns and in general of style. Finally, it has been these complex relationships between knowledge, text and context that have been demonstrated in an exploratory analysis of an editorial in the *NYT*.

References

Augoustinos, M. and Walker, I. (1995) *Social Cognition. An Integrated Introduction.* London: Sage.
Bar-Tal, D. and Kruglanski, A.W. (eds) (1988) *The Social Psychology of Knowledge.* Cambridge: Cambridge University Press.
Bechtel, W. and Graham, G. (1999) *A Compendium to Cognitive Science.* Oxford: Blackwell.

Bernecker, S. and Dretske, F.I. (eds) (2000) *Knowledge: Readings in Contemporary Epistemology*. Oxford: Oxford University Press.

Bourdieu, P. (1988) *Language and Symbolic Power*. Cambridge: Polity Press.

Breakwell, G.M. and Canter, D.V. (eds) (1993) *Empirical Approaches to Social Representations*. Oxford: Clarendon.

Britton, B.K. and Graesser, A.C. (eds) (1996) *Models of Understanding Text*. Mahwah, NJ: Erlbaum.

Clark, H.H. (1996) *Using Language*. Cambridge: Cambridge University Press.

D'Andrade, R.G. (1995) *The Development of Cognitive Anthropology*. Cambridge and New York: Cambridge University Press.

Dijkstra, T. and Smedt, K. (eds) (1996) *Computational Psycholinguistics. AI and Connectionist Models of Human Language Processing*. London: Taylor & Francis.

Farr, R.M. and Moscovici, S. (eds) (1984) *Social Representations*. Cambridge; New York/Paris: Cambridge University Press/Editions de la Maison des Sciences de l'Homme.

Fauconnier, G. (1985) *Mental Spaces: Aspects of Meaning Construction in Natural Language*. Cambridge, MA: MIT Press.

Fiske, S.T. and Taylor, S.E. (1991) *Social Cognition*. New York: McGraw-Hill.

Flick, U. (ed.) (1998) *The Psychology of the Social*. Cambridge; New York: Cambridge University Press.

Foucault, M. (1972) *The Archaeology of Knowledge and the Discourse on Language*. New York: Harper & Row (Harper Colophon).

Fraser, C. and Gaskell, G. (eds) (1990) *The Social Psychological Study of Widespread Beliefs*. Oxford; New York: Clarendon Press; Oxford University Press.

Gazzaniga, M.S., Ivry, R.S. and Mangun, G.R. (1998) *Cognitive Neuroscience. The Biology of the Mind*. New York: Norton.

Graesser, A.C. and Bower, G.H. (eds) (1990) *Inferences and Text Comprehension. The Psychology of Learning and Motivation*, Vol. 25. New York: Academic Press.

Gumperz, J.J. and Levinson, S.C. (eds) (1996) *Rethinking Linguistic Relativity*. Cambridge: Cambridge University Press.

Holland, D.C. and Quinn, N. (eds) (1987) *Cultural Models in Language and Thought*. Cambridge; New York: Cambridge University Press.

Johnson-Laird, P.N. (1983) *Mental Models: Towards a Cognitive Science of Language, Inference and Consciousness*. Cambridge; New York: Cambridge University Press.

Kintsch, W. (1998) *Comprehension. A Paradigm for Cognition*. Cambridge: Cambridge University Press.

Kreckel, M. (1981) *Communicative Acts and Shared Knowledge in Natural Discourse*. London; New York: Academic Press.

Lakoff, G. and Johnson, M. (1980) *Metaphors We Live By*. Chicago: University of Chicago Press.

Lakoff, G. and Johnson, M. (1999) *Philosophy in the Flesh: The Embodied Mind and its Challenge to Western Thought*. New York: Basic Books.

Langacker, R.W. (1983) *Foundations of Cognitive Grammar*. Bloomington, IN: Indiana University Linguistics Club.

Levy, J.P. (ed.) (1995) *Connectionist Models of Memory and Language*. London; Bristol, PA: UCL Press.

Markman, A.B. (1999) *Knowledge Representation*. Mahwah, NJ: Erlbaum.

Moscovici, S. (2000) *Social Representations. Explorations in Social Psychology*. Cambridge: Polity Press.

Potter, J. (1996) *Representing Reality: Discourse, Rhetoric and Social Construction*. London; Thousand Oaks, CA: Sage.

Ryle, G. (1949) *The Concept of Mind*. New York: Barnes and Noble.

Schank, R.C. and Abelson, R.P. (1977) *Scripts, Plans, Goals, and Understanding: An Inquiry into Human Knowledge Structures*. Hillsdale, NJ; New York: Lawrence Erlbaum, distributed by the Halsted Press Division of John Wiley and Sons.

Shore, B. (1996) *Culture in Mind: Cognition, Culture, and the Problem of Meaning*. New York: Oxford University Press.

Sperber, D. and Wilson, D. (1986) *Relevance: Communication and Cognition*. Cambridge, MA: Harvard University Press.

van Dijk, T.A. (1991) *Racism and the Press*. London; New York: Routledge.

van Dijk, T.A. (1993a) *Elite Discourse and Racism*. Newbury Park, CA: Sage.

van Dijk, T.A. (1993b) 'Principles of Critical Discourse Analysis', *Discourse & Society*, 4(2), pp. 249–83.

van Dijk, T.A. (1998) *Ideology: A Multidisciplinary Approach*. London: Sage.

van Dijk, T.A. (1999) 'Context models in discourse processing', in H. van Oostendorp and S.R. Goldman (eds), *The Construction of Mental Representations during Reading*. Mahwah, NJ: Lawrence Erlbaum, pp. 123–48.

van Dijk, T.A. (ed.) (1997) *Discourse Studies: A Multidisciplinary Introduction*. London: Sage.

van Dijk, T.A. and Kintsch, W. (1983) *Strategies of Discourse Comprehension*. New York: Academic Press.

van Oostendorp, H. and Goldman, S.R. (eds) (1999) *The Construction of Mental Presentations during Reading*. Mahwah, NJ: Lawrence Erlbaum.

Werth, P. (1999) *Text Worlds: Representing Conceptual Space in Discourse*. London: Longman.

Wilkes, A.L. (1997) *Knowledge in Minds. Individual and Collective Processes in Cognition*. Hove: Psychology Press.

Wodak, R. (1996) *Disorders of Discourse*. London: Longman.

6
Critical Discourse Analysis and Evaluative Meaning: Interdisciplinarity as a Critical Turn

Phil Graham

Introduction

The perceived need to transcend disciplinary boundaries in Critical Discourse Analysis (CDA) is a contemporary imperative throughout most social sciences (Jessop and Sum, 2001). As such, it highlights the fragmenting trajectory social science has taken, most noticeably over the last 150 years. Critical scholarship has its *raison d'être* in that fragmentation because the first imperative of any critical social science is to develop an historically grounded, comprehensive theory of social change – a 'critical philosophy' which sees humanity as an unbroken, historically embedded whole (Marx, 1843 [1972], p. 10). Prior to the emergence of social science disciplines in the mid-nineteenth century, social theory 'was an integral part of philosophy' which had underpinned 'the pattern of all particular theories of social change' throughout history (Marcuse and Neumann, 1942 [1998], p. 95). Consequently, from a critical perspective, 'social change cannot be interpreted within a particular social science, but must be understood within the social and natural totality of human life' (ibid.). Accordingly, the contemporary trend towards interdisciplinary, 'transdisciplinary' (Fairclough, 2000), or 'post-disciplinary' (Jessop and Sum, 2001) approaches to social analysis is, by definition, a critical turn.

My approach to the problem of disciplinary boundaries, which I explain more fully below, is synonymous with that of Jessop and Sum – it is 'pre-disciplinary in its historical inspiration and ... post-disciplinary in its current intellectual implications' (ibid., p. 89). In essence, it is a refusal to acknowledge the dictates of contemporary disciplinary boundaries, and thus cannot be termed 'interdisciplinary' in the usual sense of the word: that is, selecting and combining approaches (or practitioners) from within well-defined disciplines and subdisciplines of social science in order to forge problem-specific solutions (which is not to say that such approaches are either invalid or

110

fruitless). It is an approach that assumes disciplinary boundaries are nothing more than institutional and discoursal consequences of historical power struggles amongst vested interests, the political economic forces in which such interests are embedded, and the intellectual proponents and opponents thereof. Disciplinary boundaries are therefore 'discourse-historical' phenomena (Wodak, 2000). Their emergence mirrors the increasingly specialized nature of work in industrialized societies, and is quite literally an industrial phenomenon (Innis, 1942). In forging a critical approach to CDA, I draw most heavily on 'pre-disciplinary' political economy of Marx (cf. Marx, 1844 [1975], 1973; Jessop and Sum, 2001).

The central argument of this chapter is that what we call 'disciplines' in social science are historically constituted practices of evaluating the social world in different ways, and it is precisely these different ways of evaluating social phenomena that define disciplinary boundaries. However, in the formation of disciplines, it is particular ways of evaluating that get evaluated and re-'ordered' (Fairclough, 1992), specifically by propagating the *Significance* of particular modes of evaluating. Taking the broadest historical perspective, we can trace the evaluative fractures of disciplinarity to two paradoxical, closely associated histories: a historical reordering of power from the institutions of the Church and Crown to the institutions of Reason during the 'Enlightenment'; the second is a reordering of discourses propounding a static, Natural Order view of our social universe in the eighteenth century to the more dynamic, Darwinian view characteristic of the late nineteenth century (Ware, 1931).

In 'Western' scholarship, the historical shift in legitimacy from the institutions of *Divinity* (Church and Crown) to the institutions of *Truth* (Science and Reason) is obfuscatory upon close inspection, largely because of the lack of difference in the stated scope of the systems' authority (both have sought to explain and regulate the totality of human affairs), and because of their common heritage in the Church. It was Church scholastics who developed what has become known as 'the' 'scientific method', a mode of enquiry based on the 'careful analysis of experience' which left the Church 'with a refinement and precision ... which the seventeenth century scientists who used it did not surpass in all their careful investigation of method' (Randall, 1940, p. 178). The similar scope and common heritage of the institutions of *Reason* and *Divinity* – institutions with ostensibly opposed value systems – are evident when political economy first emerges as a distinct discipline (of which more below).

Outlines of a 'post-disciplinary' theoretical and analytical approach

The primary theoretical assumption of my approach is explicitly 'autopoietic': that is, human social systems are living, sociocognitive systems, the organization and reproduction of which is ultimately coordinated in the domain of language (Graham, 1999; Graham and McKenna, 2000; cf. also Maturana and Varela, 1980; Luhmann, 1995). However, to be understood as such, social systems must be understood to 'live', 'think' and 'act' at different magnitudes of time and space, and in qualitatively different ways, than their human constituents, both in terms of time and scale (cf. Lemke, 1995, forthcoming; Luhmann, 1995). They have a different order of existence than the individuals whose interactions constitute them. That is to say, social systems have a different ontology from the people who create, inhabit and reproduce them, even though social systems and the individuals that constitute them are interdependent (Lemke, 1995). The relationship between social systems and individuals is analogous – though in no way qualitatively identical – to the relationship between an organism and the cells that constitute it. An organism's cells die and reproduce while the organism lives far beyond the life of any cell, just as our most powerful social systems live beyond the lives of any individual person. A social system is no more an organism than a cell is an organism.

Such a view has a number of implications for analysis. The first of these is that analysis must deal with identifiable social units, which I define here as 'discourse communities' (after Lemke, ibid., p. 42). The boundaries of human social systems are, at least by the definition I am using here, characterized by the ways in which members of particular social systems comprehend, represent and reproduce their worlds (ibid.; cf. also Graham and McKenna, 2000). The second implication is that no comprehensive analysis can be valid from such a perspective without taking the dimension of time into account: that is, whilst having a distinct identity over a given time scale (Lemke, forthcoming), living systems have characteristics that change over time, just as people are born, grow and die while, 'like all living things, having the power to change out of all recognition', while remaining somehow 'the same' (Orwell, 1941 [1957]). Hence any critical social analysis will be historically contingent and historically grounded (Wodak, 2000). A third implication for analysis is that the genesis and maturation of social systems, their *ontogenesis*, brings environment, or context, into account, thereby orienting analysis towards a *co-ontogenetic* perspective (Maturana and Varela, 1980; Luhmann, 1995, p. 119; Graham and McKenna, 2000). Consequently analysis becomes relational as well as historical, and must therefore take into account that relationships between social systems, their constituents, and their shared histories, are intrinsic to, if not definitive of, their character; their character 'depends primarily on *connectivity*' (Luhmann, 1995, p. 119), or intersystemic 'mediations' (Silverstone, 1999, p. 13).

Seen from this perspective, the study of social phenomena differs from the study of non-living phenomena, such as the objects of many branches of physics, engineering, and chemistry. However, '[h]uman communities *are* ecosystems. Ecosystems *are* biological, chemical and physical systems'

(Lemke, 1995, p. 159). Consequently, the differences that are generally used to distinguish between the objects of 'natural' as opposed to 'social' science are probably better described as differences between living and non-living phenomena. The theoretical and analytical differences between these are first (and quite literally) a matter of time. At least as far as we know, the principles governing non-living phenomena are timeless. For instance, based on current knowledge we must assume that the laws of gravity will be the same tomorrow as they are today, and that they were ever thus. Similarly, we must assume that the principles of particle physics and, for example, thermodynamics will be, and always were, the same, even if our understanding of them changes. Living systems, while not exempt from the ahistorical principles of 'non-living' dynamics, change over time, and the changes they undergo become more complex in proportion to the connections between them and other living systems, their constituent parts and their environments. Further, the higher-order principles of living systems change as the systems themselves change (a human embryo is neither comparable to an adolescent nor to a person in old age, except at the most trivial level). From such an understanding flows 'a view of hierarchically related levels of organization' and at 'any particular level of [analytical] interest, we can see it being sustained both from below, by the actions of subsystems, and from above by its participation in a still larger system' (ibid., p. 165). Evaluative meaning can be seen to 'work' in precisely the same way (Graham, 2002a).

Evaluative meaning and the formation of disciplines

An imperative to analyse evaluative meaning flows directly from the autopoietic position I have briefly outlined above. Maturana and Varela's (1980) is a theory 'biology of cognition'. They define living systems as those entities able to make a distinction between themselves and their surroundings by means of observation (1980, p. xix; cf. also Luhmann, 1995). As far as humans are concerned, 'the act of observing *is* the act of evaluation and to separate them is to force a distinction on human practice that does not in reality exist' (Harvey, 1973, p. 15). Therefore the fracturing of human social systems, as in the formation of disciplines, is essentially an evaluative phenomenon. The false distinction between 'natural' and 'social' sciences, which in the English tradition can be traced to the formation of the Royal Society for the Improvement of Natural Knowledge (Huxley, 1893, pp. 21–3). The social, intellectual and environmental damage associated with the dissociation of human phenomena from the rest of nature should not be underestimated: when humans see themselves as other-than-natural, a false view of humanity as being supernatural, along with a perverse anthropocentrism, follows – a point not lost on Marx, who sees the dissociation of humanity from nature as the basis of alienation in all its forms (for example, 1844

[1975], pp. 326–8). What we call disciplinarity is alienation exemplified: it is the conscious production of 'otherness' for specific ways of thinking about our universe. Disciplinarity is therefore an historical process of 'reordering' intellectual discourses, an institutional, 'textual' and 'political' valorizing of particular modes of understanding which necessarily devalues others (cf. Fairclough, 1992; Lemke, 1995).

My approach to analysing evaluative meanings in texts, which I have called 'predication and propagation', is a synthesis of methods developed by Lemke (1998) and Martin (2000), among others (Graham, 2002a). I argue that evaluative meanings can be seen to happen on at least four levels of abstraction as they propagate throughout texts (Graham, 2002a):

1. The broadest and most abstract semantic levels of propagated value are *Desirability* and *Importance/Significance*, which are mutually mediating in the process of evaluative propagation.
2. At an almost equally abstract level are *Warrantability/Probability*; *Comprehensibility/Obviousness*, *Usuality/Expectability*, *Utility/Usefulness* (proposals only), *Difficulty/Ability* (proposals only), *Normativity/Appropriateness*, all of which can mediate, support and propagate the semantic categories of evaluation in (1). Which of these dimensions get foregrounded in the propagation of the categories in (1) is genre-specific.
3. Intermediate categories, again, may either be predicated of textual elements or propagated across long stretches of text. However, they cannot typically be deployed to evaluate propositions or proposals, and are 'parts' of the broader semantic dimensions in (1) and (2). As predicates of elements in language, they can also propagate the evaluative semantics of (1) and (2). The (ineffable) definitions for these labels are drawn from Lasswell (1941), Perry (1916) and/or Martin (2000). Whether as part of attributive or identifying clauses, or as parts of propositions, or otherwise embedded (intertextually or implicitly) in nominal elements or relations in the text, evaluations at this level can themselves be evaluated in terms of the categories in (1) and (2) above. They include *Power, Respect, Freedom, Efficiency; Morality, Trust(worthiness), Legality, Virtuousness; Beauty, Intelligence, Wealth, Excellence (Quality), Consistency, Balance, Happiness, Stability, Complexity, Sophistication, Coherence, Restrictiveness; Quantity, Magnitude (Scope* and *Dimensionality), Expense, Dependency, Innovativeness, Novelty*, and so on.
4. Lexical resources that explicitly inscribe an evaluation for an element in the text, literally a predicate. These are most conveniently organized by Martin under the headings *Affect, Judgement* and *Appreciation* (once again emphasizing the ultimate impossibility of separating 'fact' from 'value'). These resources for 'appraisal' are directly inscribed in the text and directly affected by the resources of 'amplification' and 'engagement' (Martin, 2000, p. 145). They are directly predicated of elements in the text, even

though they may be seen as intertextually 'evoked' or 'inscribed' (ibid., p. 154). Seen relationally, they are in 'hierarchical', or constitutive, relationships with the broader, less specific categories in (1),(2) and (3), which may also appear as predicates of textual elements (Graham, 2002a).

When grammaticalized across longer stretches of text, more and less explicit appraisals take part in 'syntaxes' of evaluation that propagate other values, the most abstract and exhaustive of which are *Desirability* and *Significance*. Specific evaluative syntaxes are mediated by the historically and institutionally specific axiologies of any social context.[1] Propagated values are those realized beyond the level of the elements in the text. These appear to be hierarchically organized, syllogistic, multidimensional, and fall under the broad categories identified in Lemke (1998) (Graham, 2002a). These last are listed in Table 6.1.

The means by which evaluations propagate depends on the grammatical status of the evaluative resources being deployed (are they nominals or part of a nominal group?); the elements being evaluated (are they construed as outcomes of Processes or as attributes of substances?); the temporal aspect of the elements involved (what are the tense and modality systems doing?; do the nominals 'contain' implied aspects of time?); and the grammatical

Table 6.1   Evaluative resources for proposals and propositions

Evaluative dimension	Positive degree	Negative degree
[D] Desirability/Inclination	It is *wonderful* that John is coming	It is *horrible* that John is coming
[W] Warrantability/ Probability	It is *certain* that John is coming	It is *unlikely* that John will come
[N] Normativity/ Appropriateness	It is *essential* that John comes	It is *inappropriate* that John comes
[U] Usuality/Expectability	It is *normal* that John is coming	It is *unusual* that John is coming
[I] Importance/Significance	It is *important* that John comes	It is *irrelevant* whether John comes
[C] Comprehensibility/ Obviousness	It is *obvious* that John is coming	It is *mysterious* that John is coming
[H] Humorousness/ Seriousness	It is *hilarious* that John is coming	It is *serious* that John is coming
[A] Ability/Difficulty [proposals]	It is *easy* for John to come	It is *difficult* for John to come
[Ut] Utility/Usefulness [proposals]	It is *useful* for John to come	It is *useless* for John to come

Source: Adapted from Lemke (1998, p. 37).

relationships (or apparent lack thereof) between textual elements (cf. Lemke, 1998; Graham, 2001, 2002a). To make matters more complex, evaluative meanings can get nominalized and appraised, as can relationships between elements, as can whole value systems (axiologies), as in the perjorative use of the term 'ideology' (Graham, 2002a).

Further complexities arise in the analysis of evaluations when we take into account the historical processes of 'mediation' – literally, the means by which community-specific axiologies are produced, reproduced and inculcated across social spaces and through time (Silverstone, 1999, ch. 1). Therefore, if we are to make 'sense' of evaluative propagation and its social force, we must share some considerable degree of knowledge about often submerged axiologies peculiar to discourse communities. Notions of 'heteroglossia', 'discourse formations', 'intertextuality', 'inculcation' and 'evaluative patterns' all refer to the historical and normative work that has gone into building evaluative 'logics' over time, space and throughout institutions in society (Firth, 1953; cf. Fairclough, 1992, pp. 12–135, 2000; Lemke, 1995, pp. 22–36, 1998, pp. 34–5; Graham, 2002a). Therefore we would expect to see an historical layering, hybridizing and textual 'chaining' of axiological traditions in any given instance (Graham, 2002a).

Genre-specific values and the formation of disciplines

In most respects, my approach to the analysis of how disciplinarity happened is 'discourse-historical' because it 'attempts to integrate much available knowledge about the historical sources and the background of the social and political fields in which discursive "events" are embedded' and 'analyzes the historical dimension of discursive actions by exploring the ways in which particular genres of discourse are subject to diachronic change' (Wodak, 2000). The analysis I present here focuses on the genre of academic journal articles that mark formal disjunctions central to the formation of various disciplines in social science. Time and space do not permit fine-grained analyses of explicit or implicit evaluations in the texts that follow. I have presented approaches to doing so elsewhere in far greater detail than is possible here (Graham, 2001, 2002a). I define the perceived value of any particular phenomenon as the 'ecosocially' constructed *Desirability* of that phenomenon (cf. Lasswell, 1927; Lemke, 1998; Graham, 2002b). Further, I assume that the perceived *Desirability* of anything is socially, linguistically, ecologically and technologically mediated (Graham, 2002b). Within the discourse communities of scientific enquiry, the two broadest evaluative dimensions that propagate and support the *Desirability* of any given body of disciplinary knowledge are *Significance* and *Warrantability*: the most *Desirable* scientific knowledge will be both true and important within a given field.

At the outset of disciplinarity, I presuppose an already broken philosophy in which the broad evaluative domains of the *True* (Logic), the *Good* (Ethics), and the *Beautiful* (Aesthetics) have been actively held apart in philosophy for centuries (Hegel, 1816 [1995], p. 407; Russell, 1946 [1991], pp. 54–5; Lemke, 1995, pp. 178–9). I further assume that any change or reordering of axiologies is intimately 'connected with a change in the social system' (Russell, 1946 [1991], p. 53). My analysis thus foregrounds the historical 'hybridization' and reordering (or 'restructuring of the order') of values along inter-institutional lines (cf. Fairclough, 1992, p. 222; Lemke, 1995, pp. 178–80).

In what follows, I provide examples from the disciplines of economics, political science, psychology and ethics. Where possible, I have used editorial introductions to first issues of journals for newly emerging disciplines to focus on the intertextual separation of new disciplines from their 'parents'. By 'intertextual', I mean the 'actual utterances' of 'distinct social *voices*' which arise from and constitute the formal and institutional 'stratification of language in actual use' (Lemke, 1995, p. 24). These stratifications are evident in 'professional jargons' of academic and professional groups (Bakhtin, 1935, cited in Lemke, 1995, p. 24). From the late nineteenth century onwards, intertextual separations within academia becomes a social function of new academic journals.

The journals I have chosen have been influential in the formation and maintenance of their respective disciplines. All continue to be published up to the present day. All are in English, although foundational scholars from non-English-speaking backgrounds in each of the disciplines I discuss here have published in the journals. While I expect the Englishness of the journals to have some associated idiosyncrasies, I have no reason to suspect that the fundamental dynamic is any different, at least in other 'Western' contexts.

I ground my investigation of disciplinarity in 'pre-disciplinary' political economy because it is the first discipline to be formally defined in post-Enlightenment social science (Jessop and Sum, 2001, pp. 90–1). Like all contemporary sciences throughout the Western world, political economy has its roots in religious scholarship (for example, Randall, 1940; Langholm, 1998). Its earliest proponents were 'polymaths who wrote on economics, politics, civil society, language, morals and philosophy' (Jessop and Sum, 2001, p. 90). In short, pre-disciplinary political economists were concerned with the production of values, in the fullest and most multifaceted sense of the term.

Political economy: the first discipline

The expansive scope of pre-disciplinary social science is clear in the earliest formulations of political economy. Early political economists believed that they had discovered

> an elucidation of natural law, and that its scope extended to all of man's dealing with man [*sic*] and nature. It was therefore a moral science governing man's social activity, much the sort of thing that John Locke once

hoped to achieve for ethics by applying to that subject the laws discovered by his friend Newton. (Neill, 1949, p. 537)

Destutt de Tracy (1801, cited in Kennedy, 1979) is exemplary of the expansive character of late eighteenth- to early nineteenth-century social science. He formulated a literal 'ideology', a 'science of ideas', that aspired to 'establish a sound "theory of the moral and political sciences"', and which embraced 'grammar, logic, education, morality, and "finally the greatest of arts, for whose success all the others must cooperate, that of regulating society"' (ibid., p. 355). It quickly became clear to vested interests that Tracy's political economy, and other systems like it, sought to replicate the authoritative scope of the Church and Crown. Consequently, such systems were roundly attacked and dispersed (ibid.).

Similarly, in the transition from the Natural Order view of the social world to that of the strong Social Darwinism characteristic of the late nineteenth century, the Natural Order was not so much destroyed as it was provided with an increasingly dynamic and 'scientific' explanation. The whole of human life came to be viewed as a struggle for survival, and only the fittest would survive: 'the Natural Order was for the eighteenth century what evolution became for the nineteenth, the common concept into which every generalisation was thrown' (Ware, 1931, p. 619). But this latter worldview would not supplant the former: a universal Natural Order was thereafter seen to emerge, not by the design of a clockmaker God, but from all-out, constant competition for survival on the part of every living thing (cf. Tylor, 1877; Ware, 1931).

Mainstream political economy began a rapid descent into a science of price during the last quarter of the nineteenth century. These were taken up, in the first instance, by the newly emerging fields of sociology, psychology, anthropology, political science and moral philosophy (see, for example, Perry, 1916). After World War I, the study of society fragmented further into the disciplines of propaganda studies, public opinion, business studies and myriad others (Graham, 2002b). This chapter seeks to undermine and transcend disciplinary boundaries that have developed and hardened over the last century and a half by identifying the evaluative means by which early disciplines were 'created'. It is informed by an historical materialist theory of value which sees the evaluative sediments of historical process in the official discourses of expert power propounded today (Graham, 2002a).

Analysis: beginning in the middle

Between the years of 1916 and 1921, mainstream political economy finally withered from being a 'science of everything' to being concerned solely with the study of prices. The following two texts are exemplary illustrations:

[1] Consider the ways in which a single object such as a book may be praised or disparaged... These various properties 'cheap,' 'mendacious,'

'ignorant,' 'edifying' and 'crude,' differ characteristically as a group, from such other properties as the book's color, weight, and size. They are the terms in which the book may be estimated ... *We need the term 'value' as a term to apply to all the predicates of this group.* We may then speak of economic values, moral values, cognitive values, religious values and aesthetic values as various species of one genus. It follows that *we should no longer speak of economics*, after the manner of von Weiser as '*treating the entire sphere of value phenomena*'; *but as one of the group of value sciences*, having certain *peculiar* varieties of value as its province, and *enjoying critical competence or authority only in its own restricted terms*. (Perry, 1916, pp. 445–6)

[2] An *eminent European* economist, writing seventeen years ago, *ascribed* the *confusion* [in economics] to our *general pre-occupation* with the theory of value. He declared in so many words that 'the *most radical and effective cure* for this confusion would be to do away with *the whole theory of value*' and to begin at once with 'an explanation of prices and the general causes governing them'. *He held this procedure to be quite possible and wholly advantageous. The thesis which at that time sounded so radical has since become almost commonplace.* (Parry, 1921, p. 123)

In texts [1] and [2] we see that within a mere five years, various aspects of value get formally 'divided up' along semantic lines amongst a *group of value sciences*, with economics finally being confined to the *explanation of prices and the general causes governing them*. The semantic residue includes, most broadly, *cognitive values, religious values and aesthetic values as various species of one genus*. Value thus becomes a superordinate abstraction in the study of human affairs, and the primary objects of social science – social activity and social change – are theoretically broken into ever-smaller pieces.

More interestingly (and typically), we see how evaluations of 'value' itself get fractured in these two passages, specifically in order to separate economics from all other modes of social enquiry by diminishing its evaluative scope (or *Magnitude*). In [1], Perry raises the concept of value to a superordinate category that pervades all aspects of human judgement, but only in order to diminish the scope of economics and ensconce the 'philosophers of value' as authorities for the remaining *sphere of values*. Perry manages this by deploying the semantic dimension of *Necessity*, the hortatory 'shadow' of the propositional semantics of *Significance*: the clause that begins *We need the term value* ... is on the borderline, containing both propositional and hortatory aspects (Graham, 2001, 2002b; cf. also Thibault, forthcoming). Using Lemke's (1998) probe, we see that the clause could be reconstrued as 'it is *Important* that we have value as a term to apply to *all the predicates of this group*' (a proposition), or 'it is *Necessary* to have value as a term ...' (a proposal evaluated for obligation), or, to foreground the implied imperative, 'we *must* use value as a term to ...' (a proposal with a high degree of obligation). In other words, what appears as a statement claiming evaluations for *Warrantability* and *Obviousness* about the nature of value also contains an imperative to see value as a superordinate category which has no particularity or wholeness. *Necessity* for seeing value in such terms is also propagated in the exercise of obligation, or *shouldness* (Martin, 2000) in the exhortation that we **should** *no longer speak of economics* as a general science of values. Perry combines the semantics of obligation and *Necessity* with the second-order evaluative dimension of *Magnitude* to achieve an evaluative split in the very concept of value, which *should not* apply to **all** *the predicates of this group ...*, to *the* **entire** *sphere of value phenomena*, but only to **one peculiar** variety enjoying *authority only in its own* **restricted** *terms*. Perry is quite literally disciplining economics, constraining its *scope* along evaluative lines by assigning *authority* over specific evaluative domains in particular disciplines.

In text [2] Parry deploys a projecting function to operationalize the evaluative semantics of *Significance, Comprehensibility, Usuality, Normativity, Possibility* and *Desirability* to endorse the theoretical move that Perry, in text [1], referred to five years earlier. *Significance* is attributed both to the **eminent European** *economist* and his **effective** *cure* for the illness of in-*Comprehensibility* (*confusion*) in economics. The resources of *Usuality* and *Normativity* are deployed to trivialize former practices (amongst economists, *confusion* is ascribed to a **general** *pre-occupation with the theory of value*), and to valorize a focus on *prices* for economics (what was once such a *radical thesis* has become *almost commonplace*). The effect is to propagate the *Desirability* of a *wholly advantageous cure* for economics, implying that the discipline had become sick from its *pre-occupation* with a *whole theory of value*. Once again, a reduction in *scope* or *Magnitude* where the concept of value is concerned has become not only *quite possible*, but *Usual, Appropriate* and *Desirable* for the study of economics. We see here, in the codification of contemporary economic theory, the element of *Time* – history – being acknowledged as a significant force in the formation of disciplines: economics previously suffered from *confusion*, a scientific illness. But later, clarity is brought to the discipline, *a cure for the illness of confusion*, by disciplining economists' conception of value – by literally abolishing *the whole theory of value* from economics.

Disciplining the social universe

The emergence of psychology is very closely related to the reduction of political economy to being merely a study of prices (Graham, 2002b). The following text is an editorial introduction from the first issue of the journal *Mind: A Quarterly Review of Philosophy and Psychology*, first published in 1876.

[3] Theoretic psychology has its practical application ... in the **balanced** *training and culture of the individual mind*, while it deals separately with *functions whose* **natural** *play stands* **greatly** *in need of regulation* ... A **true** *psychology* **ought** *unquestionably to admit of being turned to the educator's*

be the identification of *the laws which underlie **man's social life as a whole**,* as in early political economy. A general lack of *Ability* and *Comprehensibility* prevent any *general social science*: the whole of human interaction cannot possibly be understood. Therefore it is necessary to emphasize particularities within *a plurality of social sciences,* with political science enjoying a pre-eminent *Significance* amongst all of these because of its *Good*-ness.

Smith defines political science such that 'the thoughts of the definer' can be 'thought over... until the disciple has gained the same outlook over the subject as the master – and then he no longer needs the definition' (1886, p. 1). In other words, the purpose of having a defined discipline is that basic evaluative assumptions of the discipline go unquestioned so that *the disciple* can gain the same worldview as *the master.* Here we find the essence of disciplinarity: *the disciple* is disciplined not to think beyond the evaluative *scope* of the discipline. The discipline thus hides its own evaluative biases from its disciples by inculcating them as presuppositions and raising the discipline's *Significance* above all others.

These phenomena are most overt in the emergence of sociology:

> [5] Sociology is an ***advanced*** study, *the last and latest in the entire curriculum... It involves **high powers** of generalization, and ... **absolutely requires** a broad basis of induction.* It is largely a philosophy, and in these days philosophy no longer rests on assumptions but on facts. To understand the laws of society the mind must be in possession of a large body of knowledge. This *knowledge **should not be** picked up here and there at random,* but ***should be** instilled in a **methodical** way.* It should be *fed to the mind with **an intelligent purpose** in view,* and that purpose should be *the preparation of the mind for ultimately entering **the last and most difficult** as well as **most important** field of human thought, that of sociology.* Therefore, history, political economy, and the other generic branches should first be prosecuted as constituting the necessary preparation for the study of higher ordinal principles. (Ward, 1895, pp. 25–6)

Ward's sociology in [5] is, again, a science of the whole human condition. Again, it is a synthesis of already existing fields of study: *history, political economy and the other generic branches.* It is explicitly a *philosophy* that *rests on facts.* Here we see the most explicit exhortations of *Necessity* (*sociology **absolutely requires** ...*; a sociologist must have *high powers...*; knowledge ***should not be*** acquired at *random...*; knowledge ***should be** instilled* methodically); statements of *Significance* (*sociology* is ***advanced***; the *last and latest* discipline; the ***most important** field of human thought*); and ascribes the highest levels of *Ability* to sociologists. Once again, academic modes of evaluation are reordered, placing sociology at the pinnacle of all social enquiry.

Sociology met with the most resistance of all the disciplines established in the late nineteenth century, probably because of its blatant intent to

subordinate the entirety of social science – without exception – to its own principles of classification (cf. Tylor, 1877; Smith, 1886; Hayes, 1905). The elision
of the broad evaluative domains of the *Good* and the *Beautiful* from the philosophy of early sociology, or rather their total subordination to the *True*, creates paradoxes which become apparent very early in the field. The immediate
effect is that the *Good* gets cast as an *object* of sociological investigation, and
thus as an object of *factual* investigation (cf. Carrel, 1907; Hayes, 1918).

Moral philosophy (or ethics) responds to sociology with an historical rejoin-
der to regain some of its lost *Significance*. Its proponents do so by appropriating,
as the basis of morality, prevailing notions of racial betterment – eugenics –
which became the dominant paradigm for social enquiry throughout the West,
from the late nineteenth century until 1945 (Paul, 1984):

[6] In the history of philosophy *the science of morals **preceded** that of sociology...it is **the first parent** of every science, present or future*, which treats
of the actions of men. *Sociology and its branches or departments **have only**
statistical value* unless they make inductions from their researches *with
a view to racial benefit*, and *the making of these inductions is **necessarily**
moral*...There are social as well as individual morals...If sociology has
not a moral purpose, it is *an intellectual endeavor to obtain data as to the
behavior of men in society* and would take rank with other branches of
human knowledge *having no direct bearing upon the welfare of humanity*. If,
on the contrary, sociology has a moral purpose, then it appears as a
branch or offshoot of the moral stem. (Carrel, 1907, pp. 448–9)

Again, text [6] clearly attempts to reorder discourses in favour of moral philosophy along lines of *Significance*. The forensic appeal to history claims
Temporal Significance as the basis of a broad *scope* for ethics in the assertions
that ethics ***preceded** that of sociology*, and is thus the ***first parent** of every science, present or future*. Sociology gets reconstrued as merely an historical
branch or offshoot of the moral stem. In [6] we see evidence of an almost total
historical hybridization and reordering of disciplinary discourses. Carrel
fuses Social Darwinist assumptions with the practice of moral philosophy, a
scholastic remnant, and the assumptions of eugenic sociobiology and early
sociology, in an attempt to reorder disciplinary discourses that propagate the
Significance of ethics. This is a pattern repeated over and over, throughout
the social sciences, through to the present day.

Heading backwards into the future: implications and operationalization

One could proceed in far more detail, ad infinitum, tracing the continual
hybridization, fragmentation and reordering of academic discourses into
what have become the myriad disciplines of contemporary social science.

But the main implications of the general patterns thus far noted are: (1) that the discourse-historical roots of all contemporary social sciences are to be found in the institutions in which they were first developed as a coherent whole, namely the medieval institutions of the Church and Crown; (2) that at every step, each new social science has attempted to grasp the whole of human existence as its domain of authority; (3) that the continual reordering and fragmentation of academic discourses into, within and between the disciplines of social science has taken place along evaluative lines, privileging certain ways of evaluating over others by propagating *Significance* for each new discipline; (4) that because centuries of historical work has gone into fracturing social sciences into myriad fragments of linguistically sealed expertise, certain dimensions of evaluative meaning can easily be foregrounded in order to motivate masses of people, while others can be totally suppressed; and (5), because of (1), (2), (3) and (4), we would expect to see, in practically any privileged public voice, historical heteroglots – historical layers – of axiological hybrids that collapse and conflate contradictory evaluative resources from throughout history. In what follows, I give an example of how the evaluative resources developed in the formation of disciplines, and throughout human history, are deployed in contemporary discourses of power.

Latterday Princes and their historical hybridization

Today, the most powerful discourses fuse and deploy any and all historical evaluative resources without regard for their contradictory origins, probably because those resources have become generally unrecognizable. Here is a superlative example:

[7] In my faith tradition, the true prophet of God's message for humankind is the one who comes forth to say: I have been called, as we have all been called, to bring good news to the poor. To bring healing to the sick. To mend the broken-hearted. To speak out clearly on behalf of the oppressed.

Dr. King reminded us that prophetic truth is marching on.

He taught us that there is no such thing as partial freedom. All of our people must be free from economic privation, or none of our people will be fully free. In his last speech, delivered from the pulpit of Mason Temple in Memphis, Tennessee – when he told of his vision from the mountaintop – he reminded us of the urgent need to build 'a greater economic base.' (Gore, 2000)

In [7] a Vice President of the United States compresses at least five millennia of heteroglossic resources into 133 words to propagate the *divinity*, *Desirability* and *Necessity* of a dogmatically Marxist proposition. Gore's speech intertextually conflates the religious legitimacy of God, political economic expertise; liberal doctrines of freedom; Marxist doctrines of emancipatory technological development; the ancient priestly tradition of prophesy; the socialist politics of economic equality; and the Christian ethic of unselfish, sympathetic action – to name just a few. The evaluative resources Gore deploys can be detailed and understood both as phenomena with distinct historical, institutional, and intellectual pedigrees, and as resources for exercising power over societies which have been developed, refined and reproduced over many years, since the earliest stages of history (Graham, 2002a).

Concluding remarks

Today, no critical social science can function from within any of the isolated bunkers created by disciplinarity over the last century and a half. The dynamics of specialization in general are a function of a 'civilization dominated by machine industry industrialism': the fetishes of specialization and the production of excess preclude the possibility of understanding either ourselves or our place in history (Innis, 1942, p. 33). A narrowly defined social-scientific disciplinarity also precludes understanding our current civilization, because an historical totality of human values has now become an instantaneously mediated commonplace throughout an interdependently associated humanity.

Seen as artificially separated value sciences, each with authority in their own domain of human experience, the very idea of disciplinary social science is self-evidently insufficient for comprehending our contemporary world in any critical way. Each object of social science, and each compartment of social science, is itself a social subject. Each acts and impacts upon the others according to its institutional axiologies to order and reorder the *Significance* of specialized ways of seeing, being and (inter)acting (Fairclough, 2000). Each discipline is a discourse community and a social practice. Each disciplined social science has its roots in a broken language and a common charter: the language is that of broken philosophy and broken understandings of value; the charter is that of the whole human condition. Just as it has become more necessary than ever to understand ourselves as part of a global totality – as humans embedded in communities and in the rest of nature – a critical, historically grounded approach to doing so has become more necessary than ever.

If we accept that the human social environment is ultimately coordinated in meaning making, the entry point for any critical science must also be meaning making. However, in seeking interdisciplinarity, CDA risks emulating the totalizing grasp of all preceding social sciences. If we accept that social science has fragmented into disciplines along the semantic fault-lines of evaluative meaning, any critical turn in social science will begin with a comprehensive theory of value. If we are to make sense of the profound changes we are going through as a species, we must understand the nature of our species – our common humanity – not as merely psychological, economic, political, ethical or merely discoursal; we must understand the dynamics of meaning making as the dynamics of understanding and association. A genuine CDA is merely a beginning for any future critical social science, not an end.

Notes

1. For instance, the *Importance* and *Desirability* of a courtroom witness is mediated by assessments for *Warrantability*; *Truth* being the institutional standard at stake.
2. It is still called 'the Divine Science' by its disciples.

References

Carrel, F. (1907) 'Has sociology a moral basis?', *International Journal of Ethics*, 17(4), pp. 448–54.

Fairclough, N. (1992) *Discourse and Social Change*. Cambridge: Polity Press.

Fairclough, N. (2000) 'Discourse, social theory, and social research: the discourse of welfare reform', *Journal of Sociolinguistics*, 4(2), pp. 163–95.

Firth, R. (1953) 'The study of values by social anthropologists' (The Marrett Lecture, 1953), *Man*, 53 (October), pp. 146–53.

Gore, A. (2000) 'Remarks as prepared for delivery by Vice President Al Gore, Dr. Martin Luther King, Jr. Day, Benezer Baptist Church, Atlanta'. Washington: Whitehouse Publications. (<http://www.pub.whitehouse.gov/uri-res/I2R?urn:pdi://oma.eop.gov. us/2000/1/18/15.text.1>.)

Graham, P. (1999) 'Critical systems theory: a political economy of language, thought, and technology', *Communication Research*, 26(4), pp. 482–507.

Graham, P. (2001) 'Space: irrealis objects in technology policy and their role in the creation of a new political economy', *Discourse & Society*, 12(6), pp. 761–88.

Graham, P. (2002a) 'Predication and propagation: a method for analysing evaluative meanings in technology policy', *TEXT*, 22(2).

Graham, P. (2002b) 'Hypercapitalism: new media, language, and social perceptions of value', *Discourse & Society*, 13(2), pp. 227–49.

Graham, P. and McKenna, B. (2000) 'A theoretical and analytical synthesis of autopoiesis and sociolinguistics for the study of organisational communication', *Social Semiotics*, 10(1), pp. 41–59.

Harvey, D. (1973) *Social Justice and the City*. London: Blackwell.

Hayes, E.C. (1905) 'Sociological construction lines I', *American Journal of Sociology*, 10(5), pp. 623–42.

Hayes, E.C. (1918) 'Sociological as ethics', *American Journal of Sociology*, 24(3), pp. 289–302.

Hegel, G.W.F. (1816 [1995]) *Lectures on the History of Philosophy (Vol. 1): Greek Philosophy to Plato*. Lincoln: University of Nebraska Press.

Huxley, T. (1893) *Method and Results: Essays*. London: Macmillan.

Innis, H.A. (1942) 'The newspaper in economic development', *Journal of Economic History*, 2, Issue supplement: 'The tasks of economic history', pp. 1–33.

Jessop, B. and Sum, N. (2001) 'Pre-disciplinary and post-disciplinary perspectives', *New Political Economy*, 6(1), pp. 89–101.

Kennedy, E. (1979) ' "Ideology" from Destutt de Tracy to Marx', *Journal of the History of Ideas*, 40(3), pp. 353–68.

Langholm, O. (1998) *The Legacy of Scholasticism in Economic Thought: Antecedents of Choice and Power*. Cambridge: Cambridge University Press.

Lasswell, H.D. (1927) 'The theory of political propaganda', *American Political Science Review*, 21(3), pp. 627–31.

Lasswell, H.D. (1941) 'World attention survey', *Public Opinion Quarterly*, 5(3), pp. 456–62.

Lemke, J.L. (1995) *Textual Politics: Discourse and Social Dynamics*. London: Taylor & Francis.

Lemke, J.L. (1998) 'Resources for attitudinal meaning: evaluative orientations in text semantics', *Functions of Language*, 5(1), pp. 33–56.

Lemke, J.L. (forthcoming) 'Across the scales of time: artifacts, activities, and meanings in ecosocial systems', *Mind, Culture, and Activity*.

Luhmann, N. (1995) *Social Systems*. Stanford, CA: Stanford University Press.

Marcuse, H. and Neumann, F. (1942 [1998]) 'A history of the doctrine of social change', in D. Kellner (ed.), *Technology, War and Fascism: Herbert Marcuse: Collected Papers of Herbert Marcuse (Vol. 1)*. London: Routledge.

Martin, J.R. (2000) 'Beyond exchange: APPRAISAL systems in English', in S. Hunston and G. Thompson (eds), *Evaluation in Text*. Oxford: Oxford University Press, pp. 142–75.

Marx, K. (1843 [1972]) 'For a ruthless criticism of everything existing' [letter to Arnold Ruge], in R.C. Tucker (ed.), *The Marx–Engels Reader*. New York: W.W. Norton, pp. 7–10.

Marx, K. (1844 [1975]) 'Economic and philosophical manuscripts', in K. Marx, (R. Livingstone and G. Benton, trans.), *Early Writings*. London: Penguin, pp. 279–400.

Marx, K. (1973) *Grundrisse: Foundations of the Critique of Political Economy (Rough Draft)* (M. Nicolaus, trans.). London: Penguin.

Maturana, H. and Varela, F. (1980) *Autopoiesis and Cognition: The Realisation of the Living*. Dordrecht: Reidel.

Mind (1876) 'Prefatory Material' [editorial], 1(1), No. 1, pp. 1–6.

Neill, T.P. (1949) 'The Physiocrats' concept of economics', *Quarterly Journal of Economics*, 63(4), pp. 532–53.

Orwell, G. (1941 [1957]) 'England your England', in G. Orwell, *Inside the Whale and Other Essays*. London: Penguin, pp. 63–90.

Paul, D. (1984), 'Eugenics and the Left', *Journal of the History of Ideas*, 45(4), pp. 567–90.

Parry, C.E. (1921) 'A revaluation of economic theory', *American Economic Review*, 11(1), Papers and proceedings of the Thirty-third Annual Meeting of the American Economic Association, pp. 123–31.

Perry, R.B. (1916) 'Economic value and moral value', *Quarterly Journal of Economics*, 30(3), pp. 443–85.

Randall, J.H. Jr, (1940) 'The development of scientific method in the school of Padua', *Journal of the History of Ideas*, 1(2), pp. 177–206.

Russell, B. (1946 [1991]) *History of Western Philosophy and its Connection with Political and Social Circumstance from the Earliest Times to the Present Day*. London: Routledge.

Silverstone, R. (1999) *Why Study the Media?* London: Sage.

Smith, M. (1886) 'Introduction: the domain of political science', *Political Science Quarterly*, 1(1), pp. 1–8.

'ignorant,' 'edifying' and 'crude,' differ characteristically as a group, from such other properties as the book's color, weight, and size. They are the terms in which the book may be estimated ... *We **need** the term 'value' as a term to apply to **all** the predicates of this group.* We may then speak of economic values, moral values, cognitive values, religious values and aesthetic values as various species of one genus. It follows that *we **should no longer speak** of economics*, after the manner of von Weiser *as 'treating the **entire** sphere of value phenomena'; **but as one** of the group of value sciences,* having certain *peculiar* varieties of value as its province, and *enjoying critical competence or authority **only in its own restricted terms**.* (Perry, 1916, pp. 445–6)

[2] An ***eminent European*** economist, writing seventeen years ago, *ascribed* the ***confusion*** [in economics] to our ***general pre-occupation*** with the theory of value. He declared in so many words that 'the ***most radical and effective cure*** for this confusion would be to do away with *the **whole** theory of value'* and to begin at once with 'an explanation of prices and the general causes governing them'. *He held this procedure to be **quite possible** and **wholly advantageous**. The thesis which **at that time** sounded so **radical** has since become almost **commonplace**.* (Parry, 1921, p. 123)

In texts [1] and [2] we see that within a mere five years, various aspects of value get formally 'divided up' along semantic lines amongst a *group of value sciences*, with economics finally being confined to the *explanation of prices and the general causes governing them*. The semantic residue includes, most broadly, *cognitive values, religious values and aesthetic values as various species of one genus*. Value thus becomes a superordinate abstraction in the study of human affairs, and the primary objects of social science – social activity and social change – are theoretically broken into ever-smaller pieces.

More interestingly (and typically), we see how evaluations of 'value' itself get fractured in these two passages, specifically in order to separate economics from all other modes of social enquiry by diminishing its evaluative *scope* (or *Magnitude*). In [1], Perry raises the concept of value to a superordinate category that pervades all aspects of human judgement, but only in order to diminish the scope of economics and ensconce the 'philosophers of value' as authorities for the remaining *sphere of values*. Perry manages this by deploying the semantic dimension of *Necessity*, the hortatory 'shadow' of the propositional semantics of *Significance*: the clause that begins *We **need** the term value* ... is on the borderline, containing both propositional and hortatory aspects (Graham, 2001, 2002b; cf. also Thibault, forthcoming). Using Lemke's (1998) probe, we see that the clause could be reconstrued as 'it is *Important* that we have value as a term to apply to *all the predicates of this group*' (a proposition), or 'it is *Necessary* to have value as a term ...' (a proposal evaluated for obligation), or, to foreground the implied imperative, 'we *must* use value as a term to ...' (a proposal with a high degree of obligation). In other words, what appears as a statement claiming evaluations for *Warrantability* and *Obviousness* about the nature of value also contains an imperative to see value as a superordinate category which has no particularity or wholeness. *Necessity* for seeing value in such terms is also propagated in the exercise of obligation, or *shouldness* (Martin, 2000) in the exhortation that we ***should** no longer speak of economics* as a general science of values. Perry combines the semantics of obligation and *Necessity* with the second-order evaluative dimension of *Magnitude* to achieve an evaluative split in the very concept of value, which *should not* apply to *all the predicates of this group ...*, to *the **entire** sphere of value phenomena*, but only to *one **peculiar*** variety enjoying *authority only in its own **restricted** terms*. Perry is quite literally disciplining economics, constraining its *scope* along evaluative lines by assigning *authority* over specific evaluative domains in particular disciplines.

In text [2] Parry deploys a projecting function to operationalize the evaluative semantics of *Significance, Comprehensibility, Usuality, Normativity, Possibility* and *Desirability* to endorse the theoretical move that Perry, in text [1], referred to five years earlier. *Significance* is attributed both to the ***eminent European** economist* and his ***effective** cure* for the illness of in-*Comprehensibility* (*confusion*) in economics. The resources of *Usuality* and *Normativity* are deployed to trivialize former practices (amongst economists, *confusion* is *ascribed* to a ***general** pre-occupation with the theory of value*), and to valorize a focus on *prices* for economics (what was once such a *radical thesis* has become *almost commonplace*). The effect is to propagate the *Desirability* of a *wholly advantageous cure* for economics, implying that the discipline had become sick from its *pre-occupation* with a *whole theory of value*. Once again, a reduction in *scope* or *Magnitude* where the concept of value is concerned has become not only *quite possible*, but *Usual, Appropriate* and *Desirable* for the study of economics. We see here, in the codification of contemporary economic theory, the element of Time – history – being acknowledged as a significant force in the formation of disciplines: economics previously suffered from *confusion*, a scientific illness. But later, clarity is brought to the discipline, *a cure* for the illness of confusion, by disciplining economists' conception of value – by literally abolishing *the whole theory of value* from economics.

Disciplining the social universe

The emergence of psychology is very closely related to the reduction of political economy to being merely a study of prices (Graham, 2002b). The following text is an editorial introduction from the first issue of the journal *Mind: A Quarterly Review of Philosophy and Psychology*, first published in 1876.

[3] Theoretic psychology has its practical application ... in the ***balanced** training and culture of the individual mind*, while it deals separately with *functions whose **natural** play stands **greatly in need of regulation** ...* A ***true** psychology **ought** unquestionably to admit of being turned to the educator's*

purpose, and in no direction has the new journal *a more effective opening* at the present time. To speak, in the same connection, of such subjects as Logic, Aesthetics and Ethics, may seem *strange*, but there is *good reason* for so doing. The existence ... of the three distinct bodies of doctrine ... is a signal confirmation of the theoretic distinction of Knowing, Feeling and Willing which has established itself, not without *difficulty*, in modern psychology ... From a philosophical point of view it is of course *needless to justify* the consideration of *the true, the beautiful and the good* in a journal whose subject is Mind. (*Mind*, 1876, pp. 4–5)

The editor of *Mind* is concerned with propagating the *Significance* of psychology as a discipline by proposing that a *true psychology* not only embraces the entirety of individual experience, but the whole of philosophy as well. While the predicate *true* would seem to belong to the broader semantic domain of *Warrantability*, in this context it is a level 2 evaluation for *authenticity* which the author deploys to propagate the *Significance* of psychology. This is further evidenced when the author deploys the resources of *Significance* and *Necessity* by claiming that psychology is responsible for the *balanced training and culture of the individual mind*, the *natural play* of which is *greatly in need of regulation*. The evaluative chain deployed here is underpinned by the Judeo-Christian assumption that people are naturally in a 'fallen' state: that is, that the *Usual* state of the individual mind is not *balanced*, and that it is therefore *Important* to scientifically regulate people's mental development. The introduction to *Mind* acknowledges the *difficulty* already had by *modern psychology* in theoretically separating *Knowing, Feeling and Willing* into *three distinct bodies of doctrine*. It therefore acknowledges difficulties which are today inverted in the widespread quest for interdisciplinarity: contemporary social science, as this volume indicates, is struggling to overcome the difficulties created by the institutionalization of *theoretic* separations that stem from post-'Enlightenment' scholarship – those between mind and body; facts and values; subjects and objects, and, most importantly, between the various aspects of value (Harvey, 1973, p. 14). However, I reiterate that the means of disciplining social science and its objects does not stop with those separations, it begins with them as presuppositions.

The totalizing yet fragmented grasp of early psychology is repeated in the emergence of every new discipline in social science. Take, for instance, the formal emergence of modern 'political science', a term which, says Smith in his introduction to the first issue of *Political Science Quarterly*, 'is greatly in need of definition':

[4] It seems *preferable ... to recognize but one political science* – the science of the state. The relations with which this science deals *may*, of course, *be subdivided and treated separately* ... We may distinguish between the various functions of the state. But *there is no good reason for erecting these various*

> *groups of questions into distinct political sciences. The connection of each with all is **too intimate**.*
>
> ...
>
> The theory of governmental administration is largely economic; and state-finance is a part of the administrative system of the state, is based on economic theory, and is regulated by law ... *All the social relations with which politics, law and economics have to do lie within the domain of ethics. **Duty, loyalty, honesty, charity** – these ideas are **forces that underlie and support** the state; that give to law its **most effective sanction**; that cross and modify **the egoistic** struggle for **gain**.* (Smith, 1886, pp. 3–4)

We see in [4] that, like psychology, the Significance of **one** *political science* is to organize sciences which **may be** *subdivided and treated separately*: the various branches of *politics, law and economics*, the *so-called political sciences*. But that is clearly *un-Desirable* to Smith, who subsumes them under a more abstract, **general** *political science*. Smith defines the whole of political science in terms of a specific evaluative domain: the *Good*, or *ethics*, part of the semantic domain of *Normativity*. Political science is *the science of the state*. The *state* is a set of *social relations* given force by specific *ideas*, which he takes to be unquestionably *Desirable*: *Duty, loyalty, honesty, charity*. Thus, all the political sciences *lie within the domain of ethics*. While Smith is clearly propagating the *Significance* of having only **one** *political science*, he clearly deploys a wider range of evaluative resources in text [4] to do so, despite the overall claim that political science is at root a science of the *Good*.[2]

Those domains are more apparent when Smith defines political science as a group of *particular social sciences*:

> [4.1] *Social science*, in the *broadest* sense, deals with **all** the relations of man [sic] in society; more precisely, with all the relations that result from man's social life. *It may be questioned whether it is proper to speak of **a** social science. We certainly have **no general social science** in the sense that we* have particular social sciences. In politics, in economics, in law and in language, we are able to some extent trace phenomena to their causes, to group facts under rules and rules under principles. But *the laws which underlie **man's social life as a whole** have **not been grasped or formulated***. Social science or sociology, if we use the term, is therefore *simply a **convenient** general expression for a plurality of social sciences*. (ibid., pp. 1–2)

While Smith claims that political science is a science of the *Good*, the *Good* is already subordinated to the tenets of *Logic* (that is, it is first a science of the *True* conforming to the evaluative dictates of post-Enlightenment *objectivity* and *Warrantability*). *Significance* is propagated again by the devices of *scope*: **all** *social sciences* depend on empirical methods, but there is **no general** social science; there are only **particular** ones. The ultimate result of a *social science* would

Thibault, P.J. (forthcoming) 'Interpersonal meaning and the discursive construction of action, attitude and values: the global modal program of one text', in P. Fries, M. Cummings, D. Lockwood and W. Sprueill (eds), *Relations and Functions in Language and Discourse*. London: Cassell.

Tylor, E.B. (1877) 'Mr. Spencer's *Principles of Sociology*', *Mind*, 2(6), pp. 141–56.

Ward, L.F. (1895) 'The place of sociology among the sciences', *American Journal of Sociology*, 1(1), pp. 16–27.

Ware, N.J. (1931) 'The Physiocrats: a study in economic rationalization', *American Economic Review*, 21(4), pp. 607–19.

Wodak, R. (2000) 'Does sociolinguistics need social theory? New perspectives in Critical Discourse Analysis', Keynote address, SS2000, Bristol University, 27 April.

7
Texts and Discourses in the Technologies of Social Organization

Jay L. Lemke

One of the fundamental claims of Critical Discourse Analysis (CDA) is that texts play a constitutive role in social structuration. In this chapter I will develop a theoretical perspective that tries to understand this claim in both a material and a semiotic sense. Recent research on complex systems shows that typically they are organized on and across multiple timescales. In the particular case of social-ecological systems, technologies of social organization are mediated by semiotically significant material artifacts, which persist or are functionally reproduced in long-timescale processes but are created and used on the much shorter timescales of human semiotic activity. Texts, as instances of such material-semiotic artifacts, play a key role in the organization of social systems across timescales and in the widest extension of social networks. I will argue here that this role for texts of all kinds (including those written in the grammars of architecture and bodily habitus) makes them uniquely valuable as indices of historically changing modes of social control. Extrapolating from contemporary developments in textuality (for example, hypertexts and web-surfing), I try to identify emerging forms of social control in the era of globalization. Postmodern texts and social practices already exist; they mediate new forms of social control in new ways. Progressive social projects must learn both to resist them and to make use of them, and CDA needs to extend itself in a highly interdisciplinary way in order to help us do so.

Interdisciplinary approaches are critical to the success of such a project. First, there is the necessity of combining social theory and semiotics, particularly models of social change and the linguistic analyses of texts. My thesis here is that texts themselves play a key role in processes of social change because they are the link across time and space that binds a social system together; they are both material and semiotic objects, they have physical properties which enable their semantic content to span time and space. The social functions of texts also depend on how they are used in social practices, so that microsocial analysis, as well as macrosocial models of system change must be taken into account. Social systems change on all timescales at once, the microsocial events more rapidly, their macrosocial norms, contexts and typical forms more slowly. In addition to this, interdisciplinarity is required by the excess of the semiotic beyond the linguistic. Every material written text is also a visual meaning-artifact, and verbal meanings frequently depend critically on the co-occurrence of visual forms. For the purposes of linking social systems together across time and space, not all 'texts' moreover are like the verbal-visual forms of print: the human body operates also as such a material-semiotic artifact, as do all scales of technical artifacts, from machines to architectures to cityscapes.

Below, I will first sketch a complex-systems model of semiotically mediated social ecosystems (hereafter *ecosocial systems*) and discuss the general role of texts and other semiotic-material artifacts in producing the coherence of such systems across time and space. I will then outline very briefly and suggestively the history of changing ways in which texts have mediated different forms of social control in different eras. Finally, I will critically characterize emergent forms of textuality as a new order of meaning-making practices in contemporary social experience that I shall call 'traversals' and identify their distinctive role both in new modes of social control and in progressive social projects.

From complex material systems to the role of texts

The argument I present first is a brief summary of one for which I have recently given several more detailed accounts (Lemke, 2000a,b,c, 2002b). It begins from a commonplace of complex systems theory (for example, Bar-Yam, 1997): dynamical systems in which large numbers of elements interact to produce determinate but unforeseeable new phenomena – such as organisms, ecosystems, and cities – are characterized by a hierachical organization across multiple levels (Salthe, 1985, 1993), each with its characteristic timescales (for characterizing the rates of processes) and spatial-extensional scales (for typical distances, sizes, masses and energies).

In many such systems there is a physical separation of processes which take place at very different rates; they do not efficiently exchange energy, and so informational signals, with one another. But in systems where there is semiosis, that is, meaning-making through the mediation of signs or symbols, different organizational levels constituted by processes operating at vastly different timescales can become linked by the circulation of material artifacts that are 'written' and 'read' according to the conventions of some meaning-making community. Material-semiotic artifacts, such as inscriptions and written texts, tools, architectural structures and the signifying and remembering human body itself persist over much longer timescales than the ones on which the processes of creating or 'writing' them and interpreting or 'reading' them take place. The shorter-term activities of people in social systems can thus gain a measure of longer-term coherence and larger-scale integration across institutions and cultures through the circula-tion of people and things that carry meaning. The same object, of course, may take on different meanings at different moments in its circulation in a community (cf. Star and Griesemer, 1989, on 'boundary objects'), and also thereby contribute to larger-scale social organization.

Relying on this model, we can gain some insight into the 'technologies' of social organization through which it is possible for human communities, in partnership with tools and raw materials, to coordinate the building of a cathedral over a centuries-long timescale or how it is that centuries-old tra-ditions and rituals can be maintained through the actions of people and arti-facts that happen on the timescale of minutes, hours or days.

This role of texts and other material-semiotic artifacts makes them useful as windows onto the larger-scale and longer-term processes of social organi-zation, regulation and control, as well as processes of significant social and cultural change.

Modes of textuality and modes of social control: a thesis

Suppose we look at the history of the textual mediation of social control in the following broad terms. Imagine three ways in which texts and other semiotic-material artifacts have come to mediate social control, beginning with the primary integrating function of their specific informational con-tent, as in the architectural plans for a medieval cathedral or the Great Wall of China, or the transmission of sacred texts and legal texts that helped to ensure the stable repetition of rituals and formulas as guides to action over timescales of centuries. This was, I believe, the dominant mode of media-tion for a very long time following the invention of writing. But as the scales of human societies grew from unique villages and cities, each of which had unique institutions and texts, to scales on which there was a replication of standardized institutions (the same ritual of the Latin Mass across Europe, the multiple copies of the tablets of Hammurabi to standardize the laws of an empire, the same forms and practices of Chinese magistrates' courts across vast territories and stable over centuries), a second mode of textual mediation, extending the first mode, became more and more significant. This was mediation by standardized text-form or genre, whether of written texts or other artifacts.

Each of these overlapping modes corresponds, I suggest, to a distinct mode of social regulation in-the-large and social control of individual behaviour at the small scale. In the first case, unique texts and unique insti-tutions regulate particular acts in an ad hoc manner; this is the mode of *qadi* justice in the Islamic tradition. In the second case, often historically simul-taneous with the first, it is not the unique content of texts or acts alone which matters in social regulation, but the form, type, kind or genre of these acts and texts. The content of the texts and acts still matters, but their conformity to standardized, replicated forms and manners also matters, and matters increasingly as social institutions and aggregate human communities such as states, empires or multinational corporations increase in their spatial scales and operate over longer and longer timescales.

But this is not the end of the story. I believe that today we are witnessing a new enlargement in the maximum scales of organization of global society, crossing the boundaries of the modernist nation-state and indeed of all institutions, cross-linking institutions in new ways. Correspondingly there are new forms of textuality and semiotic mediation, whose emergent instances might be represented by such phenomena as hypertext and the World Wide Web. More specifically, we are increasingly making use of modernist forms and genres in hybrid media where the traditional boundaries are regularly crossed by 'traversals' as we jump through hypertexts or surf across the Web. This emergent order of textual mediation should correspond, by the general thesis I have been developing here, to new modes of social organization and social control. Critical Discourse Analysis needs to find ways of addressing not just the (still very important) relations between standardized discourses, genres or textual forms and the institutional practices and interests which they sustain, but also this newer, emergent mode of mediation, with all its implications for the emergence of new modes of social control and changing relations among the individual or activity-scale of social coherence, the institutional scale, and the new transinstitutional forms.

There are many examples to help illustrate what this new mode of 'traversals' is like in comparison to the older modes of unique texts and standardized genres:

- *hypertexts* – experienced in time as jumping from one element in one modern genre or type to another that may be quite disparate; for example, narrative to poem to diagram to table to dialogue to video to quantitative graph, and so on (Landow, 1997; Lemke, 2002a) and also linking across topics and themes that may have no typical cultural collocations
- *web-surfing* – which generalizes the simple hypertext across radically different content categories, linguistic registers and institutional domains of human activity, but with some logical connective relations at each juncture or link, and with a sense, like that for hypertext, of a coherent meaning-experience along a whole experiential trajectory
- *channel-surfing* – the immediate predecessor of web-surfing, in which the viewer jumps at various rates among the widely different television programmes and genres (adventure to cooking to news to talk show, and so on), again creating a unique and in some sense coherent meaning-making experience, in which the viewer is a more active creator of the trajectory than he or she could be in relation to any single programme
- *mall-cruising* – an architectural experience, or 'reading' of assembled space, in which, whether as shopper or social visitor, over a relatively

short span of time, individuals move from food court to clothes mart to movie theatre to furnished public space, again assembling the trajectory of a coherent visit-to-the-mall.

It is not just these sorts of relatively short-term experiences that show the increased signficance of transgenre and transinstitutional traversals of a sort that begins to transcend the organizational and regulatory logic of standardization which so characterizes modernism. There are also instances at larger scales of extension and at longer timescales:

- *hybridizing identities* – combinations serially and simultaneously of participations in and affiliations with more diverse communities; for example, serial and simultaneous bi- and multisexualities; affiliations to both Black *and* White racial groupings, to African *and* Puerto Rican cultures and communities, to being both Asian and European, and to developing and hybridizing institutional and affiliative identities on timescales from months to a lifetime
- *career-surfing* – younger, privileged individuals today do not look forward to having a lifetime career in a single institution or social sector, but to lifescale traversals across many careers in many institutions, and even to mixing and alternating roles such as engineer, musician and student on shorter and shorter timescales, even within the same day or week; it no longer makes sense to identify with a single career, profession or institution because meaningful life occurs in the traversals across multiple social formations as modernism once defined them
- *corporate chameleonism* – multinational corporations today are more often networks of diverse enterprises, with no single 'core' business; they are constituted as looser aggregates, capable of more rapid and opportunistic change on short timescales; they may have no stable structures or principles; their organizational coherence is achieved through personal links and empty or hyperreal signifiers (styles, brands)
- *transdisciplinarity* – intellectual and academic work is increasingly shifting from relatively stable professions and systems of organized practices and methodological and professional canons to simultaneous and serial mixing and hybridization across more diverse disciplinary communities and practices on shorter timescales (that is, mixing even in the same sentence or procedure, rather than only across a long career)
- *globalized urbanism* – networks of institutions and material structures within urban ecosocial systems are increasingly becoming liberated from local functional constraints as these are balanced against opportunities for global networking and use is made of the richer diversity of urban networks/resources that results; urban subgroups (such as diasporic communities) can link into global transurban networks, thereby increasing local urban diversity, permitting change on faster timescales and gaining freedom from local constraints.

Traversals and their textualities are parasitic on modernist genres and typologies; their heterogeneity is only defined relative to the different modernist categorizations of their units. But this is precisely the heart of our postmodern fascination, especially in popular and youth culture, with 'border crossings', with a greater freedom to mix the unlike, to create hybrids and perform hybridity. It is not just the mixing of unlike that increases our semiotic resources, it is the mixing of contraries; it is finding ways of being two things that in modernist terms you cannot both be (for example, racially both Black and White, or gendered as both masculine and feminine). The traversal mode undermines binary categories and laughs in the face of a modernist logic that excludes the middle, the *tertium quid*, the miscegenated monstrosity. It is a defiance of social control by purity of type. Even as social dynamics generates new discouses and registers shared across individuals and communities, the possibilities of traversals correspond to a hybridizing potential to take these discourses not as bounded, discrete wholes to remain inside of, but as elements to play with and to make new and more unique meanings and lives with.

In the emergent era of traversals, newer forms of social organization have only a stylistic unity, rapidly changing and opportunistic memberships and goals, and fluid roles and structures (see the literature on 'new corporations' and postmodern 'virtual organizations'; for example, Gee et al., 1997). Social control is shifting to become directed at producing short-term styles of mixing traditionally separated modernist modes of behaviour, retaining them only as empty signifiers disconnected from the no-longer-determinative social institutions that used to give them direct reality, and at shortening the timescales for persistence of any particular stylistic pattern, disposition or institutional loyalty or membership. It is mediated by congeries of texts originally from different discourse communities and registers that are juggled together for the purpose, or by the net effects of participation in highly heterogeneous social networks across a span of relatively shorter as well as longer timescales.

Traversals again require a fundamentally interdisciplinary approach in our theories and how we apply them. It is not just that texts of very different genres (for example, fictions and scientific accounts; advertising and artistic productions) become interlinked in hypertext webs, or that we witness the playful hybrids of postmodern architecture (for example, structurally integrating Bauhaus and Beaux Arts elements), but that in lived traversals every meaningful form that may be encountered in a day of life may be seen as contributing meaning to a whole that transcends all divisions of disciplinary specialization.

How is this possible? Until relatively recently, the overall functioning of society required the separation and mutual insulation of modernist institutions, the relative purity of their genres, confinement of individual career-trajectories to single institutions or at least institutions in the same economic and cultural sectors, and individual identities that were categorically assignable to discrete genders, ethnicities, sexualities, and so on. What has changed

I believe are the relationships among levels of organization. With the emergence of new global social and economic networks that are transnational and transinstitutional (cf. Appadurai, 1996; de Castells, 1996) there are now higher levels of relatively stable social organization which permit a greater degree of plasticity and lability at the level below. This is a general feature of naturally evolved complex systems with hierarchical levels of organization (Lemke, 2000a,b,c). An intermediate level filters noise and reorganizes variety from the level below it *as* information for the level above, and at the same time a higher level provides the relatively stable dynamical context within which variety is permissible at the level below. So long as there is something going on at the level below to provide the constitutive input to organizational patterns at the higher level, that higher level is relatively fault-tolerant toward how the input is provided or by which subsystems.

One of the most interesting features of the emergence of a higher level of organization in a complex system is that because of the filtering and buffering effects at this new level, the levels above are less sensitive to individual events and detailed variation at levels below the emergent one. Only variation at the level below which is transduced as significant variation (meaning) for the levels above, by the emergent level, counts. As a result we may picture higher levels as becoming more fault-tolerant with respect to lapses and failures in processes at lower levels.

We can for example imagine that at the level of global economic organization, it is necessary to have a certain volume and rate of circulation of global capital, but exactly which institutions are contributing how much at any given moment to the net average rate of flow matters relatively little. Similarly, with the emergence of supranational organizations such as the institutions of the European Union, the international monetary and financial institutions, or the internet, local and regional interests can be pursued in much more radical ways than could be permitted by nation-states when they themselves were the highest level of social and economic organization, which all lower level institutions had to rely on for a stable working environment. When the stability of the nation-state and its national-scale institutions was paramount, greater regulation of local and regional-scale interests and institutions was necessary. With the emergence of the transnational organization of global society and its economy, the regulatory stability of the nation-state is no longer so critical and a greatly increased variety and autonomy at the subnational level is to be expected.

Very generally, I am proposing that the modernist modes of social control and their associated standardized bureaucratic genres, which are still in existence and still necessary on some scales, are no longer as critical to the sustainability of the global ecosocial system as they were a century ago, and that it is the opening up of the modernist closure of institutional social formations (in the sense of Chandler and van de Vijver, 2000) which creates the space of possibility for hybridity, traversals, and so on.

From standardized discourses to hypertextual traversals

To the extent that the modernist paradigm of discrete and separated institutional registers, genres and discourses holds sway, overall societal organization is represented by heteroglossia and heteropraxia: each social stratum and category (for example, class, gender, age, sexuality, religion, ethnicity, occupational-institutional affiliation; collectively 'caste') is defined by and co-constituted through difference and distinction among its characteristic internally consistent and homogeneous discursive forms and signifying practices (cf. Lemke, 1995). The social system as whole is organized by this multidimensional matrix of castes and subcultures, which presents a relatively slowly changing array of structural relationships. Social control is oriented to the reproduction of discourses and practices, to the maintenance of their differences, to the maintenance of their differential social distributions with respect to age, gender, sexuality, class, subculture and culture. Social control practices seek to slow the rate of structural change at the level of the organization of the community and its differentiating discourse types and practices. They permit much faster rates of change in texts and also relatively rapid change in individual development, so long as it is along mostly predictable trajectories of socialization that conform to the typologies of the social-structural order (cf. Bourdieu, 1984, 1990, on habitus). Individual habitus is an internalization of both standardized caste-specific dispositions and of combinations which remain structured by fixed cross-caste relations.

We can formulate our larger thesis of the increasing dominance first of standardized forms and then of traversals and hybridity in these terms. For example, in the history of science the premodern or early modern epoch could be characterized as an *Age of Experiments*; each individual and unique experiment held the greatest significance and people sought to reproduce it exactly. It held the place of the unique text in our historical scheme of texts, genres and traversals, and functioned through its 'verbatim' practice-content. An individual scientist went from experiment to experiment without being constrained by the not-yet-emergent definitions of scientific specializations or professional organizations and communities, that is, the scientific disciplines which mark the subsequent epoch or *Age of Professions*. In the latter, there are research programmes and careers which are confined to, and help constitute, the disciplinary professions and their organizations. There is relatively greater homogeneity at longer timescales from the viewpoint of the individual scientist; there is heterogeneity only in-the-large, across different specialized scientific professions. This heterogeneity is materially instantiated in the few cross-science institutional relations, but mainly in the mutually supportive functions of the different sciences in industrial society as a whole. Finally, in the emergent *Age of Transdisciplinarity*, more and more scientists cross the traditional disciplinary boundaries in cutting-edge work, interact and confer more often across those boundaries, and over their careers shift more radically, relative to those professional divisions, across the sciences. Individual experiments and even research programmes can no longer be assigned easily to one discipline; new hybrid professions arise, but there is not just a finer subdivision of professions emerging, there is greater heterogeneity on each timescale: in the work of an experiment, in the course of a research programme, and in the life career of a scientific worker.

In this example, early forms of social control for experiments took the form of establishing credibility and reproducibility for each unique experiment in ways that were not yet canonical or standardized across large classes of experiments (cf. Shapin and Schaffer, 1985). It was mediated by recipe-like texts for the literal or verbatim replication of actions and observations, as well as by unique apparatus and constructions (themselves material 'texts', semiotic artifacts). The texts and artifacts functioned not as instances of types (discourses, standardized instrumentation) but as unique constellations of 'content'. The form of social organization was the local and extended (for example, in scientific correspondence) unique community, relatively more dependent on the idiosyncrasies of members. Communities arose and dissolved as 'individuals'. Credibility and reproducibility were relative to the unique memberships of the communities.

With the emergence of the modern scientific professions, social control took the form of standardized curricula for education and training, professional certifications, and standardized methodological canons and mediating instrumentations. The unique content of individual texts became less important than the production of texts that conformed to canonical discourse formations (registers, genres, thematic formations). One modern scientific textbook 'says' pretty much the same as another; differences in wording are regarded as immaterial. Individual experiments retain a unique textual component, but this is embedded within a high degree of discursive and material standardization (cf. Latour, 1987; Bazerman, 1988). It is such cross-textual semantic homogeneities and standardized apparatus and procedures that define the modern professions.

In the new era of transdisciplinarity, there is beginning to be a return to the uniqueness of experiments, apparatus, and accounts, and to highly original, non-typical work; but by and large it is still produced through mixes of standardized elements (apparatus, procedures, discourses) from the professionalized disciplines. Social control is again exercised through relatively idiosyncratic and shifting shorter-term communities (for example, key figures meeting at international conferences, online list groups) and credibility within them (as well as through resource networks, both financial and material, mediated by these communities). A new interdiscipline arises with each new thematic focus around which ad hoc groups of researchers produce connections between one line of work and another. These changing communities meet with the support of different hosting universities or institutes, and are funded year-to-year by different combinations of governmental, corporate and philanthropic institutions. Social control is mediated by these heterogeneous assemblages and by the discursive and material constellations produced by these transdisciplinary communities, which are themselves hybrids and tend to persist on shorter timescales than the older, modernist disciplines. The new transdisciplines come and go as needed and as produced by the constellations of interests of members in each other's work (cf. Stengers, 1997, on the production of interest). In the postmodern world, there is no expectation of long-term institutionalization. Transdisciplinary constellations come and go as needed; they are 'just in time' phenomena.

Timescales and textscales

I have suggested so far that as more stable levels of social organization develop at larger extensional scales and longer timescales, there is increased fault-tolerance for volatility of those forms of social organization at smaller-shorter scales which previously carried more of the burden of social stability. Modernist institutions persist, but more and more the new emergent productions valued in our communities are created across institutions rather than within them. What is done within them becomes merely the maintenance of an infrastructure which permits the emergence of novelty that arises by the hybridization of resources across different institutions, produced in the mode of activity I am calling 'traversals'.

But what of the scales of the texts and artifacts which are produced, both within institutions and between them? I have suggested that not only social organization in the large, but also social control at the scale of individuals and their activities, is mediated in part by semiotic-material texts and artifacts which circulate in communities and link large-scale, long-term processes, institutions and social formations with smaller-scale, shorter-term actions and activities. For modernist institutions it is both texts and text-types which are relevant. We can ask about the social-organizational and local-control functions of texts of different length, and about the timescales of persistence and use of both texts and text-types, as well as their spatial and social extension geographically and across social categories and numbers of people and individual institutions. Here, I would like to lay some conceptual foundations for such enquiries. In particular, I would like to raise some questions about the relations of textscales, timescales, and social scales, and their implications for issues of changing paradigms of social organization and behavioural control.

Let's look at the range of timescales associated with texts and text-like artifacts. The timescales associated with such texts/artifacts are:

- intermittent periods of production/composition
- full timespan for production
- intermittent periods of use/reading

- maximum timespan for being in use by a single user or user group
- timescale of publication, circulation
- maximum timescale for being in circulation in a community of users
- physical lifetime of the readable 'text'.

Note that the last two assume that for the meaning of the artifact to remain available it is necessary not only that the physical object remain legible in principle, but also that there are readers who are capable of interpreting it in something like its intended contexts of use. When the language has been lost, when the culture that made meaningful interpretation possible is gone (or either has changed beyond recognition), then the text loses its semiotic affordances in practical terms. 'Revived' texts and languages represent a special case (for example, for use by archaeologists and historians), but the cultural contexts are so changed that I think we must consider these to be 'new texts' in the sense that the meanings that are made with them no longer retain definite linkages with the practices of the communities (the culture) that produced them, and are now artifacts in effect of our own time and culture (Foucault, 1969). The material artifacts may be the same, but the meanings made are not. This is relevant because of the thesis discussed previously: what matters for purposes of social organization and control is the passing

Table 7.1   Timescales and material texts

Unit practice	Timescale	Typical duration	Full span of process
	10^{-1}		Edge of awareness
Read text unit	1–10 seconds		
Read	$2–10^2$	Seconds to minutes	
Write text unit R	10^3	o(15 minutes)	
Write, read	$10^3–10^4$	Hour	
Write, read	10^4	o(2.75 hours)	
Write ...	10^5	Day	Read
	10^6	11.5 days	Read, write
	10^7	4 months	Read long text
Publish, circulate	10^8	o(3.2 years)	Write long text
Use regularly	10^9	o(32 years)	Keep homologous records
Functional span	10^{10}	o(320 years)	Historical timescale; new institutions
Physical decay; unintelligibility	10^{11}	3,200 years	New cultures, languages; limit of historical records
Ecosystem, climate change	10^{12}	32,000 years	

of information between the large-scale, long-term processes of an ecosocial system and its smaller-scale, shorter-term processes and activities.

Table 7.1 suggests very generally some of the timescales associated with the use of ordinary written texts. It is important to pay attention here to the role of *intermittency*. At the human scale, interaction with an artifact (or natural object, or person, considered as a source of meaning) can rarely persist continuously or quasi-continuously for more than a day (sleep intervenes, at least). But social activities and projects can continue on much longer timescales, and the material artifact itself is an essential element in enabling a continuity or resumption of the activity, even when that activity is the writing or reading of the text itself. Intermittent, interrupted or resumed activities are the rule beyond the multihour timescale, and these are greatly abetted in their potential complexity (that is dimensions of variability) beyond the limits of human by semiotic-artifact mediation.

Each different timescale of activity, however, is likely to have different social functions, both with regard to organization (that is, contribution to a larger-scale process) and control (that is, constraints on shorter-term processes in order to make such a contribution). There is a need for CDA to enquire into this functional differentiation with regard to timescales, and an important start on such enquiries is investigating the extent to which, say, shorter vs longer texts carry different functions and mediate different kinds of social organization across scales.

The short and the long of it

The dynamics of use – writing, reading, publishing, circulating, and so on – link timescales, which are a common measure for all these phenomena, and text-scales, which are the structural-organizational units of the text itself with regard to how we use it insofar as we make meaning with it. In traditional terms, such units in written texts include the letters, spaces and punctuation marks; the words, phrases, clauses and sentences; and the larger rhetorical and typographical units such as paragraphs, chapters, volumes, and so on. These are different for other media and for hybrid media (Kress and van Leeuwen, 1996; Lemke, 1998a).

Think of the texts we read and respond to on the shortest timescales with no need to remember for the longer term, such as traffic signs or gestures in talk. We have today many more of these in our new media, such as instant messages and short emails. Read, quickly responded to, and deleted. Or ephemerality may be assumed in the medium itself, as for example with beeper messages and voicemail messages. We receive a frequent stream of very brief messages, quite unlike the long and infrequent letters of the past, or the short and even less frequent prototypes of these new media, such as telegrams. We scan newspaper headlines and website titles and banners and move on. The text may remain, but it does not function on any longer timescale for us.

We never return to it. I believe we really do deal today with more frequent jumping from one text to another one that is not intrinsically or cohesively related to the first (that is, for which there are no conventional intertextual ties; cf. Lemke, 1985, 1995). In the past our evanescent messages came by voice from people around us, but it was rare that people had so many brief messages so frequently delivered. More often we had sustained dialogues with people, so that while each turn at talk could be accounted a brief message, there was still a semantic continuity and certainly an actional one across them.

Looking to messages on the minutes to tens-of-minutes scale, there are more sustained and concentrated acts of reading, equivalent to reading a long email or a news story. We create such messages in durable media (durable on a scale at least 10 to 100 times longer than the timescale of the process of composition or expected use). The daily newspaper was probably the prototype medium for this, providing much shorter texts than those of classical essays or pamphlets. News magazines today and many popular print forms convey texts on the one- to two-page-length scale, padded out with photographs and drawings. The typical newspaper or magazine story of 75–100 years ago would have been much longer. Popular songs also tend to be of several minutes' duration.

As we approach the half-hour to hour timescale, we have the famous example of television programming, on a timescale so much shorter than traditional theatrical plays (a half-hour television series episode, minus breaks, is about a tenth the length of a serious classical play). In order of magnitude these are also not so far from the typical length of commercial films (two hours).

All activity on scales longer than a few hours, which define the social-structural continuities of modern life and go back as far as agriculture itself, are *resumptive*. We return and take up where we left off. And how do we know where we left off? How do we organize activity over timescales and for complexity greater than that for which memory is reliable? Historically, first by our arrangements of the environment, then by tallies and records, and finally by writing and drawing. We also use collective reconstructive memory, where a group, in intermittent consultation, can remember a more complex plan and what has already been done, over a longer timespan than an individual might reliably do.

Let's shift over now to the other end of the scale. What is the longest span of time over which an individual engages even intermittently with the same text-artifact? We could imagine a diary kept throughout life and regularly re-read. There are traditionally also certain sacred texts that we encounter and are exposed to again and again throughout life, at least in the context of institutional activity. Such lifespan texts are relatively rare. They are also not generally mediated by a single artifact. The technology of a text that is copied into many artifacts enables social communities not only to preserve the text against accident, but also to disseminate it so that a larger community can be linked together through it and so that individuals can re-encounter the text-content over longer timescales even if in the form of different materal objects (copies).

What other texts are we likely to re-encounter over the span of a lifetime or any significant fraction of a lifetime? Popular songs tend to link a generation to its youth and today are re-heard often throughout life. Favourite films may be watched again and again, though I think this is less common than re-reading favourite books was in the past (or is now). There are now so many works in print and other media that even a favourite is often but one favourite among many and is re-accessed very rarely. Childhood stories and books may return for one's own children, playing a role in renewal of identity for ourselves as well.

Works of visual art are more likely to be kept and re-viewed on a frequent basis. There are common visual icons and images that are made pervasive over fairly long time-periods by the workings of both popular taste and corporate marketing. Cartoon characters, product logos and packaging are now seen again and again, but except for a few classics, these too tend to mutate or be replaced by something newer on a timescale of a few years to a decade.

Favourite clothes and, perhaps even more so, favourite foods represent a strong source of material-semiotic continuity and constancy in life. Indeed, a favourite recipe or the dish made with it may be among the most long-term repeated semiotic artifacts in life. Personal photographs, or today home videos, may also be counted among the texts that we revisit on the longer timescales of our lives. But notice again that these, like the foods, tend to be themselves rather short texts. The home itself is one of the most important integrating artifacts over the lifespan for many people. Today few people live out their lives in their childhood homes, but many people do live in the same semiotic-material environment for periods on the multidecades timescale. Architecture and some furnishing remain over this timescale even as smaller items and decorations change more frequently.

Among the most recurrent texts across individual lives are the ones that also play a role in the integration of the community: for example, television series and film sequels. These are perhaps not quite 'the same text' but they share characters, settings and many elements of style; they are variations on a theme in what could be imagined to be one long text, read at intervals of days to years. Television 'soap operas' have a story continuity and in some cases continuity of characters and even actors that can approach the timescale of a human lifespan (20–30 years). They are also in some sense the longest texts ever created, and they are sustained only by the device of creating an artificial community of people and following them on an almost real-time basis (a half-hour perhaps for each day of their lives) year by year.

To a lesser degree the long-running primetime television series also have this property, though on a timescale of typically five to seven years, but with some series running ten or twelve (for example, in the US, *Bonanza*, *All in the Family*) and even 20 years (*Gunsmoke*). What is sold here is a style, a genre, a text type rather than a single very long text. There is no strong continuity from episode to episode, nor an overall developing plot or story (though developing themes, like potential love interest, or eventual solution of a life- or situational-problem can sustain them over longer periods). It is not the text itself, but the formula, the style of exposition by and for these characters that is 'read' by viewers over the longer timescale. These may not be as close approximations to being single texts as in the case of the soap operas, and it is very much the 'feel' of the programme that is being appreciated/ read. The popularity of these kinds of text, apart from the virtues of any one of them, seems to speak to the need for continuity, for invariances over these timescales in our lives. There are precious few others, except for personal social relationships.

We should also note here the phenomenon of 're-runs', in which exactly the same episode may be re-shown many times in different markets (syndication). Some 'classic' episodes are sold on videotape, and many are seen again and again and by generations of viewers (for example, *Star Trek*, *I Love Lucy*, and so on). These long-lived series do become cultural icons, points of reference, topics of commonality.

Textscales and social scales

Let's take this analysis now to the higher scale of collective or community ecosocial organization. What texts unite the greatest numbers of people in reading them? Apart from the few remaining sacred texts, popular media texts would seem the most widespread by far: television programmes, popular films, popular music and music videos or computer game-worlds. Millions of people are integrated in the sense of sharing common topical referents and attitudes and values toward these texts. It is no longer a question of the common artifact; the textual content is itself transferable and reproducible. This trend is extended by digital media and has links to the shift in social control associated with definitions of 'intellectual property' (that is, semiotic property) vs traditional material property.

What are the largest projects mediated by a single artifact or text? Perhaps small groups collectively producing a single text or drawing, up to perhaps a dozen people all working around the same large diagram or passing copies of the same text around. Beyond this people might work with multiple copies of the same text, but it seems there is a definite point in the scale of complexity of interactions and practices needed to mount a project requiring many people, such that to coordinate all these people, interactions and practices, texts of more than one genre are needed. The largest film projects (for example, *Cleopatra*, *Titanic*) mobilize and coordinate large numbers of people (hundreds to thousands) over timescales of the order of years. There are many semiotic artifacts of many different genres that mediate these large-scale projects (contracts, messages, schedules, sketches, storyboards, and so on). Of these only perhaps the scripts, scene directions, rushes and rough cuts might be considered 'the same text' throughout the process.

What are the timescales across which project integration must occur in cases where we need multiple texts and text-genres to do the job? A project does not require such more complex integration merely by dint of lasting or taking longer; rather projects that require complex integration tend to take longer because they require the coordinated work of a more diverse or heterogeneous network of people and things, mediated in their interactivity by multiple texts and genres. Bazerman's (1999) discussion of functional clusters of genres of written text and my own earlier work (Lemke, 1985) on linking principles of intertextuality (specifically, actional intertextuality) both emphasize that in medium-scale social projects (granting a patent, conducting a trial) not only different texts but different genres of texts are typically and systematically interconnected by their differentiated functions in the activities that constitute the project.

How can we now relate the mode of social control directly to the mode of integration across timescales? From our earlier hypothesis, we can imagine that one dimension of the classification of modes of control has to do with the typical length of mediating texts and the frequency with which we encounter them. Another differentiates according to the maximal span of relevance of any one text and the lifespan of conventions which establish 'sameness' across related texts. A third dimension would be the nature of the content of the texts and how this functions to integrate actions, on what timescales and across what heterogeneity in the network.

A key issue then is the extent to which the detailed content of a text matters at the next higher level of social integration. That level may be buffered or fault-tolerant, so that only some gross average characteristic is abstracted from texts at a lower level, which becomes all that is relevant at the higher level. It does not matter functionally just how we write the messages that schedule people to meet, so long as the meetings take place. But consider the difference between sending people one master schedule for all meetings vs sending them individual messages ahead of each meeting. The former appears to greatly reduce their control over longer timespans, but in fact allows them to plan around the schedule; whereas the latter makes their long-term planning impossible because they never know when the next meeting may be scheduled. This is the difference between service by appointment and being perpetually on call. This is a clear example of a difference in mode of social control being mediated by differences in the mode of textual integration across timescales.

Note that it is a particularly apt example because the detailed content of the message is directly tied to activity: invariance of day, time and place information in and across messages to participants. But there is also indifference at the higher level (where what matters on the longer, institutional timescale is only whether the meeting took place, and whether there was any output from it) to just how the meeting was scheduled. Yet it does matter at the institutional level what long-term attitudes and resentments may develop on the part of individuals who are on call vs participating by advance appointment, and this in turn may affect the content of the meeting, how long it takes for there to be output from it, and indeed whether an individual will continue to participate or not. The loss of an individual may mean the loss of embodied information important to the project, because individuals often carry critical information from activity to activity.

Traversals and social control

Our earlier discussion proposed a historical change from reliance on integration through a particular text, to integration through a text type, genre, style or discourse type, to integration through a strategy of connecting texts of very different types. This also seems to be a move from long texts frequently revisited, to shorter texts rarely revisited (but with text types being frequently revisited), to texts of variable length and type that are not revisited in the same sequence (though perhaps revisited in new sequences), where what *is* frequently revisited now is the connection strategy, or system of intertextual tying, as applied to different sequences among different texts of heterogeneous types. This last case also argues for shorter constituent texts if only because the variety of meaning that can be built by sequences using the same strategy depends on sequence length (for a given heterogeneous text resource base). Because the timescale for the total activity is roughly constant, each unit needs to become shorter.

The paradigm case of this last strategy is *hypertext* (Landow, 1994, 1997; Lemke, 1998b), in which relatively short text-units (Landow's *lexias*) are concatenated in branching systems of multisequential linkages. The user (reader-writer, meaning-maker) makes a traversal through the hypertext (that is, through the whole relational textual database, the resource system which enables all the possible traversals) and constructs meaning along the way. This traversal then passes through elements which, in the case of the Web, may be of many different genres, functioning in many different modernist institutions, and of many different media (for example, Lemke, forthcoming (a)).

Social control here corresponds not only to the control of content, which is the same as in prior modes of textual mediation, and to the well-formedness criteria of genre elements, but to the kinds of reasoning and action (cf. Kolb, 1995), including the literacies needed to write valued hypertext (Lemke, 1998c), which new members of the community must obtain as part of their 'cultural capital' (Bourdieu, 1984, 1990).

Imagining these as three 'regimes' of textual mediation of social organization and control, then in the first regime, new texts are very difficult to produce and circulate, and innovation is simply a change in the content of the text. In the second regime, new texts are easy to produce and circulate provided they are of recognized types, but the creation of new types is difficult; innovation is in the form and the content becomes less critical. Higher levels of organization are now buffered against changes in content, but not against changes in form. In the third regime, new text types are relatively easier to produce, and indeed conditions favouring this regime also favour constant innovation in text-types, with relatively little emphasis on content except as a feature of the type (that is, appropriate linguistic register). What is difficult is the production of new intertextual strategies, but not the construction of new sequences that make use of existing intertextual strategies. The higher levels of the system are now buffered against changes in text-type and text content (and more generally in institutional types and activities), but not against changes in intertextual strategy (or transinstitutional culture). Fundamental changes in the system now take place at longer timescales. The types of change at shorter timescales which were formerly significant matter much less at higher scales of organization, if at all.

From the perspective of the cultural capital which is effective and valued in the society, and so the social control which results from inculcation of a habitus (dispositions to action and evaluation) in individuals, we may say that:

- in regime 1, the dominant habitus is one whose cultural capital is tied to the exegesis of a particular text
- in regime 2, the dominant habitus affords cultural capital that is tied to proficiency with the creation of texts of particular discourse formations or types
- in regime 3, the dominant mode of cultural capital enables surfing across many genres, text- and media-types and discourse formations; what is valued is the ability to connect texts and activities, and therefore institutions, in standard ways (cf. intertextual strategies), while what is innovative, and therefore highly controlled, is the production and circulation of new kinds of connection strategy.

In the regime of this newest 'traversals' mode of textual mediation and social integration, it is not the new connections themselves that represent fundamental change (and so threat to stability) in the system at higher levels of organization, but only new strategies for making meaningful connections. It remains to be seen what forms this social control, and resistance to it, will take in the future, but it must certainly be on the agenda of CDA to be prepared to expose the relationships of social power, interest and advantage, and textual mediation of social control in this newly emergent regime.

References

Appadurai, A. (1996) *Modernity at Large: Cultural Dimensions of Globalization*. Minneapolis: University of Minnesota Press.
Bar-Yam, Y. (1997) *Dynamics of Complex Systems*. Cambridge, MA: Perseus Publishing.

Bazerman, C. (1988) *Shaping Written Knowledge*. Madison: University of Wisconsin Press.

Bazerman, C. (1999) *The Languages of Edison's Light: Rhetorical Agency in the Material Production of Technology*. Cambridge, MA: MIT Press.

Bourdieu, P. (1984) *Distinction: A Social Critique of the Judgment of Taste*. Cambridge, MA: Harvard University Press.

Bourdieu, P. (1990) *The Logic of Practice*. Stanford, CA: Stanford University Press.

Chandler, J. and van de Vijver, G. (eds) (2000) *Closure: Emergent Organizations and their Dynamics*. Volume 901, Annals of the NYAS. New York: New York Academy of Science Press.

de Castells, M. (1996) *The Rise of the Network Society*. Oxford: Blackwell.

Foucault, M. (1969) *The Archeology of Knowledge*. New York: Random House.

Gee, J.P., Hull, G. and Lankshear, C. (1997) *The New Work Order: Behind the Language of the New Capitalism*. New York: Westview.

Kolb, D. (1995) *Socrates in the Labyrinth: Hypertext, Argument, Philosophy*. Cambridge, MA: Eastgate Systems.

Kress, G. and van Leeuwen, T. (1996) *Reading Images*. London: Routledge.

Landow, G. (ed.) (1994) *Hyper/Text/Theory*. Baltimore: Johns Hopkins University Press.

Landow, G. (1997) *Hypertext 2.0*. Baltimore: Johns Hopkins University Press.

Latour, B. (1987) *Science in Action*. Cambridge, MA: Harvard University Press.

Lemke, J.L. (1985) 'Ideology, intertextuality, and the notion of register', in J.D. Benson and W.S. Greaves (eds), *Systemic Perspectives on Discourse*. Norwood, NJ: Ablex, pp. 275–94.

Lemke, J.L. (1995) *Textual Politics: Discourse and Social Dynamics*. New York: Taylor & Francis.

Lemke, J.L. (1998a) 'Multiplying meaning: visual and verbal semiotics in scientific text', in J.R. Martin and R. Veel (eds), *Reading Science*. London: Routledge, pp. 87–113.

Lemke, J.L. (1998b) 'Hypertext semantics'. Paper presented at the International Congress of Systemic-Functional Linguistics, Cardiff, 1998. Online at <http://academic.brooklyn.cuny.edu/education/jlemke/webs/hypertext/tsld001.htm>.

Lemke, J.L. (1998c) 'Metamedia literacy: transforming meanings and media', in D. Reinking, L. Labbo, M. McKenna and R. Kiefer (eds), *Handbook of Literacy and Technology*. Hillsdale, NJ: Lawrence Erlbaum, pp. 283–301.

Lemke, J.L. (2000a) 'Opening up closure: semiotics across scales', in J. Chandler and G. van de Vijver (eds), *Closure: Emergent Organizations and their Dynamics*. Volume 901, Annals of the NYAS. New York: New York Academy of Science Press, pp. 100–11.

Lemke, J.L. (2000b) 'Material sign processes and ecosocial organization', in P.B. Andersen, C. Emmeche and N.O. Finnemann-Nielsen (eds), *Downward Causation: Self-Organization in Biology, Psychology, and Society*. Denmark: Aarhus University Press, pp. 181–213.

Lemke, J.L. (2000c) 'Across the scales of time: artifacts, activities, and meanings in ecosocial systems', *Mind, Culture, and Activity*, 74, pp. 273–90.

Lemke, J.L. (2002a) 'Multimedia genres for science education and scientific literacy', in M. Schleppegrell and M.C. Colombi (eds), *Developing Advanced Literacy in First and Second Languages*. Mahwah, NJ: Lawrence Erlbaum, pp. 21–44.

Lemke, J.L. (2002b) 'Discursive technologies and the social organization of meaning, *Folia Linguistica*, 35(1–2), pp. 79–96. (Special issue)

Olson, D.R. (1994) *The World on Paper*. New York: Cambridge University Press.

Salthe, S.N. (1985) *Evolving Hierarchical Systems.* New York: Columbia University Press.
Salthe, S.N. (1993) *Development and Evolution.* Cambridge, MA: MIT Press.
Shapin, S. and Schaffer, S. (1985) *Leviathan and the Air-Pump.* Princeton, NJ: Princeton University Press.
Star, S.L. and Griesemer, J.R. (1989) 'Institutional ecology, "translations" and boundary objects: amateurs and professionals in Berkeley's Museum of Vertebrate Zoology, 1907–39', *Social Studies of Science,* 19, pp. 387–420.
Stengers, I. (1997) *Power and Invention: Situating Science.* Minneapolis: University of Minnesota Press.

8
Identities in Flux: Arabs and Jews in Israel

Marcelo Dascal

> The maxims of philosophers concerning the conditions under which
> public peace is possible shall be consulted by nations armed for war.
>
> Immanuel Kant
>
> When you know someone's race, you know nothing [about her].
>
> Toni Morrison

Preliminary considerations

I am not a sociologist, nor a political scientist, nor a jurist, nor a specialist in the affairs of the Arab minority in Israel. Although I have some training in linguistics, especially in the pragmatic analysis of discourse, I suppose I was invited to participate in the interdisciplinary 'think tank' that led me to write this chapter in my capacity as a practitioner of philosophy.[1] As such, I – for one – don't necessarily disregard the 'facts', nor do I make a point of suggesting 'unrealistic' ideas. But I can allow myself a measure of methodological freedom in taking some distance from strict subservience to a narrowly understood 'realism'. This freedom grants a philosopher the possibility of putting forth for discussion what seem to be fantastic or utopian proposals, if judged from the perspective of the present circumstances. It is my belief that, if such proposals meet the condition of being at least conceptually sound (that is, if they could exist in some possible world, where circumstances would be reasonably different), it is not unreasonable to hope that they may, ultimately, materialize. Even if they don't, they may be worth elaborating, discussing and, eventually, fighting for.

Philosophy, as I understand it, is essentially a *critical* endeavour, an effort to detect and clear up conceptual difficulties that are often responsible for what seem to be insurmountable obstacles for the solution of practical conflicts. At the level of theoretical research, the conflict between different theories may engender debates of the kind I call, in a technical sense, 'controversies', which are in my view the actual engine of intellectual progress, for they create the critical conditions for conceptual innovation.[2] However, when conflict

150

involves practical issues of existential importance, it may have – on the contrary – a paralysing effect, rigidifying and further polarizing the opposing positions, thereby preventing conceptual creativity and, therefore, the solution of the conflict. But it is precisely in these cases that an effort must be made to distance oneself from the prevalent stereotypical patterns of thought in order to find ways to reconceptualize the conflict and eventually solve it. Insofar as the conflict that is the object of the present discussion is extremely acute and cause of much suffering, I consider the analysis and eventual removal of conceptual problems that block its solution as a task of primary importance.[3]

I am happy that this task has been undertaken by an interdisciplinary and interethnic group of researchers, and I am profoundly grateful for the opportunity of being a member of this group. Our meetings have been extraordinarily rich in many respects. They have been open, sincere, sometimes even moving – as a true meeting of persons (not only of minds) should be. Although many of us came with previously established opinions about many of the issues discussed and some were quite sceptical about the value of such meetings, the discussion contributed to a better understanding of the various positions, and in some cases may also have contributed to significant changes in them. This demonstrates a willingness to listen and to understand, to make clear one's thought in the light of objections and to endeavour to come to mutual understanding, which is a precondition to agreeing on anything.[4]

Furthermore, in the course of our discussions, it became apparent that the participants did not range themselves according to the usual ethnic or political allegiances that prevail in public as well as semi-public similar meetings in Israel and elsewhere. The atmosphere of intellectual freedom and honesty permitted the emergence of important divergences and of a variety of nuances that are overshadowed in the publicly issued declarations. This fact not only illustrated the non-monolithic character of each 'bloc'. It also showed the insufficiency of such simplistic formulae to express the complexity and rich conceptual texture of the issues they are supposed to deal with. In this respect, the meetings encouraged me to perform the kind of critical analysis that follows.

Interdisciplinarity: difficulties and hopes

Although I have chosen in this chapter to approach this task at a somewhat abstract level, that is, via conceptual analysis, it should be obvious that, given its magnitude and complexity, it should be handled in an interdisciplinary way. In fact, concepts are intimately connected with their linguistic expression – both lexical and discursive – and the critical analysis of discourse should be the natural ally of the critical analysis of concepts. I say 'should' because, unfortunately, this is not always the case. In the present chapter, for example, I could not avail myself of discursive data nor the critical analysis thereof.

Although sociologists such as Sammy Smooha have studied extensively the attitudes of the Arab minority in Israel and their change over time, their main concern naturally is not the quality of the linguistic data. I am in the awkward position of preaching interdisciplinarity and not being able to implement it, for although I mention other relevant disciplines, such as discourse analysis, sociology, anthropology, psychology, literary studies, political science and history, my chapter ultimately remains narrowly philosophical in scope. This kind of failure – and this is not to excuse myself for it – is in fact quite widespread as far as interdisciplinary research is concerned. The reason for that may lie in the inherent difficulties of interdisciplinarity.

One of the major problems interdisciplinary work has to face is its attitude towards the disciplines involved in it. As a joint endeavour involving specialists coming from different disciplines, can it challenge the 'authority' of such specialists or disciplines in their respective fields? Suppose that in a cognitive science conference a linguist presents evidence supporting his or her theory about the evolution of grammar. Is a neuroscientist entitled to question the data, their interpretation, and the conclusion they are supposed to support?[5] If the answer is negative, then the joint endeavour is interdisciplinary only in a relatively mild sense. What is aimed is to compound, in a Cartesian spirit, the results obtained authoritatively by each of the disciplines through the use of its own methods and procedures. It is assumed that these results should be compatible and complement each other. No enlightenment is expected from the discussion or criticism, by practitioners of another discipline, of one's procedures, presuppositions or theories. Consequently, the dialogue hardly becomes dialectical, and the exchange of ideas remains rather limited in scope.

If, however, the answer is positive, a deeper interaction may arise. Through the eyes of the other discipline's partner, one may be led to see conceptual, methodological, or other limitations of one's disciplinary matrix, which otherwise might remain unnoticed because they are grounded in a disciplinary praxis that acquired the weight of tradition and authority. When mutual questioning across disciplines becomes possible, the rigid conceptual frameworks of each discipline are likely to be challenged in spite of the authority they are inveighed, giving rise to more subtle conceptual hybridizations, eventually more appropriate for dealing with the complex phenomena the interdisciplinary endeavour was undertaken for. Under such conditions, the emergence of what might be better termed 'transdisciplinarity' may occur.

Dichotomies and beyond

The positions presented in our discussions were framed in terms of dichotomous categories, such as universalism vs particularism, democracy vs ethnicity, trust vs suspicion, 'israelization' vs 'palestinization', identification vs identity, cultivation of difference vs assimilation, equality vs discrimination, strategic vs tactical goals and so on. In terms of such oppositions, contradictions were detected and dilemmas were formulated, both of whose horns were shown to be equally destructive. On the basis of such dichotomies and the dilemmas they engendered, violent confrontation appeared sometimes to be the only possibility ahead.

But the discussion sometimes also disclosed dissatisfaction with – and thereby the insufficiency of – the dichotomies on which it was based. In one meeting, the social worker Hawla Abu-Bakr argued that israelization is not necessarily opposed to palestinization. In another, the political scientist Yaron Ezrahi pointed out the changes that are taking place – for example, in Europe – in the concepts of citizenship and sovereignty and their impact on the range of possible relations between ethnic identities and statehood. In yet another, the jurist Ruth Gabizon argued – analysing the case of the school system in Jaffa – that the demands for equality in the allocation of resources, in the quality of education and in free access by children to all schools are justified strategic goals in the struggle for full equality, but they may conflict in practice with each other, so that the achievement of one of them may require at least the tactical postponement of the others. Regardless of whether her tactical considerations are correct or not, I think her analysis shows that 'equality' is not a monolithic notion, which either applies fully or doesn't apply at all.

I submit that we should try to pursue and deepen this process of 'de-dichotomization' that some of us have so far inadvertently applied to the categories we used in our discussions. This will reveal that most of the concepts that are crucial for the conflict we are analysing and its eventual solution are not 'classical' concepts, definable in terms of necessary and sufficient conditions, but rather 'cluster concepts', to which other forms of 'definition' are more appropriate.[6]

I will try to show that, if we employ these conceptual tools instead of their more traditional counterparts, we may be able to formulate an acceptable conception of a pluralistic society – which is, I believe, what all the participants in this group are somehow trying to reach. In such a society, both the required partnership between the different groups and the legitimacy of their (sometimes deep) differences may find their place.

How to conceptualize identity?

For brevity's sake, I will limit myself to one example, which is – I believe – illustrative of the whole set of key concepts (for example, 'democracy', 'autonomy', 'equality', 'Jew', 'Arab') we have been employing in these discussions. I have deliberately chosen the concept of 'identity', one of the most emotionally laden of the lot, because even if my analysis is incorrect, it might perhaps help to deflate a bit the emotional charge of this term.

The term 'identity' derives from the Latin *idem* – 'the same', which denotes a relation. Strictly speaking, a thing can bear this relation only to itself. The logical 'principle of identity' spells this out by allowing us only to say 'A is identical to A'. If B has *any* property that A does not have, then A and B cannot be 'the same'. The logico-metaphysical 'principle of the identity of indiscernibles', due to G.W. Leibniz, asserts that 'two' things that share all their properties are not two, but one and the same. On this view, the 'identity' of a thing is simply the set of *all* its properties and since a thing *is* the set of all its properties, its identity is not something the thing 'has'; it is the thing itself.

Obviously, when we speak of personal, professional, intellectual, ideological, collective, ethnic, cultural, national, political, and so on, identities, we are departing from the strict logico-metaphysical notion described above. For we are talking about subsets of properties that define a person's personal, professional, collective, ethnic, and so on, identities. To say that each of these subsets 'defines' an identity is traditionally taken to mean that each of the properties in the subset is a necessary condition and all of them together are a sufficient condition for possession of that identity. Furthermore, such definitions are not merely 'nominal', for they are supposed to capture the 'essence' of the identity they define. In this capacity, they should not include 'accidental' properties. Essential properties are supposed to be fixed (or at least fairly stable), intrinsically important and shared by all members of the class possessing the identity in question, whereas accidental ones are variable, peripheral and not shared by all the members of the class.[7]

Identity conceived in this way is usually assumed to be 'essential' also in a stronger sense, according to which not any set of necessary and sufficient properties (for example, those appearing in a passport or identity card) can be used to define identity. Only a special set of selected properties will do, for identity is taken to capture what grants unity and uniqueness to an entity, functioning as the substrate of that entity. In this sense, as a condition for the existence of the entity in question, which it defines exclusively, identity must be kept absolutely 'coherent', 'pure' and 'homogeneous', and diversity or plurality within it cannot be tolerated. National identity in times of war and in dictatorial regimes is often conceived in this way. For example, in the wake of the Spanish Civil War, statements such as the following ones, by ideologues of the Franco regime, were not uncommon:

> To tolerate diversity of points of view or philosophical conceptions would lead to the destruction of Spain. We will not allow this to happen to Spain ... We do not descend in any way from any posture that represents a partial attitude; following the war that has put an end to the possibility of various Spains, all assumed to be equal, ... we are positioned in the straight line of the only possible Spain ... (Pérez Embid, 1949, p. 149ff.)

> We have to maintain now in full swing the homogeneity obtained in 1939 ... We have to put an end to the pact of heterodoxies by eliminating

discrepancies. Dialogue yes; but only in order to convince, to assimilate. Therefore there can be no hesitation in the repulsion of those elements that make themselves inassimilable by the unitary, national and orthodox tradition. (Calvo Serer, 1949, p. 167)[8]

The Lebanese-French writer Amin Maalouf has felicitously dubbed 'murderous' any identity characterized in these terms (Maalouf, 1998). According to him, those who employ this notion of identity – and they are not confined to dictatorial regimes – in fact demand from individuals and groups to 'define themselves', to find out 'who they are at bottom', that is, to make up their minds about which of the many components that contribute to their identity is *the* dominant, essential or decisive one. In so doing, they presuppose that, unless such a choice is made, a person or a group is maimed at the deepest level, that of identity. But this is only so, he argues, if one uncritically makes use of a 'narrow, exclusionary, bigotry-based, simplistic conception that reduces identity to only one of its components', which then becomes 'an instrument of exclusion and sometimes an instrument of war' (ibid., pp. 14, 205). As opposed to that, he proclaims his own multiple belonging to different cultures, languages, ethnicities, traditions and nations, and defends the legitimacy of an alternative conception of a plural identity, where no component is required to be the most essential one.

Literature abounds with novels where the plurality of the components or an individual's (or group's) identity and their complex interrelations are explored. Thus, Maalouf himself depicts in his historical novels individuals that lived at the crossroads of different cultures, religions, languages or historical periods, that travelled widely and whose self was ultimately shaped by all such encounters.[9] Carlos Fuentes, in his 1967 novel *Change of Skin*, explores the mixed composition and fluidity of the identities of four individuals and two couples, in a plot that takes place in the pyramid of Cholula, a sacred place for all ancient Mexican religions, against the background of a modern Mexico unable to 'define' its identity (Fuentes, 1991). Juan Goytisolo, who lived in exile during Franco's dictatorship, reveals in *Signs of Identity* how what seemed to be the monolithic shared identity of the young members of an anti-Franco group is retrospectively called into question when many years later one of them comes back from exile to visit his friends.[10]

The natural tendency is to single out cases where plurality presents itself as a problem, which again presumes that the 'normal' state of affairs is a homogeneous and unitary identity, individual or collective, conceptualized the essentialistic terms. But why should we assume that this is the case?

The truth is that this way of characterizing identities does not fit the actual, 'natural' use of the concepts to which it is supposed to apply. From the moment we are born, our personal identity is changing, incorporating new elements and dropping old ones. A rigid, unchangeable identity seems to be the exception rather than the rule. Consider a 'cultural identity', for example. It is supposed to comprise a rich gamut of contents, including historical facts and myths, heroic figures, rituals, a canonical literature, language, gastronomic habits, holidays, typical patterns of behaviour, and so on. Each of these contents, however, may vary considerably across individuals who see themselves as belonging to a certain cultural tradition, that is, as rightfully representing a given 'cultural identity'. If we tried to define such an identity in essentialistic terms, we would be forced to determine the precise nature of each of the contents mentioned, under the constraint that they should be shared by all the members of the class. In all likelihood, we would at best end up with either a content-rich but arbitrary definition or with a content-impoverished, merely 'formal' or 'nominal' definition. The former would exclude most of the members, whereas the latter would fail to do justice to the significance the concept 'cultural identity' is supposed to have. Similar difficulties arise with the concepts of 'national identity', 'ethnic identity', and so on.

One might be tempted to view such difficulties as supporting the view that all such identities are spurious constructs, devoid of any significance whatsoever. This, in turn, would support the universalistic claim that the groups allegedly defined by means of such 'identities' cannot aspire to have any epistemic and, a fortiori, moral status and that, consequently, loyalty to them – that is, 'patriotism' – is nothing but 'the last refuge of the scoundrel'.[11]

Another possibility is to acknowledge that the concepts under discussion are not 'classical' ones and to apply to them a different notion of concept. To make a long story short, a concept such as 'cultural identity' would consist in a cluster of properties such that: (a) none of them is a necessary condition for its correct application and (b) any 'reasonably weighty' set of them is sufficient for its correct application. Not all the properties in the cluster have the same 'weight' or 'centrality', so that only subsets of properties containing at least some relatively central properties will satisfy the 'reasonably weighty' requirement. Also, the set is not closed or fixed: in the course of the concept's evolution, some properties may enter the cluster and others may leave it; and the degree of centrality of a property may also vary historically. What preserves the concept's stability or 'identity' is only a certain amount of diachronic overlapping between its different synchronic 'stages'.

On this account, there is no single subset of properties – no 'common denominator' – shared by all individuals displaying a given 'cultural identity'. It is unlikely, but possible, that two individuals who rightfully claim to possess 'the same' cultural identity in fact base their claims on non-overlapping subsets of properties underlying that concept. It is more likely, though, that the intersection between the subsets is not empty. In either case, 'cultural identity' is based on a relation Wittgenstein has dubbed 'family resemblance', according to which, although no single trait or group of traits is shared by all family members, a network of similarities between 'neighbouring' members allows one to view the whole set as a 'family'.

Admittedly, concepts characterized in this way are not as crispy as 'classical' concepts, for they don't possess clear boundaries and a tight unity. But they fit better the dynamic, fluid and relatively loose character of the concepts of identity (and related ones) we currently use. To be sure, under the pressure to make 'clear' public statements in a one-minute TV spot, one tends to simplify matters and to resort to the 'classical' formulations of these concepts. But in discussions such as ours we have a duty to seek the most adequate conceptual tools, no matter how time-consuming and complex their use turns out to be.

Horizons

Suppose I am right about the nature of the concept(s) of identity and other concepts that have played a key role in our discussions. What new horizons for the relations between Arabs and Jews in Israel does this afford?

First, it contributes to the realization by each of the two groups that their respective collective 'identities' (cultural, ethnic, national) are much more multifarious, fluid, looser and even conflict-ridden than their pompous declarations would wish the other side to believe. To be sure, both sides are aware that this is the case: after all, Israeli Arabs watch daily the skirmishes of the 'culture wars' among the Jews, and many Israeli Jews know that something similar is going on among their Arab neighbours. But somehow, due to the prevalence of the classical conceptual model (which fits stereotypical, lazy thinking), each side tends to believe in a basic underlying unity (in its own and in the other side's 'identity') capable of overcoming these 'superficial' divergences. Calls for unity on both sides tend to sustain this belief. Once an alternative conceptual model is available, according to which collective identities are intrinsically *not* tight, cohesive concepts, it can help to conceptualize and legitimize, rather than to oversimplify and ultimately deny, a situation that de facto obtains and is known to obtain.

Second, such a change in perception may reduce the feeling, which exists on both sides, of being threatened by the other side. Only a cohesive and unitary 'identity' can function as an agent capable of acting conspiratorially to undermine the position of the 'enemy'. The many voices and trends characteristic of a looser 'identity' make this much harder, especially when the doubts and arguments of such voices are likely to be the object of fierce public debate.

Third, with a reduction of the level of mutual threat, the force of 'slippery slope' arguments ('give them a finger, tomorrow they'll take the whole hand'; 'the domino effect', and so on) is reduced as well. Consequently, it becomes harder for the Jewish majority to oppose the granting of some form of autonomy to the Arab population, on the grounds that it would be a step towards a 'binational' state. Similarly, the Arab minority would be hard put to reject such proposals as that of an eventual 'civil or military service' law for all Israeli citizens on the grounds that it would mean 'capitulation'.

Fourth, stereotypical self-perception and other-perception becomes more difficult, if not altogether impossible, once collective (and personal) identities are no longer conceived in terms of a few shared defining traits. Each individual, on each side, can be perceived as legitimately choosing and constructing a personal and collective identity, not easily reducible to the 'identities' that can be picked up from extant conceptual shelves.[12] No one can be put in a predetermined and simplified box. The phrases 'Some of my best friends are Arabs' and 'Some of my best friends are Jews' lose, accordingly, their pejorative resonance and come to reflect the actual interplay of multiple-trait identities.

Fifth, in-group and out-group differences are expected on this model and, therefore, they become admissible, that is, 'tolerated'. This lays down the basis for a minimal pluralism. If, later on, differences are not only admitted, but also valued, a more substantive version of pluralism becomes possible.[13]

Sixth, different collective identities defined as clusters of properties are not isolated entities. They may share *memes* (the cultural counterparts of *genes*).[14] Groups in close interaction undergo processes of 'assimilation' (absorption of large numbers of 'alien' *memes* and their rise to a position of centrality, at the expense of the 'native' *memes*) and 'differentiation' (decrease in the number of 'alien' *memes* and rise to centrality of the 'native' ones). Both processes are part and parcel of normal cultural evolution and usually they co-occur. In this sense, 'israelization' and 'palestinization' of the Arabs in Israel, just as 'arabization' or 'levantinization' and 'jewification' of the Jews in Israel, are two faces of cultural evolution, which are not necessarily contradictory. Whether the one or the other will be enhanced in the short run depends, to some extent, on the political guidance of the leadership of both sides, but in the long run these are processes that can hardly be avoided.

Seventh, the sharing of *memes* by different collective identities enhances the possibility of mutual understanding. In particular, it is one of the means whereby members of one group can place themselves 'in the place of the other', that is, to try to see things from the other's point of view.[15] This is not an easy matter, for one either is obfuscated by the uniqueness of one's own experience, or one simply projects one's way of thinking and behaving onto the other's situation, thereby minimizing the possibly deep behavioural and cognitive differences involved, or both. Sometimes, however, with enough courage and intellectual perspicacity, such difficulties may be overcome. Ehud Barak's recent statement about enlisting in a 'terror' organization were he born a Palestinian, and Edward Said's recent acknowledgement of the profound difference between the (Jewish) Shoah and the (Palestinian) Naqba, are courageous public expressions of this phenomenon. Both demonstrate the possibility of viewing things 'from the place of the other', on the basis of an acknowledgement both of the uniqueness of that place and of its similarity to one's own place.

Eighth, in terms of the conceptual model proposed, a commitment by a minority (willing to preserve its distinctive collective identity) to the 'common good' of the citizenship of a state need not be interpreted as a commitment to a differentiating subset of traits in the majority's collective identity. Rather, commitment can be addressed to a minimal set of shared traits, or even to a neutral framework, not necessarily identified as the 'expression' of the majority's collective identity. Due to the majority–minority asymmetry, the majority has an obligation to avoid as much as possible the identification of the state's framework with traits that preclude the possibility of the minority's commitment to it.

Prospects

Someone may agree with all I said on the abstract conceptual level, and yet doubt whether this has anything to do with the grim realities of the problematic situation in which we are entrapped or with a realistic assessment of possible ways to escape from the trap. I could even be blamed with proposing utopian ideas precisely as a device designed to avoid confrontation with the actual problem.[16] I might retort that, however utopian they seem to be at first, ideas have sometimes the power to stir social change and thereby to shape reality. Or, taking a detached philosophical stance, I might simply leave the issue of realism to those who have studied the situation empirically and know its current details, recent evolution and predictable trends much better than I do. But I am also a concerned citizen of this country. As such, I owe myself, my children, our discussion group and the public at large at least some clue about my assessment of the prospects that the conceptual model proposed here might work. Any such assessment must take into account those factors working against its implementation as well as those favouring it.

Let me begin with the former. The first major obstacle is the resilience of the traditional forms of categorization. I have urged 'de-dichotomization', but the usual dichotomies are alive and well. Much of what I propose is predicated on the basis of a more flexible notion of concepts, but people persist in seeking strict defining traits, in terms of which neat inclusion and exclusion rules can be formulated and absolute contradictions pointed out.[17] Instead of acknowledging the inner complexity and diversity of concepts such as 'democracy' or 'national identity', the assumption that they have some unifying 'essence' goes unchallenged.[18] In an age that has proclaimed 'the death of ideologies', it is amazing to see how the vocabulary and tenets of old ideologies infiltrate current political talk and, presumably, thought.[19]

The second obstacle I see is the resurgence and exacerbation of nationalism in some parts of the contemporary world. Surely there are several reasons for this fact. One of them, which is important from the perspective of this chapter, is its presumable connection with the process of 'modernization'. As pointed out already by Tönnies at the close of the nineteenth century, the modernization of society entails the dissolution of 'organic' communities (the village, the extended family, and so on). As a consequence, the security and pre-established identities they afford to individuals are lost. As society moves from 'closed' to 'open', as individual mobility grows, the need for alternative poles of collective identification increases and 'national identity' comes to fulfil this function. The apparently successful satisfaction of this need by nation-states, along with the apparent failure to satisfy them in any other political arrangement, leads to a demand for 'national self-determination' in the form of either an independent nation-state or of national autonomy within existing states, by those groups that did not achieve either of them. Whatever its sources, what this phenomenon means in terms of our model is that 'national identity' occupies presently a central position in the cluster of features that defines a person's identity – especially when one belongs to a group that has recently suffered a major national catastrophe. This central position tends to become so dominant that it is often equated with the 'essence' of a group's collective identity. Unless it is satisfied, the satisfaction of any other of the traits of identity is deprived of significance. There seems to be no possible trade-off between them. Under such circumstances, the flexibility of the cluster model seems to be reduced to nil.

A third major obstacle, related to the former, is the natural fear of a completely open society, where individuals must make career, family, group, identity, way of life and other choices. Deciding, especially about such crucial matters, is a painful process, and it is natural that many will long for some framework where such choices are made for them.[20] Hence the attraction of a return to 'closed' frameworks that protect one's life from the dangers of 'openness', which is often equated with permissiveness and corruption of 'true values'. A generalized or specific 'other' is viewed as the agent of such a corruption, and strict insulation (of the other or of one's own community) is the remedy. Religious fundamentalism is only the most extreme form of such a tendency, but it has milder forms as well. Needless to say, the rise of this trend is a powerful obstacle to the implementation of the conceptual model I have proposed.

A fourth and last obstacle I would like to mention is the idea expressed by the expression 'identity crisis', widely used in referring to the situation of the Arabs in Israel. The crisis consists in being pulled in two opposite and irreconcilable directions, between which one is not free to choose. The implication is that, unless one opts for a well-defined and rounded-off identity clearly expressed by the choice of one or the other direction, one faces some sort of deficiency that ought to be overcome. This way of conceptualizing the situation clearly precludes alternatives based on some sort of combination of the two allegedly contradictory directions.

Let us turn now briefly to what seem to be factors that are favourable to the implementation of the cluster model. First, the persistence of the use of rigid categorizations simply seems to indicate that the conceptual tools of those who stick to the old dichotomies still lag behind the 'facts of life'.

The multifaceted and cluster nature of the key social notions we have mentioned in this chapter is a fact which researchers are slowly bringing to the fore and exploring, even when they do not make use of such trendy labels as 'multiculturalism', 'transnationalism' or just 'pluralism'.[21]

Second, openness of course does not imply permissiveness. Quite the contrary: since it leads the individual to make choices, it requires the exercise of the individual's autonomy and the development of the critical skills and knowledge necessary for that. True, this requirement is not easy to fulfil, and the failure to do so may lead to tragic consequences. But is the solution shutting the windows, closing one's eyes, and insulating oneself and especially one's children from the open world? Openness implies more, not less responsibility, more willingness and capacity to exercise one's right to choose one's own destiny. This does not mean the wholesale delegitimization of traditional forms of life and human groups. An 'open' society need not, by fear of falling back in tribal 'closure', become 'abstract' and deny the legitimacy of 'organic' groupings with which individuals identify.[22] The 'culture wars', insofar as what is at stake in them is to conquer the identification of individuals, must take into account *all* the components of personal identity, *all* the needs an 'identity' is expected to fulfil. In this respect, the Arab and Jewish champions of 'modernization', who employ the easy delegitimizing rhetoric revealed by the use of such terms as 'backwards', 'medieval', 'conservative', 'traditional', 'primitive', and so on, reveal also their lack of understanding of their own cause and thereby do more disservice than service to it.[23]

At any rate, the option of closure, however tempting it may be for some people, is not really viable in our digital age – and this is the third factor I would like to mention. I am speaking not only of the process of cultural, social and economic 'globalization', but also of the vehicle through which it will be accelerated beyond our imagination, namely the incredible facility of access to any sort of information by anyone having a computer and a telephone line. We are on the verge of becoming what Javier Echeverría (1995) has felicitously dubbed 'domestic cosmopolites'. Soon, without leaving our home (*domus*) we will be able to reach not only the local supermarkets, libraries, banks and TV channels, but also all the markets, data banks, financial institutions, and media programmes of the world (*cosmos*). Any attempt to curtail this facility and freedom of digital access will be very difficult, if not altogether impossible to implement.

The last factor I want to mention consists simply in the fact that hyphenated national identities and other forms of hybrid concepts have become a natural part of the social landscape, rather than an anomaly or a disease to be cured. 'Italian-American', 'African-American', 'Malayan-Chinese', 'Russian-Israeli' and 'Israeli-Arab' are no longer expressions that provoke an eyebrow. Whoever watched the last World Cup certainly noticed the hybrid 'nationality' of some of the best teams, and some spectators may have chosen to support one team or another due to his or her identification with *part* of the national identity of a player. In internet MUDs (multiple-user domains), people can experiment with their identities by varying the presentation of their virtual personae in terms of nationality, gender, age, education, profession and other components (cf. Turkle, 1995). I entirely agree with Danny Horowitz (1996) when he points out that the concept 'border line' should be replaced by 'border land' and that the phenomenon of hybrid populations of border lands as well as of diasporas is much more common and widespread than it was hitherto realized.[24] I would add that (a) the phenomenon Horowitz describes is not just a matter of trans-*nationality*, but of diluting and crossing all kinds of conceptual and other border lines; and (b) such forms of hybridization have not yet, perhaps, become the rule, but they are far from being the exception either.

I leave it to the reader to ponder carefully about the relative weight of each of this selection of pro and con considerations in order to reach his or her own assessment. Whatever the conclusion, I trust that this exercise will have brought to the reader's attention aspects of the problem and possibilities of solution he or she may not have thought of before. If this is the case, I will be more than satisfied by having thereby contributed to enriching the debate and, eventually, in helping to make it transcend its current conceptual deadlock.

Notes

1. Thinking team on the relations between 'Jews and Arabs in Israel', The Institute for Israeli–Arab Studies, Ra'anana, with the support of the European Union. The team comprised Arab and Jewish researchers, and held twelve monthly meetings in 1997 and 1998. I wish to thank Yitzchak Reiter and Adel Man'a, organizers of the think tank, for inviting me to participate, and all the participants for the lively discussions. The first draft of this chapter was discussed by the team in March 1998. Traces of the comments and critiques will be found in this version. I apologize for not being able to take into account all the suggestions that were made.
2. For my views on the role of controversies in intellectual progress, see, for example, Dascal (1998, 2000).
3. The Arab population in Israel (in its pre-1967 borders) comprises about 17 per cent of the country's population, that is, about 1.2 million people. As citizens of the state, they are entitled to vote and to be elected, as well as to all other state-provided services. They enjoy a measure of cultural autonomy (Arabic is one of the official languages of Israel, and there is an independent – although not entirely autonomous – Arab educational system), but complain about actual discrimination in several domains (and rightly so, in many cases). The fundamental problem is to reconcile the fact that Israel defines itself as a 'Jewish state' with the fact that a large portion of its citizens are not only non-Jewish, but are such that they identify themselves (ethnically, religiously and nationally) as Palestinians, who are in turn perceived by most Jewish Israelis as the enemies of the Jewish state. The extremely difficult question to be faced is how, under these conditions, Israel's Jewish and Arab citizens can forge a joint identity, acceptable to both groups, that will permit them to coexist democratically and pay allegiance to a state that each will see as 'theirs'.

4. As I prepare this chapter for publication in September 2001, the conditions in our region have deteriorated sharply. The second Intifada rages, along with the inescapable Israeli reprisals. Deep sorrow and anger, which both sides see as fully justified, lead to ever more entrenched positions. Under these conditions, the situation of the Israeli Arabs becomes, naturally, even more complex and difficult, and the basis and usefulness of a dialogue with Israeli Jews seem to be reduced to nil. Yet, I think dialogue continues to be the only realistic option, and the spirit and substance of the debates in our group should continue to serve as a model – especially in the present circumstances.

5. 'Cognitive science' is a label created a few decades ago for a 'federation' of disciplines, including linguistics, cognitive psychology, computer science, philosophy and neuroscience. Although there are already, in addition to research centres, also departments, programmes of study, and degrees bearing this label, it turns out that the disciplinary borders between the members of the federation are – in my opinion – as entrenched as ever.

6. The notion of 'cluster concepts' is borrowed from the work of the philosopher of science Peter Achinstein, who developed it in order to deal with the so-called 'natural kinds' concepts (cf. Achinstein, 1968). Other ways of showing the flexibility of concepts, as opposed to the rigidity ascribed to them by the classical view, include, for example, the description of the set or class defined by a concept in terms of a notion of 'gradual' or partial rather than discrete or 'yes-or-no' set-membership. This notion can be formalized by means of a version of non-standard logic called 'fuzzy logic', due to F. Zadeh. The idea of applying fuzzy logic to the Israeli–Palestinian conflict first occurred to me in conversations with my colleague Shaul Mishal. I want to thank Shaul for his receptiveness to the idea that non-standard ways of conceptualization are needed to understand and creatively imagine solutions for this thorny conflict.

7. For example, the property 'is an inhabitant of Jaffa', though currently applying to the author of this chapter, will not be considered part of his 'personal identity' – otherwise he would have had a different personal identity when he inhabited São Paulo, Jerusalem or Kiryat Ono. Or the property 'has a Greek nose' is unlikely to be part of the 'Greek identity' – otherwise a Greek gentleman who undergoes plastic surgery to modify his nose would thereby lose his national identity.

8. I am grateful to Quintín Racionero for this and the preceding quote.

9. See for example, his novels *Léon l'Africain* (1983), *Samarcande* (1988), *Les jardins de lumière* (1991), *Le périple de Baldassare* (2000).

10. Here is a passage of this novel worth quoting for its human and political insight: 'Your efforts of reconstitution and synthesis stumbled in a grave obstacle. Through the documents and testimony kept in the folders you could dust your memory of the events and incidents that you had considered lost and that, recovered from oblivion illuminated not only your biography, but also dark and revealing facets of life in Spain ..., but, due to your voluntary expatriation ..., the earlier communion had disappeared ... your own adventure and that of your homeland had taken different paths; you were headed towards one direction, after the ties that had linked you to the tribe were broken ...; the homeland headed towards another direction, with the group of your friends who persevered in the noble endeavor to transform it, paying with their bodies the price that you, by indifference or cowardice, had refused to pay ... Your memory was empty after twenty years of exile. How to rebuild without damage the lost unity?' (Goytisolo, 1966 [2001], p. 136; my translation.)

11. Elsewhere I have discussed this position, arguing for the moral status of loyalty to human groups that fulfil certain conditions (Dascal, 1977).

12. For a clear exposition and defence of the role of 'cultural choice' in constructing identities, see Tamir (1996).

13. On the distinction between these two senses of tolerance and their implication for inter-cultural relations, see Dascal (1989, 1991).

14. The notion of a '*meme*' was introduced by Richard Dawkins (1976) and has been extensively applied to the cultural sphere by Daniel Dennett (1995).

15. On the moral, political and epistemological importance of the maxim 'Put yourself in the place of the other', see Dascal (1993, 1995).

16. A strategy Karl Mannheim dubbed 'escape into the future', contrasting it with the appeal to 'ideology', which he called 'escape into the past' (Mannheim, 1936).

17. For example, Azmi Beshara, a philosopher and Arab member of the Israeli parliament, rejects the concept of a 'double identity' of Israeli Arabs, and claims that to be an Israeli and to be a Palestinian represents a contradiction 'at the heart of' their identity (Beshara, 1993). Yehoshua Porat, following a similar kind of logic, stresses the all-or-none character of the expression 'a country of/for all its citizens', which Beshara has promoted to central stage in Israeli political debate. According to Porat, this expression implies equality of rights but also of duties, as well as linguistic and cultural uniformity (Porat, 1998).

18. In a recent TV interview, the writer Naomi Frankel, who lives in the small Jewish quarter in the West Bank city of Hebron, was asked whether the Jewish settlements in the West Bank were not 'ideological'. Her reply was a flat 'No.' When further asked whether the fact that the settlements were based on the claim that Jews ought to take hold of the whole Land of Israel was not ideological, her reply was: 'Not at all. This premise is the essence of Judaism.' But consider also the similar uncompromising essentialist position of Haifa's Chief Rabbi, Sha'ar Yishuv Cohen (1998): ' "Jew" is a religious concept ... to be a Jew is to be a member of the Jewish religion.'

19. If, as claimed by Martin Kramer (1996), Arab nationalism or pan-Arabism 'has been finally abandoned', should we interpret Azmi Beshara's continuing admiration for Nasser and his talk of 'the great Arab nation' (interview in *Ha'aretz*, 29 May 1998) as a mere anachronism?

20. Walter Kaufmann (1973) has coined the term 'decidophobia' for the fear of making decisions, whose many forms he unveils in his book.

21. For example, the sociologist Eliezer Ben-Rafael describes three basic components in religious Judaism – 'the notions of God of Israel and His Teaching (the Torah), the commitment to a People of Israel, and the allegiance to a set of geo-historical symbols, the concept of the Land of Israel', and contends that the differences between the various forms of religious Judaism lie in 'their relative emphasis on each of the components' (Ben-Rafael, 1996, p. 192). The Jerusalem jurist Ruth Gabizon, in her attempt to demonstrate the compatibility between the predicates 'Jewish' and 'democratic' of the State of Israel, proposes two criteria for handling these predicates: (a) the meaning assigned to them should capture an important element in them, and (b) no given definition of these concepts should be used as a means to decide the normative-political issues on the agenda (Gabizon, 1998, p. 223). Her analysis takes advantage of the fact that the concepts involved comprise many components, which can be structured in different ways, so as to allow for reasonable solutions for such difficult problems as the 'Law of Return', which she proposes to replace by 'legislation that deals with the entrance [into the country]

and acquisition of citizenship making no structural distinction on the basis of nationality' (ibid., p. 276). Such a formulation, I think, matches (and develops) Said Zaidani's careful phrasing of the demand for 'cancellation or replacement of the Law of Return' (Zaidani, 1998, p. 114).

22. Cf. Popper (1966). For a criticism of Popper's tendency to characterize the 'open' society as if it had to be an 'abstract' society, see Dascal (1979).
23. For an analysis of the modalities and roles of delegitimization in conflicts, see Bar-Tal (1990).
24. On the effects of the 'border land' situation on identity dynamics, see the interesting study by Muhammad Amara of the village Barta'a, which was divided in two parts in 1948 and remained 'mentally divided' even after the 1967 physical reunion (Amara, 1996).

References

Achinstein, P. (1968) *Concepts of Science*. Baltimore: Johns Hopkins University Press.
Amara, M. (1996) 'Divided identity: political and social division in a divided village', in S. Ossetsky-Lazar (ed.), *The Jewish–Arab Relations in the State of Israel*. Givat Haviva: Jewish–Arab Center for Peace.
Bar-Tal, D. (1990) 'Causes and consequences of delegitimization: models of conflict and ethnocentrism', *Journal of Social Issues*, 46(1).
Ben-Rafael, E. (1996) 'A paradigm of Jewish identities', in Y. Kashti et al. (eds), *A Quest for Identity: Post War Jewish Biographies*. Tel Aviv University: School of Education, p. 192.
Beshara, A. (1993) 'On the issue of the Palestinian minority in Israel', *Theory and Criticism*, 3.
Calvo Serer, R. (1949) 'España sin problema', *Arbor*, 45–6.
Cohen, S.Y. (1998) ' "Jew" is a religious concept ... to be a Jew is to be a member of the Jewish religion', in T. Harman and E. Ya'ari (eds), *Relationships between Religious and Secular [Jews] in Israel*. Tel Aviv University: The Tami Steinmetz Center for Peace Research.
Dascal, M. (1977) 'Relevant loyalty', in M. Dascal (ed.), *The Just and the Unjust*. Tel Aviv: University Publishing Projects, pp. 29–38.
Dascal, M. (1979) 'Closed society, open society, abstract society', in H. Berghel et al. (eds), *Wittgenstein, the Vienna Circle, and Critical Rationalism*. Vienna: Holder-Pichler-Tempsky, pp. 253–7.
Dascal, M. (1989) 'Tolerance and interpretation', in Z. Rosen and Z. Tauber (eds), *Violence and Tolerance*. Tel Aviv: Papirus, pp. 157–72.
Dascal, M. (1991) 'The ecology of cultural space', in M. Dascal (ed.), *Cultural Relativism and Philosophy*. Leiden: Brill, pp. 279–95.
Dascal, M. (1993) 'One Adam – many cultures: the role of political pluralism in the best of possible worlds', in M. Dascal and E. Yakira (eds), *Leibniz and Adam*. Tel Aviv: University Publishing Projects, pp. 387–409.
Dascal, M. (1995) 'Strategies of dispute and ethics: *Du tort* and *La place d'autruy*', in *Proceedings of the VI. Internationaler Leibniz-Kongress*, Vol. 2, Hannover, pp. 108–16.
Dascal, M. (1998) 'The study of controversies and the theory and history of science', *Science in Context*, 11(2), pp. 147–54.
Dascal, M. (2000) 'Controversies and epistemology', in T.Y. Cao (ed.), *Philosophy of Science* [Vol. 10 of Proceedings of the Twentieth World Congress of Philosophy]. Philadelphia: Philosophers Index Inc., pp. 159–92.
Dawkins, R. (1976) *The Selfish Gene*. Oxford: Oxford University Press.

Dennett, D. (1995) *Darwin's Dangerous Idea*. New York: Simon & Schuster.

Echeverría, J. (1995) *Cosmopolitas Domésticos*. Barcelona: Editorial Anagramma.

Fuentes, C. (1991) *Cambio de Piel*, 5th edition. Barcelona: Seix Barral.

Gabizon, R. (1998) 'A Jewish and democratic state: challenges and dangers', in M. Mauthner et al. (eds), *Multiculturalism in a Democratic and Jewish State*. Tel Aviv University: Ramot, p. 223.

Goytisolo, J. (1966 [2001]) *Señas de Identidad*. Mexico: Mejores Novelas en Castellano del Siglo Joaquín Mortiz.

Horowitz, D. (1996) 'Trans-nationalism as a theoretical framework for studying the Palestinian citizens of Israel', in S. Ossetsky-Lazar (ed.), *The Jewish–Arab Relations in the State of Israel* [Summaries of a Workshop held in May 1996]. Givat Haviva: Jewish–Arab Center for Peace.

Kaufmann, W. (1973) *Without Guilt and Justice: From Decidophobia to Autonomy*. New York: Dell Publishing Co.

Kramer, M. (1996) *Arab Awakening and Islamic Revival*. New Brunswick and London: Transaction Publishers.

Maalouf, A. (1998) *Les identités meutrières*. Paris: Grasset.

Mannheim, K. (1936) *Ideology and Utopia*. London: Routledge & Kegan Paul.

Pérez Embid, F. (1949) 'Ante la nueva actualidad del problema de España', *Arbor*, 45–6.

Popper, K. (1966) *The Open Society and its Enemies*. 2 Vols. London: Routledge & Kegan Paul.

Porat, Y. (1998) 'What is a country of/for all its citizens?', in E. Rekhess (ed.), *The Arabs in Israeli Politics: Dilemmas of Identity*. Tel Aviv University: The Dayan Center for the Study of the Middle East and Africa.

Tamir, Y. (1996) 'Some thoughts concerning the phrase "a quest for identity"', in Y. Kashti et al. (eds), *A Quest for Identity: Post War Jewish Identities*. Tel Aviv University: School of Education.

Turkle, S. (1995) *Life on the Screen: Identity in the Age of the Internet*. New York: Simon & Schuster.

Zaidani, S. (1998) 'The Arabs in the Jewish state: their status in the present and future', in E. Rekhess (ed.), *The Arabs in Israeli Politics: Dilemmas of Identity*. Tel Aviv University: The Dayan Center for the Study of the Middle East and Africa.

9
Political and Somatic Alignment: Habitus, Ideology and Social Practice

Suzanne Scollon

> Before it leaves the lips, every word must be evaluated as to its
> consequences. A smile that appears at the wrong moment, a glance
> that is not all it should be can occasion dangerous suspicions and
> accusations. Even one's gestures, tone of voice, or preference for
> certain kinds of neckties are interpreted as signs of one's political
> tendencies.
>
> Czeslaw Milosz, 'Ketman', *The Captive Mind* (1955 [1981], p. 54)

Political alignment as Soma

Milosz, writing in Poland after World War II, characterizes human comportment and speech in what he calls the 'people's democracies' as acting that takes place wherever one finds oneself, even in the privacy of one's own quarters. Though a degree of acting is part of human relationships everywhere, that in Eastern Europe was 'a conscious mass play rather than automatic imitation' (1955 [1981], p. 55). Conscious acting develops the habitus until 'Proper reflexes at the proper moment become truly automatic.' The game of concealing one's thoughts and feelings in order to protect oneself, one's reputation, and one's relatives was not invented in postwar Poland or Czechoslovakia but was cultivated and termed *ketman* in the Islamic world, where the man of faith protected his faith from exposure to infidels. Though Milosz imagined that in the West the constant conscious cultivation of what he so aptly terms 'reflexes' was not necessary, it is only by comparison that a person from what he calls the Imperium finds people completely relaxed, saying whatever comes to mind, laughing out loud.

As Milosz convincingly argues, political alignment does not arise out of abstract reasoning alone but out of both conscious and unconscious alignments of the body, which merge into stances so natural they assume the nature of reflexes. After a few years in Washington, DC, and Paris as cultural attaché at the Polish Embassy, he depicts Eastern Europeans and Westerners as having different habitus. The acting with which 'everyone plays to everyone else' consists of networks of social practices linked in indirect ways with ideologies. Whether or not the actor is conscious of what he or she is doing, his or her demeanour and dress are interpreted by others, consciously and unconsciously, as indexing political alignment.

Any particular social practice has its phylogenesis within the linked social practices of a community that shares an ideology. *Ketman* is a complex of social practices that evolved both in the Islamic community and the communist countries not only in Eastern Europe but also in China and elsewhere. It is also found in the United States in different forms.[1] An individual who grows up in a community internalizes complexes of social practices tied to its ideology in individual habitus which may be regarded as a compost heap of social practices. When the individual as an adult becomes socialized to a new community with a different configuration of social practices, his or her individual habitus which is the residue of earlier life experience becomes detritus to be worn away to create humus for the ontogenesis of new social practices.

Theory and interdisciplinarity, an eclectic approach

Milosz provides an insider's perspective or member's generalization of postwar Eastern European society as well as an outsider's perspective on postwar American society through interactions with Americans. The concept of *ketman* is foreign to Americans, who assume they operate on the basis of free will, though many fear a return to the political conformism of the McCarthy period.

At the same time that Milosz wrote about *ketman*, Jurgen Ruesch and Gregory Bateson sought to understand the psychological, social and technological changes of the era by examining communication in a social matrix of communication theory, value theory and anthropological statements about culture (Ruesch and Bateson, 1951 [1968]). Their work was part of what they describe in the Preface to the 1968 edition as a convergence of psychiatry, psychology, sociology and anthropology on what became known as behavioural science. They note the emergence of general systems theories in the biological sciences from the convergence of physiology, ecology and ethology.

It was in this social matrix that I trained in psychology and Boasian anthropological linguistics. In my dissertation (S. Scollon, 1982) I used the ethnography of speaking, Batesonian epistemology, Piagetian psychology, Hallidayan linguistics and sociology of knowledge approaches to phenomenology and the construction of reality to argue that values embodied in patterns of socialization affect grammar through linguistic strategies of politeness. That is, it was an examination of the role of communicative patterns in linguistic adaptation and convergence. Central to the analysis was Hymes' (1966) argument for two types of linguistic relativity, which Ron Scollon and I advanced in our account of linguistic convergence among speakers of French, English, Chipewyan and Cree in Fort Chipewyan, Alberta (Scollon and Scollon, 1979). Hymes argued that one cannot simply assume that a language affects the cognition of its

speaker without knowing the circumstances in which the speaker came to use the language in question. We showed that the four languages spoken in the community of Fort Chipewyan had become more like each other and attributed this convergence to the reality set or worldview prevalent among members. In keeping with what we called the 'bush consciousness', speakers were inclined to calque from one language to another rather than maintain separate grammars.

In characterizing the bush consciousness we described a set of social practices relating to the use of language in teaching and learning, practices relating to what Bateson (1942 [1972]) called 'deutero learning' based on the gestalt psychologists' 'learning set'. Responding to an article by Mead (1942) on anthropology and the purposive cultivation of democratic values in which she wrote that as social scientists we need to recognize that 'by working toward defined *ends* we commit ourselves to the manipulation of persons, and therefore to the negation of democracy', Bateson (1942 [1972], p. 159) commented that Mead posed a kind of koan:

> The problem is one of very great difficulty as well as urgency, and it is doubly difficult because we, as scientists, are deeply soaked in habits of instrumental thought ... The problem which Dr. Mead – who envisages a change in such habits – raises is how habits of this abstract order are learned. (ibid., p. 162)

In describing what we called a reality set, we documented how Athabaskans learned habits of non-intervention which in interaction with habits of purposive, instrumental thought produced habits of entropy. The integrative orientation to knowledge implies a holistic mode of learning. In this research we took a genetic approach to behaviour which Cole (1995) termed 'socio-cultural-historical psychology', though our primary concern was not psychological but linguistic. The practices we observed in the field were consistent with what had been reported for Athabaskans in the region by other ethnographers earlier in the century. Relationships between language and cognition or reality were mediated by social practices of deference and holism in contrast to the componentiality of the modern consciousness (Berger et al., 1973). We further documented how our daughter learned habits of the modern consciousness embedded in practices of literacy (Scollon and Scollon, 1981).

From Grace (1981) I borrowed a concept he called the 'idiolect', which represents a synthesis of the individual's experiences with language, what amounts to a person's linguistic habitus. It includes not only knowledge of individual languages but also an interpretation of experiences associated with the use of those languages, such as translating from one to another according to participant structures. As a unit of analysis of language, the idiolect contrasts with the langue and the linguistic resources of a speech community. To discuss language from these three perspectives – langue, idiolect, and speech community – I borrowed the notion of dissipative structures developed by Ilya Prigogine and others in the natural sciences (S. Scollon, 1977). It was a useful model for analysing language and communication in a social matrix of languages, individuals and communities evolving over time.

The process by which the idiolect is formed within a social matrix is compared by Ruesch to the cutting of a river bed. 'The channel is formed by the water, but the river banks also control the direction of flow, so that a system of interaction is established in which cause and effect can no longer be isolated' (Ruesch and Bateson, 1951 [1968], p. 8).

Analogous to Hymes' argument on language and linguistic relativity, I argue that practice in Bourdieu's sense is not monolithic. That is, it makes as little sense to view an individual as having a practice as having a language. Instead, we must look at separate practices, some of which are acquired through the use of one language and others through several languages in different modes. That is, an individual's habitus is not isomorphic with the practice of any particular class. Rather, it is constructed out of experience in many primary groups, using different registers if not languages and incommensurable practices. Like linguists who focus on langue to the exclusion of parole, social theorists were influenced by Saussure's distinction in their thinking about practice.

Anthropologists also made social structure pre-eminent, and as Tedlock and Mannheim observe, in discourse analysis, like linguists, they have tended to subordinate action, which takes place in 'real time and history', to synchronic structure (1995, p. 6). Connerton notes that social anthropologists since Malinowski and symbolic anthropologists since Durkheim neglected diachronic processes (Connerton, 1989, p. 103). And sociologists, following Parsons, described static systems rather than developmental processes (Elias, 1939 [1968, 2000]). As Crossley points out, 'habit' and 'habitus' nearly disappeared from the sociological lexicon during the early postwar period (2001, p 81) until Bourdieu revived it. His teacher Mauss had observed differences in movement patterns such as walking and swimming, in time as well as place. On a trip to New York he noticed that the strange way of walking that girls in France were adopting was common in the streets of New York, transmitted to France by the cinema. He wrote in 1934:

> Hence I have had this notion of the social nature of the '*habitus*' for many years. Please note that I use the Latin word – it should be understood in France – *habitus*. The word translates infinitely better than '*habitude*' (habit or custom), the '*exis*', the 'acquired ability' and 'faculty' of Aristotle (who was a psychologist). (Mauss, 1979b, p. 101)

He thus introduced triangulation, the 'triple viewpoint', adding a psychological mediator to the biological and sociological, and a social dimension to the study of habit.

The evolution of mediated discourse analysis

In the ethnography of speaking, which began with Gumperz, Hymes and Goffman at Berkeley, Goffman's influence was felt in linguistic anthropology as well as what came to be called interactional sociolinguistics. What Goffman had done was to introduce microanalysis to urban sociology after developing his methodology in a small, stable Shetland community (Merritt, 2001). Yet, he himself did no linguistic analysis, though he cited Voloshinov on reported speech in *Frame Analysis* (Goffman, 1974). Through reading Uspensky (1973), who had introduced Goffman to Voloshinov, we began thinking in terms of dialogicality and polyphony or heteroglossia. By the time we went to Fort Chipewyan, Alberta, our anthropological linguistic toolkit had already been supplemented by Goffman, ethnomethodology and phenomenology, and Foucault.

With an understanding of Athabaskan communicative practices and how they led to complementary schizmogenesis when Athabaskans interacted with Euro-Canadians, we became critical discourse analysts in the sense that we exposed power relations between government bureaucrats including service professionals in health, law and education, who tended to be Anglo-Americans, on the one hand, and Native Alaskans as clients on the other. We described communicative practices as arising out of conflicting reality sets or ideologies and sought to explicate these conflicts for practitioners and Native Alaskans alike (Scollon and Scollon, 1981).

The basic approaches of Critical Discourse Analysis (CDA) and anthropological linguistics, then, were integrated as we became engaged and committed advocates for Native Alaskans, showing how they were being given short shrift by carriers of what we came to call the Utilitarian Discourse System (UDS) (Scollon and Scollon, 1995 [2001]; S. Scollon, 1994). Our approach could almost be called critical anthropological linguistics, as we sought to critique the UDS first from Athabaskan and then from Chinese perspectives. What began as a critique of Western alphabetic literacy emergent in the discursive practices of our two-year-old daughter led to a broader critique of the ideology and discursive formation of a globally intrusive worldview embedded in powerful institutions.

While the social practices of educators for example, including ourselves and our colleagues, were based in the literate practices assumed to be necessary for success in the contemporary world, we came to see, with others in what came to be called new literacy studies (Gee et al., 1996), that literacy, far from being the cause of success, was more a package of practices controlled by the powerful. Becoming literate in what we called essayist literacy required a restructuring of personal identity that threatened more harm than good. It threatened what Mead termed 'the moral autonomy of the human spirit' (cited in Bateson, 1942 [1972], p. 159).

Like the discourse-historical approach of CDA, we followed a principle of triangulation. However, rather than triangulating disciplines within Western academics, we triangulated the UDS within which these disciplines are embedded with the Athabaskan reality set and the discourse of East Asians literate in the Chinese script or Sinographic writing. While CDA attempts to attack institutions of power by critically analysing institutional texts, we see this privileging of text as a manifestation of the UDS.

Our approach, which we call Mediated Discourse Analysis (MDA), differs from CDA in its focus on action. Unlike CDA, which operates with a pre-supposed psychology of the individual and recruits psychologists for the discourse-historical approach, as psychologists and anthropologists we retain the concept of the person as a social actor embodied in the society of various social groups. We thus maintain the distinction between the biological person and the abstract individual made by Mauss (Mauss, 1979a; Scollon and Scollon, 1994, 1995 [2001]; S. Scollon, 1997; Weber, 2001).

Taking action as the unit of analysis forces attention to time, space, objects and the histories interwoven in these mediators of action. This principle underlies the sociocultural historical psychology of Wertsch and others (Wertsch, 1985, 1991, 1994, 1998; Cole, 1995; Wertsch et al., 1995), based in the psychology of Vygotsky.

French ethnographers have recently proposed an 'ethnography of action', and Weber (2001) argues for a 'multi-integrative ethnography' which takes interaction as primary, after Bateson (1958). A recent monograph by Chase Hensel (1996) is a model of what might be considered multi-integrative ethnography, integrating the practice and structuration approaches of Bourdieu and Giddens with anthropological linguistics with a Batesonian focus on interaction and an interactional linguistic focus on linguistically mediated interaction. Hensel defines what might be considered linguistic habitus in terms of contextualization conventions, acquired 'as a result of a speaker's actual interactive experience, i.e., as a result of an individual's partic-ipation in particular networks of relationship', citing Gumperz and Cook-Gumperz (1982, p. 18) (Hensel, 1996, p. 159). The family systems approach of Bateson, Ruesch and others helped overcome the weakness of practice theory, adding a diachronic element of learning, maintenance and change.

Having relocated culture in interaction where the structures of habitus are generated, Hensel suggests parallel structures of 'subcultural' and 'family' habitus and even 'individual' habitus (ibid., p. 156). Having overcome the individual–society antinomy, like Wertsch, it remains only to elaborate on sit-uated learning in particular networks as Lave and Wenger (1991) have done with the notion of 'communities of practice'.

MDA, a nexus of practice[2]

The primary theoretical issue addressed by MDA is the juncture between individual action and public discourse in the complex environment of contemporary societies. The question we asked was, 'How do people construct social identities in discourse and social interaction?' Taking action as the unit of analysis, we regarded speech, gesture or text as mediational means appropriated by agents to do something. In looking at media texts, we analysed how news-makers and journalists were positioning themselves and each other in producing text. We looked at how news stories spread among different populations in Hong Kong during an 'event survey', asking people what was happening while also collecting newspapers, magazines and recording broadcasts.

On first going to Hong Kong we began with an ethnography of communication approach to studying discourse in Hong Kong by trying to teach it to our students – which meant also trying to explain it to junior colleagues. This resulted in a synthesis of our earlier work among Native Americans and East Asians, which gave us a triangulation of perspectives on the UDS which was fast spawning neocapitalism (Scollon and Scollon, 1995 [2001]). We encountered a strong literate bias that was antithetical to the ethnographic method. We had earlier accounted for behaviour in contemporary Taiwanese that resembled that in the *Li Ji* (Book of Rites) in terms of systems of face relations (Scollon and Scollon, 1994). Now we had to account for differences not only between Taiwanese and Hong Kong students but also between genders and generations of Hong Kongers.

The different emphases, one on discourses of geopolitical events and how they were interpreted by political leaders and journalists, the other on social actors and what they were doing in relation to the discourses taking place around them, came together in what Ron Scollon called Mediated Discourse Analysis (1998, 2001a,b). The linguistic analysis of texts informed my analysis of the action mediated by those texts. I was able to show that verbal and non-verbal behaviour during the height of the Taiwan missile crisis could only be understood by taking into consideration news accounts of political events (S. Scollon, 2001). But the texts themselves were only clues as to what the actors were appropriating in their actions on the field as they played out through habitus the ideologies embodied in their life histories. Using MDA, I showed how actors reproduced identities of mainland Chinese communists and Hong Kong Guomindang loyalists, with the texts of journalists, politicians and DJs, part of what Bakhtin (1929 [1984]) called 'hidden dialogicality'.

I first described what we call a nexus of practice, an interlinked set of practices enacted daily by members of a group of retired people who practised Tai Chi (*taijiquan*) together at a Hong Kong park. Many of the linked practices are associated with the community of practice of Yang-style *taijiquan*. Others are practices of having tea and *dim sum* in restaurants, shared not only by Hong Kong Chinese but also by people in the neighbouring province of Guangdong. I then showed how one woman in the group, anticipating the Taiwan missile crisis, gradually began untangling the web of interwoven practices so that in the heat of the crisis she rather suddenly separated herself from the group.

The concept of the nexus of practice is prefigured, I discovered to my chagrin, in *The Civilizing Process*, published by Norbert Elias in 1939. The network of interdependencies among human beings is what binds them together. Such interdependencies are the nexus of what is here called the figuration, a structure of mutually orientated and dependent people (1939 [1968, 2000, p. 482]). In his Postscript to the English translation, written in 1968, Elias offers as the simplest example of figuration, social dances such as the mazurka, tango, or rock'n'roll. The image of mobile figurations of people on a dance floor helps eliminate the antithesis between individual and society.

MDA and CDA

Like other approaches to CDA (Fairclough, 1992, 1995; Fairclough and Wodak, 1997; Wodak, 1999), MDA began with a social semiotic grounding in Hallidayan linguistics. Unlike CDA, which focuses on texts, whether published or recorded in interviews, MDA takes language as primary but not unique among the mediators of action. The term 'mediated discourse' implies that all discourse is mediated, whether it involves two people face-to-face or multimedia productions. Action, being socially oriented, is inherently communicative and embedded in a nexus of social practice.

Like the discourse-historical approach to CDA (Wodak et al., 1999; Reisigl and Wodak, 2001; Wodak, 2001), MDA is diachronic and views all text as situated discourse, though we place more emphasis on ethnography. In practice, what I do is learn everything I can about the people I deal with, both by interacting with them directly and by reading whatever I can find that they themselves read or that is written about them as a population, which in the case of Hong Kong Chinese and practitioners of *taijiquan* meant learning to speak Cantonese and Putonghua and to read Chinese. As the colony, not to mention myself, had also been shaped by the history of the Enlightenment and Utilitarianism, this was an important area of study. What we called the UDS (Scollon and Scollon, 1995 [2001]) came into contact with Confucianism and local practices when Hong Kong was colonized, and Mao's revolution added a new twist.

By teaching courses in rhetoric, communication, pragmatics, sociolinguistics, linguistics and English language and literature to Hong Kong tertiary students and English teachers for three years, I learned about teaching and learning practices in the colony as well as patterns of language use (S. Scollon, 1995, 1996, 1997, 1999). By studying Chinese in Kunming, Yunnan, after having studied it some two decades before, I learned about Mao's revolutionary discourse and Deng's reform discourse (Gu, 1996). This provided a contrast with one year of ethnographic research in Taiwan. I found that the Mandarin I had learned at university served me better in Taiwan than in

China, where Chinese (Putonghua) had evolved during the course of Mao's modernization and continued to adapt to Deng's reforms.

In parallel with my participant observation among a group of retired and semi-retired people who practised *taijiquan* together every morning at an urban park, I was engaged with a group of colleagues in studies of public discourse as Hong Kong made the transition from British to Chinese sovereignty (Jones et al., 1997; Scollon and Scollon, 1997; R. Scollon, 1999, 2000). Serendipitously, not only did we develop theory and methods incorporating sociocultural psychology and CDA in approaching public discourse, but the database we collected happened to coincide with the Taiwan missile crisis, and I was able to make use of it to analyse the fission that took place in the group of morning exercise friends whose community of practice I was a legitimate peripheral participant in.

In analysing news stories we used CDA, showing how choice of verbs of reporting indicated sociopolitical positioning. Comparing multiple accounts of the same press conference, we showed that the same statement was filtered through ideologies of libertarian free press 'objectivity', Cold War 'China threat' or socialist modernization (S. Scollon, forthcoming (a)).

At the same time, I listened to what people on the field were discussing and observed which newspapers they bought as they went to take tea. Here I was interested in how people were aligning themselves as colonial subjects incredulous at the posturings of Princess Diana, as Hong Kong citizens anticipating return to Chinese sovereignty and considering options for emigration, as savvy business people, or as friends interested in health, enjoyment of food and *taijiquan*.

In the analysis, then, I use myself as informant, much as Gary Snyder (1972) transformed himself from anthropologist to informant in his practice of Zen. I became the subject who embodied incommensurable practices as I became socialized first to a Putonghua-speaking group in China and then to a Cantonese-speaking group in Hong Kong, with a history embodied in habitus of experiences with both languages in other places, in and out of classrooms.

Being marked as Other by elders in the group, an abnormal person with no memory, no manners, I was subject to the reversal, 'a reading in reverse of the ethnographer', discussed by Rose:

> What is possible in this space of contact, crossing over, assimilation, appropriation, juxtaposition, and fusion, has not been adequately explored; indeed, this space has no real name. What we know is that there are numerous ragged zones of contact between peoples who hold incommensurable values and beliefs, traditions and philosophies. (Rose, 1991, pp. 289–90)

Here I engage in yet another aspect of interdisciplinarity, ethnopoetics or anthropological poetics, which Rose locates at the periphery of cultural theory, as Bourdieu, Foucault, the Frankfurt School, Lévi-Strauss, Williams and the others neglected cultural difference and diversity. Taking the practice of *tai-jiquan*, I 'inhabit a zone of contact (by crossing it again and again)' (ibid., p. 291). Furthermore, I inhabit this zone with others who are also Other, exploring assimilation, appropriation, juxtaposition, fusion and fission.

From contact with Snyder before going to Asia I began thinking in organic metaphors, as he conceived of Zen meditation as cultivating weeds, of discourse as organically related to the people, animals, plants and earth it inhabits. Thus I see habitus as a compost heap of organic matter capable of fertilizing seeds, in addition to the fossilized layers of sediment visualized by other social theorists.

My analysis of the phylogenesis of practices is reminiscent of Norbert Elias' study of the sociogenesis of civilizing practices, and my analysis of the ontogenesis of my own practice as I integrate into the different groups draws on Vygotsky's notion of the Zone of Proximal Development and Bakhtin's dialogicality including hidden dialogicality.

Habitus and the boundary of consciousness

'Habit', wrote Bateson, 'is a major economy of conscious thought' (1942 [1972], p. 141). He suggested that Samuel Butler may have been the first to point out that what we know best we are least conscious of. Like Merleau-Ponty (1962, p. 143), he used the example of the blind man who appropriates a stick and incorporates it as a matter of habit, transplanting himself into the stick as he grasps it. Elias (1939 [1968, 2000]) related social and psychical habitus, showing how social and psychical transformations of habitus resulted in historical change. In the civilizing process he documented, private and public behaviour developed as separate nexus of practice as people over a period of centuries came to regulate their drives. He showed how control of urination, for example, according to time, place and the presence of other people had both a sociogenesis in English, French and German societies and a psychogenesis in the individuals growing up in those societies.

Habitus, a set of generative dispositions, has its ontogenesis in the earliest development of social and cognitive life. Ron Scollon (2001a) shows how a simple practice like handing an object to another person is constructed out of linked practices of offering food, complying with requests, and other actions, some of which are accompanied by talk, in the period during the second year of life when a child develops a sense of separation between him- or herself and the objects in his or her environment, and at the same time begins to speak. With such early beginnings, it is a rare action which is fully conscious in the habitus of the adult. That is, any single practice is linked in its ontogenesis with other practices until a similar constellation or nexus of practices and social and material conditions brings forth the action, partially intended and partially in the nature of reflex. Each action contains within it a whole history of hidden dialogicality, partly conscious, partly unconscious. As Bourdieu remarks:

> The 'unconscious', which enables one to dispense with this interrelating (of the social conditions in which the habitus was constituted to the social conditions in which it is implemented), is never anything other than the forgetting of history which history itself produces by realizing the objective structures that it generates in the quasi-natures of *habitus*. (1990, p. 56)

What Bourdieu terms 'genesis amnesia' varies not only according to specifics of time, place and social circumstances but also according to the degree to which one is socialized to be conscious of the workings of the habitus. According to Bourdieu, 'Bodily *hexis* is political mythology realized, *em-bodied*, turned into a permanent disposition, a durable manner of standing, speaking, and thereby of *feeling* and *thinking…*' (1977, p. 93). This ideology is unconscious and 'cannot even be made explicit'. Starrett (1995) takes exception to Bourdieu's assertion that the pattern of postures that make up body hexis is transmitted in practice 'without moving through discourse and consciousness' (quoted in Starrett, 1995, p. 962, from Bourdieu, 1977, p. 87). Starrett shows that Egyptian discourse about Islamic body hexis consciously teaches students to 'read ideologies into gesture, motion, and ritual' (1995, p. 964), and cautions that Bourdieu's overemphasis on practice might perpetuate the Victorian dichotomy between 'primitive' and 'developed' forms of communication. Bourdieu's assertion of the unconscious nature of hexis also perpetuates the Cartesian dualism of body and mind. It is perhaps this belief that is part of the Enlightenment ideology that is embodied in our unconsciousness of our structured dispositions and not shared by Egyptians or Native Alaskans.[3] It is considered childlike to attend to bodily hexis.

As Elias argued, Western Europeans in the twentieth century retained a 'mental habitus' of binary oppositions such as rational–irrational, spirit–nature, individual–society, which is inadequate for understanding how historical transformation takes place.

Hensel, noting that Gumperz and Cook-Gumperz locate contextualization conventions such as code shifts, formulaic expressions, departure strategies and the like below the level of consciousness, examines a subset of these conventional usages that lie at the boundary of consciousness (Hensel, 1996, p. 160). These are amenable to strategic manipulation, much like the strategies described by Reisigl and Wodak (2001, p. 44), though the latter are perhaps more conscious.

We can be jarred into attending to naturalized aspects of habitus by encounters with others who do not share our habitus. One manifestation of this is being forced to pay attention to our own accent or habits of pronunciation by people who do not catch what we say. We also notice differences in demeanour when watching film or television which has been dubbed into a language different from the one spoken by the actors, or when a person changes his or her facial expression as he or she shifts from one language into another.

Habitus as embodied ideology

As Bourdieu and Starrett suggest, habitus or hexis (Greek for the Latin *habitus*) is embodied ideology. The revolutionary government of China not only distributed land and capital, it also distributed symbolic capital by adopting a national language that was taught in all the schools and used by government officials. At the same time, it simplified the writing system to make it available to the masses. The Pinyin orthography was adopted for writing Putonghua using the Roman alphabet, and a few hundred of the most commonly used characters were simplified. Texts were written from left to right instead of from right to left, and this nexus of linked practices was inculcated in school children throughout the nation, who speak many different languages.

As Norbert Elias described in great detail in *The Civilizing Process* (1939 [1968, 2000]), the sociogenesis of the European body entailed a long process of evolution from the medieval period through the constitution of court society and continuing today. An increase in the social division of labour and monopolies of violence by ruling courts dovetailed with control and management of bodily impulses including natural functions and aggressive expression. Instrumental to this civilizing process were socialization, rationalization and individualization.

Through socialization, natural functions were defined and managed as primarily social. Bodies became transformed into locations for the expression of codes of behaviour manifest in the rules of decorum described by Erving Goffman (1959). As Shilling (1993) points out, Elias' analysis provides the basis for Goffman's account of the presentation of self. The civilized habitus allows for bathing in swimsuits in public places, a practice which would have been inconceivable in earlier times.

For Elias, the civilized body is a historical development. The embodiment of civilized practices is a product of both biological and social processes in this evolutionary development. He speaks of an interweaving of psychological functions of drive control, what he terms the 'psychic habitus', with the social constraints that developed with the changing relationships between people.

In his 1968 Postscript to the work first published in 1939, Elias attempts to account for the non-reception of his ground-breaking work in terms of widespread tendencies in contemporary sociology, primarily under the influence of Talcott Parsons and the American School, who viewed society in terms of steady states rather than development. Whereas nineteenth-century sociologists had ideological reasons to embrace a theory of progress and development, twentieth-century theorists likewise had their own ideological conceptions which kept them from considering long-range, dynamic processes. This change in the nature of social ideals he sees as symptomatic of changes concomitant with the rise of the ideology of the nation-state and the 'general conception of society as something abstracted from the reality of the nation-state' (p. 465) held by the leading sociological theorists of the twentieth century, whether conservative and liberal or socialist and communist. The obstruction posed by the predominant modes of thinking appeared to preclude the study of long-term processes without an ideological motive.

The reification of the nation as the image of society on the one hand and the image of the individual personality on the other has widely ramifying roots, in Elias' view. In nations with a strong liberal tradition, there is an often irreconcilable split between the nation as the highest value and the autonomous free individual as the highest value, reflected in the theories of society.

Billig (1995) shows how nationalism is 'enhabited' in citizens of established nations. Like Elias, he laments the double neglect of nationalism on the part of citizens and sociologists alike. Yet, in myriad linked practices of what he terms 'banal nationalism', political affiliation is flagged as citizens are reminded of their place in a world of nations. He documents how nationalism is deeply naturalized in the habitus of modern citizens. China, Taiwan and Hong Kong are no different from other nations in this respect. Every evening China Central Television broadcasts news and weather reports in Putonghua, with simplified characters and Pinyin on the screen showing temperatures on dozens of locations on a map of China. Street signs are imprinted from left to right in simplified characters and Pinyin. School children sing the national anthem in Putonghua.

In these networked practices, national languages become naturalized – Putonghua in China, Guoyu in Taiwan, English and Cantonese in Hong Kong. Guoyu or Mandarin is similar to Putonghua, the two varieties diverging half a century ago when Mao's revolutionary government undertook language reform and becoming linked with different practices in their separate histories (Chen, 1999). The same utterance may be written in several different ways, some linked with Taiwan and others with China.

For example, a bit paradoxically, in China which has a socialist ideology each individual exerciser takes care of his or her own belongings before beginning to exercise, while in Hong Kong the first one to arrive stakes out a plot of ground for the group by placing a sheet of plastic on which others place their belongings. The basic practice of individual custodianship I found in Kunming, China, is linked with social practices of the work group, egalitarian naming practices and face relations, and the use of Putonghua, while the basic practice of group custodianship in Hong Kong is linked with social practices of kinship, hierarchical and gender-based naming practices and face relations, and the use of Cantonese. Somatic alignment arising out of the habitus in times of political tension lead to attributions of corresponding political alignment.

In the politically charged environment of the Taiwan missile crisis of March 1996, previously unconscious and unnoticed social practices became signs of political tendencies that occasioned dangerous suspicions if not open accusations among members of the group in Hong Kong. Speaking Cantonese became a sign of loyalty to Hong Kong and, incidentally, the Guomindang whose supporters were numerous in the neighbourhood of the park where they met. Correspondingly, speaking Putonghua became suspect, and people who had customarily used the language for teaching and learning as well as socializing suddenly self-consciously curtailed this practice in the presence of others.

In what follows I will examine the ontogeneses of contrasting social practices that arise in the same set of actions, my own endeavour to become a member first of the group in China and then of the one in Hong Kong. I will describe the material and objective conditions within which I attempt to adapt my habitus to the social practices of each group and relate the comparative denaturalization of practices to their phylogenesis within the revolutionary and Confucian discourses of China and Hong Kong. In this I take a diachronic view of communities of practice, in contrast to Bourdieu's synchronic notion of *les champs*, the field or social space that elicits in its members a *sens pratique*, *savoir-faire*, *savoir-vivre*, *savoir-être* that becomes a kind of symbolic capital (Bonneville, 1997). As Ron Scollon (2001a) argues, any view of practice must include not only a theorization of the origins of social practice in the life of the individual (an 'ontogenesis') in the material and objective conditions within which actions take place, it must also include a theorization of the origins of any particular practice (a 'phylogenesis') within the society.

Hanging or dropping: habitus and social practice

When an ethnographer enters a community, it is the practices that most differ from what she is accustomed to that stand out. For example, the anthropologist Barbara Ward (1989) noted that Hong Kong villagers in the 1950s had a different attitude toward play than she was accustomed to in England, as was brought home to her when she brought toys as gifts for the children after a short trip home. In a community that valued work, where children performed necessary tasks and seldom played, the toys were hardly welcomed by the adults who found their use a distraction from the daily business of life. The practices of one's own group become denaturalized when they come into conflict with those of a new group.

Here, I focus on one basic social practice that reflects the different ideologies of the groups I have described entering in Kunming and Hong Kong (S. Scollon, forthcoming (b)). I argue that one group's practice was more in keeping with my own habitus, and thus easier to adopt than the other group's. As the simple practice of placing one's bag or other personal possessions is symbolic of one's membership in the group and readiness for group activity, its mastery, appropriation or resistance is significant in gaining acceptance as a potential group member. Of course acceptance is always provisional, and tolerance is not quite the same as acceptance.

When I first approached a group of retired academics and others who met every morning in a triangle of space containing trees, grass and dirt on the campus of Yunnan University in Kunming in southwestern China, I hung my bag on a tree branch before joining the group in practice. This was a practice I had learned from another group that practises together every morning in another section of the same campus, on the veranda of an old building that once housed the university library. There was a row of hooks along the wall, where individuals hung their bags and coats before beginning to exercise. It did not take any instruction or even any conscious thought for me to adopt this practice, which, given the physical arrangement seemed quite natural.

In Hong Kong I joined a group that met in a public park that encompassed four soccer pitches. There was no building, and the few trees on one edge of the grassy playing field were tall with high, thick branches. The group had their own practice of placing their belongings on a rectangular piece of plastic advertising 'Bright and Beautiful Cleaners'. As I lived right across the street from the playing field it was not until the end of the second week of daily exercise with the group that I took a bag with me and dropped it onto the pile of things on the plastic. When it was time to leave, someone handed it to me, and an older man whom I shall call Mr Yang asked me whether I'd be coming the next day, handing me the plastic rectangle. He told me to come early, saying that he came at about 6 a.m. and could teach me.

When I told my husband what Mr Yang had said, he suggested that I was being treated like a rookie on a baseball team. From force of habit, I failed to arise early enough and so was unable to do as I had been told and went instead after 7.30 a.m. There were things piled on newspapers and a few things on the ground. I put them on the plastic and thought no further about it.

With the benefit of hindsight I can say that my failure to do as I was told was an early example of what came to be described as my lack of manners, an act of resistance to becoming the low man on the totem pole. Aside from not speaking and understanding Cantonese adequately, I was marginal and unteachable because my habitus did not conform to the social practices of the group. My resistance to the taken-for-granted social practices that reflected a hierarchical face system became denaturalized for me as I noted how resistant I was to addressing the man who led the group exercise as *Sifu* (master). This person told his superior, the leader of the entire group, that he could not teach me because I did not understand Cantonese. He later told others that my memory was not normal and I lacked manners.

Since language is a technologized or objectivized cultural tool, his saying that he could not teach me because I did not understand Cantonese was in part a gloss of his perception that I lacked the appropriate manners. At a tacit level that I was not always aware of, I was manifesting my history of resistance as an American-born Chinese to what might be considered Confucian hierarchical practices. The *Li Ji* (Legge, 1967) prescribes that an inferior should be the first to greet a superior, if the latter has cast a glance in his direction. This practice, technologized as a cultural tool in the *Li Ji*, was something my grandfather tried to teach me every time I failed to greet him in the morning. My fifth-grade teacher, a Chinese American, also tried to inscribe this on my habitus by making me write a hundred times 'I will say good morning when I see the teacher' after I had passed her in the crosswalk on the way to school without saying anything. Although that school year I was awarded the trophy for being a model student at my Chinese-language school, I soon began practices of resistance that involved sins of commission as well as of omission.

It did not take long for me to master the practice of placing my belongings on the plastic or the newspapers that supplemented it or came to take its place. However, this simple enough practice was part of a whole nexus of practices that were not part of my habitus. I soon noticed that the younger women of the generation that observed Confucian, that is, hierarchical male-centred practices, took it upon themselves to move the whole array of things when it threatened to rain or when a lawnmower was nearly upon it. They also made sure to remove and discard the newspapers at the end of the practice, and hand whatever remained to its owner, as they did that day I first left my bag. They had appropriated the whole set of practices, just as they found it natural to pour tea for the men when we went to *yum cha*. They also found it natural to take places in the back row when the group lined up to practise, and to address the ones in the front row as *Sifu*. Unlike them, though I was younger than most, I did not readily appropriate these practices of moving in physical space isomorphic with social space as they had not become embodied in habitus at an earlier age.

An important difference between the groups in Kunming and the one in Hong Kong is that the former consisted of retired faculty members, each group containing members from a different university. Though the ones who taught at Yunnan University had the advantage of a sheltered meeting place with hooks for coats and bags, the other group shared the practice of hanging their own belongings. This egalitarian practice may be regarded as a carryover from the days when they worked for the same institution and even earlier to school days when as students they hung their things on hooks provided in classrooms. The group in Hong Kong, on the other hand, consisted of individuals engaged in different trades, and their practice on the field was organized more like kin or quasi-kin relations among friends than like colleagues in the same institution.

Though the Kunming groups also showed respect for their elders and especially for the one they address as *Laoshi* (teacher), they made no attempt to rank each individual member within a hierarchy the way the Hong Kong group did. That is, the hierarchy was not made explicit through the use of forms of address such as Elder Brother (for senior male student of the same *Sifu*), Elder Sister and the like. Nicknames such as *Lao X* (Old X) or *Xiao X* (Little X) refer to age rather than expertise, and the teacher is younger than the retired faculty members. In posters placed to recruit private students among foreigners and overseas Chinese, he advertised the name of his teacher, appropriating the traditional martial arts practice of grafting himself onto a lineage.

Practice as a count noun

In Bourdieu's theory of practice, specific practices are not clearly described or differentiated. Ron Scollon (2001a) argues that we need to distinguish practice as a count noun from practice as a mass noun. The practice of *taijiquan*, which in Bourdieu's usage would be a unitary practice, consists of innumerable separate practices, some common to all tai chi practice and others specific to particular communities of practice. I would consider it a nexus of practice made up of interlocking nexus of practice. Though the movement sequences performed by members of each group closely resemble that of the other and they share what I call a heritage of practice in that their movements are traceable historically to the same founder, they perceive themselves as distinct communities of practice.

A practice such as hanging one's bag on a tree branch is tied to a particular physical setting as much as to a particular kind of activity. The complex of practices that constitute exercising are linked with practices of dressing, travelling to a specific place such as a gym, undressing, showering, dressing, putting one's belongings in a locker, going to a room designated for a particular kind of exercise, warming up, and so on. Each of these practices can be further decomposed into practices acquired in other places at an earlier time.

Similarly, the practice of writing can be decomposed into practices of picking up and holding a brush, pen or pencil, sharpening a pencil, grinding ink on a stone or opening an ink bottle, placing paper on a flat surface and orienting it in a particular way, writing on or between lines beginning at the top right or top left, writing from left to right or from right to left or top to bottom, or plugging in and booting up a computer and typing on a keyboard. Each of these practices is linked to learning by imitation or explicit instruction in particular linguistic codes, spoken and/or written.

Phylogenesis in community of practice

In Kunming as well as in Hong Kong, people take outings to public parks in family as well as other social groupings. In both cities people also go as individuals to schools, offices, community centres or shopping malls. Theft is a concern in both places, and people keep a watchful eye on their own belongings. Practices for tending personal belongings in each group evolved out of existing practices among the individual members, which relate not only to the personal histories of individuals but also to the material conditions of the places in which they habitually met and the history of the group.

Pan (2000) shows that in Guangdong, a province in south China, face systems of hierarchical relationships vary depending on setting. That is, in work settings, deference depends on official rank more than on age or gender, while in family settings the traditional Confucian hierarchies of age and gender hold sway. Practices of topic introduction and turn exchange are linked in different ways to social rankings in each setting. Thus, the phylogenesis of practices for conducting business meetings takes place in the context of modern socialist ideology, whereas the set of practices for the distribution of talk at family dinners has its phylogenesis in a community of practice with a much longer history tied to Confucian social norms.

With morning exercise linked to school and work for the people in Kunming, the group activity carries associations of egalitarian relationships among members as well as individual responsibility for personal belongings. For the group in Hong Kong, interaction was patterned according to a family model, with hierarchical, gender-based expectations for collective care of individual, personal belongings.

Groups in other settings adopt similar practices for placing personal belongings for the duration of their meetings. In a *taijiquan* class held in an exercise room at City University of Hong Kong, there were benches along the wall to each side of the door. The teachers placed their belongings on one bench and students on benches along the opposite wall. This practice developed naturally in a class that met for eight sessions. In another class at a community centre in Hong Kong, the teacher placed her tape recorder and other belongings on a cloth in a corner near the door, with students arraying their things on the floor nearby.

Incommensurable practices

Hanging a bag from a hook or branch and dropping it on a sheet on the ground are incommensurable practices that cannot be done simultaneously, though they can be done in sequence. It is also possible for people in the same group to do one or the other, but since these incommensurable practices are forms of identity claims, one does not choose one or the other without associating with or dissociating from the group.

When one woman began hanging her quiver of swords from a post or tree branch at the playing field in Hong Kong, this action was linked to practices of walking backwards (an exercise to strengthen the kidneys), practising by herself rather than with the group, and gradually shifting her position from day to day in relation to the group, in a pattern isomorphic with relations between China and Taiwan in the developing tension over the Taiwanese presidential election and US granting of visas to Taiwanese officials (Scollon, S.W., 2003). By the time she began hanging her bag, she had already transformed her nexus of practice and separated herself physically from the group.

Speaking Cantonese and speaking Putonghua are also incommensurable practices that cannot be done simultaneously, and switching among members of the Hong Kong group resulted in a degree of language interference that made speech difficult to comprehend. Although there are many people in the world who can switch easily between these languages, this was not true of anyone in the group. As part of the habitus linked in webs of practice, each language embeds beliefs, values and emotions.

Styles of *taijiquan* may also be incommensurable practices. One cannot simultaneously perform more than one. Even slight variation in one movement may make it difficult to coordinate one's practice with another's. Even when practising each style separately one may interfere with the other. In theory, practice is preparation for fighting, where fixed habit patterns are a disadvantage. Thus, practising the fixed forms and fighting may entail incommensurability.

Habitus and field

Complexes of practices such as genres of speaking or movement sequences leave a residue in the habitus, which is the embodiment of a person's life experience. One's first experiences with discourse in language of whatever varieties in whatever combinations condition verbal interaction for a lifetime and, as we have argued, any change is experienced as a change in identity (Scollon and Scollon, 1981). Bourdieu emphasizes the weight of this historical force:

> ... the anticipations of the *habitus*, practical hypotheses based on past experience, give disproportionate weight to early experiences. (1990, p. 54)

Our early experience disposes us to trust people who speak and act like we do, or at least like people we have learned to trust. As I jokingly said to my first group of linguistics students in Hong Kong, I would do anything they told me to do in Cantonese because in my experience it was a language spoken by elders or school teachers, authority figures who commanded obedience. Our daughter, who was cared for by a Cantonese-speaking great-aunt, as an adult still regards Cantonese as the voice of power and authority. The feeling remains imprinted in her habitus from the days when, as a toddler, I spoke to her in Cantonese and she protested, 'Don't talk that way.'

This avoidance of Cantonese because of its association with old-fashioned authoritarianism, a personal disposition shared by all my close family members and friends with the exception of my paternal grandfather, made it difficult for me to learn to speak the language, though many of the attitudes and interaction patterns encoded in and linked with use of the language have left residues in my habitus, which also contains residues formed by resistance to these complexes of practices. I prefer 'residue' to 'capital', which implies that the agent can invest or cash it in at will.

The habitus as Bourdieu conceives it is embodied in a field of objectifiable relations, accumulated capital in a bank owned by someone else, with rules and structures that exist apart from the individual agent that continually re-enacts them. Bourdieu speaks of 'homologous *habitus,* such as those that underlie the unity of the life-style of a group or a class' (ibid., p. 55). There is a sense in which each group, in Kunming and in Hong Kong, shares a homologous habitus which arises out of common experience, however the group may be characterized. Though Bourdieu does not define 'field', we may consider participants in each group to belong to different fields or discourses. Within each group, the habitus is homologous, so that within reasonable limits members know what to expect of each other. Neither group has habitus homologous with mine, though there are overlapping practices, and both groups experience me as an outsider who is lacking in the common sense and social graces driven by the logic of shared practice.

In short, being the product of a particular class of objective regularities, the habitus tends to generate all the 'reasonable', 'common-sense' behaviours (and only those) which are possible within the limits of these regularities, and which are likely to be positively sanctioned because they are objectively adjusted to the logic characteristic of a particular field, whose objective future they anticipate (ibid., pp. 55–6).

In Bourdieu's conception, the habitus is a master hardware program, generated by and generating procedural rules within a field. As such, it accumulates symbolic capital analogous to databases, symbolic and convertible rather than hard currency.

Though he describes the logic of practice as 'soft logic', I would argue that the unconscious nature of the habitus cannot be as objective and regular as he claims. What resides in the habitus is not hard fossil remains nor abstract rules but humus and detritus, not buried treasure but compost that prepares the ground for new growth in the form of weeds as well as transplants. As Calhoun observes, 'Bourdieu's theory is at its best, therefore, as a theory of reproduction, and at its weakest as a theory of transformation. In this it shows its structuralist roots' (1995, p. 142).

Transformation and recontextualization of habitus

While Bourdieu does not rule out transformation, he gives no account of how this might take place. I view the habitus as a dissipative structure in interaction with its environment (R. Scollon, 1977; S. Scollon, 1977; Prigogine, 1984). As long as the environment remains relatively stable, fluctuating within predictable limits, the individual is disposed to operate according to established norms. The field within which the habitus develops is also a dissipative structure with its own fluctuations in interaction with its environment which includes the habitus of individuals who may have been shaped in other environments. Bourdieu assumes stability:

> the *habitus*, like every 'art of inventing', is what makes it possible to produce an infinite number of practices that are relatively unpredictable (like the corresponding situations) but also limited in their diversity. (1990, p. 55)

When a new environment produces such fluctuations that the habitus is restructured, the detritus of old practices becomes humus for new. In any particular habitus, the seed stock is limited, and new practices cannot be invented out of nothing.

Like the practice of handing, practices of becoming attached to and disposing of belongings have their ontogeneses in early childhood, in linked configurations of discursive and nondiscursive practices by which an infant becomes a person with personal belongings and later a schoolchild with a book bag. Of course, these practices can be modified as an adult goes from carrying a handbag to a backpack to wearing a moneybelt.

Becoming a member of the community of practice which exercises together, then, entails adopting linked chains of verbal and nonverbal practices. Some links in the chain were common to both groups, though linked with other practices. There were both overlapping and incommensurable practices. I will summarize the salient practices of each group and then discuss which ones were overlapping and incommensurable in my own habitus.

Kunming, Yunnan, China

In Kunming, the group shared what Gu (1996) terms a Revolutionary Discourse, predominant in China under Mao's revolution, which redistributed property with the ideology that everyone should have an equal share. Confucian hierarchical face relations were overturned, with students asserting power over teachers. Egalitarian face relations were reflected in forms of address, with people addressing each other uniformly as *tongzhi*, 'comrade', during the early years of the revolution. With the opening up of Deng Xiaoping's reform era, the honorific second person *nin* has returned in some uses, and some prefer terms like 'manager' to *tongzhi*, which has been appropriated by members of the gay community (Jones, 2001). *Sifu*, the word for 'master', is used for tradesmen like taxi drivers and electricians.

Putonghua, the language promulgated during the revolution, was used in talking to outsiders, but among the group the Kunming dialect was used. Though the teacher was accustomed to teaching foreigners, from whom he could ask fees that would be prohibitive for most Chinese, he spoke almost entirely in Putonghua. His business card was printed with his name in traditional Chinese characters, though simplified characters were used throughout China except in dealings with overseas Chinese or to signal what Gu calls the Discourse of Reform in signs over beauty salons and other businesses reflecting the new economy (Scollon and Scollon, 1998). Pinyin was also used to represent his name in the official orthography designed for spelling Putonghua.

As indicated on the teacher's card, he taught a style of *taijiquan* known as Heng style, which was practised by the group. Heng was a follower of Yang Chengfu, the originator of the widespread Yang style, and their form looked to me like a variation of the Yang style. As I have noted above, the members of the group were retired faculty from nearby universities who assembled at a particular spot every morning at about 8.30. They would chat and then line up on the sidewalk to practise the long form in unison. The teacher would arrive and critique their practice and sometimes tutor a foreigner. On weekends they would be joined by younger business people who worked during the week, and the practice of the form would be followed by pushing hands practice.

I identify social practices of greeting, chatting, lining up, practising in unison, coaching or tutoring, and pushing hands as constituting the group. Arriving and leaving on foot or astride a bicycle, participants find a tree under which to park the bicycle or from which to hang a bag, some arriving empty-handed. Figure 9.1 represents a nexus of practice made up of salient practices of egalitarian face relations, Heng-style *taijiquan*, hanging bags, speaking the Kunming dialect, and carrying over practices from the workplace.

Hong Kong

The group in Hong Kong participated in a variety of discourses including Confucianist and colonial, with nearly all members travelling in and out of

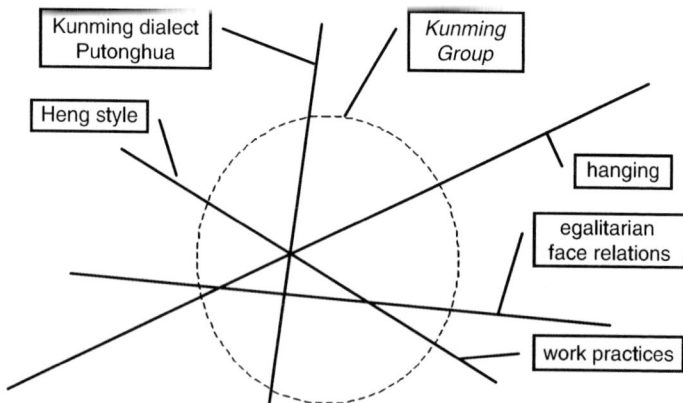

Figure 9.1   Nexus of practice of Kunming group

the colony at one time or another. Their mutual interaction was governed largely by Confucian values associated with gender-based hierarchical face relations reflected in forms of address. They practised a literate, componential style of teaching and learning, using a list of names of forms or movement patterns that they referred to frequently.

Teaching as well as most conversation took place in Cantonese, though dyads or triads would occasionally use the Qiuzhao dialect, Putonghua or English. Because of the colonial history of Hong Kong, English was respected but also feared and disliked, and used only when necessary in communicating with outsiders. Putonghua was also regarded as an outsider language, used to communicate with mainlanders or Taiwanese who were not Cantonese. During the transition to Chinese sovereignty in 1997, several members of the group attended classes in Putonghua.

The group was known as 'Friends of Tai Chi' at the restaurant where they habitually went for tea and *dim sum*. The leader of the group pronounced them 'morning exercise friends' in an effort to forestall a complicated introduction of all the group members with the appropriate quasi-kin terms some members thought should be used among the group. Although the relationships signified by these terms governed social practices within the group to a large extent, the *Sifu* was uncomfortable with making them all explicit. He enjoyed the appearance of egalitarian relations symbolized by dividing the bill among those present, aware that he could not be held responsible for distributing his teaching equally among group members as there was no economic transaction. The only one exempt from paying his share was the old retired grand-master, who always took the seat of honour at the *Sifu*'s right and was treated with respect.

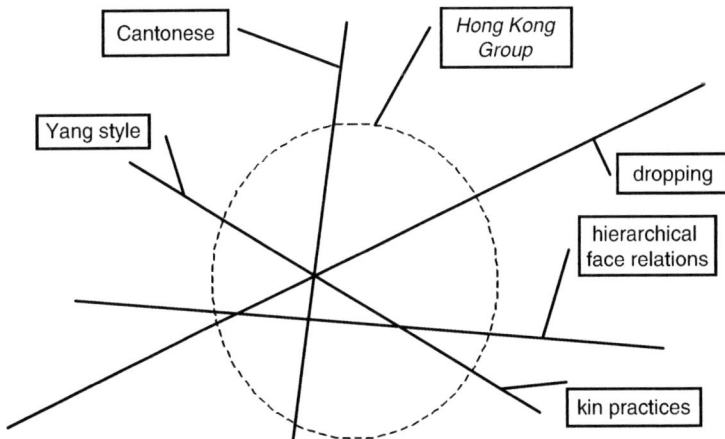

Figure 9.2   Nexus of practice of Hong Kong group

As I mentioned above, the social practices of quasi-kin relations included group custody of belongings, seating, pouring tea for others higher in the hierarchy, as well as ordering dishes for the whole group, paying the bill and asking the *Sifu* for advice regarding health and medicine. The nexus of practice in Figure 9.2 shows practices which contrast with those of the Kunming group: hierarchical face relations, Yang-style *taijiquan*, Cantonese, placing belongings on the ground, and quasi-kin social practices.

Political climate accentuates differences in habitus

In December 1995 the United States was arranging a transit visa for the Taiwanese Vice President, who stopped in Los Angeles on his way to a meeting in Guatemala. In early January 1996, China announced it would oppose any form of what it called 'transit diplomacy'. I approached the group in Hong Kong unaware of the effect this political climate would have on its members. Taiwanese flags flew on the hill which rose beside the playing field across the street from our dwelling in a formerly well-to-do neighbourhood of Kowloon.

The woman who invited me to join the group was from Beijing, had married a man from Guangzhou and settled in Hong Kong when he was transferred there ten years before. She was appropriating a social practice familiar to me from Kunming which I later encountered in Chengdu as well, inviting a stranger who showed knowledge of the group's practice to join. It later became evident to me that newcomers joined the group only by association with someone already a member. Many people watched the group practice from a respectful distance and even imitated their movements, but few became part of the group. The woman, whom I shall call Mrs Chin, was questioned about whether I was her friend.

At the end of December Mrs Chin, anticipating political conflict on the basis of news reports, started to adjust her daily routine, adding two sets of sword practice. As part of this new practice, she stationed herself in the northeast corner of the group, practising alone for the first time. Gradually, through a set of interlocking practices including walking backwards, arriving at different times and establishing a fixed set of routines, she separated herself from the group, moving at the height of the Taiwan missile crisis in mid-March to the southeast corner of the group and from there to a spot 50 yards to the south. Most significantly, during the course of this movement she stopped setting her bag on the communal pile and began hanging it from a post or tree branch.

By timing her actions in counterpoint to the established routines, the nexus of practice of the group, she set up fluctuations in the structure of the group that were amplified by political developments. When the amplification became too great, chaos resulted and order was restored by her withdrawal from the group. It is impossible to say which of her actions were calculated and which emerged out of group interaction. All that can be said is that the result was her withdrawal from the group at the height of the crisis. Bourdieu allows for this kind of strategizing.

It is, of course, never ruled out that the responses of the habitus may be accompanied by a strategic calculation tending to perform in a conscious mode the operation that the habitus performs quite differently, namely an estimation of chances presupposing transformation of the past effect into an expected objective (Bourdieu, 1990, p. 53).

What Bourdieu does not account for is the interaction of different habitus in the transformation of past habitus.

It was revealed to me in the period leading up to the Taiwanese presidential election of 23 March, after which China threatened to deploy missiles toward Taiwan, that Mrs Chin was suspected by group members of being a secret agent for the Chinese government. It did not take long for me to surmise that I was also suspect by association. As I began following her to her new location and hanging my bag there before setting it on the ground with the others, it was not long before I came under criticism, not directly for being a communist sympathizer, but ostensibly for picking up Mrs Chin's bad habits in performing *taijiquan*.

What are the social practices engaged in by Mrs Chin that became associated with ideology? One very salient one was speaking Putonghua. A few days after the *New York Times* reported at the end of January that China planned to strike Taiwan with missiles every day for 30 days beginning on the day after the elections, we were having tea at a restaurant after practice. As is a common practice, a couple of men were reading a newspaper. An editorial criticized then president Lee Deng Hui for his declaration of Taiwanese sovereignty. Mrs Chin said to me that we should speak to each other in Cantonese.

She had introduced me to the group declaring that as I was from America, I spoke English and Putonghua, but not Cantonese, like everyone there in America. Obviously it was a gross simplification if not misrepresentation of American or even Chinese-American practice, but in my case, although I had some background in Cantonese, I was far from fluent. I had studied Mandarin at university and Putonghua in Kunming, and found it easier to communicate with Mrs Chin than with others in the group, partly because she was herself marginal.

Linked in Mrs Chin's habitus to the use of Putonghua were egalitarian assumptions that led her to refuse to be addressed as *Sije*, 'elder female student under the same master', and to frequently assert that 'we are all about the same' in age and expertise. The male chauvinism of the older males rankled. She had been leader of morning exercise in middle school in Beijing, and found it natural to want to exercise with other women unencumbered by critical males. She also found it natural to be followed by males, though none went so far as to follow her to her new location.

After a visit by George Bush (Senior) to Jiang Zemin to discuss the Taiwan issue, the group split through interlocking social practices involving timing and physical positioning between those following Mrs Chin and those following her rival, and I found myself instrumental though by no means the only one to be caught in the middle of this rivalry, as different habitus produced fluctuations in the temporal and spatial positioning of the group. Several of us had, stored in our habitus, social practices homologous with those of Mrs Chin, and had no idea our actions could be linked with ideology. When the Chinese lunar New Year arrived, Mrs Chin worked hard to restore harmony to the group, but soon after there were rumours of impending war and she found it difficult to maintain her enthusiasm.

Aside from speaking Putonghua, I thought nothing of hanging my bag from a post, though I was aware of the fact that my movements were being watched. Though at first Mrs Chin differed mainly in pace and style from others in the group, the *Sifu* soon began to introduce changes that set his followers apart from her, and to comment that her practice was deteriorating. I was warned not to imitate her, and after a few months she ceased coming to the field. Her husband was reported to have asked group members why the group had split, which they found outrageous as it was their perception that Mrs Chin had split herself off.

Homologous habitus leads to attributions of political alignment

Mrs Chin, for her part, just before the Taiwanese election, had informed me of a television programme produced in Guangdong and broadcast in Hong Kong, in which a *Sifu* demonstrated Yang-style taijiquan. A particular movement she appropriated from this television *Sifu* was contested by the Hong Kong *Sifu* and identified as 'mainland style'. Another movement appropriated from a videotape of a Beijing *Sifu* had been appropriated by a rival in the group who, with me and others, had unwittingly allowed Mrs Chin to split us off from the rest of the group temporarily.

Overlapping or partially homologous habitus shared by those of us who regularly visited mainland China became markers during the Taiwan missile crisis of mainland or communist sympathies, compounded with antipathy toward anyone from the North and in particular Beijing, became highlighted. In order to remain in the good graces of the *Sifu* who had married a daughter of the Guomindang, we had to reform our habits, which is not to say our habitus. We refrained from speaking Putonghua and eventually from being seen with Mrs Chin, and were careful to imitate the gestures authorized by the *Sifu* (S. Scollon, 1998).

In conclusion, I would argue that it is no easy matter to modify one's habitus. By the time one becomes conscious of the alignments called up by one's habitus, one may be irreversibly marked as a member of the wrong group.

The basic practice of individual custodianship in Kunming is linked with social practices of the work group, egalitarian naming practices and face relations, and the use of Putonghua, while the basic practice of group custodianship in Hong Kong is linked with social practices of kinship, hierarchical and gender-based naming practices and face relations, and the use of Cantonese. Somatic alignment arising out of the habitus in times of political tension lead to attributions of corresponding political alignment.

I have argued that each particular social practice has its phylogenesis within the nexus of practice of a community that shares an ideology. That is, political alignment is deeply rooted in habitus which in turn has roots intertwined with embodied ideologies. An individual who grows up in a community internalizes complexes of linked social practices as habitus tied to common ideologies. Habitus may thus be regarded as a compost heap of social practices. When the individual as an adult becomes socialized to a new community with a different nexus of practice, his or her habitus, including embodied ideologies, the residue of earlier life experience, becomes detritus to be decomposed into humus for the ontogenesis of new social practices.

To make this argument, I documented the ontogeneses of contrasting social practices arising from comparable sets of actions, my socialization into the nexus of practice first of a group that practised the Heng style of *taijiquan* in Kunming and then of a group that practised the Yang style in Hong Kong. I showed how my habitus was partially homologous with the nexus of practice of each group. That is, I had been socialized to linguistic and other practices that partially overlapped with each nexus of practice, so that I was able to adapt my habitus to each group with some degree of consciousness. Nevertheless, I was unable to control imputations of political leanings that arose out of the unconscious workings of habitus.

In order to investigate the role of habitus, ideology and social practice in political alignment, I first examined the workings of the broad discourses of revolution and reform in China and the Neoconfucian and colonial discourses of Hong Kong. This required a diachronic approach, as these discourses have evolved over the course of centuries. As my own habitus has also evolved over the course of more than half a century, I reflected on the ways in which it came into conflict with the nexus of practice of the groups I interacted with. Needless to say, participant observation was only possible as a result of language learning and other modifications of habitus over the years.

By paying attention to action in addition to texts, I was able to detect the ways in which specific practices were linked to ideologies in different communities of practice. In this I used Mediated Discourse Analysis (MDA), which differs from CDA in its focus on action. Extending Hymes' second type of linguistic relativity, I argue that in order to discover relationships among habitus, ideology and social practice we cannot simply assume that members of a social group share homologous practice. Rather, as Ron Scollon (2001a) argues, we have to theorize the ontogenesis of any particular practice within the life of the developing infant as well as its phylogenesis within a society.

Notes

1. Jurgen Ruesch describes American conformance as stemming from the assumption of equality and thus the need to please everyone in one's reference group, which Americans recognize as the ultimate authority (Ruesch and Bateson, 1951 [1968], p. 109). On American conformity, see also de Tocqueville (1966).
2. See R. Scollon (2001a,b) for an elaboration of MDA and its nexus of practice.
3. I owe this observation to discussions with Dennis Demmert and other members of the Professional Development Seminar which I coordinated under a grant from the Mellon Foundation at the University of Alaska Fairbanks in 1980–81, as well as a conference on cross-cultural communication held in Anchorage in May 1981, sponsored by the University of Alaska Instructional Telecommunications Consortium.

References

Bakhtin, M.M. (1929 [1984]) *Problems of Dostoevsky's Poetics*. (trans. and ed. Caryl Emerson) Minneapolis: University of Minnesota Press.
Bateson, G. (1958) *Naven: A Survey of the Problems Suggested by a Composite Picture of the Culture of a New Guinea Tribe Drawn from Three Points of View*. Cambridge: Cambridge University Press.
Bateson, G. (1942 [1972]) *Steps to an Ecology of Mind*. New York: Ballantine.
Berger, P., Berger, B. and Kellner, H. (1973) *The Homeless Mind, Modernization, and Consciousness*. New York: Random House.
Billig, M. (1995) *Banal Nationalism*. London: Sage.
Bonneville, L. (1997) 'Introduction a la sociologie de Bourdieu: du role des notions d'habitus et de champ dans l'approche de Bourdieu'. <http://www.generation.net/~elbonne/luc/travail9.htm>, accessed 13 November 1997.
Bourdieu, P. (1977) *Outline of a Theory of Practice*. (trans. Richard Nice) Cambridge: Cambridge University Press.
Bourdieu, P. (1990) *The Logic of Practice*. Stanford, CA: Stanford University Press.
Calhoun, C. (1995) *Critical Social Theory: Culture, History, and the Challenge of Difference*. Oxford: Blackwell.
Chen, P. (1999) *Modern Chinese: History and Sociolinguistics*. Cambridge: Cambridge University Press.
Cole, M. (1995) 'Socio-cultural-historical psychology: some general remarks and a proposal for a new kind of cultural-genetic methodology', in J.V. Wertsch, P. del Rio and A. Alvarez (eds), *Sociocultural Studies of Mind*. Cambridge and New York: Cambridge University Press.
Connerton, P. (1989) *How Societies Remember*. Cambridge: Cambridge University Press.
Crossley, N. (2001) 'The phenomenological habitus and its construction', *Theory and Society*, 26, pp. 81–120.
de Tocqueville, A. (1966) *Democracy in America* (ed. J.P. Mayer) (new trans. by G. Lawrence). Garden City, NY: Doubleday.

Elias, N. (1939 [1968, 2000]) *The Civilizing Process: Sociogenetic and Psychogenetic Investigations* (English edition (1968) Trans. Edmund Jephcott, with some notes and corrections by the author; Revised edition ed. E. Dunning, J. Goudsblom and S. Mennell). Oxford: Blackwell.

Fairclough, N. (1992) *Discourse and Social Change*. Cambridge: Polity Press.

Fairclough, N. (1995) *Critical Discourse Analysis: The Critical Study of Language*. London and New York: Longman.

Fairclough, N. and Wodak, R. (1997) 'Critical discourse analysis', in T.A. van Dijk (ed.), *Discourse as Social Interaction*. London: Sage, pp. 258–84.

Gee, J.P., Hull, G. and Lankshear, C. (1996) *The New Work Order: Behind the Language of the New Capitalism*. Boulder, CO: Westview Press.

Goffman, E. (1959) *The Presentation of Self in Everyday Life*. New York: Doubleday.

Goffman, E. (1974) *Frame Analysis*. New York: Harper & Row.

Grace, G. (1981) *An Essay on Language*. Columbia, SC: Hornbeam Press.

Gu, Y. (1996) 'The changing modes of discourse in a changing China'. Plenary address, 1996 International Conference on Knowledge and Discourse, Hong Kong. Beijing Foreign Studies University, unpublished manuscript.

Gumperz, J.J. and Cook-Gumperz, J. (1982) 'Introduction: language and the communication of social identity', in J.J. Gumperz (ed.) *Language and Social Identity*. Cambridge: Cambridge University Press, pp. 1–21.

Hensel, C. (1996) *Telling Our Selves: Ethnicity and Discourse in Southwestern Alaska*. New York and Oxford: Oxford University Press.

Hymes, D. (1966) 'Two types of linguistic relativity', in W. Bright (ed.), *Sociolinguistics: Proceedings of the UCLA Sociolinguistics Conference*, 1964, The Hague: Mouton, pp. 114–67.

Jones, R.H. (2001) 'Mediated action and sexual risk: discourses of AIDS and sexuality in the People's Republic of China'. PhD Dissertation, Department of Linguistics, Macquarie University.

Jones, R., Scollon R., Yung, V., Li, D. and Tsang, W.K. (1997) 'Tracing the voices of Hong Kong's transition with subject-run focus groups'. Paper presented at the Second Symposium on Intercultural Communication, Beijing Foreign Studies University, 10–15 October.

Lave, J. and Wenger, E. (1991) *Situated Learning: Legitimate Peripheral Participation*. Cambridge: Cambridge University Press.

Legge, J. (1967) *Li Chi: Book of Rites*. Vol. 1. New York: University Books.

Mauss, M. (1979a) 'A category of the human mind: the notion of person, the notion of "self" ', in *Sociology and Psychology: Essays* (trans. B. Brewster). London, Boston and Henley: Routledge & Kegan Paul, pp. 59–94.

Mauss, M. (1979b) 'The notion of body techniques', in *Sociology and Psychology: Essays* (trans. Ben Brewster). London, Boston and Henley: Routledge & Kegan Paul, pp. 97–123.

Mead, M. (1942) 'The comparative study of culture and the purposive cultivation of democratic values', in *Science, Philosophy and Religion, Second Symposium*. New York: Conference for Science, Philosophy and Religion, Chapter IV.

Merleau-Ponty, M. (1962) *Phenomenology of Perception* (trans. from French by C. Smith). London: Routledge & Kegan Paul.

Merritt, M. (2001) 'The neglected ritual: from Erving Goffman's "Neglected Situation" to situated discourse and social presence'. Paper presented at American Educational Research Association, April 2001, Seattle.

Milosz, C. (1955 [1981]) *The Captive Mind* (trans. from Polish by J. Zielonko). New York: Vintage.

Pan, Y. (2000) *Politeness in Chinese Face-to-Face Interaction.* Stamford, CT: Ablex Publishing Corporation.

Prigogine, I. (1984) *Order Out Of Chaos: Man's New Dialogue with Nature.* New York: Bantam Books.

Reisigl, M. and Wodak, R. (2001) *Discourse and Discrimination: Rhetorics of Racism and Antisemitism.* London: Routledge.

Rose, D. (1991) 'Reversal', in I. Brady (ed.), *Anthropological Poetics.* Savage, MD: Rowman & Littlefield.

Ruesch, J. and Bateson, G. (1951 [1968]) *Communication: The Social Matrix of Psychiatry.* New York: Norton.

Scollon, R. (1977) 'Dissipative structures, Chipewyan consonants, and the modern consciousness', *Working Papers in Linguistics*, 9(3), Department of Linguistics, University of Hawaii, pp. 43–64.

Scollon, R. (1998) *Mediated Discourse as Social Interaction: A Study of News Discourse.* New York: Longman.

Scollon, R. (1999) 'Official and unofficial discourses of national identity: questions raised by the case of contemporary Hong Kong', in R. Wodak and C. Ludwig (eds), *Challenges in a Changing World: Issues in Critical Discourse Analysis.* Vienna: Passagen Verlag, pp. 21–35.

Scollon, R. (2000) 'Methodological interdiscursivity: an ethnographic understanding of unfinalizability', in S. Sarangi and M. Coulthard (eds), *Discourse and Social Life.* London: Longman, pp. 138–54.

Scollon, R. (2001a) *Mediated Discourse: The Nexus of Practice.* London and New York: Routledge.

Scollon, R. (2001b) 'Action and text: toward an integrated understanding of the place of text in social (inter)action, mediated discourse analysis and the problem of social action', in R. Wodak and M. Meyer (eds), *Methods of Critical Discourse Analysis.* London: Sage, pp. 139–83.

Scollon, R. and Scollon, S. (1979) *Linguistic Convergence at Fort Chipewyan, Alberta: An Ethnography of Communication.* New York: Academic Press.

Scollon, R. and Scollon, S. (1981) *Narrative, Literacy and Face in Interethnic Communication,* Norwood, NJ: Ablex Publishing Corporation.

Scollon, R. and Scollon, S.W. (1994) 'Face parameters in East–West discourse', in S. Ting-Toomey (ed.), *The Challenge of Facework: Cross-Cultural and Interpersonal Issues.* Albany: State University of New York Press, pp. 133–57.

Scollon, R. and Scollon, S.W. (1995 [2001]) *Intercultural Communication: A Discourse Approach* (revised edition). Oxford: Blackwell.

Scollon, R. and Scollon, S.W. (1997) 'Political, personal, and commercial discourses of national sovereignty: Hong Kong becomes China', in M. Lauristin (ed.), *Intercultural Communication and Changing National Identities.* Tartu: Tartu University Press, pp. 49–71.

Scollon, R. and Scollon, S.W. (1998) 'Literate design in the discourses of revolution, reform, and transition: Hong Kong and China', *Written Language and Literacy*, 1(1), pp. 1–39.

Scollon, S. (1977) 'Langue, idiolect, and speech community: three views of the language at Fort Chipewyan Alberta', *Working Papers in Linguistics*, 9(3), Department of Linguistics, University of Hawaii, pp. 65–76.

Scollon, S.B.K. (1982) 'Reality set, socialization and linguistic convergence'. Unpublished PhD dissertation, Department of Linguistics, University of Hawaii.

Scollon, S. (1994) 'The utilitarian discourse system', in D. Marsh and L. Salo-Lee (eds), *Europe on the Move: Fusion or Fission?* Proceedings of the 1994 SIETAR Europa Symposium. Jyväskylä, Finland: SIETAR EUROPA and University of Jyväskylä, pp. 126–31.

Scollon, S. (1995) 'Methodological assumptions in intercultural communication'. Paper presented at the Fifth International Conference on Cross-Cultural Communication: East and West, 15–19 August 1995. Heilongjiang University, Harbin, China.

Scollon, S. (1996) 'Cantonese discussion, English documents: professional communication in Hong Kong'. Paper presented at the conference on Knowledge and Discourse, Hong Kong University, June 1996.

Scollon, S. (1997) 'Metaphors of self and communication', *Multilingua*, 16(1), pp. 1–38.

Scollon, S. (1998) 'Identity through the embodiment of authoritative gesture: the practice of taijiquan in Hong Kong', in D.R. Heisey and W. Gong (eds), *Communication and Culture: China and the World Entering the 21st Century*. Amsterdam: Rodopi Editions.

Scollon, S. (1999) 'Not to waste words or students: Confucian and Socratic discourse', in E. Hinkel (ed.), *Culture in Second Language Teaching and Learning*. Cambridge: Cambridge University Press, pp. 13–27.

Scollon, S. (2001) 'Habitus, consciousness, agency and the problem of intention: how we carry and are carried by political discourses', in R. Wodak (ed.), *Critical Discourse Analysis in Postmodern Societies*. Special Issue of *Folia Linguistica*, pp. 97–129.

Scollon, S.W. (2003) 'Threat or business as usual? A multimodal, intertextual analysis of a political statement', in M. Dedaic and D. Nelson (eds), *At War with Words*. Amsterdam: Mouton.

Scollon, S. (forthcoming (b)) 'Anticipating crisis: habitus, agency, intention and changing nexus of practice'.

Shilling, C. (1993) *The Body and Social Theory*. London: Sage.

Snyder, G. (1972) 'From anthropologist to informant: a field record of Gary Snyder. Interview by Nathaniel Tarn', *Alcheringa*. 4, pp. 104–13.

Starrett, G. (1995) 'The hexis of interpretation: Islam and the body in the Egyptian popular school', *American Ethnologist*. 22(4), pp. 953–69.

Tedlock, D. and Mannheim, B. (1995) Introduction, in D. Tedlock and B. Mannheim (eds), *The Dialogic Emergence of Culture*. Urbana and Chicago: University of Illinois Press, pp. 1–32.

Uspensky, B. (1973) *A Poetics of Composition: The Structure of the Artistic Text and Typology of a Compositional Form* (trans. from Russian by V. Zavarin and S. Wittig). Berkeley, Los Angeles and London: University of California Press.

Ward, B.E. (1989) *Through Other Eyes: An Anthropologist's View of Hong Kong*. Hong Kong: Chinese University Press.

Weber, F. (2001) 'Settings, interactions and things: a plea for multi-integrative ethnography' *Ethnography*, 2, pp. 475–99.

Wertsch, J.V. (1985) *Culture, Communication and Cognition: Vygotskian Perspectives*. Cambridge: Cambridge University Press.

Wertsch, J.V. (1991) *Voices of the Mind: A Sociocultural Approach to Mediated Action*. Cambridge, MA: Harvard University Press.

Wertsch, J.V. (1994) 'The primacy of mediated action in sociocultural studies', *Mind, Culture and Activity*, 1(4), pp. 202–8.

Wertsch, J.V. (1998) *Mind as Action*. New York: Oxford University Press.

Wertsch, J.V., del Rio, P. and Alvarez, A. (eds) (1995) *Sociocultural Studies of Mind*. Cambridge and New York: Cambridge University Press.

Wodak, R. (1999) 'Critical discourse analysis at the end of the 20th century', *Research on Language and Social Interaction*, 32(1 & 2), pp. 185–93.

Wodak, R. (2001) 'The discourse-historical approach', in R. Wodak and M. Meyer (eds), *Methods of Critical Discourse Analysis*. London: Sage, pp. 63–95.

Wodak, R., de Cillia, R., Reisigl, M. and Liebhart, K. (1999) *The Discursive Construction of National Identity* (trans. A. Hirsch and R. Mitten). Edinburgh: Edinburgh University Press.

10
Voicing the 'Other': Reading and Writing Indigenous Australians

Jim R. Martin

Orientation

In this chapter I will look briefly at interdisciplinarity in the context of cross-cultural communication. The communication I'm interested in is between Indigenous peoples and European settlers in contemporary Australia – specifically, the ways in which the settlers' voice represents the voice of the Indigenous 'other'.

My own experience with what might be referred to as interdisciplinary work has been mainly in the fields of linguistics and education (Hyon, 1996; Johns, 2001), where I worked with linguists alongside educators developing Australia's distinctive genre-based literacy programmes (Hasan and Williams, 1996; Christie and Martin, 1997; Christie, 1999; Martin, 2000). The success of this enterprise as far as intervention in various sectors was concerned depended on overlapping expertise – the extent to which functional linguists became expert in language education and language educators expert in functional linguistics. In Australia's bilingual education programme for Indigenous languages a role was conceived for teacher-linguists, with this kind of hybrid expertise in mind. The changes we had in mind for literacy teaching would never have got off the ground without the pioneering work of our theoretically bilingual educational linguists.

As a result, it has seemed important to me that interdisciplinary work be more than a matter of cooperation across disciplines, with experts dividing up a problem according to their expertise – handing over to another discipline when one's expertise wears thin. Over time, I have tended to prefer the term 'transdisciplinary' to 'interdisciplinary' in order to focus attention on the need for shared expertise (in the case of my language in education work, shared expertise about language and education). This not only enables changes to practise at sites of intervention, but also encourages cross-fertilization across theories. The chapters in Christie (1999) display a number of such engagements, with linguists contributing to the development of

Bernstein's work on pedagogic discourse and educators contributing to our understanding of social context, via register and genre theory.

Genuine transdisciplinary dialogue is of course a costly exercise because of the time involved familiarizing ourselves with another discipline. Consequently, it is important to have theories that fit and people who want to change the same kinds of things about the world. Bernstein's work on pedagogic discourse (1990, 1996) and Halliday's systemic functional linguistics (1994) have proved fruitful partners for this kind of exchange because of their ongoing concern with issues of language and education. Bernstein is unusual among sociologists in making a place for language in his theory, just as Halliday's commitment to linguistics as an ideologically committed form of social action is relatively unusual for linguists. The scope of their perspectives means that issues can be tackled from more than one perspective at the same time, and the complementary gazes generate real dialogue. Being able to see language development as a process of socialization in the home and at school was the key to renovating pedagogy and curriculum.

In this chapter I will exemplify the benefits of this kind of transdisciplinary gaze by drawing on functional linguistics and social semiotics to analyse modernist and postmodernist representations of indigenous Australians in multimodal discourse (including verbal and non-verbal representations).

Modern initiatives

Muecke comments that the 'most "obvious" history to write is the one which celebrates the achievements of the powerful, using the language of the powerful' (Benterrak et al., 1984 [1996], p. 143) – a practice Rose characterizes as a form of denial which 'engenders a complicity with all that has gone before... the past is concealed; and the living become accomplices in the continuation of injustice' (1991, p. 259). Elision of this kind has been a long-standing concern in Critical Discourse Analysis (CDA), and is pursued in some detail for the discipline of history in Martin and Wodak (2003). Complementing this style of critique, here I will be more concerned with attempts to address this imbalance – to unleash the hidden histories of the powerless – focusing on the voice of Indigenous peoples in Australia. I will limit the scope of the discussion in the first instance by concentrating on the walk-off by Aboriginal workers at Wave Hill station in 1966, which is generally taken as the beginning of the land rights movement in Australia; and will be concerned principally with the presentation of Indigenous accounts in Aboriginal English, setting aside translations from the vernacular such as those presented in Hercus and Sutton (1986).

A useful place to start is Frank Hardy's well-known 1968 account of the walk-off – *The Unlucky Australians*. Hardy makes room in his autobiographical recount for Aboriginal people to tell what happened in their own words, with Hardy writing down their stories. Vincent Lingiari, generally positioned as leader of the Gurindji people involved, begins his recount as follows:

> I am Vincent Lingiari from Wave Hill. That's my proper aboriginal name. Tom Pisher and that Bestey* mob called me Tommy Vincent. My people are Gurindji. Who live in Wave Hill area. That we country. They live here longa time before Cudeba. I have had Gunabida ceremony. Gunabida is the mother of all the Gurindji people, and the corroboree dances tell the story of a man and him son spewed up by the rainbow snake near Wattie Creek in the Dreamtime. I am Kadijeri man of Gurindji people. But Bestey mob don't understand 'bout that.
>
> The manager of Wave Hill was Tom Pisher. Bestey man, Tom Pisher. Always when big plant start to go out from station when mustering start, they go out two, maybe three month. Aboriginal men out in bush all time. White ringers come back to station ebry Friday night. That not right. I think to mesel' about that longa time. And think them Bestey mob don't treat Aboriginal native people right way. Some them white fellas play bloody hell with black gin women, leave Aborigine natives out in bush for that. When Aborigine stockmen come back they have to pack up and go away again. That not right. (Hardy, 1968, p. 71)

As we can see, Hardy preserves many of the features of Lingiari's Aboriginal English – commenting on the spelling as follows:

> *The Gurindji language has no F or V sounds so they substitute P and B for these when talking English.

No doubt some editing has taken place in the transcription process; this cannot be a completely faithful rendering of spoken language, as anyone who has written down recorded speech will recognize. But the normalization process that has taken place is certainly comparable to that Hardy uses for speakers of standard English in his book (normalizing false starts, repetitions, interjections and the like). I think we can be confident that as far as the transcription goes, the Indigenous voice has not been unduly compromised.

It is useful to contrast this strategy with discourse that speaks on behalf of Aboriginal people, as opposed to quoting them. Middleton (1977), for example, offers a history of the Australian Aboriginal people which is politically closely aligned with Hardy's account. But the actual stories told by the Gurindji about the walk-off are left outside her text, as primary sources. Middleton mentions the Gurindji stories (italics below), but then paraphrases them for us; and she uses indirect speech to report what Lily Punai said (italics below), rather than quoting her directly. Thus Middleton tells us what happened in her own words, based on the Gurindji recounts:

> The reaction to the Commission decision was immediate and dramatic. On May 1st Aboriginal pastoral workers from Newcastle Waters station went on strike and most of them left the station with their families. They were followed shortly after by employees from Wave Hill and other Vestey stations. The majority of the strikers were Gurindji people. By the end of the month most of the strikers had moved to a temporary camp on the banks of the Victoria River near the Wave Hill Welfare Settlement. The story of the first days is still often told by the Gurindji – a column of men, women and children, the older children and adults sharing the burden of carrying the younger ones when they got tired and the babies, their blankets and what little possessions and food they had been able to bring with them; a noisy crowd, excited, some happy, some frightened, some worried, surrounded by their dogs as they walked through mile after mile of rough bush country.
>
> Lily Punai had been doing ironing at Wave Hill homestead where she was employed as a domestic. A white stockman came in and told her that everyone else had gone and asked if she would stay. She *said* she would go. She put the iron away, rolled her swag and at the age of 55 set out alone to walk about 15 miles to join her people. (Middleton, 1977, p. 113)

There is no question of denial here; Middleton is just as concerned as Hardy with telling non-indigenous Australians what happened to Indigenous peoples. But in the traditional discourses of history there is a degree of silencing, since the Aboriginal voices are not directly heard. Rather they function as evidence – the material basis for higher level interpretations. Middleton's leftist reading of the walk-off concentrates on the full award wages issue, which she interprets as directly responsible for the strike. In the outline of her argument below I have used indentation below to show her progressive movement from this interpretation through to evidence. In linguistic terms this involves a transition from evaluated (*immediate, dramatic*) abstractions (*reaction, decision*) to concrete activity (*she put the iron away, rolled her swag and ... set out ...*); Martin (1991) presents a more detailed account of transitions of this kind in history discourse.

> In addition the Commissioners decided that payment of the full award wages should not come into operation until nearly three years later... (Middleton, 1977, p. 112)
>
> The *reaction* to the Commission *decision* was *immediate* and *dramatic*.
>
>> On May 1st Aboriginal pastoral workers from Newcastle Waters station went on strike and most of them left the station with their families.

They were followed shortly after by employees from Wave Hill and other Vestey stations. The majority of the strikers were Gurindji people. By the end of the month most of the strikers had moved to a temporary camp on the banks of the Victoria River near the Wave Hill Welfare Settlement.

> The story of the first days is still often told by the Gurindji – a column of men, women and children, the older children and adults sharing the burden of carrying the younger ones when they got tired and the babies, their blankets and what little possessions and food they had been able to bring with them; a noisy crowd, excited, some happy, some frightened, some worried, surrounded by their dogs as they walked through mile after mile of rough bush country.

Lily Punai had been doing ironing at Wave Hill homestead where she was employed as a domestic. A white stockman came in and told her that everyone else had gone and asked if she would stay. She said she would go. She put the iron away, rolled her swag and at the age of 55 set out alone to walk about 15 miles to join her people. (Middleton, 1977, p. 113)

Rose (1991), in a book entitled *Hidden Histories*, addresses this degree of silencing by incorporating Aboriginal voices directly into her account – by including her primary sources as it were. Instead of subsuming Aboriginal voices like Middleton, she quotes extensively from them – indenting her quotations, separating them from her text by skipping a line before and after, and giving them prominence by placing them in a larger font than that used for her own discourse.[1]

Hobbles told of a conversation at Daguragu between Tommy Vincent Lingiari (usually styled the leader of the strike), Vestey's representatives and Welfare Officers. For an Aboriginal audience in the Victoria River country, this story is a delicious unmasking of hypocrisy – European officials telling striking Aborigines that they must return to dependence on Europeans because they will not be able to get along without European goods. In refusing, Tommy Vincent invokes remembrance as the key to independence. His words are laden with sarcasm; the very goods he is told he cannot do without are those which have been denied for so many decades:

> Lotta Vestey mob and Welfare came up, trying to get them back.
> 'You can get your money.'
> 'No, we don't worry for money.'
> 'How you going to get a feed?'
> 'Lotta feed in the bush.'
> ... [13 lines elided]
> 'Don't live here. This the one for Vestey.'

'Vestey only got cattle, horse, but not land. That's mine. Might be Vestey had me one time, but not now.'

... [16 lines elided]

In a few words Hobbles Danayarri captured the resistance which had remained covert for so long: 'Tommy Vincent told Lord Vestey: "You can keep your gold. We just want our land back."' (Rose, 1991, pp. 228–9)

Like Hardy, Rose appears to normalize the transcription to some extent while preserving distinctive features of Aboriginal English; in addition she includes in parentheses information she thinks readers might require to follow the Indigenous discourse (for example, who is speaking in reported dialogue, glosses on distinctive usage, 'missing' words and explanatory contextual information).

Rhetorically, Rose's discourse is not unlike Middleton's in its movement from interpretation to the material basis for her evaluative abstractions. We hear much more from Rose than from Indigenous speakers, both before and after they 'speak': she interprets; they are primary sources. Rose uses metasemiotic terms (italicized below) to introduce their speech, and often paraphrases it for us before presentation. Using the indenting technique introduced above to display this movement, Rose's discourse unfolds along the following lines.

Technically speaking, Rose's metasemiotic nouns and verbs (*conversation, story, words, letter; told, telling, refusing, told*) project the Indigenous voice, which then grounds her interpretation – including both her abstractions (for example, *remembrance as the key to independence*) and evaluations (for example, *delicious unmasking of hypocrisy*). Here are some further examples of Rose's interpretations of quoted material from her chapter on the Wave Hill strike (with projecting nouns and verbs in italics).

Hobbles *spoke* of Sandy Moray working on behalf of Aborigines, and Riley Young *spoke* of him travelling south and establishing contacts with unions; Riley's *story* appears to date from about 1950: '...' (1991, p. 226)

Riley *told* what Sandy Moray used to tell the unionists ... His aim, as Riley *explains* it, was to enlist union backing for a strike which would radically alter Aboriginal people's lives materially with respect to land. '...' (ibid.)

Big Mick has never gone in for modesty, false or otherwise. He *described* his role in the strike in a *letter* he sent to Bob Hawke and Clyde Holding in 1984: '...' (ibid., p. 230)

Jack Doolan was a Welfare Officer before and during the strike. He *described* the VRD mob this way: '...' (ibid., pp. 233–4)

For an example of Indigenous voices that take primary responsibility for telling the story of what happened as opposed to simply illustrating it, we can turn to Wright (1998), an Indigenous writer whose *Take Power Like This Old Man Here: An Anthology of Writings Celebrating Twenty Years of Land Rights in Central Australia 1977–1997* was commissioned by the Central Land Council, an Aboriginal agency based in Alice Springs. Her section on the Wave Hill walk-off does begin with a brief account by Wright contextualizing the texts which follow:

> Drawing the line: the Gurindji walk-off and the birth of land rights
>
> ...
>
> On 22 August 1966 the Grindji people, working as stockmen and station hands in the north-west of Central Australia, walked off Wave Hill Station, then owned by England's Lord Vestey. Soon after, they set up a permanent camp nearby on part of their traditional land at Daguragu, a waterhole on Wattie Creek. A ten-year battle led by Vincent Lingiari followed, which moved from a strike for wages and better working conditions to a political struggle that eventually led to the *Aboriginal Land Rights (Northern Territory) Act 1976.*
>
> Then Prime Minister Gough Whitlam handed over the lease to Daguragu Station in August 1975 by pouring a handful of soil into the hands of Vincent Lingiari and saying the land would belong 'to you and your children forever'. The 3236 square kilometres of land was purchased from Wave Hill Station with money provided by the Aboriginal Land Fund. However, in October 1979 the Northern Territory Government said it would resume the land in twenty-eight days because the traditional landowners had not kept the pastoral lease conditions. The Gurindji prevented the resumption when they demonstrated that not only had the lease conditions been met but the property was well managed. To secure the title to their and the Gurindji lodged a land claim over the property.
>
> Twenty years after the Gurindji walk-off, in April 1986, the Gurindji were given inalienable freehold title to Daguragu under the Land Rights Act.

This is followed by five accounts of the walk-off, the first four of which are by Indigenous Australians – two in Aboriginal English and two in Gurindji, followed by translations[2] (the fifth account is by a non-indigenous Australian involved in the struggle). Wright's introductions to these texts are minimal:

> This is Mr Inverway's story, told in 1996 at the thirtieth anniversary of the Gurindji strike at Wave Hill Station.
>
> [none for Mr Rangiari]
>
> The translation[3] from Gurindji to English has been done by Kalkaringi Resource and Language Centre.

The translation from Gurindji to English has been done by Kalkaringi Resource and Language Centre.

[none for Ted Egan, whitefella]

Wright's voice thus takes up much less space than that of other speakers, and compared with Rose there is far less interpretation. Wright functions more as an editor than a historian, compiling an anthology of Indigenous and non-indigenous voices (with Indigenous voices taking precedence over non-indigenous ones). One might argue that Indigenous voices have taken over history here, although Wright's own discourse would be hard to distinguish from that of Rose or Middleton and it does still ultimately frame the meaning of the oral history described by Wright as the Indigenous accounts.

Looking over these initiatives, we can see a spectrum of possibilities – Hardy stepping aside now and again to let an Aboriginal person be heard; Middleton speaking as sympathetically as her politics affords[4] on their behalf; Rose taking pains to explain to us what they mean; and Wright giving her own people the floor. There are various complementarities at issue here. Hardy offers more of an eye-witness account; Middleton, Rose and Wright look back across time. Middleton and Rose offer historical interpretations; Hardy and Wright let the stories speak for themselves. Hardy, Rose and Wright quote directly from Indigenous people; Middleton subsumes their voice into hers. Hardy, Middleton and Rose enclose the Indigenous voice in their own; Wright lets other voices dominate her editorial role.

It is tempting of course to see this in evolutionary terms, with writers making more and more room for Indigenous voices in their texts. And there is some truth to this. Writers *have* struggled self-consciously against silencing the 'other'. And we should not lose sight of role played by female writers here – Hannah Middleton, Deborah Rose and Alexis Wright. Looking over the complementarities reviewed above, however, it might be just as wise to read developments as an expansion of the discursive terrain, with an ever increasing play of voices replacing the denial and silencing which shrouded Indigenous history in the past. As a note of caution, modernist historians, for example, might baulk at the idea that Lord Vestey was anywhere near Wave Hill Station during the land rights struggle there, even though both Indigenous voices (in Wright's anthology) and non-indigenous ones (for example, Kelly, 1999)[5] place him there, jousting with Lingiari. For Aboriginal oral historians this is probably not a case of mistaken identity; Rose would probably be quick to explain that figures such as Lord Vestey absorb individuals, especially those representing them, in Aboriginal (and perhaps all) oral history (see Rose, 1991, p. 18, on Captain Cook's invasion of northwestern Australia). So the pastoral care given to Indigenous voices in Middleton and Rose has an important role to play in bridging cultures and avoiding misunderstandings and discreditations which might derail the fragile Australian reconciliation processes already underway.

A postmodernist intervention

Alongside this emerging play of voices, Muecke's poststructuralist intervention (Benterrak et al., 1984 [1996]) becomes ever more relevant for the ways in which it interrogates modernist initiatives – by writers like Hardy and Wright, historians like Middleton and anthropologists like Rose. Muecke's project involves himself writing as a poststructural theorist[6] compiling an *'archive* of fragments which are representative of just about everything that has been said about Roebuck Plains' (ibid., p. 256); the archive foregrounds the 'successive negations' of Muecke's poststructural theory (in words and photographic images), stories by and dialogues with Paddy Roe (as Indigenous 'other') and a series of paintings by Krim Benterrak, a Moroccan artist who studied in Paris and went to Western Australia in 1977. Muecke styles the book, *Reading the Country*, as a 'record of Paddy Roe's dreaming at its most important nexus: the country itself' (ibid., p. 19), 'sensitive to Aboriginal understandings of the country, one that wrote nomadically, constantly deferring its authority to other sites and their guardians' (ibid., p. 23).

The archive first appears in a larger 'coffee-table' edition (1984) and later on as a very slightly revised smaller book-shelf edition (1996). Promotional material on the first page of the 1996 edition describes the book as 'a new dawn of literature … radical, innovative, unparalleled … absorbing, beautifully produced … inspiring for its integrity, optimism and humility' and as having 'the quiet intelligence and turbulent tension of a poem'. From these evaluations we can perhaps see that *Reading the Country* has a different provenance from the texts we've been considering so far; indeed, Rose (1996) and Rose and Clarke (1997) do not refer at all to Muecke's archive,[7] although they are concerned with tracking Indigenous knowledge in Australian landscapes – a project which looks to a naive linguist such as myself to be closely related to *Reading the Country*'s composite desires. We can perhaps glean as well that I can only touch on some of the interrogations arising from such a multivocal initiative, which is after all a resource designed for ongoing dialogue, not closure.

Let's begin with the issue of rendering Aboriginal English, glossed over in the comments on normalization and transcription above. Writing as a linguist, Muecke comments on the phonology, grammar and semantics of Paddy Roe's variety, which he describes as somewhere between a mild accent and a full-blown creole (Benterrak et al., 1984 [1996], pp. 270–1); and he includes a glossary to deal with unfamiliar lexis. In addition, Muecke's transcription of Paddy Roe's speech tries to capture the 'orality' of his discourse – including both the rhythm of the narratives and their dialogical nature. Muecke scribes Roe's stories into paragraphs according to discourse markers, changes in content and movement from place to place; and within paragraphs he divides the text into lines, with pauses indicated by a dash at the rate of about one per second. He instructs readers to observe 'this alternation of speech and silence' when reading the texts aloud (ibid., p. 271). Here's the beginning of Roe's story about how he avoided becoming a member of the 'Stolen Generation':[8]

> P'lice was gonna pick me up –
> Well err all the half-caste childrens you know p'lice pick-em-up whole lot –
> But my mother didn't want to let me go
> *Krim: And she hide you ...*
> Yeah I went er well –
>
> When we left sheep station –
> they took me out –
> when we got –
> we got up to the last windmill anyway –
> then from there no more windmills –
> we camped there
> *Krim: Right*
>
> So –
> next morning –
> old man was still sleeping –
> mother making tea –
> before sunrise so we can leave windmill you know –
>
> An' mother look –
> We seen the –
> He[9] seen dust in the road you know –
> *Krim: Yeah*
> Yeah –
> Horse and cart road, no motor car those days (Laughs)...

As we can see, Muecke resists normalizing Roe's speech as writing, faithfully scribing 'false starts and repetitions' and including dialogue with Benterrak – the oral features elided by Hardy, Rose and Wright. And Muecke's punctuation and layout is designed to scribe the rhythm of the story as it unfolds, one wave of information per line in a serial chaining texture. This is of course an unusual presentation for written narration, perhaps foregrounding description over transcription – and authenticity over translation. At first blush, the stories look like poetry – and Muecke construes his archive in poetic terms so explicitly that naive readers would have to be forgiven for mistaking them as such.

> But with three authors one cannot imagine that the book is guided by any poetic unity or harmony. On the contrary, the poetry is of a different sort, one that responds to our times. It is a poetry of fragmentation, contradiction, unanswered questions, specificity, fluidity and change...
> (Benterrak et al., 1984 [1996], p. 15)

Paddy Roe, for instance, constantly talks about the *bugarrigarra* as story, as song, as a power he controls and as things to do with *particular places*. To talk *bugarrigarra* about these places is to talk about 'spirits' one cannot see, about the 'rainbow snake' rising up out of springs; it is to talk in a special way which disrupts the uniformity of everyday language. It is a bit like the talk which we call poetry, attributing it with special qualities of transcendence. Could it be that the dreaming is no more than this? Since, in Paddy Roe's case, there is none of the fear which has been associated with 'primitive belief' (no superstitions, no hobgoblins in the dark), only a joy in telling stories and singing songs, then haven't European Australians made a mistake in calling it 'primitive belief', and comparing it unfavourably with 'science'? Someone who talks the discourse of the dreaming deserves to be treated in the same way as a novelist or a poet, but one who comes from a particular culture.

The dreaming is not a set of beliefs which is being lost because it is no longer valid, it is rather a way of talking, of seeing, of knowing, and a set of practices, which is as obtuse, as mysterious and as beautiful as any poetry ... (ibid., pp. 18–19)

But for both Aboriginal and 'general' readers there is a pleasure in the text of *bricolage*, a pleasure in seeing the edifice of language tremble a little as it becomes a kind of poetry. (ibid., pp. 171–2)

Reinforcing such a reading is the juxtaposition of Paddy Roe's discourse with Benterrak's landscape paintings and Muecke's poststructuralist writing – originally compiled as an attractive coffee-table edition. The Indigenous voice takes its place as 'poetry' alongside fine art and cultural theory, a radical transposition if compared with the down to earth, eye-witness, bald-faced recounts in Hardy, Rose and Wright. Whatever value we might place on recontextualization of this order, Muecke's transcription problematizes the issue of representing oral history in writing for literate consumers. It makes us re-read transcription as translation, orality as poetry, storyteller as novelist, dreaming as theory, orator as intellectual and so on – interrogations Muecke would no doubt be pleased to have instigated and equally reluctant to resolve.

Questions of representation also arise in *Reading the Country* with respect to imaging. I'll set aside Benterrak's fascinating dialogue with landscape here (his tilt at windmills and horizons) and focus on Muecke's photographs, which are in many respects as interrogative as his presentation of Paddy Roe's speech. McGregor (1991) draws on Kress and van Leeuwen (1996) to survey the photographic representation of Aborigines in a corpus he has collected over several years. His framework for analysis is shown in Table 10.1. The results of his survey are not hard to predict, with a predominance of representations foregrounding values such as 'powerless, not cultivated, passive, not engaging viewer', and so on. Photos of Indigenous people in Hardy,

Table 10.1 McGregor's photographic iconology

Opposition	Iconographic representation
powerful/powerless	high/low
cultivated/not cultivated; or	seated on chair/standing
paternal/not paternal	or seated on ground
civilized/savage	clothed/unclothed
active/passive	vector/no vector
transformer/observer	tool vector/sight vector
person/thing	non-profile/profile
engage, not engage with viewer	gaze at/away from viewer
entering civilization/wilds	motion towards/away from
dominated by/dominating viewer	gaze directed up/down to viewer
person (nurture)/setting (nature)	foregrounded/backgrounded
more or less personal involvement	close-up/medium/long shot

Source: McGregor (1991, p. 130).

Middleton, Rose and Wright are infrequent, and when they do appear they are not as radically divergent from McGregor's corpus as one might expect, given the politics of those ventures.

Muecke, however, photographs Paddy Roe and his friend Butcher Joe in different terms, at times explicitly drawing attention to the oppositions in McGregor's iconology by way of deconstructing naturalized readings of them. The first photo in *Reading the Country*, for example, is a close-up of Paddy Roe (head only), who is facing us and looking sharply to his left (our right). Muecke's caption reads (cf. 'engage/not engage with viewer – gaze at/away from viewer' above):

> You are looking at Paddy Roe while he is glancing to his left. Will your gazes ever meet? If so, will you recognise each other? Will this recognition be based on sameness or difference? (Benterrak et al., 1984 [1996], p. 21)

The second photo in the book is of a camp scene, a long shot of (viewing left to right) Butcher Joe, then Paddy Roe, then Muecke (who is scribing), sitting in a semicircle on the ground. Muecke's caption (cf. 'cultivated/not cultivated – seated on chair/on ground' above):

> *Paddy Roe said: 'You want a chair? I always sit on the ground – more better, can't fall down.'* (ibid., p. 27)

In further photos we look both up and down at Paddy Roe, who may be near or far, who is clothed, active, pointing, drawing, using tools, chatting with Butcher Joe (who is himself presented laughing with Benterrak). We see in other words a powerful man in full custodial care of his land as he shares his dreaming with Benterrak, Muecke and prospective readers. Muecke's images embody Roe's discourse in place, and thereby demonstrate that giving voice to Indigenous Australians is a multimodal project in which verbiage and image (and other modalities as well) work in tandem to construct readings of the 'other' – a potential which is not really taken up in the relatively monomodal texts reviewed above by Hardy, Rose and Wright. Once again, we can value Muecke's multimodal project in various ways. One thing his clearly framed proliferation of modalities (theory, 'poetry', painting, photography) opens up is the possibility of 'tactical' readings which attend partially to his desires – simply breezing through his photos and captions, for example, or dwelling on Benterrak's artwork. Would such partial readings undermine the politics of Muecke's archive? Theoretically speaking, could he care?

This brings us to the uneasy tension of deferral and proscription in Muecke's writing, as we may have come to expect from poststructuralist postures in a highly charged politicized context such as reconciliation between Indigenous and non-indigenous peoples in Australia. I'll pursue just one succession of negations to illustrate this here. *Reading the Country* is subtitled *Introduction to Nomadology* and dedicated to the nomads of Broome. Towards the end of the book, in an interview with B.R. Coffey, Muecke comments that he has 'not, of course, made any claims for Australians having an essentially nomadic way of life. The word is used metaphorically' (ibid., p. 259). In the first section of the book Muecke comments:

> When I sought an underlying theme or a book which emphasises place, the movement from one place to the next, I found it in 'nomadology', the study of nomadism (Deleuze & Guattari, 1980). One has to admit that this philosophy is rather adventitious; Krim and Paddy were both brought up within so-called nomadic cultures and that gave us something to talk about. (ibid., p. 19)

But:

> Nomadology is not a general theory, a summary of observations... and is constantly in flight from ideas or practices associated with the singular, the uniform, the central authority, the hierarchy... (ibid., p. 20)

Without:

> ... for all that ascribing to any form of anarchy. (ibid.)

And:

> It is descriptive... it might talk about things people do in their travels... (ibid.)

That is:

> it aims to describe practices, ways of living, (ibid.)

While:

> ... avoiding the pretence of describing a whole people. (ibid.)

But:

> It is ... also analytical and creative ... About abstract journeys taking place while one is sitting down; trips in intensity which involve working with a kind of avidity to keep words and images on the move. (ibid.)

Thus:

> ... this book is not about Aborigines. We have tried to avoid the us-and-them division by having three authors, three sources of author-ity, as it were. Also the focus on reading, on the means of communication, shifts attention away from people or society (the concern of anthropology) and from the linear depictions of events in time (the concern of history). (ibid.)

But:

> In correcting some things, other gaps appear. Women's voices play only a small part in this book ... (ibid.)

And later, in the final section of the book:

> For them (Deleuze & Guattari) nomadology is the study of nomadism ... and it is a philosophy which has been developed in recent years by scholars looking for ways to contest the Graeco-Roman philosophical traditions which have grown up with advances of Western capitalism and continue to be its support. (ibid., p. 241)

A counter-strategy:

> ... is to call nomadism a practice and a knowledge potentially present in relation to any event, potentially effective in relation to any struggle for survival. (ibid.)

The play of counter-expectation in writing of this kind is designed to unsettle modernist readings and makes it impossible for me to sum up Muecke's discourse around Paddy Roe's succinctly here. I can't distil the theory; it's not there. What we have instead is a stance realized through a particular way of writing, a specific set of practices for texturing a gaze. Certainly this gaze encloses Paddy Roe, as Muecke explicitly laments (ibid., p. 258); but where he pronounces on Benterrak's paintings, he resists interpreting Paddy Roe's discourse for us – and yet he does interpret it. Looking back at Rose we could say that Indigenous voices in her history illustrate her points once she's explained to us what they mean; with Muecke there is more of a dialogue between Paddy Roe's voice and his own.[10] One informs the other, enhances the reading of the other ... but the Indigenous voice is not paraphrased, and thus in some sense owned.

How we value this is once again an important concern. It does take work to read Paddy Roe's discourse – more work than for the tamed discourse in Hardy, Rose and Wright. The layout is more time consuming, the Aboriginal English more distant, the place oriented meanings less familiar, and so on. And it takes work to read Muecke's poststructural theory. Elsewhere (Martin, 2003) I have argued that postmodern discourse takes the abstract discourse of modernity and re-embeds it, as it were, in a discourse of semiotic abstractions. So whereas modernity has abstractions acting on abstractions instead of people acting on people and things, postmodernity has discourse acting on discourse. Muecke's defence of theory illustrates this point:

> I wanted a reader who would become the prey of the text, seduced by its movement, reaching a breathless and mobile conclusion, ready for action and debate in relation to those issues which are most pressing for our survival in this country. The later fragments may seem too theoretical to some but in my opinion theory is not all that abstract, theories are the readily available frames in which certain questions and assumptions are allowed, and certain statements appear ... in this way they have concrete effects. (Benterrak et al., 1984 [1996], p. 259)

Here the text seduces readers, readers reach conclusions, frames allow questions and assumptions, and theories have concrete effects. In everyday life, processes such as *seduce*, *reach* and *allow* can be directly related to concrete events: *someone reaching home perhaps, allowing someone in, and the pair seducing one another*. Turn this into modernist abstraction and we have something more like *arrival home and subsequent entry permission led to seduction* – the discourse of professions, disciplines and institutions (Martin, 1993). Turn this into postmodern semiosis and we get text, readers, frames and theories as agents affecting readers, and effecting conclusions, questions, assumptions and concrete effects (which nominalization is, of course, anything but concrete).

Thinking about the kind of education it requires to master discourse of this order, I can feel Muecke's readership shrinking. How many of us will bother to read? Will we simply end up browsing through the pictures after all? Over coffee, while chatting with friends? And what if we aren't interested in art? Will we take the book off the coffee table? Would we buy it at all? Is the new, smaller edition of *Reading the Country* an attempt to recast it for a more rarefied academic sphere?

Readings and writings

Transdisciplinarity

In this chapter I have drawn on Systemic Functional Linguistics (hereafter SFL) and social semiotics (Multimodal Discourse Analysis, hereafter MDA, in particular) to analyse modernist and poststructuralist representations of the voice of Indigenous peoples in Australia. Functional linguistics was deployed to analyse the language used to introduce the voice of the 'other' – the kinds of projection and metadiscourse deployed, and the kinds of expansion connecting one voice to another (elaboration or extension). MDA was used to consider the use of images in relation to this verbal material. One thing a focus on imaging draws attention to is the significance of graphology as a resource for foregrounding Indigenous voices in texts that otherwise enclose the 'other'.

Although I have not foregrounded it in this chapter it is important to note that the MDA used by McGregor and myself was designed by Kress and van Leeuwen (1996) on the basis of Halliday's systemic functional analysis of English grammar. So one might argue that beyond a transdisciplinary project with overlapping expertise such as that I described at the beginning of the chapter, what we are in fact looking at is the emergence of a transdisciplinary theory – systemic functional semiotics (SFS?) transcending SFL and MDA (Lemke, 1998; Martinec, 1998, 2000a, 2000b, 2000c, 2001; Baldry, 1999; O'Halloran, 1999a, 1999b, 2000; van Leeuwen, 1999; Kress et al., 2001; Kress and van Leeuwen, 2001; van Leeuwen and Jewitt, 2001; Unsworth, 2001; Martin, 2002a, 2002b, 2003). And this raises important questions about what kind of theory can function in this way. One thing I would emphasize here is the importance of a multi-perspectival perspective – a theory that looks across modalities, using a range of complementarities such as metafunctions (modes of meaning), strata (levels of abstraction) and ranks (units of different size). Poststructuralism has served us well as far as deconstructing theories and discourses is concerned; but its successive negations make it less than effective as a tool for intervention. Perhaps it is time to begin constructing theories that transcend the grand monovocal and inherently reductive systems of modernity, with multiperspectivity as a key ingredient for practically oriented transdisciplinary work.

Voicing

We have taken just a glance at reconciliation discourse in Australia here, focusing on representations of the Wave Hill walk-off and Paddy Roe's country (Roebuck Plains). As far as giving voice to Indigenous Australians is concerned we can already see a range of disciplines involved – writers, historians, anthropologists, linguists and cultural theorists. And typically authors and editors play more than one role at a time – Hardy as writer and historian, Rose as historian and anthropologist, Muecke as linguist and cultural theorist. Whatever their composite roles, giving voice involves producing texts, and so there is a role for critical discourse analysts to play in understanding what is going on. And since the texts are multimodal ones, this analysis itself will have to be a composite one, involving analysis of both language and image (and other modalities as they arise) – implicating both linguistics and social semiotics, as these disciplines are now conceived. One thing I am trying to suggest here as far as an interdisciplinary gaze on an interdisciplinary initiative is concerned is that we look at positive developments – at sites where people strive to make the world a better place – alongside our more familiar (and perhaps more comfortable) deconstructions of semiosis as it enacts hegemony at sites of crisis and enduring malaise around the world (Martin, 2004a[2006]).

As for giving voice to Indigenous Australians, we have surveyed a range of possibilities, including discourse that subsumes their story (Middleton), that paraphrases and interprets it (Rose) and that backs off to let it stand alone (Wright). One thing we need to keep in mind in evaluating these strategies is that however hands-on or hands-off our approach, a text is still a meaning potential. It will be taken up and read in different ways, according to the interested social subjectivities involved. For example, I first read Paddy Roe's story about avoiding being taken from his mother and sent to Beagle Bay Mission as an amusing anecdote about Indigenous people outsmarting the police. Years later, now I understand a little more about the Stolen Generations issue, I read the story more as an exemplum about genocide and shudder at the cultural implications of his narrow escape and others' tragic misfortunes. Anecdotes, exemplums – these are of course my Western narrative frames (Martin and Plum, 1997); but that is just the point – I cannot not read through non-indigenous eyes. Muecke's poststructural interrogations take up this issue of interested readings in important ways. He's not just striving to let Indigenous Australians speak; he knows that that is not enough. Beyond giving voice he wants us to think about how we hear – how we read the voices that are presented to us, and how we read the discourse enacting those presentations.

How we value this range of interventions in relation to reconciliation is for me a matter of time and place. I suspect that for people struggling to move out of modernity into a postcolonial Australian world, then Rose's strategy is a supportive one. Her texture (of interpretation, paraphrase and illustration) forms a bridge from 'our' culture to 'theirs' – a path across if we want to take it. An avenue for sympathy, perhaps empathy; for respect, perhaps understanding. This is paternalistic of course; but perhaps a charitable outlook is the best that mainstream Australia can manage in these reactionary times when rapid economic change unnerves the populus and shameless politicians blame any 'others' they can find for what is going on.

Looking further ahead, Rose's strategy doesn't really involve genuine dialogue. For that we need other possibilities, including those in which Indigenous voices give voice to us. Reading through the Indigenous papers in, say, Gratton (2000), or listening to the Indigenous band Yothu Yindi (1992), I am both shamed and heartened by the generosity of their framing – 'their' willingness to share with 'us'. Yunupingu sings and writes of double power (1999), two-way education (1990) – discourse for negotiation, from which invaders have so much to learn.

Notes

1. Personally, I found this graphological foregrounding quite disconcerting when first reading *Hidden Histories*, often feeling confused about who was quoting whom – which attests in no small part to its ideological significance.
2. As noted above, translated material is beyond the scope of this discussion, but mention should be made here of Hercus and Sutton (1986) which includes two sections on the Wave Hill walk-off – a recount by Johnny Kijngayari and the 1975 handover speech by Vincent Lingiari (1986), both translated line by line from the Gurindji and annotated by Patrick McConvell. Hercus and Sutton briefly contextualize this material before handing over to the Aboriginal voices.
3. We should keep in mind of course that the transcriptions of Aboriginal English by Hardy, Rose and Wright all involve some degree of translation – across modalities from spoken language to writing, and across dialects from less standard forms to more standard ones; for discussion of Aboriginal English in trial, see Eades (1995), Hill (1999).
4. Writing from a left union-oriented position, Middleton (like Hardy), tends to read what happened at Wave Hill as a strike over wages, as opposed to, say, a protest concerning land rights and culture.
5. Paul Kelly and Kev Carmody's popular land rights anthem, 'From Little Things Big Things Grow' was released in 1991 and has certainly introduced more Australians to the Gurindji walk-off than any other account. They invent some punchy dialogue for Lingiari, who is presented as an Aussie battler taking on the British Lord (see Martin, 2002c, for discussion).
6. And occasionally as a linguist (Benterrak et al., 1984 [1996], pp. 270–2) and social semiotician (some of his readings of images throughout the book), two discourses in which he also has professional expertise.
7. Nor to Muecke (1992) for that matter.
8. As Muecke explains: 'In the first decades of this century, when the first generation of part-Aboriginal children was appearing, the practice of authorities was to collect the children and send them to Beagle Bay Mission, north of Broome. This practice effectively blocked their traditional education. This book would never have been possible if Paddy Roe has not avoided the police' (Benterrak et al., 1984 [1996], p. 264). This was the first I'd heard of what was to become widely known in Australia as the 'Stolen Generations', following publication of *Bringing Them Home* (1997); see also Bird (1998), Manne (1998, 2001), Read (1999, 2000), Reynolds (1999), Tickner (2001).

9. As Muecke footnotes, 'Aboriginal English does not indicate gender in the pronoun. "He", therefore, is "mother"' (1996, p. 264).
10. Muecke does, however, explain Butcher Joe's songs, inserting them into his section 'The song in the story' in a manner akin to Rose.

References

Baldry, A. (ed.) (1999) *Multimodality and Multimediality in the Distance Learning Age.* Campo Basso: Lampo.

Bernstein, B. (1990) *Class, Codes and Control 4: The Structuring of Pedagogic Discourse.* London: Routledge.

Bernstein, B. (1996) *Pedagogy, Symbolic Control and Identity: Theory, Research, Critique.* London and Bristol, PA: Taylor & Francis (Critical Perspectives on Literacy and Education).

Benterrak, K., Muecke, S. and Roe, P. (1984 [1996]) *Reading the Country.* Freemantle, WA: Freemantle Arts Centre Press (revised edition, 1996).

Bird, C. (ed.) (1998) *The Stolen Generations: Their Stories.* Sydney: Random House.

Christie, F. (ed.) (1999) *Pedagogy and the Shaping of Consciousness: Linguistic and Social Processes.* London: Cassell (Open Linguistics Series).

Christie, F. and Martin, J.R. (1997) *Genres and Institutions: Social Processes in the Workplace and School.* London: Pinter (Open Linguistics Series).

Eades, D. (1995) 'Aboriginal English on trial: the case for Stuart and Condren', in D. Eades (ed.), *Language in Evidence: Issues Confronting Aboriginal and Multicultural Australia.* Sydney: University of New South Wales Press, pp. 147–74.

Gratton, M. (ed.) (2000) *Reconciliation: Essays on Australian Reconciliation.* Melbourne: Black Inc.

Halliday, M.A.K. (1994) *An Introduction to Functional Grammar* (2nd edition). London: Edward Arnold.

Hardy, F. (1968) *The Unlucky Australians.* Melbourne: Thomas Nelson.

Hasan, R. and Williams, G. (eds) (1996) *Literacy in Society.* London: Longman (Applied Linguistics and Language Study).

Hercus, L.A. and Sutton, P. (eds) (1986) *This is What Happened.* Canberra: Australian Institute of Aboriginal Studies.

Hill, B. (1999) 'Driftwood: T.G.H. Strehlow and the Stuart case', *Strehlow Research Centre Occasional Paper* 2, pp. 121–70.

Human Rights and Equal Opportunity Commission (1997) *Bringing Them Home: National Inquiry into the Separation of Aboriginal and Torres Strait Islander Children from Their Families.* Sydney.

Hyon, S. (1996) 'Genre in three traditions: implications for ESL', *TESOL Quarterly,* 30(4), pp. 693–722.

Johns, A.M. (ed.) (2001) *Genres in the Classroom: Applying Theory and Research to Practice.* Mahwah, NJ: Lawrence Erlbaum.

Kelly, P. (1999) *Don't Start me Talking: Lyrics 1984–1999.* Sydney: Allen & Unwin.

Kress, G., Jewitt, C., Ogborn, J. and Tsatsarelis, C. (2001) *Multimodal Teaching and Learning: The Rhetorics of the Classroom.* London: Continuum (Advances in Applied Linguistics).

Kress, G. and van Leeuwen, T. (1996) *Reading Images: The Grammar of Visual Design.* London: Routledge.

Kress, G. and van Leeuwen, T. (2001) *Multimodal Discourse – The Modes and Media of Contemporary Communication.* London: Edward Arnold.

Lemke, J. (1998) 'Multiplying meaning: visual and verbal semiotics in scientific text', in Martin and Veel (eds), pp. 87–113.

Lingiari, V. (1986) 'Vincent Lingiari's Speech' (trans. P. McConvell), in L.A. Hercus and P. Sutton (eds), *This is What Happened*. Canberra: Australian Institute of Aboriginal Studies, pp. 312–15.

McGregor, W. (1991) 'Photographs of Aborigines and police', *Social Semiotics*, 1(2), pp. 123–58.

Manne, R. (1998) 'The stolen generations', *Quadrant*, No. 343, Vol. XLII(1–2), pp. 53–63.

Manne, R. (2001) *In Denial: The Stolen Generations and the Right*. Melbourne: Black (republished from *Quarterly Essay*, 1, 2001).

Martin, J.R. (1991) 'Nominalisation in science and humanities: distilling knowledge and scaffolding text', in E. Ventola (ed.), *Functional and Systemic Linguistics: Approaches and Uses*. Trends in Linguistics: Studies and Monographs 55. Berlin: Mouton de Gruyter.

Martin, J.R. (1993) 'Technology, bureaucracy and schooling: discursive resources and control', *Cultural Dynamics*, 6(1), pp. 84–130.

Martin, J.R. (1999) 'Grace: the logogenesis of freedom', *Discourse Studies*, 1(1), pp. 31–58.

Martin, J.R. (2000) 'Design and practice: enacting functional linguistics in Australia', *Annual Review of Applied Linguistics*, 20 (20th Anniversary Volume 'Applied Linguistics as an Emerging Discipline'), pp. 116–26.

Martin, J.R. (2002a) 'Writing history: construing time and value in discourses of the past', in C. Colombi and M. Schleppergrell (eds), *Developing Advanced Literacy in First and Second Languages*. Mahwah, NJ: Lawrence Erlbaum, pp. 87–118.

Martin, J.R. (2002b) 'Fair trade: negotiating meaning in multimodal texts', in Patrick Coppock (ed.), *The Semiotics of Writing: Transdisciplinary Perspectives on the Technology of Writing*. Brepols: Indiana University Press, pp. 311–38.

Martin, J.R. (2002c) 'Blessed are the peacemakers: reconciliation and evaluation', in C. Candlin (ed.), *Research and Practice in Professional Discourse*. Hong Kong: City University Press.

Martin, J.R. (2003) 'Making history: grammar for explanation', in J.R. Martin and R. Wodak (eds), *Re/reading the Past: Critical and Functional Perspectives on Time and Value*. Amsterdam: Benjamins.

Martin, J.R. (2004 and 2006) 'Positive discourse analysis: solidarity and change', *Revista Canaria de Estudios Ingleses* 49, pp. 179–200. Reprinted 2006 in *The Journal of English Studies* 4(14), pp. 21–35. Sichuan International Studies University, China.

Martin, J.R. (2004b) 'Sense and sensibility: texturing evaluation', in J. Foley (ed), *Language, Education and Discourse: Functional Approaches*. London: Continuum, pp. 270–304.

Martin, J.R. and Plum, G. (1997) 'Construing experience: some story genres', *Journal of Narrative and Life History*, 7(1–4), special issue, 'Oral versions of personal experience: three decades of narrative analysis', (ed. M. Bamberg (guest)), pp. 299–308.

Martin, J.R. and Wodak, R. (2003) *Re/Reading the Past*. Amsterdam: John Benjamins.

Martinec, R. (1998) 'Cohesion in action', *Semiotica*, 120(1/2), pp. 161–80.

Martinec, R. (2000a) 'Rhythm in multimodal texts', *Leonardo*, 33(4), pp. 289–97.

Martinec, R. (2000b) 'Types of process in action', *Semiotica*, 130(3/4), pp. 243–68.

Martinec, R. (2000c) 'Construction of identity in M. Jackson's "Jam" ', *Social Semiotics*, 10(3), pp. 313–29.

Martinec, R. (2001) 'Interpersonal resources in action', *Semiotica*, 135(1/4), pp. 117–45.

Reading and Writing Indigenous Australians 219

Middleton, H. (1977) *But Now We Want Our Land Back: A History of the Australian Aboriginal People*. Sydney: New Age Publishers.

Muecke, S. (1992) *Textual Spaces: Aboriginality and Cultural Studies*. Sydney: New South Wales University Press (Communication and Culture).

O'Halloran, K. (1999a) 'Interdependence, interaction and metaphor in multisemiotic texts', *Social Semiotics*, 9(3), pp. 317–54.

O'Halloran, K. (1999b) 'Towards a systemic functional analysis of multisemiotic mathematics texts', *Semiotica*, 124(1/2), pp. 1–29.

O'Halloran, K. (2000) 'Classroom discourse in mathematics: a multisemiotic analysis', *Linguistics and Education*, 10(3), special issue, 'Language and other semiotic systems in education', pp. 359–88.

Paul Kelly and the Messengers (1991) *Comedy*. Sydney: Mushroom Records.

Read, P. (1999) *A Rape of the Soul so Profound: The Return of the Stolen Generations*. Sydney: Allen & Unwin.

Read, P. (2000) *Belonging: Australians, Place and Aboriginal Ownership*. Cambridge: Cambridge University Press.

Reynolds, H. (1999) *Why Weren't We Told?: A Personal Search for the Truth About Our History*. Melbourne: Viking.

Rose, D.B. (1991) *Hidden Histories: Black Stories from Victoria Rover Downs, Humbert River and Wave Hill Stations*. Canberra: Aboriginal Studies Press.

Rose, D.B. (1996) *Nourishing Terrains: Australian Aboriginal Views of Landscape and Wilderness*. Canberra: Australian Heritage Commission.

Rose, D.B. and Clarke, A. (eds) (1997) *Tracking Knowledge in North Australian Landscapes: Studies in Indigenous and Settler Ecological Systems*. Canberra: North Australia Research Unit, Australian National University.

Royal Commission into Aboriginal Deaths in Custody (1991) *National Report of the Royal Commission into Aboriginal Deaths in Custody*. Vols 1–5. Canberra: Australian Government Publishing Service.

Tickner, R. (2001) *Taking a Stand: Land Rights to Reconciliation*. Sydney: Allen & Unwin.

Unsworth, L. (2001) *Teaching Multiliteracies across the Curriculum: Changing Contexts of Text and Image in Classroom Practice*. Buckingham: Open University Press.

van Leeuwen, T. (1999) *Speech, Music, Sound*. London: Macmillan.

van Leeuwen, T. and Jewitt, C. (2001) *Handbook of Visual Analysis*. London: Sage.

Wright, A. (ed. for the Central Land Council) (1998) *Take Power Like This Old Man Here: An Anthology of Writings Celebrating Twenty Years of Land Rights in Central Australia 1977–1997*. Alice Springs: IAD Press (Jukurrpa Books).

Yothu Yindi (1992) *Tribal Voice*. Sydney: Mushroom Records.

Yunupingu, M. (1990) 'Language and power: the Yolgnu rise to power at Yirrkala School', in C. Walton and W. Egginton (eds), *Language: Maintenance, Power and Education in Australian Aboriginal Contexts*. Darwin: Northern Territory University Press, pp. 3–6.

Yunupingu, M. (1999) 'Double power', in P. Wignell (ed.), *Double Power: English Literacy and Indigenous Australia*. Melbourne: Language Australia, pp. 1–4.

Part III

From Theory to Social and Political Practice

11
Activist Sociolinguistics in a Critical Discourse Analysis Perspective[1]

Patricia E. O'Connor

Critical Discourse Analysis (CDA) advocates interdisciplinarity in research, forging bonds *among* rather than divisions *in* research paradigms. In this chapter I propose we conjoin the linguistic and social picture, which many conference panels present, by examining applied research which more fully fleshes out and inherently repositions us as members of both a linguistic research community as well as a global community whose interests include social organizations, cultural representations, political and ideological praxis, new technologies for learning and communicating, conflict management, workplace roles, crime, justice, survival, and identity, and – if we want to dream large – an improved quality of life. How can our research add to the quality of life? John Rickford suggested in an address at the Georgetown University Roundtable on Linguistics 2000 that we linguists are at a crossroads where we must consider our parts in doing more with the knowledge we produce. This chapter takes up that challenge suggesting that an activist sociolinguistics can emerge from the empirical work we linguists do. In light of the 11 September terrorist attacks on the World Trade Center in New York and the Pentagon in Washington, DC, and their association with compelling discourses calling for violence and counter-attacks, we can see even more of an urgency to conjoin our work in understanding the connections between what we research and what we do with research, especially research such as mine that deals with discourses of violence.

To name a few recent sources on which this activist work on violence draws, we can look at prior analyses: of language of prejudice and hate by van Dijk (1989, 1991, 1993); Wodak and Matouschek (1993); Wodak (1996b); Leudar and Nekvapil (2000); Reisig and Wodak (2001); of argument and incitement to violence by Labov (1981); Grimshaw (1990); Briggs (1993); O'Connor (1994, 1995a, 1995b, 2001); of misunderstandings of culture by Schiffrin (1984) and Tannen (1990).[2] These studies further expand our questioning of the connections between talk and actions that provide uptake to charged language. We see this as well in work by critical discourse analysts such as Wodak, who is involved in new studies of institutional discourse, and Fairclough, who reminds us of critical positionings found in networks of 'dominance, difference, and resistance' (Fairclough, 2001). Wodak's *Disorders of Discourse*, in particular, asserts that critical discourse linguistics analyses power relationships and disordered discourses to promote reflection that creates 'critical agents who query the underlying assumptions of structures in our society and equip them with the linguistic tools for demystifying power relationships and de-harmonizing pseudo-harmony' (1996a, p. 180).

In my own research on maximum-security prisoners and on addicts I use CDA to examine the ways in which people agentively present themselves in autobiographical discourse, positioning themselves not only in their criminal or errant pasts but narratively constructing past selves and potentially new selves in society. I suggest that elements of agentive discourse are clustered in sites of reflexive language, particularly in frame breaks and in meta-talk or evaluative references to one's knowledge state. Such breaks interpenetrate the narratives and complicate the determination of personal, moral agency because they reveal an epistemic grappling with the action taken (in the past) while showing agentive manipulation of the story (in the present). Such constructivist work places the speaker and the linguist in an interesting nexus of practice that could effect change.

Linking our practices

Ron Scollon describes a nexus of practice as 'a network of linked practices' (2001, p. 147) and stipulates that these practices while being interconnected may be loosely linked and are only understood over time. To demonstrate this he uses the simple situation of ordering a latte at a coffee bar. A series of ordering, selecting, refining an order (non fat?, 2 per cent milk?) paying, waiting, receiving, and so on, face the purchaser with each instance of the practice, an act which can grow more complex over time and in different coffee bars. A nexus of practice within the researcher's experience doing CDA will also involve an overlapping, interconnecting, changing and developing set of actions diachronically and synchronically charged with texts and tensions for interpretation.

In 1984 I entered the nexus of practice of American incarceration and criss-crossed it with the practice of teaching and, after six years, with specific research and subsequently with more teaching. Those contexts for research as well as the larger contexts surrounding and interpenetrating that research set up the call I take up here for acknowledging activist linguistics. Activist linguistics, as I see it, does not mean that the researcher skew her or his findings to support one group or one ideology or another. Nor does it mean that a famous linguist use her or his fame to support causes.[3] Rather, an activist linguistics calls for researchers to remain connected to the communities in which they research, returning to those settings to apply the knowledge they have generated for the good of the community and to deepen the research through expansion or focus. Wodak's long-term commitment to study of discourses in community settings – therapeutic discourses, media discourses, educational discourses – shows one such model of expanding research agendas, which over time show the interconnectedness of hierarchical models of maintaining power (see, for instance, Wodak, 1996a; Reisigl and Wodak, 2001, for longitudinal analyses of prior research in current contexts).

Methods and long-term commitment

Details of what I as an ethnographic researcher did to explore the prison milieu are found in *Speaking of Crime* (O'Connor, 2000). In that work, using 101 narratives of criminal acts told by inmates in a US maximum-security prison, I analysed narratives of violent acts by focusing on reflexive moments in the discourse relating those acts. My approach was interdisciplinary, drawing from the fields of sociolinguistics, social psychology and literary theory as I examined autobiographical narratives in textual, social, cultural and personal contexts. I extended the idea of a participation framework to include the working of language on the formation and reformation of a self in society. I argued that we can see a grammar of agency within the units of discourse that speakers use in telling their autobiographies. That reflexivity can be observed *not only* in the prisoners' own epistemic considerations, but also in a 'community reflexivity' via the uptake a community takes towards those it puts inside prisons. In that respect, the research joined into a larger nexus of practice.

After a presentation of examples from institutional data, this chapter grapples with the issue of subjectivity that the previous paragraph entails when the researcher herself is part of that reflexivity in a community of uptake. In light of this positioning I discuss my methods for beginning new research projects into narratives from those in substance-abuse treatment. People in prison have often entered those walled-off places through the practice of drug use, addiction or illicit drug sales. I consider myself a critical discourse analyst by method and an activist linguist by inclination, situating my work within communities most known for their transgressive acts. My research suggests that long-term involvement in a setting leads to a thicker, richer interpretation of data that can contribute to social change. I acknowledge and emphasize the involvement I used to set up research during extensive volunteer work prior to and after collection of data on violence and violation: 18 years of teaching and service in a prison surrounded the first life story collection; seven years of administrative and academic service encompass my new project gathering life stories of substance abusers. Questions to be pursued include, 'How do attachments to (or detachment from) speakers affect data?', 'How can informants become co-researchers?', 'How do researchers form partnerships with communities?', 'Does participatory action research allow for continuing relationships of inquiry?', and 'Can we form "reciprocal" Zones of Proximal Development as researcher-learners?'

Background on prison and illegal drug use

Research into prisoners' lives requires that we situate their individual accounts within a larger, national story of incarceration. By mid-2000, 1.9 million persons populated prisons and jails in the United States (Beck and Karberg, 2001, p. 1). By end of 2000, that number had increased to 2,071,686 (Beck and Harrison, 2001, p. 1). In the last decade the rate of incarceration in the United States increased from 1 in every 218 residents to 1 in every 142 (Beck and Karberg, 2001, p. 1). Even with these large numbers, the actual personal involvement with criminal justice sentencing is much greater. Over 6.3 million people are on probation, in jail or prison, or on parole, according to the United States Bureau of Justice Corrections Statistics (2001).[4] The major precipitating causes for incarceration are drug related. The Department of Justice information estimates that '70% of all inmates in local facilities had committed a drug offense or used drugs regularly in 1998' (Wilson, 2000, p. 1). Over 50 per cent of all adult arrestees in a study of 34 sites spread over the United States tested positive for one of five drugs in the year 1999, according to the Arrestee Drug Abuse Monitoring Program (ADAM) of the National Institute of Justice (2000, p.1). Thus, the research I did into imprisonment necessarily needs *to expand* to larger precipitating forces for criminal behaviour. It also needs *to focus* on the understanding of drug use, addiction, crime and drug-related incarceration as well as recovery if I am to make an impact upon rehabilitation through the research I conduct.

Inside criminals' lives

A look at samples of discourse from maximum-security prisoners shows us something of the dangerous world of criminals and the equally dangerous world inside prisons and their connections to drug sales and drug addiction. Briefly below, I include an example[5] of the dangerous world inside prison depicted in a narrative by a man, to whom I give the pseudonym 'Edward', who was stabbed at night as he slept in his supposedly locked cell.

39   Blood was shooting out everywhere.
40   But still . . that didn't stop me.
41   I knew I had to get this knife out of his hand,
42   because if I didn't . .
43   I would have been dead in there, you know.
44   That was my objective right there.

45   I wasn't worrying about dying at the time, you know.
46   I just had to get this knife out of his hand.
47   And when I did get the knife out of his hand,
48   it fell up underneath the bed.
49   I didn't even try to reach it, you know.
50   He ran out the cell on the tier, you know,
51   and left me standing in the cell.
52   But by this time I had lost so much blood,
53   the floor look like it had about a inch of blood on it,
54   you know.
55   I had lost so much,
56   I was sliding down.
57   But I picked myself back up,
58   and walked out on the tier.

We see in this story, besides the simple narration of events, a man contemplating the actions he took which saved his life. He mentions his knowledge state, 'I knew I had to get this knife out of his hand' (line 41) and that he knew he could not stop to worry about dying (line 45). He makes a meta-comment on his action, 'That was my objective right there', in line 44. These aspects of his story management reveal that autobiographical recollection is a fruitful site for capturing reflexivity in discourse, a type of talk that has therapeutic potential.

On the streets

When the speaker is not the victim but the victimizer, can we also note moments of such useful reflection? In the following passage, an inmate I call 'Roman' describes how he came to his 40-year prison sentence for murder.[6] Of interest to this discussion is the reflective discourse with which Roman comments on the action scene he recalls in this narrative.

1 POC: What led you here?
2 Roman: . . . It was like I said,
3   we was selling drugs,
4   and I was supposed to go see some people,
5   get some more drugs.
6   And, when we got there,
7   they decided they wasn't gonna give me any drugs.
            They was just gonna take my money . .
                ould n't let it happen.
                aw one of the guys reaching for his gun,
                t both of 'em have it . .
                esses say that it was a arm,

13		they thought it was an armed robbery,
14		because I gave the guy the bag
15		with the money in it.
16		When he refused me,
17		I shot him.
18		And he dropped it.
19		Witnesses saw me pick the bag up,
20		so they thought it was a robbery.
21		They was trying to hurt me,
22		so I had to do something.
23	POC:	So what's the charge then?
24	Roman:	Murder, armed robbery, murder one,
25		murder to [commit?] armed robbery,
26		carrying a pistol without a licence.
27	POC:	And for that you got how many years?
28	Roman:	I got 40 to life.

In my early linguistic analysis of this narrative, following Labov, Schiffrin and Tannen, I noted that the speaker here reports the events in the complicating actions that we see in lines 3, 6, 10 and 11. He was selling drugs, he went somewhere to buy more drugs, he saw someone reach for a gun, and he shot two people. Surrounding this bare schema are evaluations that suggest Roman has taken a more contemplative, reflective positioning on the acts. Reflexivity comes with the immediate repetition of the narrative and subsequent amplification in the section that follows the pause at the end of line 11 'so I let both of 'em have it . .'. In lines 12–22, Roman provides more details, contemplating what witnesses suggested, claiming they had seen Roman in an act of robbery. Thus, Roman presents himself in the interview frame as a man who is protecting his business interests, not an armed robber and murderer, in spite of what witnesses and later courts decide.

How might an activist linguist proceed, beyond carefully describing components of narrative analysis based on this interview excerpt? The story's second iteration shows how the speaker rationalizes his action to shoot and orients the listener to two overlapping sets of practices: (1) the street-crime world where fast reactions protect assets and take lives, and (2) the courtroom world where witnesses make testimony for jurors to determine consequences. Later portions of Roman's interview reveal a more astute self-positioning. Toward the end of Roman's remarks he contemplates his life in general as a result of the attraction to the world of drug sales:

425	I got caught up on the life,
426	the fast life,
427	the women, the money . .
428	being able to walk through the neighbourhood,

429   and have everybody, you know,
430   who had the drug, give their respect.
431   And . . now that I think about it,
432   it's the dumbest thing I ever did in my life . .
433   It's gotten me here and so much time.
434   I'm not even 40 years old . .
435   and I got more time than I am old.

Roman mentions a key element in narratives of criminals, respect (line 430), where he pinpoints the allure of being positioned as successful in what many call 'the life, the fast life' (lines 425–6) of the streets. Earlier in the interview Roman has talked of being beaten as a child and sleeping under the elementary school steps to avoid an abusive parent. In this excerpt he calls out against his reactions to the ill-gained respect he garnered as a dealer in a most reflexive passage: 'And . . now that I think about it, it's the dumbest thing I ever did in my life' (lines 431–2). Charles Taylor (1985) suggests that humans can develop into strong evaluators. This passage suggests that now, in prison, in the interview setting with the teacher who has become researcher, Roman attempts just such a strong evaluation of the choices he made and how he, a child much neglected, was duped by 'respect'.

If the linguist had left the research site behind after this data collection, she might, however, have over-interpreted that remark as indicating change not only in Roman's worldview but also in his current actions. Several years after the taping, this inmate was found to have carried out an attempt on the life of another inmate in that facility as part of a drug-running enterprise within the prison. Thus, long-term involvement with the communities in which one researches provides more opportunity for analysis of data not only synchronically with other narratives collected, but also diachronically over time within one person's experiences and within the history of the community. If the researcher wants (as I do) to suggest ways that the data analysed can help contribute to positive change in the life of the speaker and of the community, then she or he must be ready to recontextualize data. This is particularly appealing when a researcher can work among disciplines whose worlds of practice overlap. That call for interdisciplinarity that readily applies to the field of CDA led me to probe deeper into the connections between the world of drugs and the worlds of incarceration.[7] In the passages below, from the man I call 'Martin', we see criminal behaviour develop in its overlapping nexus with the world of addiction.

The drug life

Martin, a heroin addict, had spent many of his 6–20 years sentence for armed robbery in the complex where I research. At the time of the interview he had returned to serve more of this sentence after having been paroled and having violated that parole through drug use. This narrative details how he became a runner for the drug enterprise as a child and then a seller before becoming an addict himself. Martin had mentioned leaving his parents' home at the age of 13, and continued:

(Transcript numbers indicate that this is in the middle of the 1,400 lines of his transcript.)[8]

723	MARTIN:	I left
724		But after leaving,
725		then I got caught up into a lot of different things . .
726		and . . one thing, you know,
727		led to the other . .
728		I had to have money to survive out there
729		and that led to robbing people and stuff like this, you know.
730		and . . . then it started, with the drugs.
731		And this was a guy
732		that used to live right across the street from my mother . .
733		He had me selling the stuff,
734		and I didn't know what the stuff was at first.
735		Then one day, I's, I kept looking at it . .
736		I saw . . it was in the little capsules . .
737		I said, 'Well, I'm going to try this' . .
738		You know, because I'm carrying it, you know.
739		I might as well . . .
740		So I tried it.
741	POC:	What was it?
742	MARTIN:	It was heroin.
743	POC.	Heroin.
744	MARTIN:	and . . I got so carried away . . you know, you know,
745		It was it was something totally different . . you know.
746		It changed . .
747		the course of everything, you know.
748		And I just kept on.
749		Here I'm getting it,
750		and I ain't got to pay for it . . .
751		you know,
752		I just kept on and on . .
753		And then after . .
754		the guy stopped me from selling the stuff,
755		because my people . .
756		they didn't know I was using any drugs,
757		but they didn't like the fact

758   that I was hanging out with these people, you know,
759   and, he just stopped selling the drugs,
760   after awhile himself . .
761   But . . I, you know, was still up there in the street . .
762   and . . I had stopped for a while
763   and I got this uh, with this other group here . .
764   and I tried to have my people come . .
765   to see what I was doing . .
766   and they had told me . .
767   'Well, we'll be there.'
768   and that night in the club they never showed up.
769   So that messed me up.
770   I said,
771   'Well, they don't care about what I'm doing,
772   or nothing else,' you know . .
773   But I knew . .
774   and this is a fact . .
775   that I knew that I didn't have to be out there
776   doing what I was doing . . because . .
777   my, my father was working,
778   he's working to take care of his children, you know.

Martin's story of his early use of heroin, an experience that 'changed . . the course of everything' (lines 746–7) demonstrates several features of reflexive discourse within the larger context of self reflection on a life in which auto-biographical interviews lie. Martin's originally unagentive expressions 'then I got caught up into . . a lot of different things . . and one thing, you know, led to the other . .' (lines 725–7) and his 'and that led to robbing people' (line 729) become much more self-positioning as an agent when he goes into the details of his narrative on his decision to sample the capsules of heroin he carried for the dealer.[9] ' "Well, I'm going to try this" . . you know, because I'm carrying it, you know' (lines 737–8). Important in reflexive speech are acknowledgements of one's mental states, constructed dialogue and meta-talk. In lines 772–3 we see two uses of 'know' that bear comment. The refrain-like 'you know' that often forms a pause marker and that establishes a cadence in the discourse of the prisoners is neatly contrasted with uses of the verb 'know' in its more definitional sense in lines 773 and 775. The constructed conversation that he uses to depict his own talk to himself about whether to sample the drugs enhances for the audience the interior debate Martin recalls. The meta-talk, the commentary on the statement forthcoming in line 774 'and this is a fact', feature evaluation as well as self reflexivity in narrative.[10] This mini-break in flow of the story shows the speaker affirming for his listener the seriousness of his understanding of his actions. While the facts according to Martin suggest that he did not lack necessities because his father worked extra hours, he does suggest that his call for help had been ignored when his people had 'never showed' (line 768) and that he interpreted this omission as damning.

Reflexive frame breaks

When inmates stop their action narratives to discuss mental states I refer to these as reflexive frame breaks.

773	but I knew . .
774	and this is a fact
775	that I knew that I didn't have to be out there
776	doing what I was doing.

The break in Martin's storyline with its emphatic meta-talk marking 'and this is a fact' (line 774) addresses simultaneously the interviewer and the speaker himself, inviting the interviewer into the mind of the speaker as he tries to make sense of his past. He positions his interlocutor (and now you as well) to look into his actions in the past. His information that his family did not lack for money and his information state 'I *knew* that I didn't have to be out there' pin him down as a mistake maker. How much he understands about the effect of the growing drug addiction at that time is left up for interpretation. In the world of the interview, however, we can expect the interlocutor to get that point through the juxtaposition as well as through the admission. Among African-American speakers, much is expected of listeners to take up the nuances and Martin no doubt expected the inference to be made. Saying blatantly 'I knew' may have been his way of ensuring that the white interviewer got the point.

Activist linguistics

Here is where I propose that the findings we make as linguists conducting research in workplaces, in institutions, on media, and so on, can lead to an activist stance, an agency of our own, if you will. In the prison where one's placement is directly associated with one's crime (that is, surrounded by like kinds), it may be unlikely that a person would ever consider replacing or relocating the kind of self who did indeed commit that crime. I suggest that within a participatory rehabilitative discourse with non-criminals, however, a prisoner's break in a narrative to talk about his thoughts at the time of the act might indicate that he is now thinking rehabilitative thoughts, for he is pondering about his thinking at the time and the place of the event. He may be able to begin to see himself as a strong evaluator of his acts, not as someone alien to or unagentive in his own past. He may be in a discourse that could prepare him for more morally agentive living. And if there is someone who can provide the uptake, the reinforcement for that postulation, I suggest that new actions are more likely. Fruitful uptake depends, then, upon hearing the stories and reacting to them – validating or challenging, but none the less interacting with the prisoner, not isolating him or her from the potential for changed behaviour.

An activist linguist might then participate with those in other disciplines – counsellors, criminologists, prison officials, educators, criminal justice workers – and with common citizens to set up programmes in concert, programmes informed by carefully conceived basic linguistic (and other disciplinary) research and applied to programmes with goals that promote an improvement in the community condition. This type of interdisciplinary approach invites a useful dialogue not only *about* but also *with* the incarcerated. This approach has meant looking more closely at the contributing factors to lives of crime, noting in particular the prevalence of criminals' drug addictions, working backward then into contributing factors, working closely with those who run drug treatment facilities whose goals are to change transgressors' behaviours that have led to much community mayhem and sorrow and to recurrent incarcerations.

This work has involved inviting former prisoners to participate in forming research plans along with recovering addicts and programme directors of recovery facilities, a process that by its very nature slows down research. Yet, such a slowing down is necessary as we explore the overlapping nexus of practice that prisons, drug 'cultures' and treatment centres share. My current project invites more participation in the shaping of the research to needs of these communities. I have consulted with treatment centre professionals as well as addicts and former prisoners in recovery and with volunteers in educational programmes at recovery centres to set up collections of data to track the role that discourse takes in shaping recovery. In that sense I am doing Community Based Research (CBR), an offshoot of Participatory Action Research, a term that has had recent currency popularized by Brazilian educator Paolo Freire (see Freire, 1970). Participatory Action Research, like CBR, is designed by researchers *with* those in the community that is being studied so that their interests are met by the research. For instance, Shirley Brice Heath's recent work with youths in community-based organizations has had the young people take major roles in shaping the space and design for their learning and for the research she conducts (Heath, 1998). Such research also fits well within current service learning paradigms that join college and university researchers, their student community service volunteers, and coordinators and participants at volunteer sites in community-based projects of mutual benefit. Such projects, when done well, assist us to move beyond cultural and economic barriers that have traditionally divided groups. They also provide a check on research that 'leeches' off poor communities.

In a publication by Richard Couto and his collaborators (Couto et al., 2000) we see a clear example of such Community Based (Participatory

Action) Research. In *Mending Broken Promises: Justice for Children at Risk, A Report to the Juvenile and Domestic Relations District Court, Richmond, Virginia*, Couto and his University of Richmond students interviewed not only employees of the justice department in Virginia to help design the study of at-risk youths and process its results, but also the youths themselves in the detention system and in the local Boys' and Girls' Club. The Executive Summary notes about the youths that '[t]heir insight, as expressed in their words and artwork added inestimably to the report' that shows that underlying causes of delinquent behaviour in youth offenders include 'poverty, racism, unemployment, "war zone" neighborhoods, mental impairment, school failure, and child abuse and neglect' (ibid.). Other examples of work that carries an activist application are found in the AIDS research of Rodney Jones in China and Hong Kong. In Jones' discourse analysis of identity construction of the 'AIDS celebrity', he studied public identities in Hong Kong 'where both Eastern and Western values exist side by side and interact' and where the 'media, the government, the public, and the PWA[11] himself' build their 'own "theories" regarding the self and communication' (1998, p. 309). Jones suggested that the interaction and negotiation between the groups was most significant in forming effective policies 'for the global movement for PWA rights which seeks to improve the lot of people living with HIV and AIDS in cultures with widely varying norms and traditions' (ibid., p. 332) where power dynamics among groups and ideological stands by groups can thwart effective treatment policies. He noted that identity constructions assigned to PWAs and research about them must 'go further in examining the link between such "theories" and the larger issue of power relationships between negotiators in the construction and the types of strategies they use to assert their ideological agendas' (ibid.). Thus Jones moves beyond the data study to the use of the research in society.

Linguist Keller Magenau (2000) studied jury member discourse and analysed how a group reaches consensus in the heretofore closed deliberations of an American court. Practical applications of this discourse analysis can have far-reaching results in how judges can instruct juries. The whole issue of citizens understanding their rights, obligations and protections was also examined in work by discourse analyst Curtis Renoe (2000) who studied Indonesian court proceedings. In Indonesia, the use of formulaic questions and answers in criminal proceedings may well mirror a country's culturally appropriate insistence on procedure, but information about those procedures needs to be more common knowledge, especially when the frames of operation are imitated from non-Indonesian sources. Coulthard's (1996) research into British police interrogation reports revealed discrepancies in officers' recollections and representations, and showed how social and cultural frames for interpretation of suspects' remarks shaped the transcription of remembered interviews as well as so-called verbatim sound recording transcriptions. Such forensic uses of linguistic analysis hold great promise for transformation of miscarriages of justice long associated with criminal justice secrecy.

In reference to racial discourse matters, sociolinguist John Rickford recently teamed up with his lawyer son Russell to write a volume on Black English. Published in the wake of controversy over Oakland, California's school district's use of/refusal of Black English Vernacular, this volume written for a general audience suggests that the distinctive identity that comes with speaking what they call 'spoken soul' makes the language of blacks worth treasuring:

> It marks a black identity; it is the symbol of a culture and a lifestyle that have had and continue to have a profound impact on American popular life; it retains the associations of warmth and closeness for many blacks who first learned it from their mothers and fathers and family members; it expresses camaraderie and solidarity among friends; it establishes rapport among blacks; and it serves as a creative and expressive instrument in the present and as a vibrant link with the nation's past. (Rickford and Rickford, 2000, p. 10)

Thus, while Rickford conducted basic language research over several decades, research that carefully established the speaking patterns of African-Americans, he sees new importance and application of his findings in the day-to-day understandings of blacks, an understanding that links back to historical, geographical and political ramifications, but most importantly to familial structuring and ties. In his call then, to 'do more', with which I opened this chapter, he has expanded his basic research paradigm and his nexus of practice. I suggest that seeds for such work can be found in the working papers presented at many conferences. The follow-up, however, may be at some risk to the young researcher.

At recent symposia organized to look at identity and agency, I have seen interesting discourse analyses whose applications interrogate the criminal justice system and its role in the lives of its victims, its accused, its guilty, and in those affected by the punishments. Researchers who, as I do, delve into linguistics and crime are at a minimum adding to knowledge about the criminal justice process from linguistic perspectives: how words in criminal justice permeate broader society (Ukrainian prison research by Antonia Berezovenko, 2000); how speech acts like 'testifying' and 'questioning' are open to interpretation and to confusion (Valerie Fridland's work on rape trials, 2000); how community perceptions of justice dictate praxis (Keller Magenau, 2000); how personal responsibility can be encoded or deflected in linguistic choices (O'Connor, 2000). Such research also contributes to an understanding of the effects of criminalization on the communities at large in which we researchers also share space. We see how common occurrences like imprisonment in Washington, DC, do not normalize the family's experience of incarceration but do point out what Branham (2000) calls the 'silence of society to cope with massive effects caused not only by crime but by incarceration as well'; how opening up the closed (such as jury proceedings), or the enclosed (such as prisons and prison routines of life) leads to potentials for greater understandings, potentials for change.

Does descriptive knowledge-making go far enough? What is the uptake on this kind of knowledge? If we consider the making of knowledge as a kind of macro speech act, who then participates in (to extend Austin, 1975) the perlocutionary uptake suggested by the illocutionary force of this act of research, this act of knowledge-making? Beyond rebuttals in journals, who will do that work? At what risk does a researcher take on an activist stance?

Roger Shuy closes his 1998 *The Language of Confession, Interrogation and Deception* with this remark: 'law and medicine can no longer ignore the fact that to achieve the ultimate goals of justice and health, practitioners must develop their abilities in language interaction' (p. 194). He suggests that training and workshops (based on discourse analysis) for those in the legal business would make for more efficacy as well as justice. Consider also that the discourse analysts' tools could be used to better acquaint the citizenry as well as the police and courts with their rights and obligations, and also their contributions to society.

The importance of such an act of locating agency rests not only in analysing the data from a speaker or a testimony; it also rests in raising our own epistemic considerations into a 'community reflexivity' via the uptake a community takes towards those involved in the criminal justice system. We who research are not exempt from 'community' membership, as has been made uncomfortably clear by recent terror attacks. How can, how should, linguistic research contribute to a community of uptake? First of all, long-term involvement and immersion in a setting leads to a thicker, richer interpretation of data and can contribute to social change. Shirley Brice Heath (1998) discusses the richness of her eight-year study of how 'at-risk' youth are learning. Currently, 18 years surrounds the research I've done on prisoner narratives. This immersion into at least a part of prison life and its routine has given me not only access, but also a place for repositioning the very knowledge I have gained on prisoners' epistemic understandings of their acts of crime. It helps me to find ways to assist in making a life cohesive (Linde, 1993, 1997) and to work toward making sense of lives and institutions (Linde, 1999).

Broadening the nexus of practice

Critical Discourse Analysis has called for researchers to work interdisciplinarily such that narrow foci and single-minded interpretation of data can be avoided. CDA also calls for researchers to focus on issues of social importance, issues that contribute to reduction of harm, to promoting social justice. Caldas-Coulthard and Coulthard state that CDA is 'essentially political in its intent with its practitioners acting upon the world in order to transform it and thereby help create a world where people are not discriminated against because of sex, colour, creed, age or social class' (1996, p. xi). Thus an engaged citizenry of researchers should ensue. I suggest that CDA shake hands with Participatory Action Research to form tighter alliances that remove the distancing of scholars from the subjects of research by forming 'reciprocal' Zones of Proximal Development as researcher-learners.

Lev Vygotsky in his research on learning (1934 [1986]) stated that we are in Zones of Proximal Development when we take on new concepts. We are brought into the new understanding by being acquainted with a new concept just beyond our grasp by someone in our community realm of discourse, by trying it out in our private sphere of understanding, and then by presenting it in the public sphere – in essence checking its correct applicability by the public response and, when effective, our understanding joins into the communal understanding that shapes others' concepts as well. Thus we are shaped by and shaping others when we take on a new concept, a word, an activity.

Too often, as researchers, our new understandings remain static because we short-circuit the flow of knowledge to its public applicability. We remain content to imagine our 'public' as that which sits on the editorial boards of journals, select presses or tenure review committees. I suggest that an activist linguistics will broaden the notion of community to a continuum of possibilities – if we apply the knowledge in efficacious ways with the community in which the research was conducted and broadly interact with researchers and workers in the fields in which we situate our engaged citizenry. Research in the beginning of a project may only shed new light, give new understandings of old problems. In its thicker, richer, more in-depth and interdisciplinary applications, research of peoples' ways with words should be joining us all in a community of uptake, making of us agents for solutions and not merely investigators of systematic details.

Notes

1. Special thanks to Viveka Adelsward, Jana Holsanova, Ruth Wodak, Chris Bulcaen, Teresa Alves and Teresa Cid for opportunities to meet with researchers in Linkoping, Lund, Vienna, Ghent and Lisbon to discuss aspects of this work and its critical discourse perspectives. Thanks also to the International Pragmatics Association for inclusion of part of this work at the meeting in Budapest where it enjoyed lively discussion.
2. This list is merely suggestive of the interesting prior and concurrent work.
3. Noam Chomsky's views on anarchy and free speech indicate the perils of a world-famous linguist speaking out on political matters. See Barsky (2001).
4. The number of prisoners shocks less, however, than the demographic makeup of the current incarcerated population which includes dramatic over-representation of people of colour. According to the Sentencing Project, a non-profit organization

located in the nation's capital, for males aged 20–29, one in fifteen whites, one in eight Hispanics, and one in three blacks is currently under criminal justice supervision (web page).
5. Transcript conventions used include:

,   Commas represent sentence falling intonation at a slight breath group pause.

. .   Periods represent longer breaks with each successive period indicating an increase in pausing of a half second.

—>   Arrows point out lines to be discussed in particular.

=   Latching of phrases together is shown by = which indicates that the speaker does not pause even when might be expected.

LOUD Loud emphasis is shown by using ALL CAPS.

hhhh   Laughter is indicated by hhhh; more h's meaning longer laughter.

/ /   Simultaneous speaking is represented by slash marks / / on each line where it overlaps with the other speaker on the line below.

{ }   My remarks on the text appear within curly brackets {door slams}.

[?]   Unclear or inaudible words appear within straight brackets, guesses are sometimes put inside the brackets [church?].

6. Full discussion of Roman's story appears in Chapter 2 of my *Speaking of Crime* (O'Connor, 2000).
7. I face difficulty in doing follow-up work with this particular prison population because the facility in which I researched has been closed and the prisoners, including Roman, have been distributed to facilities in other states.
8. This is one of the longest of the 19 in-depth interviews conducted inside maximum security prisons during 1991–92.
9. Carrying drugs for dealers is a common entry-level job for young children befriended by dealers. While the children receive small amounts of cash, the dealer has the benefit of a juvenile being arrested rather than the dealer since possession of the drug on the dealer's person is avoided in the event of a shakedown by police.
10. See Schiffrin (1980) and O'Connor (2000) on meta-talk.
11. PWA = Person With AIDS.

References

Arrestee Drug Abuse Monitoring Program (ADAM) (2000) '1999 Annual Report on Drug Abuse Among Adult and Juvenile Arrestees', NCJ 181426. Washington, DC: National Institute of Justice.

Austin, J. (1975) *How to do Things with Words* (2nd edn) (ed. J.O. Urmson and Marina Sbisa). Cambridge, MA: Harvard University.

Barsky, R. (2001) 'The Chomsky effect: episodes in academic activism', in S.H. Ali (ed.), *Beyond the Ivory Tower: Public Intellectuals, Academia and the Media*. Online draft available at <www.mit.edu/~saleem/ivory/ch6.htm> (accessed 21 November 2001).

Beck, A. and Harrison, P. (2001) *Prisoners in 2000*. Washington, DC: Bureau of Justice Statistics.

Beck, A. and Karberg, J. (2001) *Prison and Jail Inmates at Midyear 2000*. Washington, DC: Bureau of Justice Statistics.

Berezovenko, A. (2000) 'Prison, gender and "bottom up" language change'. Conference paper for 'Discourse Analysis of Criminal Justice' panel. Georgetown University Round Table, 6 May.

Branham, D. (2000) 'Living lies and telling truths: stigma in families of prisoners'. Conference paper for 'Discourse Analysis of Criminal Justice' panel. Georgetown University Round Table, 6 May.

Briggs, C. (1993) ' "I'm not just talking to the victims of oppression tonight – I'm talking to everybody": rhetorical authority and narrative authenticity in the African-American poetics of political engagement', *Journal of Narrative and Life History*, 3(1), pp. 33–78.

Caldas-Coulthard, C.R. and Coulthard, M. (eds) (1996) *Texts and Practices: Readings in Critical Discourse Analyses*. New York: Routledge.

Coulthard, M. (1996) 'The official version: audience manipulation in police records of interviews with suspects', in C.R. Caldas-Coulthard and M. Coulthard (eds), *Texts and Practices: Readings in Critical Discourse Analyses*. New York: Routledge.

Couto, R., Stutts, N.B. and Associates (2000) *Mending Broken Promises: Justice for Children at Risk, A Report to the Juvenile and Domestic Relations District Court, Richmond, Virginia*. Dubuque, IA: Kendall Hunt.

Fairclough, N. (2001) *Call to Action*. 'Language in the New Capitalism' website: <http://www.uoc.es/humfil/nlc/LNC_ENG/lnc_eng.html> (accessed 11 December 2001).

Freire, P. (1970) *Pedagogy of the Oppressed* (trans. Myra Bergman Ramos). New York: Herder & Herder.

Fridland, V. (2000) 'The sociolinguist in court'. Conference paper for 'Discourse Analysis of Criminal Justice' panel. Georgetown University Round Table, 6 May.

Grimshaw, A.D. (1990) *Conflict Talk: Sociolinguistic Investigations of Arguments in Conversation*. Cambridge: Cambridge University Press.

Heath, S.B. (1998) 'Working through language', in S. Hoyle and C.T. Adger (eds), *Kids Talk: Strategic Language Use in Later Childhood*. New York: Oxford University Press, pp. 217–40.

Jones, R.H. (1998) 'Two Faces of AIDS in Hong Kong: Culture and the Construction of the "AIDS Celebrity" ', *Discourse & Society*, 9(3), pp. 309–38.

Labov, W. (1981) 'Speech Actions and Reactions', in D. Tannen (ed.), *Analyzing Discourse: Text and Talk*. Washington, DC: Georgetown University Press, pp. 219–47.

Leudar, I. and Nekvapil, J. (2000) 'Presentations of Romanies in the Czech media: on category work in television debates', *Discourse & Society*, 11(4), pp. 487–513.

Linde, C. (1993) *Life Stories: The Creation of Coherence*. New York: Oxford University Press.

Linde, C. (1997) 'Narrative: experience, memory, folklore', *Journal of Narrative and Life History*, 7(1–4), pp. 281–9.

Linde, C. (1999) 'The transformation of narrative syntax into institutional memory', *Narrative Inquiry*, 9(1), pp. 139–74.

Magenau, K. (2000) 'A jury's duty'. Conference paper for 'Discourse Analysis of Criminal Justice' panel. Georgetown University Round Table, 6 May.

O'Connor, P.E. (1994) ' "You could feel it through the skin": agency and positioning in prisoners' narratives', *Text*, 14(1), pp. 45–75.

O'Connor, P.E. (1995a) 'Speaking of crime: "I don't know what made me do it" ', *Discourse & Society*, 6(3), pp. 429–56.

O'Connor, P.E. (1995b) 'Discourse of violence', *Discourse & Society*, 6(3), pp. 309–18.

O'Connor, P.E. (2000) *Speaking of Crime*. Lincoln: University of Nebraska Press.

O'Connor, P.E. (2001) 'The prison cage: African American men and prison', *Journal of African American Men*, 6(1), pp. 71–87.

Reisigl, M. and Wodak, R. (2001) *Discourse and Discrimination: Rhetorics of Racism and Anti-Semitism*. London: Routledge.

Renoe, C. (2000) ' "Just tell us the truth": interaction, language, ideology and the nature of testimony in an Indonesian criminal trial'. Conference paper for 'Discourse Analysis of Criminal Justice' panel. Georgetown University RoundTable, 6 May.

Rickford, J.R. and Rickford, R.J. (2000) *Spoken Soul: The Story of Black English*. New York: John Wiley and Sons.

Schiffrin, D. (1980) 'Meta-talk: organizational and evaluative brackets in discourse. Language and social interaction', (Special issue) *Sociological Inquiry*, 50, pp. 199–236.

Schiffrin, D. (1984) 'Jewish argument as sociability', *Language in Society*, 13(3), pp. 311–35.

Scollon, R. (2001) *Mediated Discourse: The Nexus of Practice*. New York: Routledge.

Shuy, R. (1998) *The Language of Confession, Interrogation, and Deception*. Thousand Oaks, CA: Sage.

Tannen, D. (1990) *'You Just Don't Understand': Women and Men in Conversation*. New York: William Morrow, Ballantine.

Taylor, C. (1985) *Human Agency and Language*. Cambridge: Cambridge University Press.

United States Bureau of Justice (2001) Corrections Statistics, 16 January 2001: <http://www.ojp.usdoj.gov/bjs/correct.htm> (accessed 2 July 2001).

van Dijk. T.A. (1989) 'Mediating racism: the role of the media in the reproduction of racism', in R. Wodak (ed.), *Language, Power and Ideology: Studies in Political Discourse*. Philadelphia: John Benjamins, pp. 199–226.

van Dijk, T.A. (1991) *Racism and the Press*. London and New York: Routledge.

van Dijk, T.A. (1993) *Elite Discourse and Racism*. Newbury Park, CA: Sage.

Vygotsky, L.S. (1934 [1986]) *Thought and Language* (Trans. and ed. Alex Kozozulin). Cambridge, MA: MIT Press.

Wilson, D.J. (2000) 'Drug use, testing, and treatment in jails'. Washington, DC: US Department of Justice.

Wodak, R. (1996a) *Disorders of Discourse*. New York: Longman.

Wodak, R. (1996b) 'The genesis of racist discourse in Austria since 1989', in C.R. Caldas-Coulthard and M. Coulthard (eds), *Texts and Practices: Readings in Critical Discourse Analysis*. New York: Routledge, pp. 107–20.

Wodak, R. and Matouschek, B. (1993) ' "We are dealing with people whose origins one can clearly tell just by looking": Critical Discourse Analysis and the study of neo-racism in contemporary Austria', *Discourse & Society*, 4(2), pp. 225–48.

12
Discourse at Work: When Women Take On the Role of Manager

Luisa Martín Rojo and Concepción Gómez Esteban

> When a woman is placed in a position in which being assertive and forceful is necessary, she is faced with a paradox; she can be a good woman but a bad executive or professional, or vice versa. To do both is impossible.
>
> Robin Lakoff, 1990, p. 206

Introduction

This chapter is part of an interdisciplinary research project into management models and gender (see Gómez Esteban et al., 2000). The main aim of the study is to explore whether and to what extent new theoretical models of management are encouraging the promotion of women to positions of responsibility in companies and thus leading to a correlative improvement of the image of women managers. There is a lot of literature on these theoretical models, taught in business schools, and influential in organizational practices (management, organizational tasks, selection and promotion), where they regulate the functions of management and the way power is wielded in companies. In fact, we have found that these new models defend a more democratic view of management, and emphasize, for instance, communicative and relational skills (showing empathy and requesting compliance) versus an assertive style. We expected that the inclusion of these features would contribute to breaking the 'double bind' women face regarding professionalism and femininity (given the fact, found in previous research, that assertive women in high positions are perceived as less feminine, while non-assertive women in these positions are perceived as less competent). However, from the beginning of our work we also saw that two factors were making it difficult to answer these questions: (1) the lack of consistency and internal coherence of these theoretical yet influential models, and (2) the way in which such models have been transformed and adapted to Spanish organizational culture and to the situation in the workplace. The analysis we present in this chapter focuses on the way people adapt these models to our situations – showing differences depending on whether the managers are men or women – and on the effects of these adaptations on the image of women managers.

We are interested in this topic because of our belief that a real knowledge of how the prevailing theoretical models of management are incorporated in and adapted to the Spanish workplace today is crucial not only in order to put into practice participative policies but also to introduce positive action to end the discrimination experienced by female managers and indeed the entire female workforce.

In order to understand why, despite the changes undergone in the world of labour in Spain, the inclusion of women in positions of authority is still very unusual, we will examine and problematize the role of gender in organizational structures. However, we believe that the role of gender in organizations should be framed within a broader study of power and authority. This is in fact an essential object of interest in sociological studies; the role of gender in the analysis of the social life cannot be ignored.

At the same time, our approach is also discursive. We focus on discursive practices and the ideological production, reproduction and justification of the gender relations of domination. Following this sociodiscursive approach, discursive practices are viewed as an expression of organizational structure as well as the means by which organization members create this structure and give coherence to everyday practices (for a summary of the current research and a comprehensive bibliography, including feminist studies of organizational discourse, see Mumby and Clair, 1997). However, as in other critical studies, the organization is understood here not only as a social collective where shared meanings and practices are produced, but also as a 'battlefield' where different groups compete to try to shape the organization in ways that serve their own interests. Gender is clearly involved in this competition, and thus organizations appear as fundamentally gendered structures. This is why our analysis focuses mainly on how discursive practices contribute to structure, exercise and reificate gender relations of domination and subordination (see also, among others, Jaffe, 1989; Acker, 1990; Mills and Tancred, 1992).

The sample analysed consists of two kinds of material:

1. The discourses present in the formative materials used by two of the most important business schools in Spain in their courses for managers.
2. The discourses produced by 18 interviews with managers and people involved in the selection of managers and directors, people with responsibility for human resources and training, and also people about to assume positions of responsibility.

In this chapter, we begin by presenting some of the data obtained in the study of the management models. This is the sociological framework for the subsequent analysis of the discourses produced in the interviews. The analysis of these discourses focuses on the configuration, perception and evaluation of these models and of those who perform these roles, especially women. It is, in fact, an examination of the connections established between roles, attributes and genders. We then look at how gender differences are perceived and evaluated and, finally, examine the perception of the female boss and the different images she embodies.

Interdisciplinarity: an attitude

We consider interdisciplinarity not as the mere superposition of analyses, by different disciplines, of the same object of study, but as the attempt to integrate them. Following this view, in this and other research, we have tried to produce and develop a shared space of research and an analysis which brings together the different disciplines involved.

From the beginning of our programme of research on gender in 1993, as a group we brought together different approaches – psychoanalysis, anthropology, sociology, discourse analysis and sociolinguistics – and also very divergent intellectual and personal backgrounds. We have gradually moved closer intellectually with our object of study also progressively emerging. The interdisciplinary task has been, in consequence, developed over time: from a shared design of research projects in which each researcher elaborated a specific part, using his or her specialized knowledge, to the construction of a shared object of study which has been defined and developed jointly. Our topic, then, is social representations. On the one hand, we look at how these representations are discursively built and socially shared, and, on the other, we look at the social implications of these representations, how they result in social discrimination; for instance, the representation of women managers we examine in this chapter.

What underlies this sociodiscursive approach is the shared assumption that to reduce the complexity of phenomena to a single disciplinary approach or level of analysis means reducing the comprehension and interpretation of social life. At the same time, the construction of the object of study and the analysis itself are based more than ever now on an ongoing discussion of the basic concepts and principles we are using and on which we are reaching an integrated position. This discussion starts from a shared theoretical perspective which assumes the reflexive nature of social life (in consequence, we are interested in Bourdieu's and Giddens' approaches, including the differences between them), and is accompanied by the adoption of qualitative methods of research (although we use mainly sociological tools in collecting data, like groups of discussion and open interviews, and the discursive perspective is more decisive in the analysis).

It is important to emphasize that one of the most valuable contributions of this interdisciplinary programme has been the discovery that many social conflicts and problems we have studied in the world also appear at the level of the production of knowledge. For instance, in the case of a piece of research like this, the hierarchical ranking among disciplines, according to their social consolidation and legitimization, has played an important role in the construction of the object of study, and even in getting the funding necessary to carry it out. We even found that differences in authority according to gender in society play their part in the same way in the legitimization of disciplines and the researchers' contributions.

In conclusion, we are aware that we have not yet reached a satisfactory and integrated approach. However, we do think that we have at least reached an integrated frame within which to work, designing a research project which covers an interdisciplinary study of social representation. For the moment, we consider interdisciplinarity in our team more as an attitude, a process, than as something completely achieved.

Management models: gender and role stereotypes

Theoretical and training models

In order to determine what the prevailing management models are and how they are introduced in workplaces, our research focused on the theoretical models used in the training courses offered by two of the most important business schools in Spain. The influence of these models is attested to by our interviewees, most of whom have followed business training courses, and who naturally refer to them. We therefore consider that these theoretical models could provide the basis for both interpretations of specific practices and the emergence of correlative applied models in the workplace.

The most significant assumptions that the analysis of these training materials reveals is the need to adopt new management models (the so-called democratic and transformer models), and the need to avoid old ones (all of them hierarchical models – the authoritarian, the assertive). Differences between old and new models are clearly related to the exercise of power. In new models, managers have to be able to organize and plan tasks and activities in a cooperative way ('power over' a particular domain or activity), without imposing their decisions and criteria ('power to' control another's actions and participation). Is this particular feature capable of facilitating the incorporation of women in these positions in the organization?

However, an in-depth discourse analysis also reveals that new models are not always clearly defined and are sometimes inconsistent. In fact, the analysis of these materials reveals an underlying confusion not only over what a manager is and what he or she should be, but also over the differences between traditional models and new ones. There are a number of terms which coexist and which often appear to be synonymous, although they refer to different positions, tasks and attributes. This is despite the fact that the criteria on which they are based are different. These are the terms which focus on attributes ('leader'), tasks ('manager') and hierarchical position ('boss'). Their correlatives are in the taxonomy 'follower', 'employee' and 'subordinate' respectively.

Besides this confusing coexistence of designations, certain inconsistencies are also found in the exhaustive description of their attributes. Thus, for example, in the presentation of the *democratic and transformer models*, the 'personality cult' or having influence on others (charisma) is regarded negatively. Why? A charismatic leader is defined by his psychological qualities, in particular by the ability to influence and persuade his 'followers'. But this is not a democratic way of behaving. It is also a long way from the ability to 'get the best out of his subordinates', the definition of the transformer model. But despite this explicit rejection, an in-depth study of the features attributed to these new models reveals the permanence of an underlying charismatic component. In fact, both in training materials and everyday discourses in organizations, an up-to-date version of the charismatic leader is present in every personality profile of a leader offered by the different typologies of leadership we have found.

In order to show this, we have extracted from the training materials what seems to be the prevalent picture of the ideal manager – someone dynamic who can inject energy into an organization. Social and verbal skills, a sense of humour, the ability to take things calmly – all these are stressed. Thus the ideal manager has to transmit enthusiasm and serenity at the same time.[1] However, the understanding of communication skills is reductionist and places 'clarity' as the most significant feature. The leader not only has to be able to put across a project, he must also be able to communicate it in clear, specific orders. The significance attributed to clarity shows the maintenance of an informational model of communication (versus a relational one) which emphasizes the unidirectional transmission of information and not interactional skills. Furthermore, it is precisely the ability to transmit a personal project that requires charisma.

The permanence of charisma is paradoxical in business schools, given that it does not fit in with the idea of training and modelling leaders (in fact, the emphasis on charisma questions the very rationale of a human resources policy). The training of an effective leader is undervalued. The continued role of charisma indicates an essentialism absent since the 1950s, when leadership became depersonalized. Finally, it preserves old models of management and gender alongside the new.

What is certain is that the permanence of an implicit charismatic component in the training of future managers promotes a man as the new prototype. The warning to women is clear, even in the definition of the so-called 'transforming leader', the one which could increase women's managerial presence.[2] Thus, in one of the lessons introducing this new model, we read: 'The leader, an "experienced man" with boundless gentlemanliness ... full of "bonhomie" but also "silent and shy"' (EPRI, *Liderazgo transformador*, 'Transforming Leadership', p. 10). As in this example, the prototype seems always to be a man, with the exception of some training materials and articles written by women (see, for instance, Loden, 1987; Chinchilla et al., 1999). As a result, neither in the theoretical models nor in the ideal images that emerge from the work context are women associated with the exercise of leadership. In fact, the existence of a distinctive style of feminine management is not even recognized – except negatively, as will be seen – and the specific identity of the female manager is rarely recognized.

In consequence, an in-depth analysis of these materials shows inconsistencies and lack of internal coherence in these theoretical and influencing models. We detect, in fact, a 'double discourse' which, on the one hand, promotes democratic values consistent with prevalent democratic and equalitarian ideologies, but, on the other, masks the maintenance of traditional models, only partially and superficially updated. 'Double discourses', inconsistencies and lack of coherence particularly appear during periods of sociopolitical and ideological change, and derive in part from the inclusion of new values and proposals and from the readjustment of the previous values and views, in this case of management practices and power, both still deeply associated with men: is this a local (Spanish) feature, or a general feature?

What is unequivocally local or national is the way in which these models are transformed and adapted to the Spanish workplace situation and the Spanish organizational culture. Indeed, interviewees often considered new models to be an imported and non-effective reality in the Spanish workplace. And, in this case, if theoretical models do not promote fully the presence of women in management, the current labour context is even more restrictive. As interviewees claim, day-to-day reality in organizations reinforces this tendency, maintaining traditional features and behaviour (the charismatic component). As they often say succinctly, 'One thing in theory and another in practice.' What is required in practice is the exercise of leadership in an unstable context, focused on the immediate competition, where the results are short-term. Thus the manager has to be the best person to deal with a crisis. As a result, what is valued above all is decision-making ability. Total availability and loyalty to the organization and its norms are also stressed. Women are seen not to quite fit in because of the differing norms and obligations of the home and the workplace.

In conclusion, it should be emphasized that new models of management have been introduced in business schools, and that these new models see power and authority as 'power over' (the ability to organize and plan activities in a particular domain). However, the contradictions found in their presentation reveal the survival of a concept of authority as 'power to' (the effective control of others' actions and activities) (for this distinction, see Tancred, 1997; see also Wolf and Filgstein, 1979; Jaffe, 1989; Hopcroft, 1996). The emphasis on charisma is inextricably linked to this and not easily compatible with women's performance and image in the workplace. In the following we will see how this particular adjustment is part of the dominant culture in the Spanish workplace, which associates authority and maleness, and how it both expresses and preserves the cultural system of power and privileges (for similar remarks, see Helmer, 1993; Tannen 1994, p. 167). Following our interdisciplinary and sociodiscursive approach, we will not study all the dimensions involved in these adjustments. We will focus on the study of social representations, and in particular on the way the manager's role is understood and on the images of women managers in workplaces.

Management models in interviews

From a critical perspective, discourses are not only considered as the expression of a corporate culture but also as meaningful practices framed within a complex set of class- and gender-based social relations. From now on, we will focus on the study of how people adjust new models to old beliefs, showing differences depending on whether the managers are men or women, and the effects of this adjustment on the image of women managers. The principal aim is to see to what extent changing the traditional view of managers demands the discarding of traditional links between gender and role stereotypes – and it is precisely the resistance to this that seems to be the problem.

In fact, one of the constants observed in the analysis of interviews is the survival of a vision of the workplace as something intrinsically masculine, where the accepted and dominant forms are those attributed to and associated with that gender.

[1] Muchas no porque no ha habido muchas, pero he conocido mujeres en puestos de alta responsabilidad tremendamente masculinizadas en su forma de desempeñar su rol de mando, y son tremendamente duras, muy damas de hierro ... quizás era la cultura a la que ellas estaban accediendo, y entonces uno (las mujeres en puestos de responsabilidad) copia aquello que ve, en lo que está inmerso, son las pautas de funcionamiento que ve que son las que sirven para triunfar. (Directiva en la Administración, p. 14)

[1] I've not known many women ... because there haven't been many, but I've known women in positions of high responsibility tremendously 'virilized' (real pseudo-males) in their way of carrying out their managerial role, and they are tremendously hard, real iron ladies ... Maybe because it's the culture they're moving into, so that they (women in positions of responsibility) copy what they see, what they're surrounded by, the performance models which they realize are the ones which will help her to succeed. (Woman, high-level civil servant)

This example summarizes many of the findings of this study. It is true that all the discourses analysed establish a division between private and public spheres. They all show how the tasks and objectives pursued are different in each sphere. Thus decision-making skills, pragmatism, self-control and the ability to communicate ('being able to transmit clearly') are considered as naturally lacking in the case of women, but demanded. In comparison, other abilities like negotiating skills, consideration towards the other person, sensitivity to the interpersonal dimension ('doing it together and establishing affective relationships') and communication skills, more traditionally related to women, do not appear as valued when they are present in women. The 'manager we need' in the ever-changing world of day-to-day business is still seen as being a man.[3]

This reveals the contradiction women face in the workplace, where men usually control the power structures. Even when women reach high positions, they are required to subordinate themselves to men. In the case we are examining, this subordination process involves women adopting 'male' practices in order to compete at work. Other researchers, such as Martin et al. (1983), Helmer (1993), Kendall and Tannen (1997) illustrate a different strategy in the subordination process: women adopting behavioural and discursive practices that are deferential to subordinates, and particularly to men.

Many studies address the question of how women and men enact authority in managerial positions. In fact, in some cases we found a different style in the way women enact authority – appealing to equality and consensus, minimizing status differences, reinforcing connections, and so on. In our view, a complex and comprehensive explanation of this different style should be given, considering at the same time the internalization of a lack of social authority, in spite of the high position held by these women in the organization (as in other examples of 'double status') and a related tendency to enact authority in a different way (such as the authoritative strategy of motherhood, a controlling and authoritarian strategy to achieve particular aims, found by Wodak, 1995, p. 54). A comprehensive explanation allows us to take into account the inseparable link between social practices and social structures: understanding social practices as both constrained by social structures, and an active process of production which transforms social structures. And it also allows us to explain the emergence of differences, which can be seen as a rather positive and creative adaptation, to social structure and social organization. Tannen rejects the lack of authority as an explanation, even if she considers that the way women in position of authority speak is influenced by both gender and status (Kendall and Tannen, 1997, p. 89).

However, in this chapter, we do not study the effective communicative behaviour of women in managerial position, but the image of them which emerges from interviews. In relation to this, we see a very complex displacement in the perception of these women, which appears clearly in example (1): masculine attitudes and behaviour are perceived as more valued and as necessary for success in the dominant organizational culture. As stated in this example, women imitate models which have been produced by men. In this complex and negative displacement a link is established between gender and social spaces and roles, instead of them being associated with tasks or personal attributes (workplace norms are masculine norms). This displacement reinforces the traditional division of social spaces, activities and obligations in terms of gender. The effective carrying out of specific roles in the public sphere (management) does not appear to require specific qualities or attributes, merely a specific gender. Thus, as has been pointed out by Echebarría Echabe and González Castro, such a division undermines the perception of the personal attributes of those who hold the positions. The result is that 'a public context (professional activity) elicited more masculine self-image in women and men whereas private contexts (close relationships) led to more feminine images of themselves' (1999, p. 287). The same thing occurs with the ideal images, more masculine at work and more feminine at home, but, as in example (1), it seems that there is no change in the understanding of managerial tasks and positions. However, we have found the evocation of new models of management in more abstract discourses about management, and have also seen their influence in male managers' descriptions and image. This is not the topic of this chapter, but we have observed clear changes in the images of male managers. These changes allow the incorporation of new features, such as interactional skills, and even a more democratic style. As a result of this, the traditional displacement from role stereotypes to gender stereotypes seems to be particularly active in the case of women. This fact explains why, if women and men do speak and behave in similar ways, they are likely to be evaluated differently. As example (1) and other examples in this chapter show, behaviour that transgresses gender-related cultural norms may be perceived in respect to the norms, which provide, as Cameron states, a 'rigid regulatory frame' (Cameron, 1997, p. 49) In example (1), when women are viewed through the 'lens of gender polarization', by means of which women's and men's behaviour is seen as completely opposite, they are perceived as behaving like the other gender (see Bem, 1993; West, 1995; Kendall and Tannen, 1997, for a complete explanation). However, our research shows that women managers are not only perceived as men, but also as authoritarian male managers. They are presented as reproducing old and rejected authoritarian models of management instead of new ones. As we will see below, some differences can be found in the adjustment of new beliefs and views on management to old ones in relation to both genders.

As a result, women are in a 'no-win' situation. Attitudes and behaviours identified as 'typically female' are *disadvantageous for women* (intuitiveness, helpfulness, understanding and awareness of other people's feelings, interactional skills, passion), even when they are positively valued in new models of management, and even if in the case of men they are not equally rejected. On the other hand, women assuming more masculine traits are seen as deviant. Both keeping traditional features or assuming traditional masculine traits leaves women looking unworthy of promotion. As a result, the prevalent position of men in organizations is not threatened but effectively updated, and in consequence reinforced. The interviews show the several contradictions experienced by social actors. Below, we will look at these contradictions, by means of which new models of management have come to renew the image of male managers, but not to promote women's incorporation into these positions. Discourses show how gender stereotypes play a significant role in the configuration and maintaining of role stereotypes in the case of women (men can be either assertive or democratic managers, while women cannot be effective managers: they are too assertive or too weak). Role stereotypes are responsible for the continued existence of the so-called 'glass ceiling'.

Analysis of the interviews

This analysis focuses on the discursive representation of women managers and on the adjustment of new models that seem to have had a negative rather than a positive effect for the incorporation of women in high-ranking business roles. In this analysis we consider the most outstanding discursive strategies involved in the representation of women managers: greater visibility, contrast or comparison, and assimilation. These strategies are linked to the 'tokenization' of women managers. When women comprise less than 15 per cent of an organization's workforce they can be considered 'tokens' and are probably going to be seen as symbols of their gender rather than as individuals. In the following our analysis focuses on:

- *Inferential processes, involved in these phenomena: greater visibility, and particularly in contrast and comparison.* We study conversational and non-conversational inferential processes and their cognitive effect on the negative evaluation of differences between genders.
- *Comparative structures and presuppositions.* Male and female discourses are full of comparisons that state 'how similar women are to men'. This structure shows how the association between the role of manager and the male stereotype is still prevalent.
- *Conversational inferential processes,* which show how those features which are promoted by new models of management are not seen as positive in the case of women managers. Differences are seen as delegitimizing features.
- Among the *discursive strategies involved in assimilation,* we study metaphor, which appears as the more effective procedure in the 'virilization' (being perceived as a man) of women who become managers. This presentation of women managers as authoritarian men is coherent not only

with the previously referred to negative perception of differences, but it also (and this seems to be more relevant) connects the way women perform this role with an old and generally rejected model of management, the authoritarian model.

These discursive strategies are interconnected and provide considerable evidence of the displacement, examined earlier, by means of which female gender stereotypes and role stereotypes appear as inextricably entwined. Great visibility and comparison show how organizations are gendered social structures where masculine usages and models continue to predominate. The third discursive strategy, assimilation, shows how women are in a 'no-win' situation: attitudes and behaviours identified as 'typically female' are *disadvantageous for women*, even when they are positively valued by the new models of management, and the incorporation of features traditionally associated with men by women managers is also considered negatively, given the fact that these features are associated with old models of management. Finally, metaphor shows the effects of this restricted and particular adjustment on the images of women managers.

The feminine gender, the branded gender

As Deborah Tannen (1994) has observed, the feminine is the branded gender, not only grammatically but also symbolically. For Tannen, North American culture brands the feminine gender, making it intensive, whether it be dress sense, tone of voice or the titles and forms of denomination (Mrs or Miss), and adopting the husband's surname after marriage. All these brands compose each woman's image and allow her to appear as representative of her gender.

Other authors have already pointed out how this phenomenon is particularly acute in the workplace. For Kanter (1997, p. 130), one of the first women to study this phenomenon, as long as women comprise less than 15 per cent of an organization's workforce they can be considered 'tokens' of their gender rather than individuals. This becomes especially obvious when they hold positions which are different from the established roles (woman = secretary/nurse; man = boss/doctor). A woman is not judged as an individual but as 'Woman', as a representative of her gender.

Kanter also points out that when women are seen as 'tokens' they are subject to three perceptual tendencies: greater visibility, contrast or comparison, and assimilation (1997, p. 130ff.) (see above).

Greater visibility goes hand-in-hand with the 'surprise' effect: people in Spain are still surprised that women achieve these jobs, so that neither her presence nor her performance will go unnoticed. Men, though, have the freedom to choose to be or not to be 'non-branded' (within organizations), to calling attention to themselves or not, to be judged or not – the right, in fact, to choose to be unnoticed.

Every woman will have her ability and behaviour observed and judged as to suitability. This means that all women are judged on the performance of one, and will be affected by what she does. If her performance is considered negatively, then the whole gender is discredited (think of the furious attacks on high-ranking female civil servants, even cabinet ministers). The cause of the lack of ability is attributed to the group (women cannot do this job correctly), not to the individual.

This equivalence between individual and gender is made manifest through a constant process of generalization, typical of all stereotyped representation. These generalizations work explicitly or implicitly, involving complex inferential processes, as in the following example.

[2] Yo me acuerdo *una chica* graciosísima que fue, pues surgió un tema, ella llevaba unos contenedores para basura, yo no sé qué hacía una chica vendiendo o alquilando contenedores para basura, bueno pues como era tan absurda la situación, a mí me resultaba extraño pues que una chica mona y tal, con un medio uniforme, una chica muy graciosa, intentara alquilarte o venderte unos temas de contenedores de basura pues yo te digo francamente que a mí eso pues me descentraba, yo sabía lo que costaba lo que podía llegar el precio lo que no y tal, pero el que fuera ese tipo de chica y no sé que pues no la veía en ese momento y de alguna forma me sentía raro, *yo creo que ellas lo utilizan*, imagino que el director de márqueting o de comercial de esa empresa utilizaba chicas en ese sentido porque eran mucho más, no se, entraban más, o vendía un producto tan extraño como ése pues con una rapidez. (Grupo de discusión, profesionales: 19)

[2] I remember *a girl*, she was very charming and she was selling rubbish containers. I don't know what a girl was doing selling or hiring out rubbish containers, because the situation was so absurd. I thought it was strange that a pretty girl, with a kind of uniform, a very charming girl, should be trying to hire or sell you rubbish containers; frankly it knocked me off balance, I knew what the price was and all that, but the fact that it was this kind of girl and I really didn't see it at that moment and in some way I felt strange, *I think that they use that.* I imagine that the marketing manager of that firm used girls in that way because they were much more, I don't know, they made more impact, or sold such a strange product like that one with speed. (Discussion group, professionals: 19)

The visibility of the woman because of her unusual job allows the speaker in this anecdote to make a generalization out of a specific case: a pretty girl becomes all women, 'they use it'. Although not mentioned explicitly in the discourse, the division 'men/women' is active/present ('they'), gender being once again the element which organizes the structure of both collectives. And it is not made explicit what 'it' refers to or what it is that defines this

group of women and their behaviour in the workplace. However his interlocutors could easily have obtained this information if they had activated
shared knowledge; in this case a female stereotype who uses her 'feminine
weapons' and a female stereotype who regards it as absurd that women
should be doing an activity like selling containers. The inference makes
interlocutors activate shared knowledge to enable interpretation. In this way
a sales model becomes a sexual interchange model, in which 'they' use their
charms to try in some way 'to trick us'. Once this discourse has been interpreted, interlocutors could oppose the vision of the events being transmitted. But this will be made difficult by the fact that nothing has been affirmed
explicitly and, even more so because of the greater effort that will have to
be put into the processing and in detecting the arguments present in it.

Underlying this and other examples is the problem of the uneven salience
of the attributes in the different social groups, which in its turn refers to
social identity. The expectations about what is 'normal', usual in these cases,
leads to the interpretation of an event on the basis of the stereotypes of role
and gender. The result is that this young woman, but also all women, appear
as non-professional.

What has been seen so far goes a long way towards explaining both the
stress and anxiety and the feeling of being permanently watched that
women in posts of responsibility usually experience. This leads on to a second perceptual tendency – the *comparison*.

Asymmetry in linguistic, social and cognitive comparison
Comparisons have been particularly revealing in this analysis. Given the fact
that they establish a relation between genders and specific attributes and
behaviours, they reveal how the view on managerial positions is still
gender-biased. Finally, focusing on their linguistic, social and cognitive
dimensions, we find a clear asymmetry between the terms involved in the
comparison; these terms are always 'men' and 'women'.

The linguistic dimension

[3] nosotros partimos de la idea de que las *mujeres* formadas están...
umm... tienen *la misma formación o mejor o responden mucho mejor que* los
hombres eh... Aquí no se pone ninguna traba a las mujeres por lo menos
que yo sepa ¿eh? ojo. (Directiva)

[3] we start from the idea that trained women are... umm... *have the same*
training or better or *respond much better than* men... No obstacles are put
in the way of women here, at least none that I know of, but... (Female
Manager)

In this and other examples the term of reference in the comparison is always
men or the masculine. Thus the direction of the comparison is always from

women to men, independently of whether the person talking is a woman or a man. This fact is very significant, as people usually perceive themselves and their groups as prototypes in a social comparison. In this case, women's weak social position in the public sphere means that they put themselves in the place of the other and see themselves from someone else's point of view. This, without doubt, is linked to the traditional social distribution of spaces and roles, which continues to shape both role and gender identities.

Both facts reveal that the yardstick in relation to management is masculine, from the moment that these traits and attitudes are taken for granted in men. The comparatives presume that 'men have training, respond, are able to command'. In fact, in a sentence like 'they can command/organize the same as or better than a man', the comparatives can be considered as presupposition-caring construction by which it is presumed that 'men respond, they are able to command'. Paradoxically, instead of evaluating some traits traditionally associated with women as positive for management – as new models of management suggest – interviewees emphasize that women are like men, and that traditional male traits and skills are also present in women. This seems to be considered as a way of making their image positive and of assuring them a space in the workplace.

The social dimension

These comparative structures are not reversible. It would be almost ironic to say 'men run companies/governments as well as we do', 'men can also be good bosses', 'at work men are the same as or even better than us', because in no case is this fact questioned socially.

Comparisons also show the asymmetrical distribution of social spaces between genders: men are the point of reference when the space under discussion is the public one. However, this is not the case when the discourse centres on the home. In this second case, it would not be strange to find interviews where women set themselves up as the element of reference: 'men look after the children less than we do'.

Focusing on these different levels, we realize that differences between genders are rarely admitted. If a woman in an interview says 'women are/we are the same as or better than men', the reason is that they are like men, and their success and efficiency in the workplace would seem to be guaranteed. The problem is that these skills and attributes are taken for granted in the case of men. Emphasis on the case of women introduces an element of doubt. Women need even more of the same skills for them to be taken for granted.

All this has very important consequences. In the first place, in the discourses analysed it is not questioned that these attributes and abilities are the most suitable and effective ones for the performance of the managerial role. Nor, second, is the fact that these are more characteristic of men questioned. The fact that the standard continues to be masculine also has further consequences. It means that the criteria used in comparisons are also masculine, thereby establishing the complex displacement already pointed out between the carrying out of role attributes and tasks associated with a specific gender. Given the link established between social spaces, attributes and abilities and a specific gender, the point is not whether women at work are good or are trained but whether they work like men and have the same training and qualities as men. Hence accepting this standard and these criteria carries with it men's over-representation and women's under-representation in the most powerful and prestigious social roles and occupations (for similar observations, see Echebarría Echabe and González Castro, 1999, p. 301).

The cognitive dimension

From the cognitive point of view, the comparative structures are also very revealing. People usually take themselves and their groups as prototypes in a social comparison, but in this case the perspective from which the perception is oriented and the capacity measured is from the second term of the comparison, that is from men: 'women are as capable as men'. The same thing happens in the description of a particular role. The reason is that attributes which play an important role in self-perception are insisted on as the ones necessary for the carrying out of a role. In this case, women's weak position in the labour domain means that they see themselves from someone else's point of view. Thus there is here a clear example of how androcentricism underlies cognitive comparisons.

Asymmetry also seems to be pervasive in building the managerial role: social space is decisive in one's perception of oneself and of others, and thus is a definition of identity. Men are the point of reference in the public space, and particularly in the labour world: the result is that 'a public context (professional activity) ellcited more masculine self-image in women and men whereas private contexts (close relationships) led to more feminine images of themselves' (Echebarría Echabe and González Castro, 1999, p. 287). The problem for women seems to be that 'virilization' (becoming/being perceived like a man) appears to be rejected by both genders, and appears associated with dictatorial behaviours, which are also rejected.

Finally, it should be pointed out that the proliferation of these comparisons can be explained as an interdiscursive and polyphonic device, which shows the need for interviewees to challenge still-dominant discourses in which those attributes seems to be denied to women. As a consequence these attributes and skills are emphasized. Thus in the interviews the sequence of comparisons ends up building a representation of women in the workplace which is felt to be positive. Both women and men refer to it, but in many cases it is as doubtfully positive as the ones already mentioned.

Negative evaluation of the difference in conversational inferential processes

One of the most relevant phenomena, linked with the previous one, is how the comparison between women and men, in which men are still the pervasive reference, leads to a negative perception of difference. Thus, as is made obvious in example (4), the mere possibility that women might be different from men, which is often presupposed from the interviewers' questions, is interpreted by the interviewees as a demerit or a weakness, a negative trait or failure in women. This is why, when the interviewers' questions refer to the existence of gender differences, all the interviewees rejected such a possibility and affirmed the no-difference, as happened in comparative structures ('the same as or better than men').

[4] A. ¿EXISTE ESA INCOMPATIBILIDAD (entre ser mujer y ser un jefe autoritario) O NO LA VES?
B. Las mujeres pueden mandar así, *pues si somos malísimas*, vamos podemos mandar como se nos ponga en las narices, no pero yo creo que hay que ser racionales ¿no? hay que dejar a un lado la...(risas) la época premenstrual (risas) dejar...porque eso. (Directiva)

[4] A. IS THERE ANY INCOMPATIBILITY (between being a woman and being an authoritarian boss) OR ARE YOU NOT AWARE OF IT?
B. We women can give orders, because *we are very hard*. Yes, we can be if we have a mind to be, no but I think that you have to be rational, you have to leave to the side the...(laughter) the PMS [pre-menstrual syndrome] (laughter) leave...because of this. (Female Manager)

To understand the misunderstandings that often arise in this respect between interviewers and interviewees, let us refer to the Gumperz theory of conversational inference.

Gumperz (1992, p. 223) establishes three different levels in the inferential process; contextual indexes play an important part in all of them:

- *First level: The perceptual plane* at which communicative signals are perceived, received, categorized, and gathered into information units.
    Inferences at this level provide information: turn-taking units, foregrounding and backgrounding of items of information, separating known from new information, distinguishing main points from side sequences.
- *Second level:* Local assessment of 'sequencing' and 'speech act implications'.
    Inferences at this level yield situated interpretations of 'communicative intent'.
- *Third level:* A more 'global level of framing' which signals what is expected in the interaction at any one stage.
    Inferences at this level yield global predictions and expectations about possible outcomes of an exchange, about suitable topics, and about the quality of interpersonal relations. At this level ambiguities at the perceptual or sequential levels can be resolved.

At the first level, the *perceptual level*, the signals are received and categorized. The inferences become oriented to the carrying out of communication (tone, speed, turns of speaking) and the management of information (to stress something or not, to distinguish between new and given information). In the interviews analysed, the questions and specifically the presuppositions included would thematize and emphasize differences between genders: 'women rule organizations in a different way', in example (4), and in (5) 'their communicative style is different'. This raises the question of gender differences, which then become the subject of the question, of the answer and therefore of the whole communicative event.

[5] A. ¿Y LAS MUJERES EN LA EMPRESA EN LA QUE TÚ ESTÁS EN LA RELACIÓN, EN LA FORMA DE HABLAR, EL TIPO DE RELACIONES, SON DISTINTAS? ¿LAS QUE ESTABLECEN ENTRE SÍ? ES DECIR POR EJEMPLO HABLAN CON MÁS CONFIANZA SE?

B. Sí aquí las mujeres que trabajan en nuestra compañía son mujeres (silencio) con mucha potencia a todos los niveles, te quiero decir que nunca va a ser despreciada porque sea mujer al contrario.

A. TE DIGO LAS RELACIONES NO ...

B. ¿Las relaciones entre ellas?

A. SÍ.

B. ¿O con los hombres?

A. SÍ ENTRE ELLAS, LA FORMA DE HABLAR, DE HABLARSE, SI HAY ALGUNA MANERA ... PORQUE SE HABLA DE QUE SI LAS MUJERES EN LOS CENTROS DE TRABAJO HABLAN MÁS DE COSAS PERSONALES, TIENEN UN ESTILO MÁS ... CÁLIDO DE ALGUNA MANERA ...

B. Eso es cierto yo lo noto eh ... es cierto, o sea al final siempre terminamos hablando de trapos no siempre pero ... (Directiva)

[5] A. AND THE WOMEN IN YOUR FIRM, HOW DO THEY TALK, HOW DO THEY COMMUNICATE? HOW DO THEY MAKE CONTACTS? ARE THEY DIFFERENT? AND THE RELATIONSHIP AMONG THEMSELVES? FOR EXAMPLE, DO THEY TALK MORE FREELY?

B. Yes here the women who work in our firm are women (silence) with a lot of power at every level, I mean that they are never going to be disparaged because they're women, quite the reverse.

A. I MEAN THE RELATIONSHIPS ARE NOT ...

B. The relationships among women?

A. YES.

B. Or with the men?

A. YES AMONG THEMSELVES, THE WAY OF TALKING, OF COMMUNICATING, YES THERE IS A PARTICULAR WAY ... BECAUSE IT'S ABOUT IF WOMEN IN THE WORKPLACE TALK MORE ABOUT PERSONAL THINGS, THEY HAVE A MORE ... A MORE WARM STYLE IN SOME WAYS ...

B. That's true, I've noticed it ... it's true, that is, eventually we always end up talking about clothes and fashion, not always but ... (Female Manager)

In order to understand how and why these misunderstandings occur, it is necessary to bear in mind the role of questions in interviews. First, questions introduce the topics which the interviewee will have to talk about so that they can organize the answer. They are, therefore, as Ribas Bisbal suggests (2000), thematizations which organize the communicative exchange. This is why, from the cognitive point of view, they have important consequences: they schematize a situation and force the interviewee to focus on the question from the interviewer's point of view. In example (4), the question, 'IS THERE ANY INCOMPATIBILITY (between being a woman and being an authoritarian boss)?' presupposes that there is a female style of management, or at least some difference in the way women manage an organization. This means that questions restrict not only the freedom of speech but also the freedom of representation.

The derived presupposition refers to specific social representations (women have a different style of management), which in turn are associated with values and ideologies (see also, Ribas Bisbal, 2000). However, as we see at the next level, interviewers and interviewees may not share the evaluation and the ideology associated with these representations (gender differences).

It is at the second level established by Gumperz, *speech act implications*, that the inferences are related to participants' communicative intentions, beyond what is said. Thus, in the interviews mentioned, from questions like 'do women talk/manage/behave in a different way?' interviewees seem to infer that they are required to say something against women. However, this is not the intention of the interviewers. What makes this inference possible is a specific ideological context.

In example (5), differences are understood by the interviewee as weaknesses: B's answer 'they are women (silence) with a lot of power at every level' is presented as an argument against possible differences between both genders. And, in fact, she tries to defend the value of women, paradoxically answering: 'No, no, we can't be very hard.'

In example (5), when the interviewer asks if women in the workplace talk more about personal things; if have they a style, which is warmer, the interviewee confirms her recognition of a certain difference: 'we always end up talking about clothes and fashion, not always but ...'.

The difference – in this case, a feature traditionally linked to frivolity and domestic responsibilities – is recognized but it is valued negatively.

The interviewees, as a general rule, given the fact that both models and standards are still masculine, seem to understand the recognition of difference as weakness. Thus, in (5) although B's answer begins with yes, it does so only to affirm women's capacities, as if this is being put in doubt by the question: 'they are women (silence) with much power at every level'. Rejecting the possibility of difference between genders, male/female interviewees try to promote a non-sexist image, as they recognize and defend the value of women and women in their totality ('No, no, we can be very hard'). It can be seen here that there is no recognition or any evaluation of the difference, only an internalization of a dominant androcentric and sexist culture in the workplace: women should be like men, and this model is not questioned at all. In this ideological context, equality of opportunity would seem to require homogenization and adaptation to prevalent patterns. New models of management seem to be ignored.

Thus, presuppositions in interviewers' questions present a particular representation as unquestionable truths and allow the speaker to introduce assertions without the need to justify them; this is why they become a strategy full of signifiers and therefore an argumentative strategy. However, the evaluation of this representation (there are differences) and the ideology associated with it may not be shared by participants, as happens in examples (4) and (5).

At the third level established by Gumperz, *a more global level of framing* (after Goffmann), the inferences affect the understanding of the activity in which the interlocutors are taking part, in this case, the interview and its purpose: what is expected in it, what can be obtained from it and what are suitable subjects and behaviour. These inferential processes establish, in fact, the ground on which the ambiguities in the two preceding levels can be resolved or maintained, as in the present case under discussion.

Questions about differences between male and female styles of management, and in general all the questions regarding the situation of women in companies and in selection processes, are used by the interviewees in their contextualization process of the interaction. The very question seems to be received with suspicion, as if the interviewer is trying to find the sexism hidden in the interviewees' ideologies and in those of their firms. The interviewees on many occasions appear to feel the need to defend themselves against two possible accusations: being sexist, and working for a sexist organization (for example, in (5): 'in our firm there are women (silence) with a lot of power at every level, I mean they are never going to be disparaged because they're women, quite the reverse'). It seems that merely to introduce the situation of women as a topic can lead to a veiled accusation of sexism. Thus, the interviewees seem to feel obliged to safeguard both their image and that of their firm.

As we have pointed out on other occasions (Martín Rojo and Callejo Gallego, 1995), a man or a woman who openly admits to discriminatory practices (for instance, in the selection process, or in promotion) cannot count on having a positive social image.[4] The position of these men and women is made difficult, almost untenable: how can they maintain the idea that both genders are equal and simultaneously not support and demand the free access of women to the workplace and, in particular, to managerial positions? How can they argue that success in life is based on professional success, on personal achievements but that what satisfies women should be looking after children? Inhibited sexism minimizes and hides these contradictions, but does not sustain them.

In addition, for some reason affirmation of difference is still regarded as sexist and is therefore avoided. That may be due to the fact that the speaker takes

as reference a specific traditional ideological framework. Here difference continues to be understood as faults or imperfections, and is used for the affirmation of negative traits and qualities in women (weakness, lack of criteria
and independence, insecurity), arguments which question their training and
worth. The view of difference as imperfection is inextricably related to the fact
that the norm is built upon traditional patterns which involve male stereotypes. Taking this ideological context as a point of reference, interviewees cannot acknowledge gender difference without running the risk of being
considered sexist. Consequently, as has already been seen, what is affirmed is
that women possess a quality which is taken for granted in men, at the same
or even to a greater degree. At the same time, the idea that they possess different attributes, skills and behaviours (women are more demanding than
men) is rejected. Of course, it is almost impossible to explain the existence of
these differences without resorting to essentialist explanations – often
regarded as sexist, and generally avoided – or to sociopolitical ones, which
relate these differences, now socially valued, to differences in social status,
social position or socialization. The recognition of such differences not only
entails the presentation of stressed or discriminated against women, but also
the admittance that there are discriminating organizations and social conflicts. Without recognizing discrimination, it is almost impossible to explain
why, if there are no differences in ability and skills, the number of women
highly placed in organizations is so small. In order to escape from these contradictions, women often appear as the agents of their own exclusion.

Given this ideological framework, most of the female interviewees do not
appear to have yet taken on board new trends in feminist thinking, in particular about cultural differences (linked to sociopolitical conditions) and
sexual difference. On the contrary, the interviewers' questions are framed in
a different ideological context, that of feminist thinking, and this ideological stance is not in opposition to the theoretical enquiry of studying the
suitability of feminizing workplaces by promoting a female style of management. Note how, in example (5), the interviewer is taking as reference the
work of Tannen when asking the question, and how in the answer the difference is interpreted as synonymous with weakness. On the other hand, in
example (6) the interviewer is assuming that there is discrimination, and is
trying to determine the obstacles women have to face. This view is rejected
by the interviewee, who again denies discrimination and difference between
genders.

[6] A. HAY UNA COSA QUE NOS HA LLAMADO LA ATENCIÓN QUE SE DICE ... LO DIGO
POR ESTA CUESTIÓN DEL HORARIO. QUE SE DICE QUE LAS MUJERES NO LLEGAN A ESOS
PUESTOS ALTOS PORQUE POR EJEMPLO TIENEN MÁS LIMITACIONES DE HORARIO.
B. Puede ser, puede ser, yo no sé, yo no tengo esos problemas porque
no estoy casada entonces no tengo hijos ni nada y tengo un puesto de
dirección en esta empresa perooo podría suceder. No se da el caso aquí,

tenemos mujeres, tenemos bastantes y son jóvenes y... y todas trabajan fenomenal pero además igual o mejor que los hombres o sea que que en esta, aquí no tenemos esos problemas... (Directiva)

[6] A. THERE IS ONE THING THAT HAS ATTRACTED OUR ATTENTION... IT'S ABOUT THE TIMETABLE. IT'S SAID THAT WOMEN DON'T GET THESE HIGH-LEVEL JOBS BECAUSE THEY HAVE MORE RESTRICTED HOURS.
B. Possibly, possibly, I don't know. I don't have these problems because I'm not married so I don't have children and I have a managerial post in this firm but it could happen. It doesn't happen here, we have women, we have a lot of women and they are young and... and all of them work marvellously, as well as or better than the men so that here we don't have these problems... (Female Manager)

The analysis of the conversational inferences of this and those in example (7) show that not only is work considered incompatible with family life (González et al., 2000), but also that workers have to be completely devoted to their work. Curiously, private life is understood to be the same as having children.

[7] A mí me da igual quedarme aquí hasta las 7 que hasta las 10, a mí me da igual, yo tengo mi vida privada y tengo mis amigos pero no tengo un niño que me está esperando en casa. (Directiva)

[7] It makes no difference to me whether I stay here until 7 or until 10 p.m., it makes no difference at all. I have my private life and I have my friends but I don't have a child who's waiting for me at home. (Female Manager)

This leads to a cul-de-sac. In the first place, if every hint of an affirmation of a feminine style (6) or even of women's particular needs or restrictions (7) (the exigencies of family time) is either considered negatively or as an accusation that one has to defend oneself against, this implies that style, models and requirements continue to be masculine. Second, denying the survival of sexism provides no indication of how the present situation responds to the differences in power and status, to women's different social position and the discrimination suffered. Thus the door remains open to essentialist explanations, but these are not an adequate basis on which to question the correlation established between a specific gender and specific attributes, preferences and conduct. If the presence of women and their difficult adaptation to posts of responsibility are not explicable by social conditions and different social positions, it is much less possible to challenge the traditional link between power and masculinity.

In conclusion, misunderstandings are due to the relevant role played by ideologies (sexism/feminism) in the construction of a positive self-image through discourse. These different positions are related to the different answers individuals can give against exclusion. In women interviewees we have seen how different answers are possible, from denying the differences to abandoning the wish to join. As Griffiths (1995, p. 91) argues, 'if someone has been rejected as result of attributions of race, class, gender or disability, she finds it necessary to construct a new identity which accommodates the rejection'. In the case we are examining, the differences are denied.

We also see that, in the carrying out of managerial duties, women are not only observed but are also compared with the existing – masculine – models. Out of this arises a situation recognized by both the men and the women interviewed: women have to show their value in the job, as people and also as a gender – they show that they are aware that the other group does not consider them competent at their job.

[8] B. Pues pues yo creo que todavía nos toca seguir demostrando que valemos más de verdad, todavía no,
(...)
A. ¿AUTOEXIGENCIA, DICES?
B. Autoexigencia para demostrar a los demás que...que puede hacerlo... que puede hacerlo, que puede hacerlo pero yo estoy convencida de que las mujeres pueden hacer lo mismo que los hombres, lo que pasa es que es cierto que es una sociedad machista y en la que nos cuesta todavía estar integradas, machista entre comillas, ojo yo no me quejo porque estoy en una compañía que dentro de lo que ... (Directiva)
[8] Well I think we still have to show that we are really worth more, not yet no,
(...)
A. DO YOU MEAN THEY ARE VERY DEMANDING OF THEMSELVES?
B. Very demanding to show the others that...that you can do it...that you can do it that you can do it, but I'm convinced that women can do the same as men, what happens is that it's true that it's a chauvinist society in which it's still an effort for us to be integrated, chauvinist in inverted commas, careful I'm not complaining because I'm in a company which within what...(Female Manager)

This commonplace in feminine discourse shows the self-exigency with which women face the work experience. This becomes similar to the awareness that minority groups have; they know the stereotypes that weigh on them when they are in contact situations (see Martín Rojo, 1998b).

This leads onto the third tendency, *assimilation*. Another commonplace in the narratives about women's managers examined is imitation.

The effects of assimilation: 'virilization', isolation and lack of female role models

Apart from a few exceptions, all the discourses point out the lack of feminine models of management. This means that the descriptions of the female managers revolve around two poles. They can adapt and keep some of the features of their gender stereotype: the maternal-boss, demanding but looking to help and train; the seductress, who has reached a position because of her sexual attractiveness and her seductive tricks; the pet-manager, at a middle level, being decorative and subjected to patronizing comments. The second possibility arising out of the interviews is the rejection of the gender role stereotyping alignment: in high-responsibility jobs, women adapt or are considered to have adapted to the prevailing traits and behaviour, but in an excessive and distorted way, and in consequence they are regarded as deviant examples, virilized ('pseudo-men'), and authoritarian; that is, bad managers.

Like many other authors in earlier research, we pointed out that the attribution of a prevalent position in social spaces (public and domestic spaces) to each gender underlies a discourse that marks the boundary between the 'natural' and its degeneration (deviancy). The characterization and evaluation of women's image at work is reminiscent of the culinary triangle described by Lévi-Strauss (1964) which includes the 'raw', the 'cooked' and the 'rotten' because the three items described act as poles around which a variety of values and attitudes revolve (see Martín Rojo and Gómez Esteban, 1996, for further discussion).

It has already been pointed out how the woman who competes in the workplace is often seen as a non-mother woman, something artificial, a degeneration of the mother-woman (nature). In Spanish organizations, successful women in high positions of authority are presented as women 'without' (partner, children, and home). In previous research we have shown how every aspect of these women is valued negatively in comparison with what is natural: they either 'have a moustache' or their beauty is malignant (if they are pretty, they are dangerous because they 'use their sexual weapons'); they are sterile; they are heavy-handed and display surly behaviour ('sergeant'); their wish to be promoted is personal and vindictive; they exercise asphyxiating authority. This shows the perception of an inability of women to combine professional value with femininity (Martín Rojo and Callejo Gallego, 1995). This is due to the difficulty of accepting the rapid social change of identities and spaces. Workplace culture and communications demand a style of women managers which shows the attitudes and practices typical of men; in short, that they become 'virilized'. However, in this research we also see how, besides this 'virilization', women are not presented as bad managers: when they exercise power, they adopt a very out-of-date style. Assimilation is considered an effective procedure in order to reach the highest positions in organizations:

[9] Sí. Pero quizá las mujeres que he conocido que llegan a jefas o que son directoras, son esas que asumen el, que imitan el papel masculino ... (Alto cargo en la Administración)

[9] Yes. But perhaps the women I've known who become bosses or managers, they are the ones who accept it, who imitate the masculine role... (High-ranking Civil Servant)

Nevertheless, as we will see below, this tends to be rejected. Women who follow this model are considered failures both as women and as managers.

Authority (power), a disguise that does not suit women

An analysis of the interviews shows several images of women managers. Here, we present an approximate typology, considering the cluster of metaphors documented. All the types share the feature 'virilized', but also the feature 'authoritarian'. The one which is most rejected is that of the *'pseudo-man'* (*the phallic-virilized woman*), described as authoritarian, competitive, cruel and physically virilized, as reflected in the following example.

[10] Las mujeres ... cuando son autoritarias son la leche... yo me acuerdo, pues fíjate cuando estaba en el banco, había una directiva de Banesto, pero bueno pues se fue a una empresa de bebidas de gran consumo, de refrescos y luego se incorporó a otro banco..., y de esta persona decían sus colaboradores que no podía llevar minifalda porque se le veían los cojones (Risas) y yo que llegué a conocerla – y además es que después a la empresa a la que se fue, pues una amiga mía compañera del máster, bueno pues la conoció también ¿no?... pues es que era brutal, o sea, era tan despiadada como el hombre más despiadao... ¿no? Hombre a lo mejor es un caso un poco especial ¿no?, porque es una tía que mide un metro noventa también ¿no? (Directivo Banco)

[10] Women... when they're authoritarian they're bloody awful... I remember when I was working in that bank, there was a female manager but she went to a soft drinks firm, a very popular drink, and then she joined a different bank... Well the men who worked with her said she couldn't wear a mini-skirt because her balls would show (Laughter) and I got to know her – and also that after the firm she went to a woman I know, we did the MA together, well she also knew her... well, she was brutal, as heartless as the most heartless man ... Perhaps it's a special case, isn't it? I mean, she's a woman one metre ninety tall... (Male Bank Manager)

This is the woman known colloquially as 'the one who wears the trousers'. These images keep the association of power and the phallic; the women who exercise power are seen as freaks, or at least as non-women.

The rest of the established types of virilized women are not so extreme, nor so rejected. They belong to the group of disguised women, who have been the object of much less study despite their relevance and interest.

The only woman manager that is visible and recognizable is the *virilized woman disguised as a man*: she imitates a style which is not her own and which does not suit her. This image is embodied in the metaphor of disguise, and it plays a key role in the construction of a representation of women managers.

[11] Que las mujeres están, cuando llegan a niveles de jefatura adoptan roles o papeles de hombre, ¿no? Entonces se visten como los hombres, usan chaqueta y utilizan corbata y: quieren hacer las cosas pareciéndose a los hombres, como imitar ¿no? Y yo te digo, desde un concepto, desde mi perspectiva, yo creo que no tienen que imitar a nadie. Tienen que ser ellas mismas. Y simplemente, con un buen nivel de competencia técnica y con una habilidad para conducir a las personas y nada más. (Formador en Escuela de Negocios)

[11] That the women are, when they reach managerial levels they adopt male roles. Then they dress like men, they wear a jacket and tie and they want to do things the way men do them, like an imitation. Let me tell you, from my perspective, I think they don't need to imitate anyone. They have to be themselves. Just with a good level of technical competence and with an ability to manage people, nothing else. (Management Trainer)

The appearance of this cluster of metaphors (the incorporation of women to high-level jobs like the putting-on of a disguise) structures and articulates (on allowing the integration, categorization and visualization of these elements like a conceptual structure cf. Grize, 1974) the social representation of women bosses.

This figurative core also allows the anchorage, that is, their insertion on previous social representation. Hence, their basic functions are possible: interpreting reality, orienting behaviour and social relations, as well as the cognitive integration; the insertion of these representations in the consciousness.

[12] Pero yo creo que no siempre es así, porque yo he conocido muchas mujeres ... Muchas no porque no ha habido muchas, pero he conocido mujeres en puestos de alta responsabilidad tremendamente masculinizadas en su forma de desempeñar su rol de mando, y son tremendamente duras, muy damas de hierro. Por eso no me gusta decir que la mujer manda de una manera o de otra porque no siempre he visto eso. (Miembro de la Junta Directiva de un Banco)

[12] Well I think that it isn't always like that, because I've known many women ... Many not because there have been many, but I've known highly-placed women tremendously virilized (pseudo-male) in their way of carrying out their managerial role, and they are tremendously hard,

real iron ladies. That's why I don't like to say that women have their own style of commanding, because I haven't always seen it. (Member of the Board of Directors of a Bank)

As can be seen in these examples, the figurative nucleus established around the 'disguise' metaphor not only allows the representation of managerial women but also enables them to be given a sense by means of which they are evaluated as a social object. This is closely linked to the assigning of values (as, for example, here, 'Women when they imitate men behave like them, but in an incorrect and thus worse way; women make worse bosses').

These values are different depending on the social groups. In this case, however, it seems that men as well as women reject the woman 'disguised as a man'. This figurative nucleus allows a specific integration of 'novelty' – that of women in top management posts, which is assimilated socially in a very special way. With the presentation of women top-managers disguised as men, the novelty comes into contact with a previous system of representation,[5] the association between power and masculinity, which has traditionally provided the image of the pseudo-male woman ('a woman who wears the trousers'). The 'familiarity of the strange' implies learning the new in terms of the acquired standards.

However, the metaphor of the disguise is interpreted and used in another sense, the *virilized woman disguised as a woman*. It appears in special cases, in those interviewees who recognize a differentiating trait in the female style of management: the lack of an authoritarian style and a style of management which emphasizes 'us', that is, the team, and not hierarchical differences. This is the only case where a possible female style is recognized. However, in at least one case, this is immediately disqualified and neutralized (presented as a disguise). In this way, female behaviour is once again placed in the shadow of the traditional gender stereotype. Here is the example.

[13] Si el modelo es democrático y todo el mundo estamos de acuerdo en que es democrático y es de verdad democrático el modelo funciona. Ahora si tú intentas disfrazar de una u otra cosa lo que no es una u otra cosa al final acabas teniendo problemas ¿no? y sí que las mujeres son probablemente más hábiles a la hora de disfrazar un modelo autoritario, pero simplemente habilidad a la hora de disfrazar ¿no?, o sea, ¿por qué?, pues porque a lo mejor, pues no sé, porque lo hacen mejor, pero al final los problemas y las tensiones son iguales o incluso mayores ¿no? No, yo no creo que las mujeres sean menos autoritarias ¿no?, a lo mejor lo saben en algún, en un momento determinado disfrazar mejor, pero no no no, porque además date cuenta que en una organización en la que a lo mejor impera el modelo autoritario solamente puede escalar una mujer que acepte el modelo autoritario ¿no?, con lo cual ahí me da un poco lo

mismo el hecho de que sean hombres que que sean mujeres. (Miembro de la Junta Directiva de un Banco)

[13] If the model is democratic and everyone agrees that it is democratic and it really is democratic, then the model works. But if you try to disguise it as one thing or another when it isn't one thing or another in the end you're going to have problems, aren't you? And if women are probably more skilful at disguising an authoritarian model, but they're simply skilful at disguising, aren't they? But I mean, why? Well perhaps because, I don't know, because they do it better, but in the end the problems and the tensions are the same or even greater, aren't they? No, I don't think that women are less authoritarian, perhaps they know at a specific moment how to disguise it better but no no no, because as well bear in mind that in an organization in which perhaps the authoritarian model prevails a woman can only climb if she accepts the authoritarian model, can't she? So that as far as I'm concerned it makes no difference whether they're men or women. (Member of the Board of Directors of a Bank)

Hence, any feature of female style, whether incipient or adapted to a new situation, is disqualified as it confuses and manipulates. Thus, it is not valued as consequent or part of a new model of management, but it is rejected. This means that no style appears to find favour with women; they cannot adapt to the existing models nor can they find a suitable basis for creating new ones. Without doubt, the question of styles is another component which contributes to the creation of the glass ceiling.

All these examples reveal the tendency to avoid the distinction between power and the relationship of domination. While women in positions of responsibility have the power and the authority conferred by the position they occupy ('power over' policies, activities, areas in the organization), they are socially delegitimized, and their ability to exercise power – or at least to exercise it without exhibiting dominatory and authoritarian tendencies – is questioned. This contradiction may explain why the question of power is one of the main issues in current gender and organization research (see, for example, Loden, 1987; Jaffe, 1989; Sekaran and Leong, 1992; Hopcroft, 1996; Silver, 1996; and in the field of linguistics, see, among others, Lakoff, 1990; Wodak, 1995, 1997; Kendall and Tannen, 1997; Gómez Esteban et al., 2000).

Concluding remarks

This research has shown how critical analysis of organizational discourse provides insight into the processes through which struggles over competing interests are discursively shaped. The struggle over high-level jobs takes place in several dimensions, including the symbolic one.

We have seen that the strong links established between social spaces, roles and traditional gender attributes and tasks contribute to the shaping of models of management by gender stereotypes. New models of enacting power in companies are adjusted to old beliefs and values, the prevalence of charismatic models, and the powerful and still persistent link between power and masculinity. This powerful correlation explains the maintenance of the male management models and the lack of feminine models. Male style and norms are so deeply rooted in organizational culture that the effect of the partial assumption of new models is also unbalanced: it allows the updating of male forms and style, while promoting the perception of women's communicative behaviour as deviant and as the performance of old and rejected models of enacting authority. At no time is such correlation between gender stereotypes and role stereotypes (and in consequence the different evaluation of women and men) recognized as the result of a situation of inequality and of social conditions which still oppose the incorporation of women into positions of responsibility. Gender stereotype shaping role stereotypes promotes essentialist discourses that attribute specific worth and possibilities to the genders and favour the survival of such a pernicious association. As a result, we see that organizations are gendered and everyday discourses in organizations reproduce traditional gender stereotypes.

Given the perception of social space, role, tasks and attributes regarded as masculine, it is difficult to assimilate new models of management which defend a democratic style and the incorporation of features traditionally attributed to women. However, we find a 'double discourse' which, on the one hand, promotes democratic values, consistent with prevalent democratic and egalitarian ideologies; but, on the other, masks the permanence of traditional models, only partially and superficially updated. 'Double discourses', inconsistencies and lack of coherence particularly appear during periods of sociopolitical and ideological change and derive in part from the inclusion and 'anchorage', and following adjustment, of new values and proposals to the previous views of management practices and power. In this sense, the discourses and knowledge produced by men and women in interviews about organizations reflect the asymmetric adjustment of these new models (the so-called democratic and transformer models) to the prevalent androcentric views in Spanish organizations. In consequence, there is an ongoing production and justification of a male-defined way of management, now adapted to the new values and models. But there is also a restriction of access and a strong rejection of the female manager. In the case of women, traditional features, such as social and communicative skills or the emphasis on 'power over' (a particular domain or activity) without stressing hierarchies or without imposing decisions and criteria ('power to' control another's actions), are still seen as weaknesses. Role stereotypes and gender stereotypes seem to be particularly bonded in this case. Furthermore, once women reach these positions they are often assimilated and perceived as pseudo-males or as manipulators of their femininity. Then, the influence of new models of management appears again, but as evidence of women's tendency to adapt old and rejected models of management, the authoritarian or assertive model.

As long as this particular adjustment of new models of management continues, the genuine integration of women into the world of work will be difficult. This is particularly clear in the rejection of the existence of a specific female style of management or in the negative evaluation of the existence of differences between genders. It is necessary to create the conditions so that the models and the representatives are not only masculine. In Tancred's words:

> Si l'on tient compte du fait que les femmes pourraient bien exercer l'autorité et le pouvoir d'une autre façon que les hommes, à d'autres niveaux de l'entreprise, et dans des domaines autres que la direction des employés, nous obtenons une image beaucoup plus riche et plus nuancée de l'autorité et du pouvoir dans l'entreprise. (1997, p. 22)[6]

Unfortunately, not only everyday discourses in organizations but also training materials and academic research reflect a traditional view of the organization, focused on efficiency, rationality and control. This reproduces a male-centred understanding of power and authority, and an authoritarian and charismatic way of running organizations which is so deeply rooted that changes and new proposals cannot easily be integrated.

Notes

1. As we will see later, it is often said (a) that women do not give orders calmly but in an excitable way (hysterically, it is claimed), and (b) that women do not react well under pressure; that in fact they increase it instead of filtering it away from the team. The person who knows how to command is the person who does it in a relaxed, in a 'natural' way, and according to the new models of management.
2. See the pioneering article by Rosener and Schwart (1980).
3. A popular study edited by ESADE (1995), and to which many authors contribute, singles out, as positive for future leadership, personal qualities which are always attributed to women: conviction vs command, ability to relate, intuition. The study also adds: 'living in peace, ethics, aesthetics, or team spirit vs competitiveness'. However, the study even ends up saying that 'the manager of the future will have to be able to show great sensitivity towards the strategic role played by people in the achieving of this success'. However, despite all of this, none of it has ever been recognized as part of a female style of management.
4. This happens whenever fields in which there is a highly dominant discourse model are studied (for example, to consider oneself 'democratic' in the field of politics, 'non-racist' in the field of social relations, or, in the case under study, to consider oneself 'non-sexist'). The participants tend to rationalize the discourse and try to

present their own behaviour as 'democratic', 'non-racist' or 'non-sexist', hiding their 'non-democratic', 'racist' or 'sexist' attitudes.

5. 'The cultural change can affect the models of thought and behaviour which modify in a profound way the experiences through the representations' (Jodelet, 1988, p. 491).

6. 'Taking into account the fact that women could exercise power and authority in a different fashion than men, at other levels of the company, and in other domains than the employees' management, we will draw a richer and finer image of the power and authority in the company.'

References

Acker, J. (1990) 'Hierarchies, jobs, bodies: a theory of gendered organization', *Gender and Society*, 4, pp. 139–58.

Bem, S.L. (1993) *The Lenses of Gender: Transforming the Debate on Sexual Inequality*. New Haven, CT, and London: Yale University Press.

Bolinger, D. (1997) *Neutrality, Norm, and Bias*. Bloomington, IN: Indiana University Linguistics Club.

Cameron, D. (1997) 'Performing gender identity: young men's talk and the construction of heterosexual masculinity', in S. Johnson and U.H. Meainhof (eds), *Language and Masculinity*. Oxford and Cambridge: Blackwell.

Chinchilla, N., García, P. and Mercadé, A. (1999) *Emprendiendo en femenino*. Barcelona: Gestión.

Echebarría Echabe, A. and González Castro, J.L. (1999) 'The impact of context on gender social identities', *European Journal of Social Psychology*, 29, pp. 287–304.

ESADE and Andersen Consulting (1995) *El directivo del futuro*. Madrid: ESADE and Andersen Consultino.

Gómez Esteban, C., Callejo Gallego, J. and Martín Rojo, L. (2000) *Modelos y prácticas de mando: El papel de la mujer en los puestos de dirección*. Research Report. Programa I+D (MEC)/Women's Institute.

González, B., Solagaistua, K. and Pérez-Montero, V. (2000) 'Conversational Inferences'. Paper presented at the European Worldwide Narratives Conference, EURESCO.

Griffiths, M. (1995) *Feminism and the Self: The Web of Identity*. London: Routledge.

Grize, J.-B. (1974) 'Recherches sur le discours et l'argumentation: travaux du centre de recherches sémiologiques de l'Université de Neuchâtel', *Revue Européene des Sciences Sociales*, special issue, 32(12).

Gumperz, J. (1992) 'Contextualization and understanding', in A. Duranti and C. Goodwin (eds), *Rethinking Context*. Cambridge: Cambridge University Press.

Jaffe, D. (1989) 'Gender inequality in workplace autonomy and authority', *Social Science Quarterly*, 70(2), pp. 375–90.

Jodelet, D. (1988) 'La representación social: fenómenos, concepto y teoría', in S. Moscoviti et al. (eds), *Psicología Social* II. Barcelona, Buenos Aires, México: Piadós, pp. 469–94.

Helmer, J. (1993) 'Storytelling in the creation and maintenance of organizational tension and stratification', *Southern Communication Journal*, 59, pp. 34–44.

Hopcroft, R.L. (1996) 'The authority attainment of women: competitive sector effects', *American Journal of Economics and Sociology*, 55(2), pp. 163–84.

Kanter, R. (1997) *Men and Women of the Corporation*. New York: Basic Books.

Kendall, S. and Tannen, D. (1997) 'Gender and language in the workplace', in Wodak, R. (ed.) *Gender and Discourse*. London: Sage, pp. 81–105.

Lakoff, R. (1990) 'Why can't a woman be less like a man', in *Talking Power: The Politics of Language*. San Francisco: Basic Books.

Lévi-Strauss, C. (1964) *Mythologiques*, Vol. I: *Le crut et le cuit*. Paris: Librairie Plon.

Loden, M. (1987) *Dirección femenina. Cómo triunfar en los negocios sin actuar como un hombre*. Barcelona: Hisaponeurpa.

Martin, J., Feldman, M., Hatch, M.J. and Sitkin, S.B. (1983) 'The uniqueness paradoxes in organizational stories', *Administrative Science Quarterly*, 28, pp. 438–53.

Martín Rojo, L. (1998a) 'The politics of gender: agency and self-reference in women's discourse', in J. Blommaert and C. Bulcaen (eds), *Political Linguistics*. Amsterdam: John Benjamins, pp. 231–54.

Martín Rojo, L. (1998b) 'Intertextuality and the construction of a new female identity', in M. Bengoechea and R. Solá Buil (eds), *Intertextuality/Intertextualidad*. Alcalá de Henares: Universidad de Alcalá de Henares.

Martín Rojo, L. and Callejo Gallego, J. (1995) 'Argumentation and inhibition: sexism in the discourse of Spanish executives', *Pragmatics*, 5(4), pp. 455–84.

Martín Rojo, L. and Gómez Esteban, C. (1996) 'Imágenes de la mujer en situaciones de competitividad laboral', in C. Bullet and P. Carrasquer (eds), *Sociología del género*. Madrid: Instituto de la Mujer, pp. 129–36.

Mills, A. and Tancred, P. (1992) *Gendering Organizational Analysis*. London: Sage.

Mumby, D. and Clair, R.P. (1997) 'Organizational discourse', in T.A. van Dijk (ed), *Discourse Studies*. Vol. 2, *Discourse as a Social Interaction*. London: Sage.

Ribas Bisbal, M. (2000) 'Discurs parlamentari i representacions socials'. PhD thesis, University of Barcelona.

Rosener, L. and Schwart, P. (1980) *Women, Leadership, and the 1980s: What Kind of Leader do we Need?* RoundTable Report on New Leadership in the Public Interest, New York: NOUW Legal Defense and Education Fund.

Sekaran, U. and Leong, F. (1992) *Womanpower. Managing in Times of Demographic Turbulence*. London: Sage.

Silver, A.-L.S. (1996) 'Women who lead', *American Journal of Psychoanalysis*, 56(1), pp. 3–16.

Tancred, P. (1997) 'Les femmes dans l'organisation: rapports au pouvoir et à l'autorité', *Les cahiers du Mage*, 1, pp. 17–23.

Tannen, D. (1994) *Talking from 9 to 5: How Women's and Men's Conversational Styles Affect Who gets Heard, Who gets Credit, Who gets Done at Work*. New York: William Morrow.

West, C. (1995) 'Women's competence in conversation', *Discourse & Society*, 6(1), pp. 107–31.

Wodak, R. (1995) 'Power, discourse, and style of female leadership in school committee meetings', in D. Corson (ed.), *Discourse and Power in Educational Organizations*. New Jersey: Hampton Press, Inc.

Wodak, R. (ed.) (1997) *Gender and Discourse*. London: Sage.

Wolf, W.C. and Filgstein, N.D. (1979) 'Sex and authority in the workplace: the causes of sexual inequality', *American Sociological Review*, 44(2), pp. 235–52.

13
Cross-Cultural Representation of 'Otherness' in Media Discourse
Carmen Rosa Caldas-Coulthard

Introduction

The topic of this chapter is the language of the news. As I finish writing it four days after the 11 September terrorist attacks on the World Trade Center and the Pentagon, reports of the events are being broadcast continuously. People from the four corners of the earth are glued to their television sets or radios following the development of events that surprised us all. Each new hour brings a new state of affairs. The many voices we hear, the many perspectives on the events, will construe different states of affairs. At this sad moment, as Paul Chilton suggests,

> what happens next will be the outcome of talk and text (cabinet meetings, public statements, media representations, individual utterances) and the text and talk will be governed by cognitive and interactive habits. Under stress pre-wired patterns of thought come into their own. Policies and the orders to execute them are linguistic acts with psychological, social and ethical underpinnings. These we can't least try to be aware of as potential impediments to just and effective response. (email message, 12 September 2001)

It is important to mention that, in the discourses of the media, politicians refer to 'we' *the civilized* world, the *'free democracies'*, *'the West'*, *'the free world'*, in contrast with 'the other' Eastern countries, where the terrorists may come from. This bipolarization or dichotomy relates to metonymic processes, as Paul Chilton (ibid.) suggests, 'whereby one element (the USA) stands for another entity – a supposed collectivity labelled "free democracies", whose real world reference however, is not determinate', but excludes or classifies negatively the 'others'.

What will the outcome of these representations be, we may ask?

At this moment of world crisis, more than ever we can say that *the language of the media* is one of the most pervasive and widespread discourses that people from all sorts of literate societies are exposed to. With the advances of technology within communication systems and networks, the production of written and spoken news invades our lives daily. The attack on the World Trade Center in New York and the Pentagon in Washington, DC, on 11 September 2001, is at this moment an ongoing narrative retold by many voices. Different people are reporting that they cannot but watch television or listen to the radio. This addictive aspect is the unexpected – what will happen next? The suffering, the death tolls are reported minute by minute and we watch the television or listen to the radio in order to understand what is going on.

News therefore, has a social, a political and an educational role. By being exposed to news, people make connections and try to understand and explain how events reported in the media relate to society as a whole.

However, news is the *report* or *recontextualization* of an event. The treatment of any topic will always depend on who is chosen to comment and whose opinions and definitions are sought. Journalists follow a series of criteria to determine what is newsworthy. News therefore, is not an objective representation of facts – news is a cultural construct that encodes fixed values. These values help journalists to determine what is newsworthy and therefore what gets reported.

In this chapter, using a multimodal approach to analyse texts and images from publications collected during the months of April and May 1997 and July and August 2000, as well as concordances and frequency counts from the Bank of English,[1] I will compare how certain evaluative and interpersonal strategies used by British and Brazilian newspapers deal with the question of representing the other. Media texts are here considered as multimodal since not only the written language but also the visual input contributes to the overall message. I will examine modes of representation of key cultural themes related to the representation of otherness. My main aim is to discuss, using a critical and interdisciplinary approach to the phenomenon of social discrimination:

- how events, people and social practices are recontextualized from two very different perspectives
- how national identities are constructed in the press, either through texts or through images.

My main theoretical and methodological principles are discoursal and linguistically oriented (I will mainly be using recontextualization and naming or referential analysis, corpus linguistics and appraisal theory as methodological instruments). Drawing on a concept of discourse proposed by van Leeuwen (1993b, 2000), van Leeuwen and Wodak (1999), and Kress and van Leeuwen (1996), I will look at the verbal and verbal-visual ways in which different social actors are represented in the media.[2] Discourses, in this chapter, are knowledges which are at the same time:

> knowledges of practices, of how things are or must be done (and at the level of discourse these two merge, or are two sides of the same coin), together with specific evaluations and legitimations of, and purposes for, these practices;
>
> linked to and activated in the context of specific communicative practices.

This entails that people may, at different times and in different contexts, draw on different discourses about the same practice or practices, choosing the one they see as most appropriate to their own interests at the given moment and in the given context (Caldas-Coulthard and van Leeuwen, 2001, p. 158).

I will also be relying on insights and concepts from other areas like news analysis, social semiotics (analysis of images) and postcolonial social theory. It is one of my key assumptions that the discourses of the media are culturally dependent and reflect what 'goes on' in society in many aspects. An interdisciplinary perspective, therefore, enriches the analysis and 'reveals' hidden agendas that are not explicit at first sight.

The special status of news as discourse

News is not a natural phenomenon emerging from facts in real life, but socially and culturally determined. News producers are social agents in a network of social relations who reveal their own stance towards what is reported. News is not the event, but the partial, ideologically framed *report* of the event.

News in the written press is a specific kind of mass media discourse which for many people enjoys a privileged and prestigious position in our culture's hierarchy of values. In Western societies, people are exposed to media language probably more than any other kind of language, since its production is immense. People watch or read 'news' because they think 'news' is about reality. The implication is that if you are exposed to news you are more knowledgeable about social facts.

Within media discourse, *news* is the most dominant *register* in terms of *generic* structure (see Butt et al., 1995 for a detailed discussion on 'register theory'). Hours of radio and television and many pages of newspapers are dedicated to the report of events that happen in the world. However, as Bell points out, there was a time when news was not a dominant genre.

> The year 1930 was early days for radio. The youthful British Broadcasting Corporation (BBC) sometimes found there was a shortage of news deemed worthy to be broadcast. If this happened, no attempt was made to fill the gap. The announcer just said: 'There is no news tonight.' (Bell, 1991, p. 1)

We cannot imagine this happening nowadays. There are always topics to be reported. In fact, news carries the daily stories of our times.

The concept of *news* is ambiguous. It implies in the first place that a given source will display some kind of new information to a general public, and in the second place that this new information is passed on objectively and from an outside point of view. Many of us watch the major television news or read the daily newspaper for information and 'believe' that what we listen to or read is a faithful account of recent events happening in the world. *News*, nevertheless, is a reconstruction of reality through the eyes of many people. The reality observed depends on how it is looked at.

In recent years, the professional journalist's self-image on the question of impartiality has come under strong examination from students of the media (see, for example, the work of the Glasgow University Media Group (1976), the University of Birmingham Centre for Contemporary Cultural Studies (Hall et al., 1980) and the publications of authors like Hartley (1982), van Dijk (1987) and Fowler (1991)). The question of faithfulness and impartiality has been challenged definitely.

News as recontextualization

News is a discourse about a social practice which always takes place outside the context of that practice and within the context of another one. This process of including one social practice into another is a *recontextualization* (Bernstein, 1981; van Leeuwen, 1993a) or

> a sequence of communicative activities which make the social practices explicit to a greater or lesser degree…Social practices are things that people do, with greater or lesser degree of freedom, fixed by custom or prescription, or some mixture of these two. (van Leeuwen, 1993a, p. 30)

Social practices are made up of elements which are integrated in a dynamic whole.

According to van Leeuwen, in all social practices there are:

1. *participants* – some have more choice to what they may do than others
2. *activities* – which may be concurrent and are related to performance indicators. In other words, there are a set of eligibility conditions which qualify participants (age, dress, place, time, objects, materials and tools)
3. *goal orientation*
4. *relationships* (ibid.).

For van Leeuwen, (ibid., p. 46) 'these are the concrete, material elements of the social practice as it actually happens'. Texts are representations of given practices not the practices themselves. The problem lies in the relation between practices and discourses about them. Van Leeuwen also distinguishes, based on Bourdieu, what he calls *participant knowledge* and *outsider knowledge*.

As an outsider, my knowledge passes through the mediation of texts. A participant's knowledge is knowing how to do something, to act and react. This knowledge is tacit, implicit, subjective, and it allows participants to achieve goals.

An outsider knowledge is *knowing that*, a knowledge of rules, of abstract schemata that can be applied to a variety of situations seen as objectively the same. This is a knowledge of a completed whole, which can be analysed into its components. It is articulated, explicit. (ibid., pp. 49, 50)

As soon as one writes or speaks about any social practice, one is already *recontextualizing*. The moment we are *recontextualizing*, we are transforming and creating other practices.

Media texts are recontextualizations that not only represent social practices, they also have to explain and legitimate; in other words, they have to make explicit the 'why' of their representations (the use of the voices of experts, for instance, is one of the legitimatory strategies frequently used in journalistic discourses).

Other important points are that recontextualizations always add *evaluation* to the social practice they refer to and that the *goal* of a given social practice can be entirely different from its recontextualization.

The ways in which goals and evaluation are made explicit in media discourse is never transparent, but they depend on the participants of the recontextualizing social practice, on how they relate to each other, and so on. From a multimodal perspective, images add evaluation to the semiotic representation in the same way as the linguistic code does.

Recontextualizations involve *substitution*, *deletion* or *addition* of elements of a given social practice (van Leeuwen, 1993a,b). Events and people in each new recontextualization are represented according to the goals, values and priorities of that communication. This raises questions of truth, bias and manipulation. It is important therefore to distinguish between social practices and *discourses* about social practices. I want to claim that there is no direct and transparent relationship between what actually people do in their public and private lives and the textual reference to their social practice.

Another important point is that the relationship between the ones that are in control of media discourse, like producers and presenters, and the receivers of the messages is highly asymmetrical – there are only a few recontextualizers who produce and present 'news' to a too-large audience, who in a sense, receive messages passively. The controllers of the semiotic (images and scenarios) and the linguistic production (the texts) can therefore establish norms and values without being questioned.

Criteria of newsworthiness

Events do not get into the news simply by happening. They must fit into a system of priorities laid down by the institution of news-making. Events need to be recognized as worthy of reporting and they should come from a known and representative source. Therefore, they need to fulfil a number of criteria. Journalists use a paradigm of what Hartley (1982, p. 76) calls *news values*.

Galtung and Ruge (1965) put forward a series of conditions applicable to news selection, which they list as 'general news values':

- frequency or the time taken by an event
- threshold or the size of the event
- unambiquity or the clarity of the event
- meaningfulness or cultural proximity
- consonance – the predictability of an event
- unexpectedness or the rarity or unpredictability of an event
- continuity or the running story
- composition – mixture of different kinds of events
- reference to elite persons
- reference to elite nations
- personalization
- negativity.

I want to focus especially on the last three categories in my analysis: **reference to elite nations, personalization and negativity.**

Since most of the news is derived from First World countries, it is not surprising that the elite nations would be referred to in the press. I checked in the newspaper section of the *Bank of English corpus* (323 million words) just to see the extent of this statement. The papers I looked at are the ones stored in the corpus and they are from the years 1992 to 1995. These are mainly quality papers (*BBC World Service, Independent, The Times* and *Guardian*, with the exception of *Today*, a tabloid, which does not exist anymore). I simply looked at names of a selection of major European and South American countries in order to compare their citation in the press. Table 13.1 illustrates the difference in the way in which First World and Third World countries are talked about.

Clearly, in purely quantitative terms, the image of the Latin American is underrepresented, especially if we consider the size of the countries and

Table 13.1   Reference to elite nations

Total occurrences	BBC World Service 8,714,743	Independent 5,034,893	The Times 10,358,64	Guardian 12,598,266	Today 6,606,537
France	5,892	4,727	5,147	5,676	4,059
Italy	2,594	1,658	1,943	1,988	2,320
Brazil	1,862	384	311	535	857
Argentina	1,843	500	341	466	462
Chile	649	142	163	174	83

Table 13.2   Area and population

Country	Area in km²	Population (year 2000) (000s)
Brazil	8,511,965	172,860
Argentina	2,766,890	36,955
Chile	756,950	15,154
France	547,030	59,330
Italy	301,230	57,636

their populations. Table 13.2 shows the individual countries in terms of area in square kilometres and population (data from Geological Survey, <www.geobop.com> and from US Census, <www.census.gov/ipc>).

Chibnall (1977) suggests that the dominant values of the ideology which provide criteria for evaluation of forms of behaviour in the press are the following:

Positive legitimating values
Legality
Moderation
Compromise
Cooperation
Order
Peacefulness
Tolerance
Constructiveness
Openness
Honesty
Realism
Rationality
Impartiality
Fairness
Firmness
Industriousness
Freedom of choice
Equality

Negative legitimating values
Illegality
Extremism
Dogmatism
Confrontation
Chaos
Violence
Intolerance
Destructiveness
Secrecy
Corruption
Ideology
Irrationality
Bias
Unfairness
Weakness
Idleness
Monopoly/uniformity
Inequality (pp. 21–2)

Positive evaluation by the press derives from the positive legitimating values, while negative evaluation is associated with problems.

In Britain, Brazil is constantly represented via fixed associations. The major references are football and other sports, the Amazon, the rainforest, children and poverty. In terms of evaluation, sports – especially football – tend to get appraised positively; the appraisal means 'capacity in social esteem' (White, 1998; Martin, 2000). Football players and famous sports personalities such as the late Ayrton Senna, Ronaldo, Pele and more recently the tennis player Gustavo Kuerten are positively viewed. The *Sunday Times* published, for example, in one of its sports pages, a text entitled 'Boys from Brazil play it their ways' (1 June 1997), illustrated by a photograph of the famous Brazilian footballer Ronaldo playing with other Brazilian footballers. They are dressed in bright yellow and green colours, running for the ball, as if lifted in the air, obviously in advantage. The background colour is blue and the grass is green. Happy moments.

Using Hallidayan Systemic theory to analyse visual communication, Kress and van Leeuwen (1996) say that visual representations have modality realized in different ways in the visual medium. For them, one of the crucial issues is the question of the reliability of the message. Is what we see or hear true, factual, real, or is it a lie, a fiction, something outside reality? Modality in images therefore refers

> to the truth-value or credibility of statements about the world. Visual images can represent the world as though it is real, naturalistic or as though it is fantastic, imaginary. Naturalistic reality is defined on the basis of how much correspondence there is between the visual representations of an object and what we normally see of that object with the naked eye. (ibid., p. 160)

They continue:

> Modality clues are motivated signs – signs which have arisen out of the interest of social groups who interact within the structures of power that define social life and also interact across the systems produced by various groups in a society. (ibid., p. 159)

We attach more credibility to some kinds of messages than to others. Photographs, they say, do not lie, but how the photographer edits reality through his or her own point of view is another matter. The authors claim that a social semiotic theory of truth cannot establish the absolute truth or untruth of representations. It can only show whether a given proposition is represented as true or not. Modality in this sense is essential in accounts of multimodal representations, since they can represent people, place, things as though they were real or fantastic, caricatures or perfect copies of the 'real'. Reality is defined on the basis of how much correspondence there is between the visual representation and what we normally see of that object with the naked eye, Kress and van Leeuwen say (ibid.).

The newspaper photograph referred to above is of 'real people' but the question is how they are presented. In this case, the Brazilian player Ronaldo is in prime position, running for the ball, in control of the situation. Another favourable aspect of this representation are the colours chosen (the newspaper could have chosen to publish the actors in black and white, but did not).

Kress and van Leeuwen (ibid.) put forward the idea that one of the ways reality is modulated in visual communication is through colour, focus and depth (perspective), which may be idealized to a greater or lesser degree. Colour plays a role in all coding orientations. You can have abstract colour (for example, uniform pinkness for faces, or greenness for grass). You can have naturalistic colour. And you can have sensory colour – colour becomes sensory to the degree it 'exceeds' naturalism. Colour is also a source of pleasure and produces (or not) affective meanings. We all recognize the emotive and sensual value of colours. Through different shades, the principle of pleasure is enacted. We react positively to colours that attract us. And colours in general are loaded with social signification. This is exactly the case in this photograph – the colours 'mean' positive and affective evaluation.

After the 1998 World Cup, photographs of Ronaldo appeared everywhere in England, in newspapers, magazines and advertising. One large British street billboard in 1999 presented him as flying over Copacabana Bay, with open arms in a crucifix format, replacing Rio's Christ. In this visual recontextualization, Ronaldo is portrayed as God.

Another recurrent representation is with the concept of 'latinidad' (Latinness). An interesting example related to Brazil is the recurrent citation in the British press of Carmen Miranda, a Brazilian singer and dancer of the 1950s, who became internationally famous after going to Hollywood. Carmen Miranda is not referred to very much in the Brazilian press discourses, but she continues to be an icon in the construction of 'foreignness' in British representations. I found a photograph of a woman (*Sunday Times*, June 2000) dressed in (again) bright yellow and red Carnival costumes, with bananas on her head, illustrating the Money pages of the newspaper. The intertextual reference to Carmen Miranda was evident.

Although this representation could be interpreted positively (bright colours, beautiful and smiling face, direct interaction with the viewers (Kress and van Leeuwen, 1996), it is paradoxical in the sense that it also has to do with carnivalization or reversal of social norms which implies negative 'social sanction' in terms of 'judgement' (White, 1998; Martin, 2000). Carnival, represented in the *Sunday Times* image described above by the colours, the costume and the textual quotation of 'song and dance', is associated here with the financial world. These two discursive formations are nevertheless incompatible – the carnivalesque denigrates the possible seriousness of the topic. For Bakhtin (1984), the carnivalesque is a counter-hegemonic tradition which

> embraces an anti-classical aesthetic that rejects formal harmony and unity in favour of the asymmetrical, the heterogeneous, the oxymoronic, the miscegenated... Within carnival, all hierarchical distinction, all

barriers, all norms and prohibition are temporarily suspended. (cited in Stam, 2000, p. 18)

This image of an unknown woman recontextualizes the practices of carnival through dressing and the use of bright colours, therefore questioning veracity, credibility and propriety in the world of economics. Although in some instances Brazil is recontextualized as a happy place (and this has to do with the dimension of 'affect' (Martin, 2000), it is also and mainly recontextualized as corrupt, in debt, criminal – and this has to do with questions of truth and ethics (the category of 'social sanction'; ibid.). The vast majority of representations of Latin America also tend to be associated exclusively with negative values; especially corruption, poverty, inequality. The recurrent negative evaluation constructs the Third World as poor, strange, foreign, distant from the point of view of the recontextualizer of the First World. The foreigner is the other, different, ugly, poor and stereotyped.

The *Sunday Times Magazine* (13 may 1997) printed, for example, shocking images taken by the famous Brazilian photographer, Sebastiao Salgado. Poor children, poor farmers, and ugly women in black and white send messages of despair, isolation and poverty. Why were these pictures chosen, we may ask?

The press seems to continue to reproduce, through these images, a colonial discourse of denigration, reinforcing stereotypical views in order to produce a positive *civilized* image of the First World – 'they' are like that; 'we', the civilized world, are not.

Linguistic recontextualizations

In order to see how far the lexical supports the visual representations, I looked at 700 concordances of the words 'Brazil' and 'Brazilian' in the Bank of English newspaper corpus, extracting 200 examples from the BBC World Service corpus and 100 from the other newspapers. The major references from these concordances are predictably to sports (football and motor racing in particular). There are also references to the Amazon and to the rainforest, to children and to poverty. Quotations related to the world of finance and politics are less frequent. Some illustrative extracts taken from the data are the following:

Carmen Miranda with their images of *Brazil as a happy place*
Gal Costa dressed as a Brazilian *dance queen should with red dress and red* ...
Investigation into *corruption* in Brazil accuses 18 congressmen
... 5,000 children were *murdered* in Brazil between 1988 and 1991 and most of ...
BRAZILIANS EAT HUMAN REMAINS FROM HOSPITAL WASTE

The last example is specially interesting. The idea of cannibalism associated to the indigenous, tribal societies is reinforced in this assertion. One of the major tenets of colonial discourses is that the Third World is undeveloped and wild – it is primitive. The utterance above reflects a third worldism view of the country being represented. It evokes the still residing original inhabitants before colonialism. As Stam very well points out, this kind of critical generalization is made 'in a situation of patronizing non-reciprocity, with negative consequences' (2000, p. 283) which possibly provokes the sensation of horror in the reader.

Alongside the investigation of the computerized corpus, I also collected stories related to Latin America mainly from the major British broadsheet newspapers – *The Times*, the *Guardian* and the *Independent* – a total of 15 texts in which Brazil was referred to and 13 texts related to other countries in Latin America. These were the only texts I could find in my daily searches of international news during a period of two months. The numbers are in fact very low compared to the great quantity of texts which refer to First World countries. The topics almost mirror the topics of the concordance lists: sports (7 texts), politics/social issues (6 texts), finance (1 text), music review (1 text).

The headlines are indicative of the themes and of the criterion of *negativity*:

Corruption claims shake Brazil's faith in Lula's party
Brazilian police *expelled*
Burning issue for Brazilians – a *homeless* Brazilian who *died after being set on fire*
Sell-off sparks *fury*

The headlines referring to other Latin American countries are no different:

Nazis, child abusers, or just good, clean-living workers? Police move in on Chile's *secretive* and *controversial* Dignity Colony
Argentineans *clash* over jobs – Argentinean *riot police* fire *tear gas* and *rubber bullets* ...
Figures *to die* for Argentina: A. Faiola reports from Buenos Aires, the world capital of *eating disorders*
Colombian *drug lord* extradited
Bolivia back former *dictator*
Former *strongman* of Bolívia scents gentler route to *power*
Aged 71, General Hugo Suarez has lost none of *his hunger for power*
Lima *turns heat* on judges
Corruption and *kidnaps* hold city to *ransom* [Mexico]

The linguistic classificatory system (van Leeuwen, 1996) is always linked to the question of how participants are recontextualized.

If we examine the British newspaper headlines quoted above, we can see that the words in '*bold italics*' always add some kind of negative evaluation to the topic being treated. They refer to a situation that indicates problems (Hoey, 1983) and semantically, they construe negative interpretations.

Lexical choices such as *corruption, drug lord, to die for, clash,* are therefore highly loaded.

Another linguistic category, *generalization* (van Leeuwen, 1996) is used by journalists to categorize Latin American participants according to their country of origin: Argentina, Bolívia, Brazil, Chile, become generalized discursive agents replacing people as social actors in the discourse. The personal classifications once more corroborate the negative evaluations – *Nazis, child abusers, drug lord, dictator.*

In general, First World recontextualizers of social practices that occur in Latin America have knowledge about these practices exclusively through the mediation of other texts. They therefore understand these practices only as 'outsiders', and consequently what gets reproduced is based on 'outsider knowledge', which is constructed on assumptions already biased – hence the negative evaluation. The audiences that receive these texts will base their outside knowledge on these negative evaluations. The media in this way legitimates its own position of superiority, reinforcing the distance between 'us' and 'them'. The analysis below exemplifies in more detail how the recontexualization of facts can influence the construction of 'otherness'.

José Tadeu: a case study

In April 1997, the tragic story of a Brazilian living in London was published in one of the London tabloids, the *Evening Standard*. This person had AIDS at the time of publication and died later.

The initial sensationalist text was recontextualized (retold through a different perspective) even by the quality press and many versions were reproduced. As Reisigl and Wodak (2001, p. 1) forcefully point out, 'racism, as an ideology, manifests itself, discursively ... Through discourse, discriminatory exclusionary practices are prepared, promulgated and legitimised.'

In his discussion of how social practices are transformed in recontextualizations, van Leeuwen (1996) suggests that there are possible choices ot a systematic network to represent social actors. They can be *included* or *excluded* in texts. If included, they can be *personalized* or *impersonalized.* When personalized, they can be *determined* in many ways. They can be *categorized* or *classified* in terms of their *identity* (age, gender, social class, physical appearance).

They can also be identified by their *function* in society (by their profession or social activity). Social actors are also *nominated*, formally or informally, by honorifics or by family relations. Through these representations, social actors can therefore be evaluated positively or negatively. Evaluation, as I suggested earlier, is a very important category in narrative discourse (Labov, 1972). Evaluations can appear at any point in the report and it is through this category (linguistic or through images) that the narrator or focalizer shows his or her involvement in the action. He or she also shows his or her

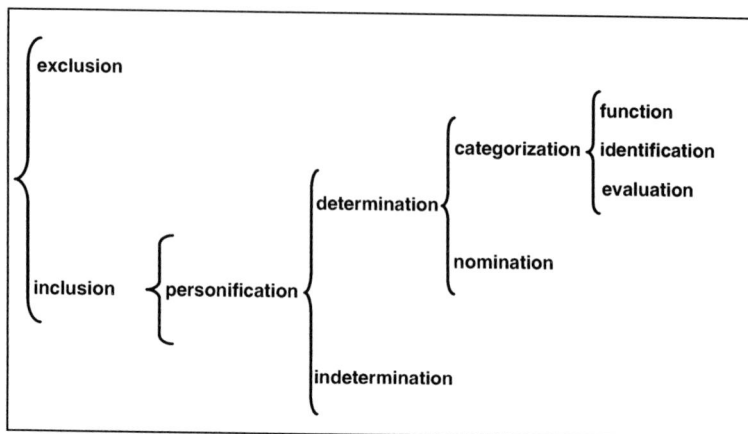

Figure 13.1   Representation of social actors in discourse
Source: Adapted from van Leeuwen (1996, p. 66).

knowledge about the expectations of the audience in relation to the reportability of the reported events. It is also through evaluations that ideological values are transmitted. In the discourse of the media, evaluative choices, like the categorization of the social actors, are an entrance point to hidden agendas. Figure 13.1 summarizes how social actors are represented in discourse.

José Tadeu's story

(Parts of the text published by the *Daily Mail*, 15 April 1997)

[Headline] YOU PAY, A SCROUNGER STAYS
[Subheadline] This is an illegal immigrant suffering from AIDs, syphilis and TB. He has so far cost the taxpayer an estimated £250,000 in benefits and medical treatment. Yet under Home Office policy he is in an unfit state to be deported and, despite his diseases, is free to wander the streets of Britian.

José dos Santos was born on 28 October, into a poor family in the city of Salvador, in the impoverished northeast of Brazil. He **eked** out a living as a musician, and **bummed** extra money from the tourists who came to see the fine old churches and the white sandy beaches. Then, as the 1990s began, and José hit his 30th birthday, his luck changed. He met an English woman called Camilla.

Camilla was a bit of a **hippie. Blonde and middle-aged,** she was fond of alternative lifestyles and had become an expert in herbal medicines. She wore long floaty skirts and could often be seen riding her bike round London's Portobello area ...

> In 1990 Camilla decided to travel…She chose Salvador, home of the **black magic cult of candomble** and the erstwhile centre of Brazil's booming **slave trade**. Salvador was the **real** Brazil.
> Camilla hit off with José immediately…They quickly became lovers.

The story continues revealing that Camilla returns to England and afterwards, send for José in 1992. He arrives in Europe without any money and without work, but Camilla is responsible for him, according to the text. The newspaper continues to describe José as follows:

> **Speaking no English**, he spent his time playing music with other Brazilians and **smoking marijuana**. **He had no money** and no intention of working. Eventually Camilla told him to get out. José was back to **living off** friends, **sleeping rough** and generally hanging out.

> After six months his tourist visa expired, along with his right to remain in this country. José kept away from the Police. Despite being homeless, it was a good time. He played a few gigs…and was quite a success with girls.

In 1993, according to the newspaper, José finds out he has AIDS. His friend Rudolf Stanling is introduced in the narrative and comes in his rescue. This is the way Rudolf is recontextualized:

> **Grey-haired and blue-eyed, Rudolf Stanling doesn't look Brazilian.** … Outside working hours, he devotes a lot of energy to his fellow countrymen. He says there are 50 HIV positive Brazilians in London.

The writer now gives voice (see Caldas-Coulthard, 1987, 1995, for the concept of 'accessed voice') to Rudolf who supposedly says he had tried to make contact with Camilla, but she was not interested in José's situation:

> 'These English women. They like brown bodies. They go abroad and see these bodies, but they don't think about the brain, the person in the body.'

José goes into hospital and receives all the treatment necessary. He is also given a flat to live in. The accusation is therefore that a foreign illegal immigrant abuses the system and that the taxpayer has to pay. The writer continues to evaluate José:

> José **speaks no English**. He **cannot write or read** in his native Portuguese. *He had no right to reside in Britain.*

The report reveals, paradoxically, that José had been in London for five years and that the Health Service had given him not only assistance, but also an NHS card. This means that he had acquired rights as an immigrant when the story was published – a person needs to be in the country for five years to get 'leave of stay' or permission to live and work there.

DLA amounts to around £115 per week, but it also triggers a number of associated payments. José's rent continued to be paid for by local authority housing benefit likewise his council tax. He has been given free access to local authority facilities... He is also able to claim free travel.

Antonio, a Brazilian friend who used to share José's flat with his Brazilian girlfriend, Limiana, is not impressed. **Sitting among the debris and junk inside the Hackney flat**, Antonio is quick to condemn the British system: 'He (José) had a very bad time here. He's had to work very hard for what he has. Yeah, the Government gives him money, but it's not enough, and it doesn't increase.'

By 1995, José had full-blown AIDS. He was still to be seen in London's many Latin clubs, smoking marijuana.

The long text continues introducing the amount of money spent by the government on José. It also continues to denigrate the Brazilian (the embolded utterances point to negative social sanction (White, 1998; Martin, 2000)):

José has never **completed his medication course**...

He was **arrested** in November 1995, walking down Oxford Street in the early hours of the morning **smoking a joint.**

He was too **infectious** to be put on a plane, but not apparently too infectious to be released back to the streets of London.

By January this year (1997) he was back in hospital once more, **swearing** at the nurses. He was very unhappy because they wouldn't let him **smoke marijuana on the ward.**

Rudolf Stanling says José needs money to go back. '**He comes from a very poor background, no shoes, no electricity, no nothing.** He can't go back to that.'

The story ends with these accusations:

José needs money for medical treatment and money to have a good life for one or two more years. Thousands of pounds. Without this money, then he will die here, and **Britain will have to pay for it.**

Britain has already done a great deal of paying. Financially, it is hard to assess, but **José has probably cost at least £250,000**, if not more. We cannot tell how many Londoners have been exposed to the three diseases he carries.

It seems unreal that an impoverished Brazilian musician has been allowed to wreak such potential havoc. Who is to blame? Not us, says the Home Office, it's a health matter. Not us, say the Department of Health, an immigration matter. Not us, say Social Service, his document is in order. Rudolf says Britain is to blame. **'You have robbed countries all over the world. Now it's your turn to pay back'.**

The argumentative strategies (see van Dijk, 1987) of negative other-presentation – the outsider Brazilian exploiting the British system (and causing havoc) versus positive self-presentation – 'we' the taxpayer or, more generalized, Britain (having to pay the bill), exemplifies the racist discourse: 'the generalized and absolute evaluations of differences that is advantageous to the accuser and detrimental to his/her victim' (Reisigl and Wodak, 2001, p. 5).

Other texts recontextualized through their point of view of the same story:

[*Daily Star*, 15 April 1997]
NO WAY JOSÉ – **Illegal** immigrant has AIDS, TB, and VD ... but can we kick him out of Britain?
Sleazy José Tadeo dos Santos has cost British tax payers a cool £250,000 – and we are **stuck** with him. We can't kick him out of the country.
We're too laid back
The Brazilian **lover boy** of a middle-aged, **sex-happy** English **hippy** is allowed to live here for six years.

[*Daily Telegraph*, 17 April 1977]
£250,000 bill for Aids immigrant 'too ill to leave'

[*Guardian*, 7 July 1997]
The Threats began after my story appeared. Now they say they'll throw acid in my face.
A front-page exclusive has unleashed a campain of hate against the young London reporter who wrote it
Interview with the author of the story.

The magazine *Leros* (August 1997), published by Brazilians living in London, came out in José's defence. It revealed that the author of the original text had in fact been married to a Brazilian from Bahia (Northeast of Brazil) and who, most important of all, was José' s friend. The writer herself had been to Bahia where she met her husband.

According to the magazine, the two friends had had some kind of fight. Jo Ann obviously had known José for many years. In defence of her husband, she decided to write her **'personal'** story.

The Analysis

The sensationalist story of a sick Brazilian reveals many aspects of how foreigners/immigrants are represented by the British press. The report produced by the writer of the initial text is based on many recontextualizations and interpretations.

The social actors represented in the text are José, Camilla, Rudolf, Antônio, his girlfriend and Brazilians (the categories analysed below are in bold in the text above).

José is personified, categorized and evaluated in many ways: he is black, poor, Brazilian, a musician without a job, he smokes marijuana, he does not speak English, he cannot read or write, he is promiscuous, he is sick. The implication of these arguments are telling – this person does not deserve to live in England.

His photograph, published with the text and taking up half the second page, reinforces the same negative evaluation carried by the text. In this photograph, José's eyes are semi-open (indicating a drugged state), has a non-conformist *rastafari* hair style (again, intertextual links with the practices of black people and drugs) and he does not interact through eye contact with the reader – the semiotic representation signifies distance and non credibility (Kress and van Leeuwen, 1996).

His friend Camilla is identified by her age, by the way she dresses and for being a hippie. She is also evaluated negatively in terms of social sanction since she goes to a primitive country looking for sex. Although the text was written by a woman, it recontextualizes Camilla in extremely sexist discourse.

Rudolf is identified by his physical appearance – he has blue eyes and he is blond. By this identification, the writer generalizes her bias against Brazilians – for her, all Brazilians should be black or brown.

Antônio and his girlfriend are nominated by their first names, they do not have a profession and they live in a horrible place.

By these representations, we can see how *Brazilians* are *generalized* in the discourse – they are poor, illiterate, ill, drugged and consequently socially unacceptable.

Brazil, as a country, is also recontextualized through a biased point of view since it is identified with magic and poverty. The discriminatory and sexist evaluations and classifications hence construe Brazilian people in general negatively.

These texts are examples of nationalistic and racist discourses where not only the general narrative but also the argumentative structures, the referential, the predicational and the framing strategies point to exclusionary practices that are legitimized by nationalistic points of view – the other is the outsider, different from 'us'.

The counter-discourse

The Brazilian press is aware of the negative representations in the European press and explicitizes the way an 'outsider look' constructs Brazil. The text in Illustration 13.1, published in one of the most popular weekly magazines in Brazil, *VEJA* (26 January 2000), exemplifies this point.

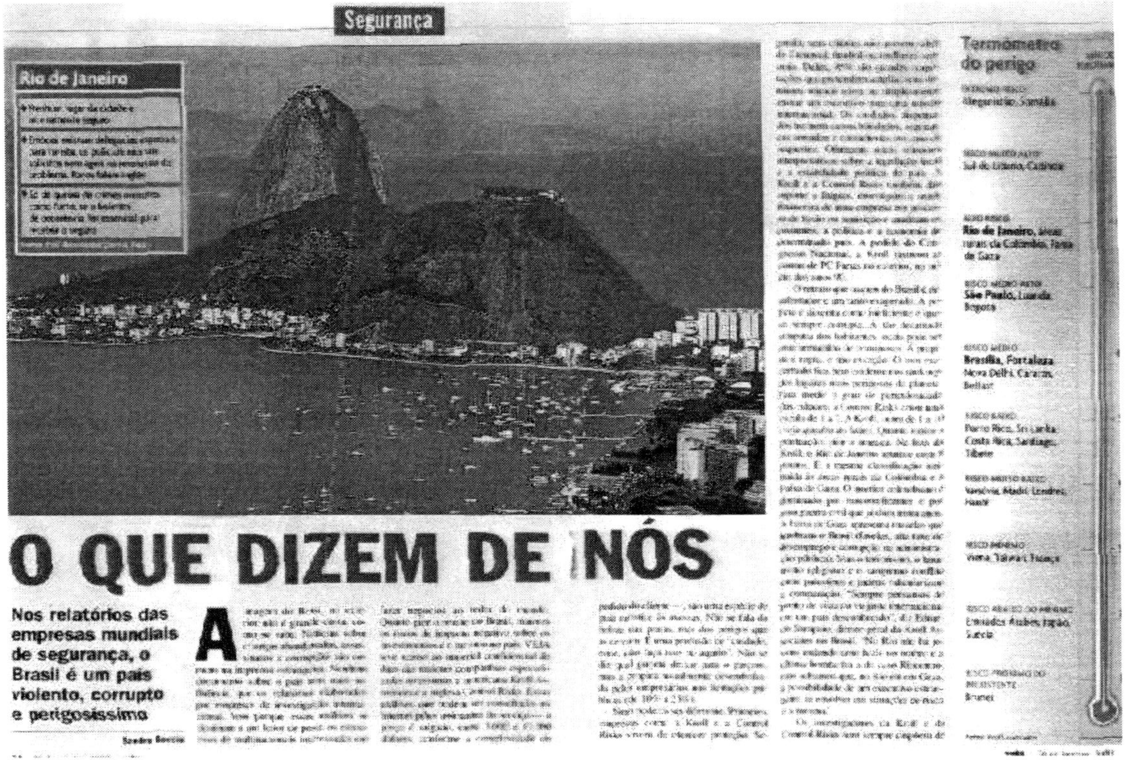

Segurança

Rio de Janeiro

O QUE DIZEM DE NÓS

Nos relatórios das empresas mundiais de segurança, o Brasil é um país violento, corrupto e perigosíssimo

Termômetro do perigo

Rio de Janeiro

São Paulo, Luanda, Bogotá

Brasília, Fortaleza, Nova Délhi, Caracas, Belfast

Porto Rico, Sri Lanka, Costa Rica, Santiago, Tibete

Emirados Árabes, Japão, Suécia

Brunei

Illustration 13.1 *VEJA* (26 January 2000)

The headline says:

WHAT DO THEY SAY ABOUT US?

The lead continues:

> In the reports produced by multinational security firms, Brazil is a poor, violent, corrupt and very dangerous place. (my translation)

This text claims that most news about Latin America in the foreign press is news about abandoned children, murders and corruption. There is a vested interest in the negative report of Third World countries, according to Sandra Boccia, the writer, because this brings profit to multinational security firms (like the English Control Risks and the American Kroll Associates). The more the First World reports on crime, the more security products these companies sell to executives of multinationals that do business around the world.

The text then continues saying that positive values are not invoked, like the beauty of the beaches of Brazil. If beaches and their beauty are referred to at all, they will be associated with some kind of crime. The tone of the article is one of indignation since, the writer claims, in terms of general evaluation, Rio de Janeiro is compared to Gaza. What the composition of the image tells us, in Kress and van Leeuwen's (1996) view, is however, another story.

Here is beautiful Rio, attractive and also 'rich' as in the First World term (many boats, many high-rises). The picture occupies the left to centre space, the already given, self-evident, commonsensical (Kress and van Leeuwen, 1996), which the reader is assumed to know about as part of his or her culture – *Rio is beautiful and it is good to live here*. The text, surrounding the image and to the right, therefore, is the new information (ibid.), the problem, what should be contested. The image is also more salient than the text, the most eye-catching element in the composition; and, since there is no framing, the elements of the image are all connected. The visual positive evaluation (contrary to the visual negative evaluation of the British texts), adding to the textual message is therefore:

> *they (the international press) do not know about this beauty.*

From a postcolonial perspective (Spivak, 1987; Xavier, 1996, 1998; Stam, 2000) Brazilians, colonized by the Europeans in the main, from very early on, developed discursive strategies of resistance and practices to deal with the colonizer. Slaves, for example, who could not fight openly with guns, created a form of dance, called *Capoeira*, which is in fact, a martial art using the legs. They also created Carnival, which, as theorized by Bakhtin (1984) and mentioned earlier,

> embraces an anti-classical aesthetic, and turns conventional aesthetics on its head in order to locate a new kind of popular convulsive, rebellious beauty, one that dares to reveal the grotesquerie of the powerful and the latent beauty of the vulgar. (cited in Stam, 2000, p. 18)

In Carnival, all hierarchical distinctions, rules and regulations are temporarily suspended. Through song and dance, common people dress as kings and queens in order to mock the higher classes. *Humour* and *mockery* are therefore part of the Brazilian identity and a form of discursive resistance.

Elite nations, as one would expect, are often referred to in the Brazilian press. However, in many recontextualizations, one feels a form of aggression built in the discourse about others – this is done through parody.

Consider the visual recontextualizations of British practices and events – royalty is always a site for laughter (see Illustration 13.2).

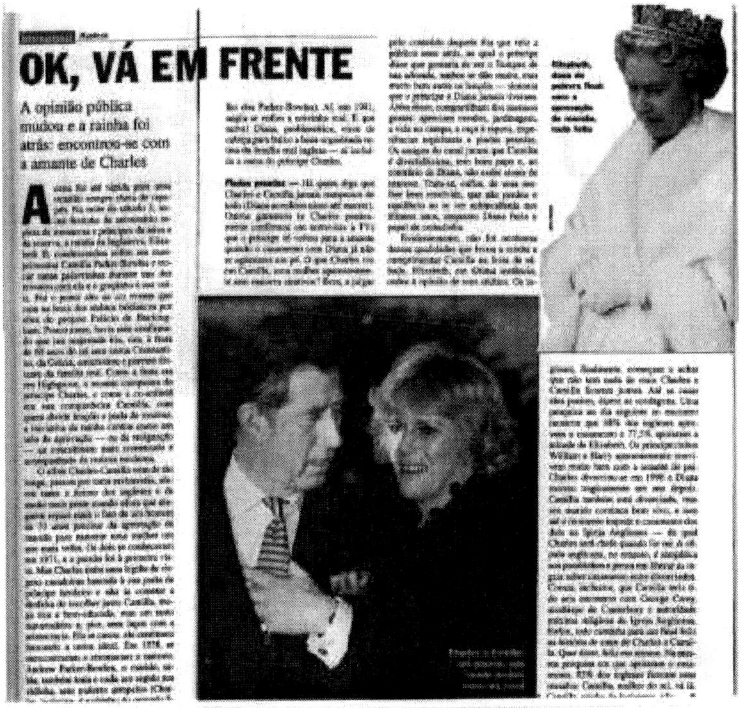
OK, VÁ EM FRENTE

A opinião pública mudou e a rainha foi atrás: encontrou-se com a amante de Charles

Illustration 13.2 *VEJA* (July 2000)

The headline says:

OK, GO AHEAD

The caption accompanying the Queen's photograph says:

Elizabeth, owner of the final word – without mummy's approval, nothing done.

The text refers to the event that the Queen now agrees to meet the Prince of Wales' new partner; not out of her own will, but to please her subjects. The writer classifies the social actors in the following ways:

The queen is nominated by first name: *Elizabeth*, or *mummy*, or *the Queen of England*.

Charles is *the king without a crown, the prince, the heir, Camilla's lover*.

Camilla is *the mistress, the partner, rich and well-educated* or simply *Camilla*.

Mummy and *the king without a crown* are ironic categorizations; *Camilla's lover, the mistress* are simply derogatory. Charles, in the same way, is reported as a little boy who needs the approval of his 'mummy'.

The text is full of diminutives, which take away the importance of the people involved – festinha (little party), *palavrinhas* (little words), *grupinho* (little group), *pombinho* (little dove). There is also reference to the well-known Tampax episode.

Camilla, however, is recontextualized in more positive terms – she is independent and more self-assertive.

If we examine the pictures, the message is very much the same.

The Queen, on the right, not looking at the reader, is the new message (Kress and van Leeuwen, 1996). The picture of Charles and Camilla, however, in the centre of the text, puts them in a more prominent position. For Barthes (1977, pp. 20–5), there are six procedures through which photos connote: trick effects (alteration and combination), pose, objects, photogenie (looking good), aestheticism (artistic quality), syntax (the placing of the photograph). The trick effect and the syntax in the photographs that accompany this text have to do with the way the positioning of the photos signifies mockery – the son is dominated by the mother. In terms of aestheticism, all social actors do not look their best. Their posing, especially Charles', is odd. The Queen looks upset through her angle of vision. In all, therefore, the photographic composition adds negative evaluation to the text, but this time in terms of parody.

Another example of mocked royalty is represented in Illustration 13.3.

The headline says:

HIGH ARISTOCRACY – IN OLD DAYS, ROYALTY HAD POWER. NOWADAYS, THEY HAVE SIZE.

In the final example, two women are contrasted – Jerry Hall and Luciana Gimenez, both connected to Mick Jagger (Illustration 13.4).

Illustration 13.3   VEJA (June 2000)

Illustration 13.4   VEJA (July 2000)

The Brazilian is the new mother of his youngest son. The two women are compared in terms of their beauty and their bodies. The headline reads:

ONE TAKES OFF, THE OTHER PUTS ON (CLOTHES).

Once again, the photos connote mockery through processes of photogenie and aesthetization. Although both photos are syntactically parallel in terms of vision, the positive evaluation is given to the Brazilian (who looks attractive). Textually, the American woman is represented through sexist and sarcastic assertions such as *old, ugly* and *bad actress*. Under the photograph of Jerry Hall, which appears next to the photograph of Luciana Gimenez, comes the caption:

Jerry takes her clothes off – everything is bad [reference to her acting], *including her little body* [use of diminutive again].

In the photo, Jerry Hall does look unconfident; she is naked and standing awkwardly.

Through text and image, the representations evaluate the social actors in different ways. The hidden message is: what is Brazilian is much better.

Conclusion

Through processes of recontextualization, the two worlds look at each other in different aggressive ways:

- the First World uses colonial discursive practices to represent the other through processes of denigration and difference
- the Third World uses postcolonial forms of resistance through humour and sarcasm.

In both cases, the representations are never neutral, without a point of view. In the age of globalization, the international distribution of power tends to make the First World culture a powerful transmitter of ideas and ideologies.

By using theories coming from interdisciplinary areas like media studies, Critical Discourse Analysis and postcolonial thinking, my analysis has tried to demonstrate that we should be aware of the power of representation and of the goals and evaluations of any given recontextualization.

Media discourses construe states of affairs that can be harmful to many people. The awareness of their processes, strategies and points of view is of utmost importance.

The discursive-analytical view taken in this chapter, together with key notions of intertextuality and multimodality, allowed me to deconstruct discrimination through language and image. By examining textual and visual evidence, nationalistic, racist and gender-biased discourses could be unravelled.

I will finish this chapter by quoting a letter written to *The Times* on 16 September 2001, five days after the terrorist attacks on the World Trade Center and the Pentagon. The writer says:

Despite the fact that Muslim communities throughout the world have condemned the terrorist attacks and have joined in with the rest in mourning and praying for the families of the victims, they have been harassed and verbally abused. Using the word Islamic with words such as terrorists, extremists, etc. paints the whole community and Islam as being terrorist and extremists.

We in the press, have a responsibility to ensure that our intemperate report-ing doesn't lead to any more incidence of abuse and threats of violence against people sharing a sense of shock and outrage. (Ahmed Versi, Editor, *Muslim News*; my emphasis)

In these post-attack days, many loaded words and pictures are repeated ad nauseum in front of our very eyes through different media discourses.

The ultimate consequence of talk and text, as Paul Chilton suggests, is peace or more war. Words together with visual representations, at this stage, are the most significant weapons.

Notes

1. Data is drawn from the Bank of English corpus created by COBUILD at the University of Birmingham.
2. Readers could reasonably expect a chapter concerned with the analysis of images to be profusely illustrated; indeed, the pre-final draft was. Unfortunately, at a later stage, it became apparent it would have cost an exorbitant amount to get permis-sion from the copyright holders to reproduce all of my exemplificatory illustra-tions, even though the intended audience is academic and small. Selling copyright to illustrations is now a big money-spinner for the media barons. Ironically, the poor Brazilians whose images are being sold almost certainly never benefit from these payments. Hence, few of my illustrations survived and the excluded ones had to be described verbally.

References

Bakhtin, M. (1984) *Rabelais and His World*. Bloomington, IN: University of Indiana Press.
Barthes, R. (1977) *Image, Music, Text*. Glasgow: Fontana/Collins.
Bell, A. (1991) *The Language of the News Media*. Oxford: Blackwell.
Bernstein, B. (1981) 'Codes, modalities and the process of cultural reproductions: a model', in *Language and Society*, 10, pp. 327–63.
Butt, D., Fahey, R., Spinks, S. and Yallop, C. (1995) *Using Functional Grammar – An Explorer's Guide*, Sydney: National Centre for English Teaching and Research, Macquarie University.

Caldas-Coulthard, C.R. (1987) 'Reporting speech in narrative written texts', in R.M. Coulthard (ed.), *Discussing Discourse*, Discourse Analysis Monographs, No. 14, ELR, University of Birmingham, pp. 149–67.

Caldas-Coulthard, C.R. (1995) 'Man in the news: misrepresentation of women speaking in news as narrative discourse', in S. Mill (ed.), *Language and Gender: Interdisciplinary Perspectives*. London: Longman, pp. 226–38.

Caldas-Coulthard, C.R. and Coulthard, M. (eds) (1996) *Texts and Practices: Readings in Critical Discourse Analysis*. London: Routledge.

Caldas-Coulthard, C.R. and van Leeuwen, T. (2001) 'Baby's first toys and the discursive construction of childhood', in *Folia Linguistica*, 35(1–2), Berlin: Mouton de Gruyer, pp. 157–82.

Chibnall, S. (1977) *Law and Order News*. London: Tavistock.

Fowler, R. (1991) *Language in the News*. London: Routledge.

Galtung, H. and Ruge, M.H. (1965) 'The structure of foreign news', in *Journal of Peace Research*, 2(1), pp. 64–91.

Glasgow University Media Group (1976) *Bad News*. London: Routledge.

Hall, S., Hobson, D., Lowe, A. and Willis, P. (1980) *Culture, Media and Society*. London: Hutchinson.

Hartley, J. (1982) *Understanding News*. London: Methuen.

Hoey, M. (1983) *On the Surface of Discourse*. London: Allen and Unwin.

Kress, G. and van Leeuwen, T. (1996) *Reading Images: The Grammar of Visual Design*. London: Routledge.

Labov, W. (1972) 'The transformation of experience in narrative syntax', in *Language in the Inner City*. University Park: University of Pennsylvania Press, pp. 354–98.

Martin, J. (2000) 'Beyond exchange: appraisal systems in English', in S. Hunston and G. Thompson (eds), *Evaluation in Text*. Oxford: Oxford University Press, pp. 142–75.

Reisigl, M. and Wodak, R. (2001) *Discourse and Discrimination: Rhetorics of Racism and Antisemitism*. London: Routledge.

Spivak, G. (1987) *In Other Worlds: Essays on Cultural Politics*. New York: Routledge.

Stam, R. (2000) *Film Theory: An Introduction*. London: Blackwell.

van Dijk, T.A. (1987) *Communicating Racism*. London: Sage.

van Leeuwen, T. (1993a) 'Recontextualisation of social practice', unpublished manuscript.

van Leeuwen, T. (1993b) 'Genre and field in critical discourse analysis', *Discourse and Society*, 4(2), pp. 193–223.

van Leeuwen, T. (1996) 'The representation of social actors', in C.R. Caldas-Coulthard and M. Coulthard (eds) *Texts and Practices: Readings in Critical Discourse Analysis*. London: Routledge, pp. 32–70.

van Leeuwen, T. (2000) 'The discursive construction of purpose', in S. Sarangi and R.M. Coulthard (eds), *Discourse and Social Life*. London: Longman, pp. 66–81.

van Leeuwen, T. and Wodak, R. (1999) 'Legitimising immigration control: a discourse-historical analysis', in *Discourse Studies*, 1(1), pp. 83–119.

White, P. (1998) 'Telling media tales: the news story as rhetoric'. PhD thesis, University of Sydney.

Xavier, I. (1996) *O Cinema no Seculo*. Rio de Janeiro: Imago.

Xavier, I. (1998) *Allegories of Underdevelopment*. Minneapolis: University of Minnesota Press.

14
Interaction between Visual and Verbal Communication: Changing Patterns in the Printed Media

Christine Anthonissen

It is common cause that we refer to Critical Linguistics (CL) and Critical Discourse Analysis (CDA) as interdisciplinary areas of research with no pretence of being *autonomous*, of having a 'sole mandate' in analysing, describing and explaining a clearly delineated set of objects, entities or phenomena. The interdisciplinary approach of CDA allows us to consider a wide variety of communicative methods and media from different perspectives in a way that does justice to the complexity of linguistic, extralinguistic and contextual components of authentic, real-life communication. An academic focus on patterns of language use in public and institutional discourses that reflect unequal power relations, is singularly characteristic of CL and CDA.[1] So, a unifying principle in CDA is to be found in its specific interest in discourses that take place in contested domains, such as the domains of nuclear energy, of human and civil rights of citizens and foreigners in modern states, of respectable educational opportunities, and so on.

Also singularly characteristic of CDA is agreement on the perspective that discourses are situated in, shaped by and constructive of circumstances that are more than and different to language. The context that contributes to deciding the meaning of a given text, is much more than purely linguistic (cf. Wodak, 1989). This has prompted acknowledgement of interdependency in relation to other disciplines such as philosophy, sociology, psychology, history, anthropology and literary theory. In identifying CDA as a typically interdisciplinary approach to analysing discourse, there is recognition of the value that advances made in these disciplines may have for improved understanding of the functioning of language in society.

This chapter is interested in texts published under conditions of strict censorship. The domain of language use is contested in that censorship occurs where a strong public institution, the government of a country, lays down rigid rules for conducting public media discourse and these rules are not readily accepted. Media producers such as broadcasters and newspaper publishers are also strong public institutions. To be effective in their functions of circulating information, testing and shaping opinions, weighing opposing ideas, debating suggested solutions to community related questions; in short, of establishing and protecting democracy, the media need and generally also claim a considerable degree of independence. In focus here particularly is a theory that allows for analysis of communicative devices employed in the printed media in circumstances where censorship has been imposed.

To describe and explain the interactive patterns that emerge under conditions of censorship, it is useful to bear in mind two levels at which interdisciplinarity in CDA is manifest. First, the relation between CDA and critical approaches taken in other disciplines or subdisciplines such as sociology, mass communication, literary analysis, and the like, needs to be considered. Critical Theory does not belong to a single discipline; rather it has something to contribute to our views on the *nature of knowledge* in whichever field we happen to be working. Second, CDA has an interest in *phenomena* such as communication patterns in public institutions, media discourse, the constitution of individual and group identity, which it shares with other disciplines as well as with other fields within Applied Linguistics. This compels one to consider particular themes and methods of research that other disciplines have developed and that may be accepted, contested, adapted and meaningfully put to use in CDA.

Of the variety of theories available for analysing news media discourse, one that has recently introduced a new dimension to our understanding of the nature of discourse is Kress and van Leeuwen's 'grammar of visual design'. In *Reading Images* (1996) they present a framework for analysing and understanding visual images, and the interaction between verbal and visual components, in media discourses. In addition, their work invites continued reflection on the nature of texts and discourses. This appears to be particularly useful for considering media representations where stipulated forms of discourse and explicitly outlined topics are prohibited.

In studies of verbal communication the distinction between *text* and *discourse* as instances of written or spoken language use has become eroded (cf. Fairclough, 1995a, p. 4; Titscher et al., 1998, pp. 37–8). Communicative conventions that determine which linguistic and textual forms are appropriate for given functions, are being challenged and changed. Established forms are given new functions, and new forms are developed to perform regular, established communicative functions. In an analogous manner, Kress and van Leeuwen's theory suggests that with changing patterns in mass communication, the boundaries between language and image in printed matter are becoming less pronounced. In science textbooks, for example, graphs, boxes and arrows are 'read' and understood with as much (or more) facility as verbal exposition.

This chapter will consider instances of communication in the printed media, in which genres untypical of news reporting were used, where information in the conventional form may have resulted in criminal liability of the reporter and publisher. It will also consider the way in which words become images and images function in a manner comparable to words. Illustrative material is taken from South African newspapers, 1986–87. First I shall give a summary of those aspects of Kress and van Leeuwen's theory that are pertinent to the interpretation of the selected censorship-restricted texts.

Kress and van Leeuwen on the 'grammar' of visual design

In the past ten years Gunther Kress and Theo van Leeuwen have considered semiotic modes other than language that go with the verbal in various kinds of discourses. This has resulted in their comprehensive theory of visual communication in which a wide range of mass media materials are referred to.

Kress and van Leeuwen (henceforth K&VL) have noted recent changes in writing practices which they interpret as changes in the relative value assigned to different semiotic modes. They point out that all texts are multimodal (1998, p. 186) in the sense that spoken language is always accompanied by paralinguistic means of communication such as speech-sound, rhythm, intonation, facial expression, gesture and posture, and that written language is always also a visual arrangement of marks on a page.

In developing a framework for the analysis of visual communication, K&VL assume at least two things. First, they assume that *language is one of a variety* of semiotic modes available to people for creating meaning. Referring to this they suggest that modes other than language, such as visual images, have been insufficiently explored in various forms of communication. Second, they assume that *forms of communication are constantly in flux.* Referring to this they indicate how the way in which language as well as visual images are used currently, shows marked change to the way these semiotic modes were used relatively recently. To illustrate, they consider how images, as a semiotic mode alternative to language, are used in a variety of texts, such as children's books, science textbooks and newspaper front pages. They also develop theoretical tools with which to describe and explain the perceived order and regularity in visual communication. Where censorship prevails, semiotic modes other than language have to be investigated. Established discursive structures that cannot be used freely have to be reconsidered; various forms of representation are available – disallowed forms may be adjusted and replaced by existing or newly developed alternatives.

The relation between analysis of visual design and Critical Discourse Analysis

Critical Discourse Analysis seeks to show how the apparently neutral, purely informative discourses of newspaper reporting, government publications, social science reports, and so on, may in fact convey ideological attitudes, just as much as discourses which more explicitly editorialize or propagandize. This discipline specifically shows how language is used to convey power and status in contemporary social interaction. Most work done in CDA has been focused on verbal texts, or on the verbal parts of multimodal texts (cf. Bell and Garrett, 1998). K&VL's grammar of visual design is intended to broaden the approach suggested by CDA, to include particularly the structure and use of images. They pay close attention to those trends in public communication where there is a notable incursion of the visual into many domains where formerly language was the sole and dominant mode. And they draw attention to the fact that images of whatever kind are not natural or neutral, but that they fall as much within the realm of ideology as any other mode of discourse.

Recognizing Halliday's metafunctions of language, K&VL consider the form and functions of visual communciation, by giving detailed attention to, inter alia, the following:

- patterns of representation available for people to encode experience visually
- patterns of interaction available for people to do things to and for each other through visual communication; this refers to the relations between makers and viewers of visual texts
- the capacity of images to form texts, the way in which signs cohere both internally with each other, and with the context in which they are produced
- the materiality of visual signs; tools and materials that signmakers use, and their contribution to making meaning.

The relation between visual communication and language

The important role of images in current newspapers, magazines, public relations materials, advertisements and various kinds of books, is noted (K&VL, 1996, p. 15). These media involve a complex interplay of written text, images and other graphic elements that combine into visual designs by means of layout. Analyses of multimodal texts that give prominence to the written word and denigrate the emergence of visual media as if images constitute a semiotic mode inferior to written language, are called into question.

K&VL (ibid., p. 16) take issue with Barthes' (1977) view that the meanings of images are always related to and in a sense dependent on a verbal text. They dispute it that images alone are 'too polysemous' to arrive at a definite meaning and that consequently 'language must come to the rescue'. Barthes distinguishes two kinds of image–text relations, namely (i) where the verbal texts extends the meaning of the image (or vice versa), adding more information, and (ii) where the verbal text elaborates the meaning of the image (or vice versa), giving an illustration or more precise restatement.

K&VL find that this distinction fails to recognize that the visual component of a text is an independently organized and structured message, connected to the written component, but not necessarily dependent on it. For them (K&VL, 1996, p. 18) the verbal and visual modes represent two sets of meaning that are 'neither fully conflated, nor entirely opposed'.

K&VL's approach to communication starts not from a mentalist or grammatical perspective, but from a social base. They hold that meanings expressed by speakers, writers, printmakers, photographers, painters or sculptors are first and foremost social meanings, which arise out of the society in which the individuals live and work. Because societies are not homogeneous, different media through which texts are constructed, will show social differences. K&VL note how a multimodal text using images and writing may carry differing and even conflicting meanings – the writing may convey one set of meanings and the images another. This is well illustrated in circumstances of censorship where certain types of reference; for example, critical reference to security forces, are forbidden. A verbal text that pays lip service to media regulations, may be contradicted and corrected by a visually linked image.

A perceived change in the conventional roles of language and image in printed texts is illustrated and explained. K&VL (ibid., pp. 26–7) note a move 'towards a decrease of control over language and an increase in codification and control over the visual' in various kinds of texts – books, films, and other forms of public language. Interestingly, this shift has also been recognized in other fields of research, such as Cultural Studies, where emphasis on analysing 'what the text says' is being replaced by emphasis on 'how different audiences read the same text'.

K&VL (ibid., p. 30ff.) find at least partial explanation for a contemporary semiotic shift in considerations of entertainment and immediacy of apprehension. Other critical discourse analysts (notably Fowler, 1991; Fairclough, 1995b) have noted this kind of shift in identifying processes of 'conversationalization' and 'marketization'. In censorship the most pertinent consideration for reverting to the visual mode (or vice versa) is to avoid liability that may arise from a verbal representation. In such circumstances visual images may operate in a manner similar to verbal imagery or indirect verbal representation. This serves to support an earlier claim that boundaries between verbal and visual are not as firm and unassailable as they have until recently been made out to be.

Finally, there is the question as to whether the move from verbal to visual is a loss or a gain. K&VL present no simple answer. They argue that different semiotic modes, visual, verbal or gestural, each have their potentialities and limitations. Different modes may be more or less useful for different matters that are to be represented. For example, it is possible that visual representation may be more apt to the 'stuff of science' than language is. Even when a shift toward visual representation is not occasioned by considerations of censorship, it seems clear that the world as it is represented visually in the mass media, is a different world, and produces different citizens, from the world formerly represented in language only. Changes in semiotic patterns necessarily raise questions about the changing nature of societies. K&VL (1996, p. 31) consider the possibility that the volume and nature of information has become so vast and so complex, that perhaps it has to be handled visually, because the verbal is no longer adequate.

Visual design in news representation

In a critical analysis of newspaper layout, with close attention to the layout of front pages, K&VL (1998, p. 186ff.) illustrate the signifying systems of conventional, contemporary layout patterns. In considering and illustrating how various modes are integrated in the layout, K&VL show how information value and salience are signalled. They also show how framing devices are used to contrast or connect certain news items. They note how news writing involves close attention to typeface choices and layout, and how different semiotic modes in such texts interrelate in different ways:

1. The written text may remain dominant, with the visual highlighting important points.
2. The written text may become less important, with the message articulated primarily in the visual mode.
3. The visual and verbal components may duplicate in expressing the same meanings.
4. The visual and verbal components may complement and extend each other.
5. The visual and verbal components may clash and contradict each other.

These different kinds of relation between verbal and visual will be followed in analysing self-censored, regulation-challenging discourses.

News representation under censorship

Here, I indicate how news reporting during successive States of Emergency in the 1980s in South Africa illustrates and to some extent elaborates the K&VL theory discussed above.

Social and historic context

In June 1985 the South African government announced a State of Emergency in various specified magisterial districts of the country, thereby indicating that protest against their rule had become a threat they could not manage by ordinary means of civil control. In terms of the regular Emergency Regulations this immediately put a number of media regulations, that is, a limited degree of censorship, in place. However, soon these regulations proved to be inadequate for stopping a flow of information about the extent of the protest as well as the manner and intensity of measures taken by the police and the military. Media reports voiced and fuelled indignation and outrage at government action in the areas affected by the Emergency Regulations. The government responded by imposing special measures of media control.

At the beginning of 1986 there were more than 100 laws circumscribing what journalists in South Africa may write about (cf. *Guardian*, 21 December 1986). Without official permission no information was to be published about matters such as defence, external military actions, liberation wars in southern Africa, nuclear activities and fuel supplies. Much of the sensitive information related to the state was 'considered secret unless proved otherwise'. In November 1985 the Minister of Police, Mr Louis le Grange, took specific action against the media by instituting regulations[2] that denied journalists access to the 38 magisterial districts under emergency regulations, except where special permission had been obtained. Making or publishing photographs, sound recordings and even drawings of restricted data, was prohibited, except with the permission of a police officer. The only reason given for such control of the professional practices of journalists was the government's concern that 'the presence of television and other camera crews in unrest situations ... proved to be a catalyst to further violence'.

On 12 June 1986, a few days before the ten-year commemoration of the Soweto uprising, a countrywide State of Emergency was declared. On 13 June as the newspapers were being delivered to points of sale, all copies of the *Weekly Mail* and *The Sowetan* were seized. On 27 June Mr Zwelakhe Sisulu, editor of *New Nation*, was arrested and detained (*Sunday Times*, 29 June 1986). The government's Bureau of Information was authorized as the only institution that could provide local and foreign media with unrest related information, photographs and other material.[3] Publication of potentially sensitive material obtained from any other source was disallowed.

The Bureau of Information censored information in various ways. Not only did it withhold information, it also gave details selectively, edited particulars of events, and forbade publication of details that were apparently known to journalists. So, for example, the names of people detained in terms of the emergency regulations were not released for publication, and the exact number of people detained at the time (mid-June, 1986) was withheld, although the director of the Bureau felt compelled to state that suggestions of 4000–4500 detainees were exaggerated.

More than emergency regulations were resorted to in the process of trying to dictate what the press may or may not say. Certain sections of the Police Act (1953) and the Internal Security Act (1982) were invoked from time to time, either to actually silence critics or to threaten action which would deter defiant journalists and editors (cf. *Daily Dispatch*, 4 July 1986).

On 11 December 1986 the government imposed a new set of restrictions. The new rules made it illegal to participate in or report on most forms of peaceful protest, such as rent-strikes or consumer boycotts. Details of the arrest of opponents of the government could not be reported without the government's approval, nor was it allowed to announce their subsequent release. Without approval, it would be an offence to report speeches which the government deemed likely to incite hostility to it. The then President, P.W. Botha, justified the measures as necessary to forestall a wave of 'revolutionary violence' allegedly planned for Christmas and the New Year by the African National Congress–South African Communist Party 'terrorist alliance' (*Guardian*, 21 December 1986).

Penalties for breaches of the regulations were such that the editor of a newspaper publishing subversive material could be imprisoned and a fine big enough to wreck the publication could be imposed. A maximum fine of R20,000 or a ten-year term of imprisonment was possible.

Given such censorship it is understandable that dissenting journalists would try to find alternatives to ordinary news reports for communicating information they felt to be in the public interest. One interesting effect of the editors' response of 'experimenting' with genres not generally associated with news reporting, was that this opened the possibility for denying that the formal conditions set in legislation had been violated. Where words and images such as photographs or sketches were forbidden, editors resorted to alternative textual structures to circumvent the official regulations. K&VL's theory is particularly useful in explaining how the latter kind of editorial choice achieved its communicative goal.

Avoiding and defying censorship

The following is a discussion of the specific examples shown in Figures 14.1–5. This serves to illustrate some of the ways in which visual and verbal signs came to interact in the publication of censorship-defying news and news comment.

Before the December 1986 regulations, blank spaces and black lines were used to signal that information was being withheld not due to bad journalism or agreement with an ideology of concealment, but merely to avoid the punitive measures attached to a breach of the imposed media restrictions. Figures 14.1 and 14.2 show the visual effect of such practices. Figure 14.1 gives the conventional layout of the middle page where a comment cartoon is placed directly next to a comment article and above the letters column. Figure 14.2 gives the same layout with which readers were familiar, but with omission and obliteration of potentially offensive material, as well as a special block announcing that the material had been censored as a result of emergency regulations.

If the editor had simply chosen an inoffensive topic for his comment column, or had given only material provided by the Bureau of Information, the

Figure 14.1

Source: *Weekly Mail* (5–11 December 1986).

media regulations would have had their intended effect. Tabooed news would have been kept from public consideration to the extent that many readers would not suspect or believe that anything of note was being withheld. To avoid any such misdirection many newspapers engaged in the practice of inserting a little block in every edition, reminding their audience of the censorship that interfered with the process of news production. Black lines and empty spaces simultaneously added a visual reminder, apology and protest. Also, these signs patently signalled how messages become distorted when censorship is applied.

In the framework provided by K&VL such use of visual signs would fall within the category of texts where 'the written text may become less important, with the message articulated primarily in the visual mode'. However, the visual component is not in the customary form of an illustration, a photograph or a diagram. Here the visual highlights the importance of written text: the verbal component should have been prominent and accessible. Instead, words become bold black stripes and sketches become large white spaces. Visual means are employed to signal the imposed 'silence', the forced removal of words and images along with the information they communicate.

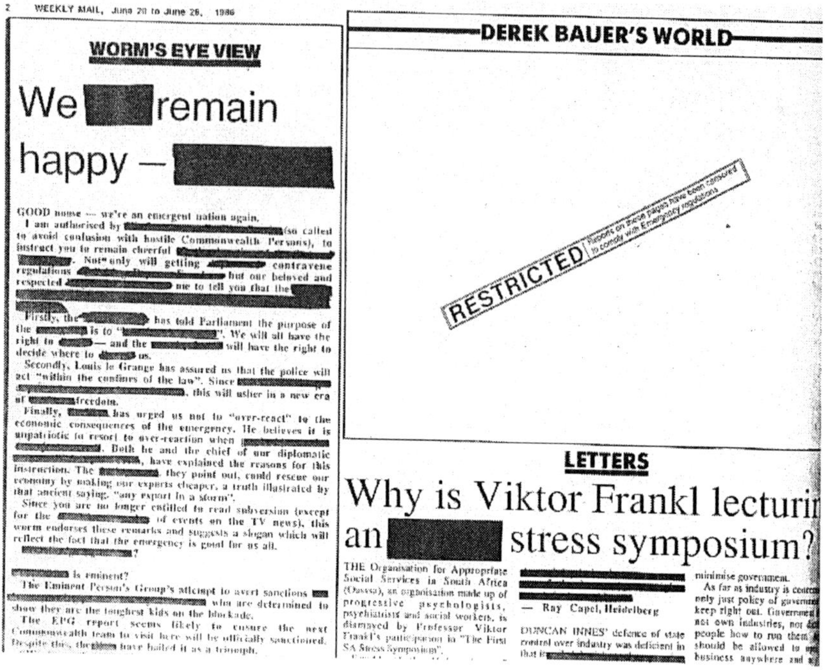

Figure 14.2

Source: *Weekly Mail* (20–26 June 1986).

Lines and blank squares used in this way are printed equivalents of involuntary verbal restraint; they are graphic metaphors of gagging.

The December 1986 regulations outlawed the use of blank spaces and black lines. Instead, large letters giving light, ironic comment were used to fill the space and, for example, the names and telephone numbers of government officials whose permission was required for any public discussion of 'tabooed' topics were boldly announced as an implied encouragement for the public to request such permission. Such use of 'laughter'[4] was balanced by more serious reports relaying the details of the government proclamation in the conventional format. Here the discursive relation between various components would fall within the category where 'the written text may remain dominant, with the visual highlighting important points'. To some extent 'the visual and verbal components may duplicate in expressing the same meanings'. Under a heading such as THE EMERGENCY MADE SIMPLE large print refers to one effect of the regulations, namely control of public debate on controversial topics. A written report with more typical generic features reiterates and elaborates on the details and effects of such control.

Detention in terms of emergency regulations was one of the tabooed topics. Figures 14.3–5 illustrate some of the alternative discursive structures editors and sub-editors selected for conveying limited information such as how many people were in detention, the reasons and alleged reasons for these detentions, and concerns about the treatment of the detainees. My contention here is that when reporting of sensitive matters is forbidden, journalists experiment with other genres than conventional reports to relay the restricted information. News reports generally represent a genre structured for the function of conveying established facts (even if from a non-neutral point of view). Other text types such as open letters and cartoons have generic features that give lesser prominence to the statement of facts. Their primary and direct function is not that of 'reporting or commenting'. Compared to front-page articles and editorials the information that such texts carry is, at least to some extent, disguised.

Early in 1987 the Minister of Law and Order, Mr Adriaan Vlok, was obliged due to opposition pressure to table in parliament the names of people detained under the emergency regulations. Interestingly, these figures

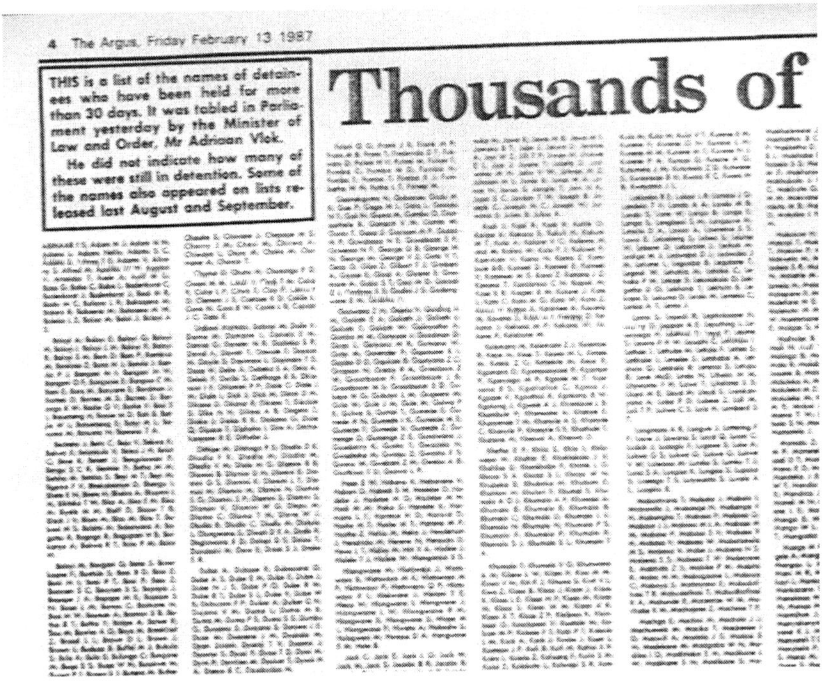
4 The Argus, Friday February 13 1987

Thousands of

THIS is a list of the names of detainees who have been held for more than 30 days. It was tabled in Parliament yesterday by the Minister of Law and Order, Mr Adriaan Vlok.

He did not indicate how many of these were still in detention. Some of the names also appeared on lists released last August and September.

Figure 14.3

Source: *The Argus* (13 February 1987).

Figure 14.4

Source: *The Argus* (13 February 1987).

confirmed what the director of the Bureau for Information had denied six months earlier, namely that about 4000 (3857) people were being held. Emergency regulations forbade comment that could be constructed as criticism. Figure 14.3 shows the way in which the full list of names of people detained for more than 30 days was published. Simply publishing a full page of names in small print is an innovative form of comment. Clearly the publisher's intention is not that the whole page should be read like any other, word for word from top to bottom. Here words have become images; the visual aspect of the printed page is more important than the verbal. This illustrates a category of visual-verbal interaction where, even with no pictures, no stripes or open spaces, the visual is dominant and the written text is subsidiary in getting the message across. The seemingly endless list of names functions to announce and underscore the vastness of the number of detainees, and the magnitude of the deception. It is a cynical response to the Minister's statement that 'the number of people being detained were far fewer than had been alleged'. In this instance the visual-verbal category K&VL identify as one where 'the written text may remain dominant, with

SOUTHERN AFRICAN CATHOLIC BISHOPS' CONFERENCE

DATED: First Sunday of Lent.

OPEN LETTER TO ALL DETAINEES

We, the members of a special consultation of the Catholic Church gathered at Hammanskraal to assess the present state of affairs in our country, want to send a message to all detainees. It is clear to us that our country has seldom witnessed such a wave of repression and such an extensive denial of basic human rights. We condemn this in the strongest possible terms and accuse the present South African government of a serious abuse of power. This is evident in the number of people who are detained, in the failure to give them access to due process, and most distressingly, the detention of children. We can find no justification for this continuing inhuman oppression and we warn that it is a measure that does great damage for the present and the future.

To all of you in detention we send the assurance of our solidarity in your suffering. In your struggle for the liberation of all the people you have been willing to sacrifice your own freedom. In condemning violence and injustice we admire and support you. We recognise in your suffering, especially those of you who have been physically assaulted and who suffer solitary confinement a very important contribution to our struggle for liberation. We will continue the work that you have been doing and we will continue to give all the support we can to your friends and relatives. To our brothers and sisters in detention we promise our prayers and whatever pastoral care we can give.

We are particularly concerned about those of you who are children and we are encouraged by the news that some adults in detention do try to take care of the children.

We will also continue to work for your freedom and we pray that God our Father will give us the wisdom, courage and strength to work continuously for the liberation of our country.

Yours in Christ,

Bishop W F Napier, OFM (President)

Cardinal Owen McCann

Archbishop D Hurley, OMI

Bishop R Orsmond

N Bruyns

Bishop M Rowland

Bishop M Coleman

Bishop J Brenninkmeijer

Archbishop P Butelezi

Bishop H Lenhof, SAC

Bishop P Nkhumishe

Bishop D Verstraete

Archbishop S Naidoo, CSsR

Fr E Farrelly, SDB

Sr Brigid Flanagan, IHF

Archbishop G Daniel

N Malalile

N F Stott

J Baulle

Fr A Nolan, OP

Professor B Gaybba

Sr Cecilia Smit, OP

Figure 14.5

Source: *Weekly Mail* (13–19 March 1987).

the visual highlighting important points' is inverted. The written text is more image than language; words are used in an unconventional way to communicate a message that is far more than a list of names.

Figure 14.4 shows a cartoon that has as its topic the Minister's disclosure of the number of detainees, and a citation of his words. A cartoon can hardly be construed strictly as a report or as comment as it does not give new information, and it is, in keeping with the conventional features of this genre, meant to be taken lightly. Nevertheless, 'many a truth is said in jest', humour often has a sting. The cartoon represents a genre that over many years has become a regular feature of the leader page. It is an instance where images say as much if not more than words. A challenge to a cartoon in terms of emergency regulations, would be completely petty. This visual mode lends itself well to implication and comment of a kind that in a verbal mode may have been offensive.

Figure 14.5 shows an open letter to all detainees that was published a month after the names and numbers of people in detention had been released. An open letter of this kind functions as a vehicle for a message of writers other than the newspaper's own reporters or editors. Although the newspaper has to take responsibility for what it publishes, it is less directly implicated in an open letter than those who drafted it. Of note here is the format, which once again is not that of the regular news report. A framed letter with the logo of the South African Catholic Bishop's Conference is adressed to all detainees and expresses concern about the 'wave of repression' and 'extensive denial of basic human rights'. Although the letter is addressed to detainees, it is open, and thus intended for a wider readership that includes relatives and supporters of detainees as well as the government and all officials in charge of the detention system. This is more than an assurance of 'solidarity in (detainees') suffering', more than a pledge of support, of prayers, of pastoral care, and of concern about children that are being held – it is additionally a form of public protest. The list of real signatures forms part of the visual message and assists in personalising a message that has an institutional character – the Bishops represent an influential institution, but they are also concerned individuals.

Conclusion

In summary, it is clear that different genres have different verbal and visual features. Where the verbal is unduly restricted it is not surprising that the visual will become foregrounded as a medium of communication. This appears to me to provide further evidence to K&VL's claim of current shifts in the ways in which the verbal and the visual interact in the media. These shifts encompass greater dependence on an underutilized communicative mode. There are circumstances in which it seems that visual media can say more than the verbal. Extending the visual in communication is not an accidental development or simply a curious attempt at doing something rare or novel. Some kinds of information may be more directly communicated visually than verbally, some have no choice but to rely on the visual. Particularly it seems that censorship provokes the use of semiotic modes other than language, and that the printed media provide a suitable context for using more than the written word in communicating sensitive material.

Notes

1. As Critical Linguistics (CL) and Critical Discourse Analysis (CDA) are terms that are often used interchangeably, and CDA has recently been used more often, I shall continue to use only the latter.
2. See Gavin Stewart's (1985) article published in the *Sunday Tribune*, 10 November 1985.
3. Details of the effects of these regulations are set out in the *Weekend Argus* of 14 June 1986.
4. Cf. Bakhtin's notion of *laughter* in his 'Laughter and Freedom' (1940 [1989]).

References

Bakhtin, M. (1940 [1989]), 'Laughter and Freedom', in D. Latimer (ed.), *Contemporary Critical Theory* (1989). New York: Harcourt, Brace, Jovanovich, pp. 300–7.
Barthes, R. (1977) *Image, Music, Text* (trans S. Heath). New York: Hill & Wang.
Bell, A. and Garrett, P. (1998) *Approaches to Media Discourse*. Oxford: Blackwell, 1998.
Fairclough, N. (1995a) *Critical Discourse Analysis*. London, New York: Longman, 1995.
Fairclough, N. (1995b) *Media Discourse*. London, New York, Sydney: Edward Arnold.
Fowler, R. (1991) *Language in the News*. London, New York: Routledge.
Kress, G. and van Leeuwen, T. (1996) *Reading Images – the grammar of visual design*. London: Routledge.
Kress, G. and van Leeuwen, T. (1998), 'Analysis of Newspaper Layout', in A. Bell and P. Garret (eds), *Approaches to Media Discourse*. Oxford: Blackwell.
Stewart, G. (1985), 'The Walls of Jericho', *Sunday Tribune*, 10 November 1985.
Titscher, S., Wodak, R., Meyer, M. and Vetter, E. (1998) *Methoden der Textanalyse*. Wiesbaden: Westdeutscher Verlag.
Wodak, R. (ed.) (1989) *Language, Power and Ideology*. Amsterdam: John Benjamins.

Index

316 *Index*